PETER B. KENEN
Editor

MANAGING THE WORLD ECONOMY
Fifty Years After Bretton Woods

Institute for International Economics
Washington, DC
September 1994

Peter B. Kenen is Walker Professor of Economics and International Finance and Director of the International Finance Section, Princeton. He is the author of numerous books and articles, including *EMU After Maastricht* (1992), *Managing Exchange Rates* (1989), *Exchange Rates and Policy Coordination* (1989), and *The International Economy* (second edition 1989). He serves on the Executive Committee of the Bretton Woods Committee and the Advisory Committee of the Institute.

INSTITUTE FOR INTERNATIONAL ECONOMICS
11 Dupont Circle, NW
Washington, DC 20036-1207
(202) 328-9000   FAX: (202) 328-5432

C. Fred Bergsten, *Director*
Christine F. Lowry, *Director of Publications*

Cover design by Naylor Design, Inc.
Typesetting by Alpha Technologies/mps
Printing by Automated Graphic Systems

Printed in the United States of America
97 96 95 94   8 7 6 5 4 3 2

Library of Congress Cataloging-in-Publication Data

Managing the world economy : fifty years after Bretton Woods / Peter B. Kenen, editor.
     p. cm.
Includes bibliographical references.

  1. United Nations Monetary and Financial Conference (1944 : Bretton Woods, N.H.)—History—Congresses. 2. International finance—History—20th century—Congresses.   3. Foreign exchange—History—20th century—Congresses.   4. Currency question—History—20th century—Congresses.   5. International economic relations—Congresses.   6. Economic history—20th century—Congresses. 7. Economic forecasting—Congresses. 8. Twenty-first century—Forecasts—Congresses.   I. Kenen, Peter B., 1932– .
HG205.M36 1994
332'.042—dc20
                                         94-22350
     ISBN 0-88132-212-1   CIP

Marketed and Distributed outside the USA and Canada by Longman Group UK Limited, London

The views expressed in this publication are those of the authors. This publication is part of the overall program of the Institute, as endorsed by its Board of Directors, but does not necessarily reflect the views of individual members of the Board or the Advisory Committee.

Contents

Preface

Throughout its history, the Institute has devoted considerable attention to the major international economic institutions. Our very first conference and publication analyzed *The Lending Policies of the International Monetary Fund* (August 1982), and a number of our subsequent studies, such as *A New SDR Allocation?* (March 1984) and *The Exchange Rate System* (revised 1985), also focused on central aspects of the functioning of the Fund. Our authors have studied a number of aspects of the GATT, the global trade institution, in such releases as *Trading for Growth: The Next Round of Trade Negotiations* (September 1985) and *Completing the Uruguay Round: A Results-Oriented Approach to the GATT Trade Negotiations* (September 1990). We addressed the role of several of the institutions in *Economic Policy Coordination: Requiem or Prologue?* (April 1991).

The Institute has also taken a look at the possibilities for creating new international economic institutions, as in Daniel C. Esty's proposals for a comprehensive environmental organization in *Greening the GATT: Trade, Environment, and the Future* (July 1994) and the suggestions for a "GATT for Investment" in our forthcoming *The Globalization of Industry and National Governments* by Edward M. Graham and myself. We have assessed some of the key regional, as well as global, institutions in studies such as *More Free Trade Areas?* (May 1989), *NAFTA: An Assessment* (revised October 1993), and *Reviving the European Union* (April 1994).

On the 50th anniversary of the original postwar economic organizations—the International Monetary Fund and World Bank—we decided to undertake a comprehensive review of the institutional framework for international economic cooperation. Such a review must of course rest on two analytical foundations: an assessment of the future needs of the world economy and an appraisal of the present regime as it has evolved over the past half century. We decided that this review should range beyond the institutions created at Bretton Woods in 1944 to encompass the entire set of structures—both global and regional—that now exist or might usefully be envisaged for the future.

Such an effort extends well beyond the capacity of any individual researcher, or even any single research center such as the Institute, so we held a conference on the topic in 1994. We were deeply gratified by the high quality of the papers and commentaries that resulted, which we present in this volume. We hope that they will make a useful contribution to public thinking about the critical issues involved, and to the intergovernmental consideration of systemic reform launched by the Group of Seven industrial democracies at their annual summit meeting in Naples in July 1994.

I am particularly grateful for the major contribution of Professor Peter B. Kenen of Princeton University in designing and executing the conference, and subsequently in editing its results. Professor Kenen is one of the world's leading experts on the entire range of international economic issues and was uniquely qualified to undertake this wide-ranging project. He has been an active and deeply valued member of the Advisory Committee of the Institute since its inception, and it was a great pleasure in both professional and personal terms to work so closely with him on it.

The Institute for International Economics is a private nonprofit institution for the study and discussion of international economic policy. Its purpose is to analyze important issues in that area and to develop and communicate practical new approaches for dealing with them. The Institute is completely nonpartisan.

The Institute is funded largely by philanthropic foundations. Major institutional grants are now being received from the German Marshall Fund of the United States, which created the Institute with a generous commitment of funds in 1981, and from the Ford Foundation, the William and Flora Hewlett Foundation, the William M. Keck, Jr. Foundation, the Andrew Mellon Foundation, the C. V. Starr Foundation, and the United States–Japan Foundation. A number of other foundations and private corporations also contribute to the highly diversified financial resources of the Institute. The Center for Global Partnership and the John D. and Catherine T. MacArthur Foundation provided partial support for this project. About 12 percent of the Institute's resources in our latest fiscal year were provided by contributors outside the United States, including about 5 percent from Japan.

The Board of Directors bears overall responsibility for the Institute and gives general guidance and approval to its research program—including identification of topics that are likely to become important to international economic policymakers over the medium run (generally, one to three years), and which thus should be addressed by the Institute. The director, working closely with the staff and outside Advisory Committee, is responsible for the development of particular projects and makes the final decision to publish an individual study.

The Institute hopes that its studies and other activities will contribute to building a stronger foundation for international economic policy around the world. We invite readers of these publications to let us know how they think we can best accomplish this objective.

C. FRED BERGSTEN
Director
August 1994

I

THE PAST

Managing the World Economy under the Bretton Woods System: An Overview

BARRY EICHENGREEN AND PETER B. KENEN

In the five decades following World War II, the world achieved a remarkable record of economic growth. In the first 25 years after the war, advanced industrial countries grew nearly twice as rapidly as in any comparable period before or since. In the next 25 years, a number of newly industrializing countries joined the "convergence club." The productivity slowdown in the industrial countries, the rise in unemployment, especially in Europe, and the challenges posed by the end of the Cold War all raise the question of whether the postwar period constitutes an exceptional half century that has now drawn to a close.

We need to understand this remarkable period to anticipate what the future holds and provide advice to those who will have to cope with it. In this overview, we analyze the postwar period as a distinct historical epoch, with the goal of identifying factors responsible for the persistence and spread of economic growth. We argue that an adequate explanation must focus on the international institutions that defined the framework for the decisions, public and private, that fostered economic growth. We distinguish Institutions with a capital "I" from institutions with a small "i". By "Institutions" we mean the organizations that shaped and conditioned the behavior of governments, such as the International Monetary Fund (IMF), the World Bank, and the General Agreement on Tariffs and

Barry Eichengreen is John L. Simpson Professor of Economics and professor of political science at the University of California at Berkeley and Peter B. Kenen is Walker Professor of Economics and International Finance at Princeton University. The authors thank C. Fred Bergsten, William R. Cline, Jeffrey Frankel, Rex Ghosh, Robert Gilpin, Joanne Gowa, C. Randall Henning, Kenneth Rogoff, and John Williamson for their helpful comments.

Trade (GATT). These organizations served as the conservators of the rules, conventions, and understandings that structured international economic relations, although they were not always able to enforce them. By "institutions" we mean the rules and understandings themselves, whether articulated formally or acknowledged implicitly, that molded national economic policies and fostered international cooperation.[1]

Our emphasis on the importance of institutions echoes recent work by North (1993) and others on the New Institutional Economics and by the contributors to Krasner (1983) on international regimes, but departs from it in significant ways. Postwar institutional arrangements were successful, we argue, because they effectively combined rigidity and flexibility. Rigidity was needed to solve commitment and coordination problems.[2] Rules of the game were needed to discourage opportunistic behavior such as the beggar-thy-neighbor policies of the interwar years. The rules served to coordinate the transition to current account convertibility and the liberalization of international trade, which allowed the industrial countries to rely collectively on export-led growth; no single country could benefit from it unless others pursued it simultaneously. The framework served to prevent individual governments from reneging on their initial commitments and also encouraged them to enter collectively into new commitments.

We depart from previous work in arguing that the postwar institutional order was not just sturdy but remarkably adaptable. It was sufficiently flexible to cope with unanticipated events and rectify mistakes. In response to unanticipated opposition, the plan for an International Trade Organization (ITO) was replaced by the General Agreement on Tariffs and Trade. In response to the unanticipated size of the dollar gap, the task of providing finance was transferred from the International Monetary Fund and World Bank to the United States under the Marshall Plan. In response to the unanticipated severity of the coordination problem impeding the move to current account convertibility—a problem dramatized by Britain's failed dash to convertibility in 1947—the European Payments

---

1. Political scientists debate whether international economic interactions simply reflect the economic and military power of the contending nations or whether the understandings and institutional structures that constitute a regime serve as intervening variables between basic power and ultimate outcomes, amplifying some influences, dissipating others, and solving commitment and coordination problems that might otherwise lock nations into a suboptimal equilibrium. The importance we attach below to US economic power indicates that we see some merit in both views, but it will become clear that we are inclined toward the second interpretation.

2. Throughout this paper, we use "coordination" in the way the word is commonly used by economists. It denotes the need for a synchronized change in behavior by governments or other economic agents. This usage includes (but is broader than) the meaning attached to the term in discussions of international policy coordination, which focuses on ways of obtaining agreements among governments on mutually beneficial policy changes.

Union (EPU) was grafted onto the Bretton Woods system and was managed by the European countries rather than the IMF. What is most remarkable about the first half of the postwar period is that institutional arrangements, even those meant to be permanent, were successfully adapted to new circumstances without impairing their integrity and hence their capacity to foster coordination and commitment. That was not always the case in the second half of the period, when the Bretton Woods Institutions were asked to take on tasks for which they had not been designed, with adverse effects on their integrity and effectiveness.

Four factors, we argue, lent strength and flexibility to postwar institutions. The first was the capacity and willingness of the United States to make side payments and apply sanctions. The United States emerged from World War II as the world's dominant economic power; it was the source of about 50 percent of global industrial production in the immediate postwar years, and it had an exceptional capacity to make the side payments needed to bring other countries on board when the institutional arrangements were designed and when it was necessary to change them. And the advent of the Cold War gave the United States a powerful incentive to exert its influence and gave other countries reasons to be receptive.

The second factor contributing to the strength and flexibility of postwar institutions was the small number of countries involved in designing them and the economic and political homogeneity of those countries. Although the countries of Latin America and those that became the Eastern bloc were present at Bretton Woods in 1944, the United States and a handful of European governments dominated the negotiations. In fact, they did much of the work beforehand. Early institutional innovations, including the Marshall Plan, the GATT, and the EPU likewise involved fewer than a score of advanced countries. The interests and attitudes shared by those countries, even before they were reinforced by the common security concerns of the Cold War, provided the common outlook and language needed to establish and successfully adapt institutional arrangements.

A third factor responsible for the early success of postwar institutions was the closed nature of domestic economies. The autarchic policies of the 1930s and the controls on trade and capital movements imposed during World War II left countries less exposed to international trade and factor flows than in the 1920s and even less open than before World War I. While the contrast should not be exaggerated, the difference was there. Controls on trade and financial flows allowed governments to pursue domestic policy goals, most notably full employment, without seriously violating international rules. They could tailor their fiscal and monetary policies to domestic needs, take welfare-state initiatives, and still meet the objectives and obligations embodied in the postwar institutions, including the commitment to liberalize their trade and payments.

The fourth factor was the success with which governments managed change domestically. In most countries after World War II, domestic interest groups agreed explicitly or tacitly to a settlement concerning the distribution of income and the organization of the economy. The establishment of welfare states and social-market economies created a web of domestic commitments and side payments that locked in cooperative behavior. The resulting political stability and support that governments enjoyed at home buttressed the credibility of their international undertakings. As economic conditions evolved thereafter in response to many factors, including the growing openness of national economies, governments could compensate those interest groups that suffered negative repercussions without preventing change from running its course. The domestic settlements from which governments derived support were not fatally undermined by their international commitments or by the domestic ramifications of those commitments.

These broad generalizations necessarily gloss over important differences in the efficacy of various institutional arrangements. The International Monetary Fund served as the embodiment of the rules and understandings that shaped the conduct of international monetary policies and constituted the Bretton Woods regime. The GATT functioned similarly in the trade domain. But policies toward economic development lacked a comparable framework. There was neither a formal institution with a capital "I" nor a set of informally accepted conventions to give them coherence and prominence.

The World Bank was established to finance development as well as reconstruction but was something of an afterthought at Bretton Woods, and its domain was limited. It was meant to intermediate between the capital markets of industrial countries and the governments of developing countries and to focus chiefly on the financing of individual projects. It did undergo adaptation, acquiring two affiliates—the International Finance Corporation (IFC) to engage in investment banking functions and thus promote private investment and the International Development Association (IDA) to provide concessional financing to low-income countries. Nevertheless, development policy operated in an ad hoc manner that worked to no one's satisfaction. US aid programs evolved out of the Marshall Plan. European programs focused on former colonies. No international agency was charged with the comprehensive surveillance of long-term capital flows and the stabilization of commodity prices, nor was there a consensus among governments on the need or way to take on these tasks.

There are two explanations for these differences in these institutions' effectiveness. One is the differing extent to which the main constituencies for the "outputs" of the institutions were present at the creation of those institutions. Much of the developing world was not directly represented at the Bretton Woods Conference. It was not clear at that point, moreover, that the advanced and developing countries had common interests and concerns important enough to produce agreed objectives and obligations.

The other explanation is the differing extent to which the postwar institutions relied on formal structures (institutions with a capital "I") and ideas (institutions with a small "i"). The International Monetary Fund was a formal structure intended to enforce an explicit set of rules; its Articles of Agreement contained a detailed list of international monetary do's and don'ts and established enforcement capabilities. Some of the rules were not enforceable, however, and they failed to anticipate all the subsequent problems. The General Agreement on Tariffs and Trade, by contrast, was an ad hoc agreement intended mainly to provide a framework for pursuing nondiscriminatory, multilateral trade liberalization. Many observers would now conclude that the GATT was the more effective arrangement. The strength of a formal arrangement such as the IMF is its rigidity; that of an informal, ideas-based institution such as the GATT is its adaptability. The greater success of the GATT thus illustrates the importance for postwar economic performance of an adaptable institutional framework.

If the Bretton Woods institutions were so important to the economic prosperity of the first 25 years after World War II, why then did they fail to support an equally rapid rate of growth in the advanced countries over the next 25 years? Part of the explanation, we will argue, is that the success of the postwar system gradually undermined the durability and adaptability of the system itself. By promoting economic growth in the industrial countries and its spread to much of the developing world, the system reduced the capacity of the United States to make side payments in order to gain support for existing institutions and for their further adaptation. The United States was no longer the dominant industrial power. The end of the Cold War reinforced this process by diminishing the incentive for the United States to make those side payments.

The success of the IMF, the World Bank, and the GATT also encouraged more countries to join, complicating negotiations and sharpening cleavages between developed and developing countries, between exporters of manufactures and of primary products, and between international borrowers and lenders. These cleavages became manifest in calls for a New International Economic Order and other challenges to existing rules. Again, the end of the Cold War, which has seen the admission to the GATT and the Bretton Woods Institutions of new countries with new aims and needs, is just the latest stage in a long process. The increased heterogeneity of the international community is one reason for the proliferation of regional arrangements; they represent a quest for homogeneity at the expense of universality, which may be needed to achieve consensus, articulate new rules, and build new institutions.

The success of postwar institutions in fostering trade and financial liberalization also opened up individual economies, which made it more difficult for governments to reconcile their international obligations with their domestic policy objectives. The early growth of international trade, the more recent growth of international capital mobility, and the prospective growth of international migration have all heightened the need to choose between adherence to international rules and independent pursuit of domestic economic and social policies. This conflict has weakened support for the existing institutions, has tended to make some of them more rigid and brittle, and has made it harder to marshal support, domestically and internationally, for the further reforms and adaptations needed to prevent obsolescence.

The opening of individual economies had another consequence. In its early stages, opening chiefly concerned the dismantling of explicit controls and restrictions on cross-border transactions. As those barriers came down, however, it became increasingly apparent that other important barriers lurk behind them—rules and arrangements deeply imbedded in domestic legislation, as well as private-sector practices, that have the effect of discriminating against international trade or investment. These are far harder to bargain away by the familiar methods used to reduce tariffs and other explicit cross-border restrictions. As firms involved in trading goods and services, in multinational production, and in international financial transactions encountered these more subtle barriers, they demanded measures aimed at achieving a "level playing field" and expressed dissatisfaction with the results of efforts to reduce conventional cross-border barriers. Governments responded in various ways: by putting unilateral pressure on their trading partners to modify domestic laws and practices, by finding ways to negotiate reciprocal changes in domestic arrangements, globally and regionally, and by trying to harmonize domestic regulations.[3]

The rest of this paper has four main sections. The first recalls how the international system was organized at the end of World War II and the adaptations made when its founders' expectations were challenged by unforeseen events. The second examines the evolution of the system and of the world economy during the 25 years after World War II. The third section looks at ways in which the system changed over the next 25 years—and ways in which it failed to change. The concluding section tries to look forward by drawing out the implications of this survey for adaptation and reform during the next half century.

Origins and Early Adaptations

The Historical Background

Governments had already tried once, after World War I, to reconstruct international economic arrangements. Almost as soon as it was created, the League of Nations established a Financial Commission to oversee

---

3. The measures taken by the United States under section 301 and "super 301" to punish other countries' "unfair" trade practices illustrate the unilateral approach; the steps taken by the European Community to create a "single internal market" under the terms of the Single European Act and the effort to liberalize trade in services during the Uruguay Round illustrate the reciprocal approach; and the Basel agreement on uniform capital-adequacy standards for commercial banks illustrates the attempt to harmonize domestic regulations.

lending to the defeated powers and the Eastern European successor states, and it worked with committees of officials and experts responsible for reconciling reparations with financial stability. The League also held a series of tariff truce conferences designed to reduce trade barriers. The Brussels and Genoa Conferences of 1920 and 1922 were convened to reconstruct the international monetary system. Central bankers such as Benjamin Strong of the Federal Reserve Bank of New York and Montagu Norman of the Bank of England cultivated contacts with the goal of harmonizing international monetary conditions.

The failure of these initiatives can be attributed to a combination of circumstances, prominent among which was the recalcitrance of the United States. Although it emerged from the war as the world's leading industrial power, the United States resisted responsibility for the development of international economic relations.[4] It refused to join the League of Nations, robbing that institution of authority. It limited its representatives at Brussels and Genoa to observer status. Spokesmen for the Harding administration criticized Strong for his foreign entanglements. In the resulting vacuum, the French and British vied for influence in Central and Eastern Europe—France seeking control of the League's Financial Commission, Britain attempting to capture its responsibilities for the Bank of England.

At a superficial level, these manifestations of US isolationism all shared a common cause: the fear that other countries would insist that the United States forgive their war debts to restore international economic stability. A deeper question, however, is posed by the sharp contrast with the post–World War II period. Why was the United States willing to take this step in the 1940s when it had been unwilling to do so in the 1920s? Learning from experience is surely part of the answer. The United States emerged from World War I with little if any experience in managing the international system and little appreciation of the implications of its economic might for international stability. Two decades of living with its economic power, not to mention the international economic disasters of the 1920s and 1930s and the experience of being dragged into a world war for the second time in a generation, understandably transformed its outlook.[5] Furthermore, domestic interest groups standing to benefit from more outward-oriented policies had learned to mobilize and lobby, and the very scale of World War II helped to transform the domestic political balance. Massive military procurement had stimulated the growth of the ship-

---

4. This is the theme of Kindleberger's (1973) influential analysis of the interwar period. It is important, however, not to overstate the extent of US isolationism. Hogan (1977) provides an account that portrays the US government as relatively active in the 1920s.

5. In fact, international engagement was not entirely unprecedented for the United States. It had convened a number of the international conferences held to deal with bimetallic controversies in the second half of the 19th century, but its lack of a central bank and its dependence on other countries for international financial support circumscribed its role.

building and aircraft industries on the Pacific Coast and in the South; these regions became more export-oriented and sympathetic to foreign policy commitments and defense expenditures than they had been previously (for details, see Seidman 1953). Still, it was far from clear that these forces would prevent the United States from retreating again into isolationism; ensuring against that contingency became a priority for European negotiators at Bretton Woods.

Lack of leadership by the United States weakened the international system established after World War I and deprived it of the capacity for adaptation. No international regime, in the sense of rules and understandings adequate to guide international economic policies, developed in the 1920s.[6] No institution was established to coordinate the stabilization of European currencies or oversee the transformation of the international monetary system from a gold to a gold-exchange standard. Countries stabilized individually, and some reverted from gold-exchange to gold-based reserve arrangements, with deflationary consequences.[7] No country was prepared to delegate authority over commercial policy to the organs of the League, and there was thus no way to achieve a coordinated shift to greater openness. The stated desire for trade liberalization remained less than credible. More generally, the absence of clearly defined rules and forums meant that the whole range of economic issues was thrown open whenever an attempt was made to deal with any single issue. Faced with these high transactions costs, governments hesitated to open negotiations. In this context, the isolationism of the United States was particularly costly. It did not use either carrots or sticks to prod other governments toward reform—the only devices that might have induced them to shift from their suboptimal equilibrium.

The failure after World War I to solve commitment and coordination problems internationally reflected a deeper failure to develop a domestic policy consensus.[8] After World War II, as we shall see, domestic interest groups reached an accommodation concerning the distribution of the national income. This distributional settlement was sealed by the

---

6. Strong and other US officials increasingly pressed for the development of the international monetary system along traditional gold-standard lines, while Norman pushed for a gold-exchange standard under which other countries held reserves in financial centers such as London. Yet the choice between a gold standard and gold-exchange standard had vital implications for the definition of acceptable monetary policies, and there was therefore deep disagreement about them.

7. The stabilization of the French franc in 1926 at an undervalued rate is frequently said to have intensified the deflationary pressures experienced by other countries. France and the United States were the most important countries to revert from the gold-exchange standard to the gold standard in the final years of the 1920s, although the liquidation of foreign exchange reserves became widespread starting in 1931.

8. This is a theme of Eichengreen (1992).

government's commitment to full employment and the welfare state.[9] Having achieved agreements at home, in ways that were broadly compatible across nations and thus consistent in their implications for the conduct of national economic policies, governments could enter credibly into international commitments. They could agree to create a single set of international economic institutions with which all could live.

The Bretton Woods Settlement

The disastrous depression of the 1930s made clear the huge costs of the failure to develop rules and understandings as well as organizational structures to guide the conduct of economic policies. The inability of politicians and officials to agree on an appropriate response to the crisis hindered international cooperation. The absence of an institutional framework allowed countries to pursue opportunistic policies that compounded their neighbors' problems. The results included the deep and persistent slump, the implosion of trade, the collapse of the international monetary system, and the termination of international lending.[10]

This experience, along with the difficulties of reconstruction after World War I, influenced British and American officials from the start of World War II. They saw the need to articulate rules and understandings to guide national policies following the war, so as to facilitate the pursuit of common objectives and discourage beggar-thy-neighbor policies. They agreed on the need to embody those rules and understandings in explicit agreements to which other countries could subscribe and to establish international organizations, not only as repositories for those agreements but also to enforce them. They viewed as vital a device for dissuading the United States from again reverting to political and economic isolationism. Out of their discussions emerged proposals for the IMF, World Bank, and ITO.

Nevertheless, the British and American negotiating positions were informed by the different situations of their countries and by different concerns. The United States sought to avoid international problems like those of the 1920s, when exchange rate instability and trade protectionism impeded the reconstruction of trade and finance. It favored fixed exchange rates, the removal of quantitative import restrictions, and nondiscrimination in trade to prevent a recurrence of the problems of the 1920s. The United Kingdom, in contrast, sought to avoid problems like those of the 1930s: high unemployment and an international system vulnerable to collapse. It advocated adjustable exchange rates and the limited use of trade controls to facilitate the pursuit of full employment at home, as well as tariff preferences to strengthen ties among subsets of countries such as

---

9. This is how one of us (Eichengreen 1994a) has characterized the rise of the welfare state.

10. O'Dell (1989) and Eichengreen (1992) emphasize how the absence of common rules and understandings blocked cooperative responses to the Depression.

those of the British Commonwealth as an alternative to dependence on an unreliable global trading system.

Given these differences, why did the negotiations succeed? Ikenberry (1993) argues that a small group of British and American policy specialists "articulated a set of ideas about monetary order and the organization of the postwar economy" that helped them identify "a set of normative and technical positions that was later embraced by wartime British and American leaders." Because these specialists were able to envisage a coherent institutional order, the two countries' policymakers were able to find common ground, despite their different concerns and the different circumstances of their countries. This is an important insight, but it is incomplete. The fact that Ikenberry's own treatment focuses on just two countries, the United States and the United Kingdom, points to another important factor, the small number of countries that had to reach agreement. The United States, as the leading player in the international arena, and the United Kingdom, as its closest ally and the second key-currency country, hammered out many of the details even before they joined some 40 other countries at Bretton Woods. Enemy powers such as Germany and occupied countries such as France necessarily had little say. Nor did representatives from Latin America or what was to become the Eastern bloc have much influence on the outcome. Both the small number of players and their homogeneity facilitated negotiations.

While the United States did not control the negotiations completely— Britain could influence the outcome by claiming to speak for most of the globe—the dynamism of American leadership contrasted sharply with the recalcitrance displayed after World War I. In part, this difference reflected belated US recognition that political isolation could not insulate the United States from future threats to world peace and that America's own prosperity depended on recovery and prosperity in Europe and other parts of the world. In part, the US role reflected the mobilization of American export interests, which had suffered heavily from the protectionism and exchange rate instability of the 1930s and the resulting implosion of trade.

International agreements once negotiated had to be ratified. They had to enjoy sufficient support domestically to be regarded as credible commitments on the part of the participating governments. Here the domestic commitment to full employment was key. Prominent among the ideas articulated during the negotiations was the belief that postwar international institutions should accommodate and indeed promote Keynesian stabilization policies and social welfare goals.[11] This generalization glosses

---

11. Thus, Keynes's final speech before the House of Lords, in which he reassured his colleagues that the Bretton Woods system was not a gold standard that would constrain the government's pursuit of full employment, is said to have played a pivotal role in the British ratification debate.

over differences between US and UK negotiators; the Americans, having the most room for maneuver within fixed exchange rates, evinced the least sympathy for proposals to allow easy recourse to parity adjustments. Yet the explicit commitment to full employment was a significant departure from previous international agreements. It allowed governments to promise their citizens that they would pursue policies to minimize unemployment, thus subduing conflicts between capital and labor. It facilitated the building of domestic coalitions that allowed for both ratification of the international agreement and subsequent implementation.

Negotiators reconciled competing objectives by emphasizing a small set of unifying principles: that trade liberalization should be pursued multilaterally and should eliminate discrimination, that transactions on current account should be freed of controls but capital movements could be restricted, that exchange rates should be pegged, and that their adjustment was a matter of common concern. Significantly, however, the power and scope of those principles differed across issue areas.

Success was most complete in the international monetary area. Many of the officials who formed the transnational policy coalition were monetary specialists, and their disagreements about the appropriate degree of exchange rate flexibility, the enforcement powers of the IMF, and its ability to create international reserves were minor compared with the matters on which they agreed. They agreed on the need for pegged exchange rates, for flexibility under exceptional conditions (including circumstances where the pursuit of full employment threatened a balance of payments crisis), for capital controls, for multilateral oversight, and for a reliable source of reserve credit. Under the Articles of Agreement, members of the IMF were required to peg their currencies to gold or to the dollar (which was pegged to gold at $35 an ounce). The IMF had to approve the initial exchange rates and most changes made thereafter, and its approval of such changes was to be conditioned on evidence that a country faced a "fundamental disequilibrium" in its balance of payments. Convertibility on current account was to be restored after a three- to five-year transition period. Finally, the Articles of Agreement attempted to provide a reliable source of reserves by endowing the IMF with a pool of national currencies to be made available to deficit countries. Each member's contribution to the currency pool was governed by its quota, which also determined the amount it could draw and its voting power in the IMF.

In the trade area, by contrast, British and American negotiators were deeply divided from the start. The US State Department subscribed fully to the principle of free trade, as US industries were competitive internationally and their main problem was securing access to foreign markets. The enthusiasm of British negotiators for free trade was tempered by the specter of the dollar shortage, concern about the sterling balances, a desire to preserve imperial preference, and fear of an inflexible external constraint inhibiting the pursuit of full employment.[12] This conflict had been finessed in wartime negotiations by skirting it in favor of monetary issues, in the vain hope that a consensus on monetary matters might spill over to trade matters. The monetary provisions of the Bretton Woods agreement did indeed provide some comfort for proponents of free and managed trade alike. On the central matter of principle, however, the United States and its negotiating partners remained as far apart after the war as they had been during it.

Even in the postwar negotiations, an attempt was made to dispatch the problem by avoiding it. Adopting the time-honored device of drafting an agreement that was too ambiguous to offend anyone, the negotiators succeeded merely in alienating everyone. Some countries such as the United States saw the ITO Charter as too interventionist. The US Congress, in particular, feared that the ITO would meddle in domestic economic affairs and refused to ratify its charter. Other countries objected to the charter's numerous exceptions and qualifications, which deprived the basic principles of operational effect.

We noted earlier that the World Bank received comparatively little attention at Bretton Woods. Despite having formally christened it the International Bank for Reconstruction and Development, its creators underestimated the needs of European reconstruction and neglected those of Third World development. The Bank's capitalization and operating procedures, decided in 1944, proved to be inadequate to the needs of postwar reconstruction, largely because the United States, from which most of the capital would have to come, wanted to minimize its financial obligations (as it had by insisting on the White Plan for the IMF rather than Keynes's more ambitious proposal for an International Clearing Union). The prostrate economies of Europe were in no position to object, and much of the developing world had not even gained the sovereign right to register an opinion.

This last fact helps to explain the failure at Bretton Woods to deal effectively with other North-South issues. Apart from establishing a presumption that the World Bank would not lend to countries in default on their external debts, its constitution provided no mechanism for rescheduling debts or managing international capital flows. This omission is puzzling, given the importance that negotiators attached to the stabilization of capital markets in light of their experience with debt defaults in the interwar period and the all-but-complete collapse of international lending in the 1930s. And nothing came of Keynes's proposal for a fourth international institution to stabilize the prices of primary commodities, although the ITO was meant to have some responsibilities in this realm. This was

---

12. The sterling balances represented amounts acquired by other countries in the course of helping Britain finance its war effort. British officials feared that their rapid liquidation under a regime of unregulated trade would produce unmanageable balance of payments deficits.

perhaps because the price slump of the 1930s was seen to reflect a secular trend in commodity prices rather than a problem of short-term instability, but it was also because many of the primary producers were not represented at Bretton Woods.

Early Adaptations

The adaptability of the Bretton Woods Institutions quickly came to the fore. When unanticipated problems arose, the operations of the organizations proposed to regulate trade, investment, and monetary affairs were modified without undermining their ability to resolve the problems they had been designed to address. The resilience of the principles articulated by wartime and postwar negotiators even allowed the organizations to be bypassed temporarily without undermining adherence to those principles.

The Marshall Plan

The most dramatic illustration was the Marshall Plan. The IMF and the Bank were obvious sources of the funds that Europe required: the former insofar as the problem reflected the need for balance of payments financing, the latter insofar as it reflected the need for long-term capital. Yet leading histories of the period barely mention the Bretton Woods Institutions. In its first five operating years, the Fund's currency transactions totaled only $851 million, of which $606 million was drawn in the first year.[13] Although the Bank extended more credit to Europe than to any other continent during its first seven operating years, its total loan commitments to Europe amounted to only $753 million between May 1947, when its first loan was made, and December 1953, a period that bracketed the Marshall Plan; they amounted to little more than a twentieth of Marshall aid. When the magnitude of the European problem was revealed clearly and the advent of the Cold War impressed upon the United States the importance of solving it, the Truman administration chose to extend Marshall aid unilaterally rather than inject additional capital into the Bank and Fund.

To have funneled aid on the scale of the Marshall Plan through the Bank and Fund would have required a fundamental recasting of those organizations rather than a marginal adaptation. The Bank was supposed to encourage international investment and supplement it at the margin. It was not supposed to suffer losses on its loans, which were meant to finance

13. The IMF barred countries receiving Marshall aid from using the Fund's resources, arguing that those countries should keep their drawing rights intact for use when the monetary system was functioning normally, not use them to finance abnormal transitional needs.

individual projects shunned by imperfect capital markets, and it was not to make grants or highly concessional loans. The Fund was supposed to provide short-term credit to finance temporary balance of payments deficits or buy time for countries to deal with long-lasting shocks. The Marshall Plan, in contrast, represented a large-scale, multiple-year commitment made in response to the recognition that Europe's problem could not be solved quickly.

The Fund was supposed to possess some direct authority or influence over its members' policies, but the Bank had none. Yet Marshall aid came with conditionality of a sort that not even the creators of the IMF had envisaged. Each recipient was required to sign a bilateral pact with the United States, agreeing to balance its budget, restore internal financial stability, stabilize its exchange rate at a realistic level, and develop a program for removing quotas and other trade controls. Each expenditure of Marshall aid had to be negotiated with the American authorities, a process that allowed the latter to promote price decontrol and discourage nationalization.

Related features of the Marshall Plan are worthy of note. The United States encouraged the recipients to pursue European integration. They had to do more than affirm their support for this goal; they were obliged to develop collaboratively a plan for allocating American aid. This requirement forced them to coordinate their national reconstruction plans and to establish an institution for that purpose: the Organization for European Economic Cooperation (OEEC), which became the Organization for Economic Cooperation and Development (OECD). The OEEC Secretariat became important as a venue for the exchange of information but also as a repository of collective memory.[14]

Furthermore, the United States was willing to countenance discrimination against American goods. Although it required recipients of Marshall aid to relax their restrictions on imports from the United States, it allowed them to do that more gradually than they relaxed restrictions on intra-European trade. This should be viewed as a price that the United States was willing to pay to achieve its Cold War objectives.

Three assessments of the Marshall Plan are found in the literature.[15] The first attached great importance to its role in stimulating the investment, financing the imports, and repairing the infrastructure that were required for the resumption of growth. The second, revisionist interpretation dismissed the plan as having been too small to contribute significantly to recovery through these channels. The third, most recent generation of studies has rehabilitated the Marshall Plan by arguing that US aid helped

---

14. The same functions can be ascribed to the secretariats of the other international institutions under discussion.

15. Citations will be found in Eichengreen (1994b).

Europe to achieve the domestic consensus on which it based its subsequent growth and—not incidently—its support for the new international rules.

That domestic consensus rested on three pillars. The first was the distributional settlement between capital and labor that had been so lamentably absent after World War I. Once there was agreement about who would pay taxes and who would receive transfers from government, budgets could be balanced and prices could be decontrolled. By providing aid equal to 2.5 percent of European GNP, the Marshall Plan reduced the sacrifices necessary for distributional compromise.

The second was an agreement that the European economies would be based on the price system and private property. Nationalizations and price controls there might be, but their scope was limited. In the turbulent aftermath of World War II, when Socialist and Communist parties were powerful in several European countries, this outcome was far from assured. The Marshall Plan was designed to promote market-oriented policies and helped to tip the balance in their favor.[16]

The third pillar was the commitment by governments to pursue growth as the best way to compensate those who were making the initial sacrifices and to protect those who could not protect themselves from the chill winds of the market. These goals were to be achieved through the pursuit of full employment and the development of the welfare state. The Beveridge Report in Britain and the Full Employment Act of 1946 in the United States symbolized these aspirations and committed governments to them. The Marshall planners accommodated them by not objecting when European governments intervened more extensively in their economies than was customary in the United States. They facilitated the pursuit of full employment by acquiescing in the maintenance of exchange controls and tolerating trade discrimination against the United States. They encouraged European industry to reorganize along American lines by adopting the management techniques and consumer-oriented products US enterprise had developed, and they used Marshall aid to bring Europeans to America to learn state-of-the-art techniques on the factory floor.[17]

---

16. The program's very design—which established an independent US government agency, staffed it with private-sector managers, linked it to private-sector groups by a network of advisory committees, and then encouraged the recipient countries to replicate this administrative structure—sought to maximize the role of market forces (Hogan 1987, 19).

17. As Hogan (1987, 23) put it, "Greater productivity . . . would adjourn the redistributive struggles that fueled extremist political parties in Western Europe. . . . [B]enefit would come from translating the problem of economic growth into a technical problem soluble by adopting American methods of private production, including American engineering, manufacturing, and marketing techniques and American strategies of labor-management teamwork."

With political stability at home, European governments were free to enter credibly into international commitments. And with the terms of the domestic settlement broadly similar across countries and compatible with the rules of the Bretton Woods system, they were able thereafter to make the particular commitments required to draw on the Bretton Woods Institutions for the support of their domestic policies. It is likely that both more extreme dirigiste and more extreme free-market policies would have proved incompatible with the Bretton Woods Institutions. Planning that was more than indicative would have clashed with the liberal trading system, as revealed even by France's limited experimentation with the Monnet Plan. A dash to current account convertibility through the adoption of a floating exchange rate, as Britain contemplated in the early 1950s, would have come into conflict with the essential provisions of the Bretton Woods agreement and threatened the progress of European integration.

The European Payments Union

The story of the European Payments Union, another early adaptation, is similar in many respects.[18] Rather than moving quickly to restore current account convertibility, Western Europe established a regional payments union, which operated through the end of 1958. The IMF was largely successful in getting its members to adopt and maintain par values, but the rapid return to current account convertibility envisaged at Bretton Woods was delayed, and official financing for intra-European payments deficits was not provided by the IMF but by the EPU, which operated with the help of the Bank for International Settlements (BIS) and OEEC.

The EPU facilitated the multilateral clearing of trade-related payments within Europe and provided partial financing for net imbalances.[19] Its rules, however, minimized the risk of a country using EPU credits to exploit its partners by remaining in persistent deficit. No conditions were attached to a country's drawings on its EPU quota, which was equal to 15 percent of its intra-EPU trade (although the fraction of any deficit that it could finance with EPU credit fell as its total indebtedness rose). But additional credits could be obtained only if a country agreed to strict conditions set down by the EPU's managing board. Discussions were initiated before a country's quota was exhausted, and it was made clear that the provision of exceptional assistance would depend on the country's early adoption of adjustment policies. Officials of governments

---

18. On the establishment and functioning of the EPU, see Triffin (1957) and Kaplan and Schleiminger (1989).

19. It should be noted that EPU clearings and credits covered more than intra-European trade, as they included transactions with Europe's colonies and with the rest of the sterling area.

requesting such assistance had to appear before the board for questioning and submit memoranda regarding their progress.

The essential function of the EPU, however, was to solve the commitment and coordination problems faced by European countries contemplating moves toward greater openness, first on a regional basis, then on a nondiscriminatory basis. Investing resources along lines dictated by comparative advantage could prove to be an expensive mistake if one's trading partners failed to do likewise. Having incurred the costs of shifting resources into the production of exportable goods, countries might find foreign markets blocked, rendering their investments uneconomical. Before reallocating resources in that fashion, each government therefore had to be convinced that its partners were committed to similar policies. Otherwise, each country would be tempted to adopt an "after you, Alphonse" strategy, leading to a classic coordination problem. The GATT, adopted as an interim arrangement pending ratification of the ITO Charter, could not resolve this problem perfectly because its scope was limited. It was concerned mainly with tariff reduction, and it did not require the rapid dismantling of trade and payments controls imposed for balance of payments reasons. Furthermore, Europe faced two special obstacles to coordinated liberalization.

One was "the German problem": recalling the Schachtian policies of the 1930s and war years, other European countries were particularly skeptical of Germany's commitment to openness. Yet Germany had long been Europe's dominant supplier of capital goods. Therefore, other European countries needed to be sure that they could count on Germany to export the equipment needed to expand and modernize their industries and to import the consumer goods and other merchandise that their industries would then export. Absent adequate assurances of this sort, it might be sensible to them to sacrifice efficiency in favor of self-sufficiency. Institutions that could lock in Germany's commitment to intra-European trade could thus help importantly to reconstitute the traditional pattern of comparative advantage and end the dollar shortage.

The other obstacle was Britain's hesitancy to restore convertibility. The failed attempt of 1947 was traumatic, and the problem behind that failure, the sterling balances, remained even after the 1949 devaluation. Proposals were made periodically in Britain for a unilateral dash to convertibility, but these were rejected because it was believed that it would require massive devaluation and an unacceptable erosion of working-class living standards.

The EPU provided an institutional solution to these problems of commitment and coordination. The participating countries proceeded simultaneously with the elimination of quantitative barriers to intra-European trade. To coordinate their initiatives, they negotiated a schedule called the Code of Liberalization. By February 1951, less than a year after the EPU went into effect, discrimination within Europe was to be eliminated. In addition, participants had to liberalize their quantitative barriers to intra-European trade so that by 1955 no more than 10 percent of intra-European trade would be burdened by quotas. The OEEC monitored compliance with the Code of Liberalization. A country failing to comply or employing policies aimed at manipulating the terms or volume of trade could expect to be denied access to EPU credits.[20]

Marshall Plan administrators supported the EPU by providing $350 million of working capital to finance its operations and by deflecting the objections of the US Treasury to the discrimination inherent in EPU arrangements. In effect, the United States used its leadership to promote flexible application of the rules it had advocated at Bretton Woods. The lure of Marshall aid enabled the United States to convince a reluctant Britain to participate in the EPU, and the supportive US role helps to explain why the EPU did not fatally undermine the authority of the IMF.[21] The United States saw the EPU as a temporary arrangement, after which the IMF agreement would come into full force. It made sure that the provisions of the EPU, other than the departure from current account convertibility, were compatible with Bretton Woods.

The acceptability of a regional payments union that discriminated in favor of intra-European trade was enhanced by the fact that it operated in the context of a GATT process that was gaining credibility and momentum.[22] The United States organized the first GATT tariff-cutting round long before acknowledging that the ITO Charter was dead. Delegates from 23 countries met in Geneva in 1947 to make product-by-product bargains on a bilateral basis. The tariff cuts resulting from this process were then generalized to the other participating countries via the most-favored nation (MFN) principle.

The General Agreement, signed on 30 October 1947, included the results of 123 sets of negotiations covering 50,000 items, as well as a general code

---

20. The Schuman Plan, which led to the European Coal and Steel Community (ECSC) and the first steps toward European integration, can be seen in the same light. The ECSC created a common market in coal and steel, and it established a high authority to monitor compliance with the agreement. Within certain limits, the authority's decisions were binding on the governments and private citizens of the participating countries. Hence, the ECSC enhanced the credibility of Germany's commitment to openness by assuring the French steel industry of access to Ruhr coal, which was indispensable to its survival, and assuring German steel producers of access to the iron ore of Lorraine.

21. The IMF's consistent opposition to the EPU was nonetheless "a major factor contributing to the decline in the reputation of the Fund in the 1950s" (Kenwood and Lougheed 1971, 263).

22. The same can be said of the ECSC and, later, the European Economic Community (EEC). Extensive arrangements were made to ensure that the ECSC was GATT-compatible. The waiver of the GATT rule against sectoral free trade arrangements, as distinct from comprehensive customs unions, was conditional on the adherence by ECSC members to certain rules and requirements. Their observance was reviewed annually by the GATT, to which other GATT members could bring complaints of excessive discrimination.

of conduct based on multilateralism and nondiscrimination and requiring the elimination of quantitative restrictions. These principles were not dissimilar from those embodied in the ITO Charter; some of the language used in the GATT was in fact drawn directly from that document (see van der Wee 1986, 349). Hence, the articulation of a set of commonly agreed rules once again facilitated negotiations and was ultimately codified as an international agreement.

Although the Annecy Round of 1949 and Torquay Round of 1950–51 did not make tariff cuts comparable to those achieved at Geneva, further progress was made, and the successive GATT rounds created a presumption that trade liberalization would become a continuing process in which reputation would matter and participants would hesitate to renege on prior commitments.

Early Achievements and Emerging Problems, 1945–70

Economic Performance in the Industrial World

Industrial production in Western Europe rose by nearly 10 percent per annum during the Marshall Plan years (1947–51). In Japan, where the heavy hand of the US occupation was similarly lightened by US aid, sustained recovery began after the application of the Dodge Plan to control inflation in 1949, and it accelerated sharply during the Korean War, when Japanese industry was encouraged to supply the needs of UN forces. Table 1 summarizes the course of growth in Europe, North America, and Japan over many decades. It shows clearly that the postwar rise in the (unweighted) average annual growth rate of output in Western European countries, which reached 4.4 percent in the 1950s and 4.8 percent in the 1960s, represented a dramatic break with the previous trend. In the United States, where postwar growth was less rapid, the case for continuity with earlier periods is easier to make. There can be no question, however, that the postwar growth miracle in Japan was entirely different from any earlier experience.

Rapid output growth and rising living standards helped to sustain support for the postwar institutions. When incomes were rising and prospects were bright, it was easier to call for the sacrifices needed to bring domestic economic arrangements into line with international requirements. Unemployment rates fell to low levels everywhere (except in Italy, where they averaged 7.9 percent in the 1950s and 3.3 percent in the 1960s); with labor markets tight, the domestic adjustments imposed by external liberalization were less objectionable. Nevertheless, some countries resisted adjustment.

Table 1 Average annual rate of growth of selected industrial countries, 1870–1989 (percentages)

Country	1870–1913	1913–50	1950–59	1960–69	1970–79	1980–89
Western Europe	2.3	1.6	4.4	4.8	3.1	2.00
Belgium	2.7	1.0	2.9	4.9	3.3	1.86
France	1.6	0.7	4.6	5.8	3.7	1.95
West Germany	2.9	1.2	7.8	4.8	2.8	2.17
Italy	1.4	1.3	5.8	5.7	3.2	1.94
Netherlands	2.2	2.1	4.7	5.1	2.9	1.33
Norway	2.2	2.7	3.2	5.0	4.7	2.39
Sweden	3.0	2.2	3.4	4.6	2.0	1.92
United Kingdom	2.2	1.7	2.7	2.8	1.8	2.41
Canada	3.8	2.8	3.9	5.6	4.2	3.02
Japan	2.4	1.8	9.5	10.5	4.9	3.77
United States	4.3	2.9	3.2	4.3	3.0	2.96

Source: van der Wee (1986) and authors' calculations.

The obvious explanation for more rapid growth in Europe and Japan than in the United States is the "catch-up" Abramovitz (1986) emphasized. Two decades of depression and war had opened up gaps between growth rates vis-à-vis both the United States and Europe's own prewar trend, and these gaps offered exceptional scope for growth after 1945.[23]

Aside from catch-up, the proximate cause of the postwar growth miracle was high investment. Investment rates in most countries after World War II were fully 50 percent higher than those attained on average in 1914–49 (table 2). Japan's investment rate, while unexceptional in the 1950s, rose by about 50 percent in the 1960s, when growth was fastest. The United States and United Kingdom, where growth was slowest, exhibited the lowest investment rates. Clearly, there was two-way causality: investment stimulated growth but was particularly attractive in countries that were growing rapidly for other reasons. Postwar growth was thus characterized by a virtuous circle.

---

23. But cross-section regressions relating growth rates to differences in levels of per capita GDP show that "catch-up" and "spring-back" explain only part of the postwar acceleration in Europe; even after allowing for this effect, European growth from 1950 through 1973 was still more than 50 percent faster than it became thereafter. Crafts (1992) calculates the growth bonus due to "catch-up" vis-à-vis the United States and "spring-back" to prewar levels. His results show that, purged of catch-up and spring-back, growth rates for eight European countries fell from 3.1 percent in 1950–73 to 1.9 percent in 1979–88. For further details, see Baumol, Blackman, and Wolff (1989).

Table 2 Total gross domestic investment as a percentage of GNP in selected industrial countries, 1900–93 (period averages)

Country	1900–13	1914–49	1950–60	1961–71	1972–82	1983–93
Western Europe	n.a.	n.a.	21.0	23.2	21.7	19.9
Belgium	n.a.	n.a.	16.5	21.0	20.9	17.1
France	n.a.	n.a.	19.1	24.6	22.3	20.1
West Germany	n.a.	14.3	24.0	26.0	21.4	20.2
Italy	15.4	13.5	20.8	20.4	19.9	20.3
Netherlands	n.a.	n.a.	24.2	25.6	20.7	20.1
Norway	12.7	15.4	26.4	26.9	30.3	24.3
Sweden	12.3	15.5	21.3	23.0	20.4	19.2
United Kingdom	7.7	7.6	15.4	18.3	18.0	17.5
Canada	25.5	16.0	24.8	22.2	22.7	20.4
Japan	n.a.	n.a.	24.0	35.1	32.1	29.6
United States	20.6	14.7	19.1	16.8	18.2	17.2

n.a. = not available

Source: van der Wee (1986, 196), and authors' calculations.

One source of the productivity growth that made investment so attractive was the expansion of trade. The volume of exports expanded faster than output, by more than 8 percent per year in Europe 1950s and 1960s, by an astounding 16.5 percent in Japan, and by 5.3 percent in the United States. The growth of trade tended to concentrate investment in the sectors where it made the largest contribution to productivity growth. As nations could exploit their comparative advantage, the level and allocation of investment was not constrained by the composition of domestic demand.

Here again, causality ran in both directions; it was, as we said, easier to liberalize trade when rapid growth made it relatively easy to bear the adjustment costs. But the dramatic contrast between export and output growth rates suggests that other forces must have been at work. Table 3 shows that the elasticity of exports with respect to output was 1.5 in the United States, higher still in every Northern European country other than Britain, and a remarkable 6.6 in Japan. The obvious explanations are trade liberalization in the frameworks of the GATT and the EEC and the relatively stable exchange rates of the Bretton Woods system, to which we now turn.

Commercial and Monetary Achievements

Six rounds of GATT negotiations were completed by the beginning of the 1970s. The most important were the first—the Geneva Round of 1947,

Table 3 Import and export growth rates, relationship to output growth, and share of goods and services in GNP, by countries

| Country | Growth rates of merchandise trade at 1963 prices, 1950–52 to 1977–69 | | Growth elasticities of trade with respect to GNP[a] | | Goods, services, and factor income as percentage of GNP at current market prices | | | |
| | | | | | Credits | | Debits | |
	Exports	Imports	Exports	Imports	1950	1970	1950	1970
Europe	8.4	8.6	1.8	1.9	26.4	31.1	26.8	30.7
Belgium	8.6	8.3	2.5	2.4	29.4[b]	48.2	29.1[b]	45.1
France	7.3	8.7	1.5	1.7	16.4	17.0	15.6	16.6
West Germany	12.0	12.6	1.9	2.0	11.6	22.0	12.9	20.2
Italy	13.1	11.1	2.4	2.1	12.0[c]	20.2	13.4[b]	19.6
Netherlands	9.3	8.8	1.9	1.8	43.1	52.2	49.6	53.4
Norway	7.3	7.8	1.8	1.9	47.4	42.4	45.9	43.9
Sweden	6.8	6.7	1.7	1.6	24.2	24.4	23.5	24.9
United Kingdom	3.1	4.4	1.1	1.6	26.9	22.6	24.6	21.8
Japan	16.5	n.a.	6.6	n.a.	n.a.	n.a.	n.a.	n.a.
United States	5.3	n.a.	1.5	n.a.	n.a.	n.a.	n.a.	n.a.

a. Rate of growth of exports (or imports) divided by the corresponding rate of growth of GNP at constant prices. Growth rates for output (not shown here) have been taken from Economic Commission of Europe, 1972, *The European Economy from the 1950s to the 1970s* (New York), table 1.2, p.4.
b. 1953.
c. 1951.

Source: Zacchia (1976) and authors' calculations.

when the United States reduced its tariffs by an average of 20 percent on all dutiable imports—and the last, the Kennedy Round of 1967, when the major participants reduced tariffs by about 35 percent on their nonagricultural imports (which represented about 80 percent of the industrial countries' dutiable imports). These reductions were impressive by any standard, but especially by contrast with the worldwide increase of tariffs after World War I. The results for agricultural trade were less impressive; apart from grains, which received special treatment, only half of the industrial countries' agricultural imports were affected, and the tariff cuts on those were little more than half as large as the cuts on manufactures.

Two other achievements underscore the importance of the Kennedy Round. For the first time, the negotiators sought to regulate antidumping practices by agreeing to a code that led the United States to expedite its antidumping procedures, Canada to adopt an injury requirement, and EEC countries to harmonize their antidumping regulations. Other codes were to be negotiated in subsequent GATT rounds. Furthermore, the Kennedy Round adopted a new method for cutting tariffs. In previous rounds, we have noted, bilateral agreements were negotiated product by product and multilateralized under the MFN principle. This became cumbersome as the number of participants grew. (It had reached 82 in the Kennedy Round.) Hence, the Kennedy Round aimed at "linear cuts" (i.e., across-the-board tariff reductions on industrial products), from which only a small number of exceptions might be made by each country. In effect, the negotiators bargained about the products on which cuts would *not* be made rather than haggling over each and every cut. Here again, US leadership was key. The US Trade Expansion Act of 1962 authorizing American participation had given American negotiators broader tariff-cutting powers.

More generally, the Kennedy Round can be understood as an American response to the most important trade policy development of the period: the advent of the European Economic Community. The United States had encouraged European integration, viewing it as a source of economic strength to fend off the Soviet threat and a means of binding Germany into Europe. The Marshall Plan had encouraged Europeans to form the OEEC, EPU, and ECSC to qualify for American aid. In 1957, the six members of the ECSC signed the Treaty of Rome, committing themselves to establish a full-fledged customs union as a way station on the road to deeper integration. Although the customs union was not completed until 1968 (albeit ahead of schedule), and its common external tariff was not higher than the previous national tariffs of the member countries, the United States had become concerned about the potential for trade diversion, prompting it to initiate the Kennedy Round.

The growth of international trade was accompanied by increasing capital mobility. American multinational firms had begun to invest heavily in Europe in the 1950s (table 4). Intra-European direct investment was also

Table 4   New US direct investment abroad, net outflows plus
retained earnings (millions of dollars per year)

Period	Total	Europe	EEC	United Kingdom	Canada	Japan
1950–52	1,376	129	100	101	506	21
1953–55	1,572	271	107	127	694	19
1956–58	3,016	583	229	302	926	10
1959–61	2,687	1,032	375	453	746	37
1962–64	3,388	1,460	736	323	772	92
1965	4,960	1,867	854	559	1,452	68
1966	5,259	2,239	1,245	574	1,626	80

Source: Adapted from Cooper (1968, 83).

growing, stimulated by the formation of the EEC. There was also an increase of international portfolio investment, and the mobility of short-term capital had been encouraged by the restoration of current account convertibility at the beginning of 1959 and the relaxation of controls on banking transactions in Europe. These developments also facilitated the growth of the Eurodollar market, in which London-based banks accepted dollar deposits and thus bid funds away from American banks, whose deposit rates were capped by Regulation Q. This is one reason for the increase of net private portfolio capital outflows from the United States, which rose from $1.1 billion in 1957 to $4.1 billion in 1964. All of these innovations tended to tighten the links among national financial markets, as is evident in the convergence of short-term interest rates in the 1960s (Cooper 1968, 112 and 141).

With the restoration of current account convertibility and termination of the EPU, the Bretton Woods system began to operate fully, although capital movements were probably freer than its architects had intended. The exchange rates of the major industrial countries were kept within narrow bands; they could not depart from their dollar parities by more than 1 percent. The only significant parity adjustments in the 1960s were the small revaluations by Germany and the Netherlands in 1961, the devaluations by Britain and France in 1967 and 1969, respectively, and the revaluation by Germany in 1969 after a brief float.[24] Even Canada, which had allowed its currency to float in 1950, returned to a pegged exchange rate in 1962. Devaluations by developing countries were more common but typically taken under duress (see Cooper 1971).

The IMF assumed a more active role as a supplier of reserve credit. It encouraged countries to draw on the Fund rather than tighten exchange

---

24. The circumstances surrounding these exchange rate changes are described by Solomon (1982).

restrictions to deal with balance of payments problems, and it made extensive use of standby arrangements. These arrangements, pioneered in negotiations with France in 1956, made very large amounts of reserve credit available to bolster confidence in a country's currency. In effect, the Fund recognized that, with the easing of controls on capital movements, a country seeking to defend a pegged exchange rate could quickly exhaust its own reserves and would need large amounts of IMF credit. To supplement the Fund's own resources, the 10 largest industrial countries set up the General Arrangements to Borrow, under which they would lend the IMF as much as $6 billion.

These expanded resources, however, might not be sufficient if the dollar, to which the Bretton Woods system was anchored, came under attack, and that possibility grew. In the late 1950s, the US balance of payments had moved into persistent deficit. American exporters were not uncompetitive, but capital outflows were growing due to the factors described above.

The new situation was dramatized in 1960 by a flurry of speculation in gold and was met by a series of ad hoc measures designed to finance the US balance of payments deficit by encouraging other countries to build up their dollar reserves rather than buy gold from the United States. One of these was the gold pool, under which the monetary authorities of the major countries, including the United States, agreed to sell gold in the London market to keep its price from rising above the official price of $35 an ounce. These measures, however, did not reduce the balance of payments deficit itself, leading the United States to take additional measures. It sought to limit the costs of stationing US troops abroad and to reduce US capital outflows. In 1963 it imposed an interest equalization tax on American purchases of foreign securities, in 1965 it imposed "voluntary" limits on foreign loans by American banks and direct investments by American firms, and in 1968 it made those limits mandatory.

Disquietude over these developments promoted discussion of changes in the Bretton Woods system. The most prominent debate surrounded proposals to create new reserve assets under IMF management, which came to be known as Special Drawing Rights (SDRs). The US Treasury opposed the idea initially because it wanted to preserve the reserve role of the dollar but shifted its position sharply in 1965 and called for negotiations on an amendment to the IMF Articles of Agreement allowing the Fund to distribute SDRs. The first distribution began in 1970, just as the stock of international reserves was about to rise hugely, due to a sudden widening of the US payments deficit.

Mounting Strains

Despite the accomplishments of the 1950s and 1960s—or, more accurately, partly because of them—the international system was beginning to experience severe strains. The dismantling of controls on trade and payments, the GATT rounds of tariff cuts, and the increase of capital mobility resulting from the restoration of convertibility rendered economies more open to flows of goods and capital. Hence, the external constraint became tighter, sharpening the conflict between internal and external objectives.

In France, this conflict emerged as early as 1952, when dirigiste policies, specifically the Monnet Plan for investment in strategic sectors, ran up against the balance of payments constraint, and the government was forced to suspend its plan to meet the targets set forth in the OEEC Code of Liberalization. France started again to remove import quotas in 1955, but the payments problem resurfaced, forcing France to devalue in 1957.

In Britain, a series of balance of payments crises forced the government to rein in demand, producing a sequence of "stop-go" episodes, and the government decided belatedly to devalue in 1967.

The United States began to confront the conflict in the early 1960s; the Federal Reserve was kept from cutting interest rates to the extent dictated by the recession of 1960–61 because of the size of the capital outflow and the weak balance of payments. Domestic agendas that might have been viable in less open economies were increasingly constrained, and the reluctance of governments to confront the new reality intensified the strains on the Bretton Woods system of pegged exchange rates.

In France, dissatisfaction with the Bretton Woods system was manifest in attacks on the dollar-based gold-exchange standard and calls for a return to a traditional gold standard. Elsewhere, the dissatisfaction was reflected in proposals for more exchange rate flexibility, but governments disavowed them because they were publicly committed to defending the existing pegged rates. Official rhetoric in the years leading up to the breakdown of the Bretton Woods system in 1971–73 was uncannily similar to official rhetoric in the years leading up to the crises of the European Monetary System (EMS) in 1992–93.

Import penetration, especially by Japanese goods, led to protectionist rumblings in Europe. Even in the 1950s, a number of European countries, including Britain and France, had discriminated against Japanese goods. When Japan gained full GATT membership in 1955, those countries invoked an exception allowing them to withhold MFN treatment from Japan. Other developments underscored the limitations of the GATT. For example, the EEC and the United States obtained waivers allowing them to impose quotas on agricultural imports when they restricted domestic agricultural production, which is what EEC did under the Common Agricultural Policy (CAP).

With Europe growing half again as fast as the United States and Japan growing three times as fast, the United States was no longer confident of its industrial dominance. Even in the 1950s, Congress had broadened the definition of injury that could be invoked by domestic producers to justify relief from import competition, and a number of tariffs were raised as a result of findings of injury made by the US Tariff Commission in response to petitions filed by domestic producers. In addition, the United States persuaded its trading partners to adopt "voluntary" restraints on certain of their exports, including Japanese and European carbon steel exports. And Congress came close to adopting the highly protectionist Mills bill in 1970. These developments reflected the increasingly divisive nature of domestic trade politics, as interest groups learned how to manipulate political levers in pursuit of their particular economic agendas.[25]

Existing institutions were ill-equipped to cope with these pressures. The GATT had achieved a significant reduction of tariffs and was fairly effective in requiring the industrial countries to abolish outright import quotas, apart from those on agricultural goods. But it could do little to combat the proliferation of "voluntary" agreements. The GATT even became involved in managing the Multi-Fiber Arrangement (MFA), the framework for a network of national restrictions on imports of textiles and apparel from the developing countries.[26] The GATT was supposed to monitor and disseminate information about members' trade policies, but this became increasingly difficult as trade barriers took new forms whose tariff equivalents were not easy to measure.[27]

Similarly, the Bretton Woods system of pegged exchange rates was ill-suited to withstand the pressures brought to bear by the increase in capital mobility. It had become far easier for investors and others to withdraw their capital from a country in anticipation of a devaluation to avoid capital losses. Hence, the first hint of an impending devaluation could precipitate a crisis. Cognizant of the danger, weak-currency countries became increasingly reluctant to contemplate exchange rate changes or even to acknowledge in principle that they may play a useful role in correcting balance of payments problems. The monetary system became rigid just when the need for adjustment was growing.

The result was mounting tension in foreign exchange markets. Britain staggered from one crisis to another until the pound was devalued in 1967. Demonstrations and strikes in the spring of 1968 provoked capital flight

---

25. Protectionist coalitions were not the only groups active in this process. The very success of the GATT produced new interest groups, such as dealers in imported cars, who lobbied equally hard for continued liberalization.

26. The MFA was adopted in 1974 and grew out of bilateral restrictions imposed by the United States, first on imports from Japan, then from other countries. Fearing that the developing countries' exports might be diverted to their markets, other industrial countries imposed similar restrictions. The MFA was designed to set standards for the bilateral restrictions and guarantee that they would be liberalized gradually, but the developing countries have argued that this liberalization has occurred too slowly.

27. It was not until after the Kennedy Round that GATT members, with the assistance of the GATT secretariat, began compiling an information base on nontariff barriers (Winham 1986, 59).

from France, which devalued unilaterally one year later. These events, in combination with rumors of a German revaluation, raised doubts about the stability of the dollar. Even before the French devaluation of 1969, governments participating in the gold pool had to sell $3 billion of gold against dollars and then to dissolve the pool itself, so that a two-tier gold market emerged in 1968. The failure of three large IMF drawings to prevent the British devaluation and France's decision to devalue without consulting the Fund were blows to the IMF's prestige.

By this time, however, the IMF had become a different institution than the one foreseen at Bretton Woods. It never acquired the veto power over parity changes on which American negotiators had insisted. France was far from alone in failing to secure the Fund's advance approval for an exchange rate change. Canada's decision to float its currency and Peru's refusal to declare a par value are other examples of the IMF's limited ability to enforce its Articles of Agreement.[28] While increases in IMF quotas and the use of standby arrangements had increased the Fund's financial leverage, many of the monetary innovations of the 1960s, such as the gold pool and the swap agreements among industrial countries, were developed and managed outside the Fund. The IMF was less an enforcer of rules than a repository for the understandings on which international monetary collaboration was based.

The Emergence of the Third World

In the early part of the postwar period, the inward-looking strategies of many developing countries limited their integration into the international system and their involvement in managing it. The merchandise exports of developing countries had grown by only 3.1 percent per annum in the 1950s. By the end of the decade, however, a shift toward export promotion had begun; developing countries' exports grew at a much more impressive rate—from the standpoint of certain industrial nations, a disquieting rate. It averaged 5.9 percent in the 1960s (calculated from Reynolds 1985, table 8). When they began to look outward, moreover, the developing countries started to take an active role in the management and adaptation of the postwar system.

Having failed to convince industrial countries of the need for a network of commodity agreements to stabilize the prices of primary products, they agreed somewhat reluctantly to the creation within the IMF of a Compensatory Financing Facility (CFF) to provide reserve credit without onerous conditions to primary-producing countries that faced unanticipated short-

---

28. The most notorious instance occurred in 1971, when the IMF managing director learned of the US decision to close the gold window only as President Richard Nixon announced it in a televised speech.

falls in their export earnings.[29] Shortly thereafter, at the start of negotiations that led to the creation of the SDRs, the developing countries demanded participation in the negotiations and a share of the new reserve assets. The negotiations had been initiated by the industrial (Group of Ten) countries, which sought internal consensus before presenting a proposal to the entire IMF membership. Going further, they decided to propose that the new reserve asset should be distributed to a small number of core countries; all others would receive conditional credit facilities financed by the core group. If given SDRs, they argued, the poorer countries would splurge on imports, and all of the SDRs would then wind up in the coffers of the industrial countries, which would, in the process, have to give up goods and services. The developing countries objected strenuously, and turned to the United Nations Conference on Trade and Development (UNCTAD) for help with the liquidity problem.[30] The negotiations stalled until the G-10 countries dropped their plan and agreed on allocating SDRs to all IMF members in proportion to their quotas.

The developing countries were equally active in matters pertaining to trade. They protested the failure of early GATT rounds to reduce agricultural tariffs, a process that did not get under way until the Kennedy Round. They complained that the GATT had failed to neutralize the political pressures in industrial countries that had caused them to make smaller tariff cuts on imports of labor-intensive manufactures, in which developing economies had a comparative advantage, than on imports of capital-intensive goods. They charged that the GATT was poorly designed to cope with the developed countries' reliance on quantitative restrictions for protecting domestic producers of goods made by unskilled labor, such as textiles and apparel.

The GATT responded to these complaints by appointing a panel of experts, chaired by Gottfried Haberler, to study the trade problems of developing countries. Its report to the GATT in 1958 led to the establishment of a series of committees. Their chief accomplishment was the 1964 decision to waive the GATT rule against new preferences in order to allow advanced countries to discriminate in favor of imports from the developing economies. This was less than the developing countries expected, and they sought redress outside the GATT, by having the UN General Assembly convene the first UN Conference on Trade and Development in 1964. The second UNCTAD meeting in 1968 improved market access for the

---

29. The origins and operations of the CFF and other special-purpose IMF facilities are examined in Kenen (1986).

30. They even tried to turn the tables on the G-10 countries by proposing that all of the SDRs be given initially to the developing countries, so that the industrial countries would have to earn their SDRs by exporting more to developing countries. This was the so-called "link" between reserve creation and development assistance.

developing countries by initiating the Generalized System of Preferences (GSP).

New Problems and Responses, 1971–93
Changes in the Economic Environment

The initial design of the Bretton Woods system and the adaptations after World War II owed much to the unique situation of the United States. Its economic and military strength, combined with other countries' concern that the United States not relapse into isolation, gave it great influence over decisions about the organization and functioning of the system. Its strength gave it the self-confidence to make bargains and accept arrangements that were seen as being disadvantageous to its narrow economic interests or those of particular sectors in the US economy.

This situation was bound to change with the recovery of other industrial countries. Even in the early 1960s, the Kennedy administration had spoken of the need for a better-balanced partnership between the United States and Europe in defense and economic matters alike. By the end of the 1960s, moreover, the Vietnam War had eroded US self-confidence and raised questions abroad about the quality of US leadership, underscoring the need to reassess roles and responsibilities.

Unfortunately, the attempt to redistribute burdens internationally took place in an economic environment that posed a growing threat to the postwar bargain about domestic distribution. Growth would slow in the 1970s. The oil shocks of 1973 and 1979 would reduce real incomes in the oil-importing industrial countries. The costs of the welfare state would rise, diminishing fiscal flexibility. And attitudes toward government would shift sharply at the end of the 1970s, resulting in challenges to the legitimacy and efficacy of tax and expenditure policies aimed at redistributing income, along with widespread attempts to reduce the size of government and its involvement in the economy. This ideological change had mixed effects on the Bretton Woods system.

On the one hand, the ideological change favored the further freeing of trade and capital flows in the 1980s. The most dramatic example was the 1985 decision of the European Community to create a single internal market. It was based on a shared commitment to deregulation and was facilitated by the substitution of "mutual recognition" for an attempt to negotiate a common regulatory regime. The most fundamental effect, however, was the change in the aims and policies of many developing countries, which began to shift from inward-looking import substitution and public-sector investment to outward-looking export promotion and private-sector investment.

On the other hand, the ideological change impaired the ability of governments to respond constructively to the domestic dislocation produced by liberalization itself and by one of its consequences—the tighter integration of national economies and resulting increase in their sensitivity to changes in comparative advantage and other external shocks. Hence, governments became more vulnerable to domestic political pressures from those who sought relief from the painful effects of international competition and economic change. It became harder for governments to abide by the rules and understandings of the Bretton Woods system. Furthermore, the deterioration of macroeconomic performance in the 1970s gave credence to the view that activist monetary and fiscal policies can do great harm but little good, and an international corollary became influential in the early 1980s: if each country would "get its own house in order," there would be no need for governments to coordinate their policies.

These trends and views emerged gradually in the 1970s and 1980s, but there was a sharp shock to the Bretton Woods system in 1971, due to the change already apparent in the relative position of the United States, the growth of international capital mobility, and the evolution of the monetary system in the 1950s and 1960s.

The Dollar Crisis and the Shift to Floating Exchange Rates

There were several balance of payments crises in the 1950s and 1960s, but they were not systemic crises. In 1971, however, the United States tried to solve its own balance of payments problem in a way that produced a major change in the international monetary system. To interpret that episode, it is necessary first to recall how the system had evolved in the 1950s and 1960s.

A system of pegged but adjustable exchange rates should meet three needs. First, it should provide reserves and reserve credit in amounts sufficient for governments to keep their exchange rates pegged. Second, it should solve the "N^{th} country" problem, which arises because a system covering N countries contains only N-1 exchange rates, so that the N countries cannot all pursue independent exchange rate policies, and there is the risk of policy conflict. Third, the system should "anchor" its members' monetary policies in order to prevent global inflation or deflation.[31]

The system designed at Bretton Woods was able to meet the first need. The IMF offered reserve credit, using the pool of national currencies subscribed by its member countries, and the size of the pool was to be reviewed periodically. The IMF Articles of Agreement also set out a procedure for changing the price of gold in terms of all national currencies, which would alter the value of all reserves held in the form of gold. The

31. McKinnon (1993) uses a similar list of needs as the framework for his history of the Bretton Woods system and for comparisons with other systems.

First Amendment to the Articles of Agreement went further, authorizing the creation of SDRs to supplement existing reserve assets. Yet most of the actual growth in reserves took the form of dollar balances built up gradually by central banks and governments. Some of them bought gold from the United States, which was committed to buy and sell it at $35 per ounce; the US gold stock fell from $22.7 billion in 1950 to $17.8 billion in 1960 and to $10.7 billion in 1970. But foreign official holdings of dollars grew by much more than foreign gold holdings, reaching $26.1 billion in 1970.

Under the arrangements adopted at Bretton Woods, the Nth country problem was to be solved by requiring that governments obtain IMF approval before changing their exchange rates. In other words, it would be solved politically by international consultations in the IMF. We have noted, however, that the obligation to obtain IMF approval was not taken seriously, and the Fund had little influence over the exchange rate policies of the industrial countries. Policy conflict was avoided in practice by the passivity of the United States, which did not pursue an explicit exchange rate policy until the mid-1960s. Even then, moreover, it sought to implement its policy by trying to discourage other countries, such as Britain and France, from devaluing their currencies against the dollar, rather than trying to achieve a general change in the value of the dollar against other currencies. Under prevailing practices, there seemed to be no choice. As most other countries pegged their currencies to the dollar, not to gold, a general change in dollar exchange rates would have required a coordinated change in those other countries' rates.

There are three ways to anchor monetary policies: by tying the value of each country's currency to an outside asset, which was the rationale for the gold standard; by imposing or adopting a policy rule or commonly agreed procedure to coordinate national policies; or by following a leader whose revealed policy preferences promise to provide the desired degree of economic stability. Some interpretations of the Bretton Woods system claim that it was meant to work in one or another of these ways and evaluate the system under that supposition, but those interpretations are hard to defend.[32] The primacy of the commitment to full employment, the importance Keynes and others attached to the adjustability of exchange rates, and the widely expressed fear that the United States might lapse into recession after World War II all remind us that the architects of the Bretton Woods system aimed at conferring autonomy on national policies, not at imposing a common discipline.[33] Yet the size of the US economy, combined with the practice of pegging to the dollar, produced an asymmetric

---

32. For a gold-standard view of the system, see Bordo (1993); for a view closer to the one set out in the text below, see Giovannini (1993).

33. The US Treasury did insist on a prominent role for gold, but mainly to reinforce the presumption in favor of exchange rate stability, not with any clear notion about anchoring national policies.

system. Other countries did not gladly emulate US policies or, in the language of the recent EMS literature, seek to "import credibility" from the United States. Nevertheless, the United States became the macroeconomic leader, and the other industrial countries followed, sometimes under protest.[34]

Many years before the 1971 crisis, Robert Triffin (1960) had warned that the monetary system was intrinsically unstable. It could not rely on US balance of payments deficits to meet the global need for reserves without eventually impairing confidence in the US commitment to sell gold for dollars, because other countries' holdings of dollars would come to dwarf the US gold stock. This warning was the rationale for creating the SDR. But eliminating the US payments deficit proved to be more difficult. Surplus countries might try to force the United States to modify its monetary and fiscal policies by refusing to build up their dollar holdings and demanding gold instead; that is what France had tried to do in the early 1960s, but it could not succeed by itself. Such pressures, moreover, might provoke an unwanted response by the United States. Instead of adopting expenditure-reducing policies, it might adopt an expenditure-switching policy—an attempt to engineer a general devaluation of the dollar by closing the gold window. And that was the option it chose in 1971, after its balance of payments deficit had increased sharply.

Even today, there is disagreement about the underlying causes of the increase in the US deficit. It is often blamed on US monetary policy, which, it is said, raised the US inflation rate relative to rates in other countries. It is sometimes blamed on US fiscal policy because the Congress refused to raise taxes to pay for the Vietnam War unless domestic social programs were cut, and the Johnson administration would not agree to cut them. It is sometimes ascribed to a gradual deterioration in the competitive position of the United States, resulting partly from the recovery of Europe and Japan, partly from faster inflation in the United States, and partly from other countries' devaluations. But it is less important to pinpoint the causes than to recall the consequences. On 15 August 1971, the Nixon administration closed the gold window and thus put other governments on notice that any additional dollars they might purchase in an effort to keep exchange rates from changing could not be presented for conversion

---

34. The leadership of the United States was reinforced in the 1950s by the dollar shortage. It was not much weakened in the 1960s, however, when the United States ran balance of payments deficits, as some other industrial countries continued to run deficits of their own and had to key their policies on those of the United States in order to limit or eliminate those deficits. The global influence of US policies was amplified, moreover, by the increasing rigidity of the exchange rate regime; countries with balance of payments deficits had to keep their macroeconomic policies in line with US policies if they were to avoid devaluations. Here again, there is a striking similarly between the Bretton Woods system in the 1960s and the EMS in the late 1980s. On the nature of the US role and the debates about it, see Solomon (1982) and Artis and Ostry (1986).

into gold. At the same time, it imposed a 10 percent tariff surcharge but promised to rescind it as soon as "unfair" exchange rates had been corrected.

The United States was not seeking to shift the world from pegged to floating exchange rates. It was trying to solve the coordination problem posed by the organization of the exchange rate regime. As it could not devalue the dollar unilaterally, it had to resolve the Nth country problem by negotiation and had thus to find a way of starting the bargaining process. In December 1971 at the Smithsonian Institution in Washington, the industrial countries agreed on an exchange rate realignment involving a significant devaluation of the dollar.[35] Some deplore the tactics and rhetoric employed by President Richard Nixon and Treasury Secretary John Connally. "The dollar," said Connally, "may be our currency, but it's your problem" (quoted in Volcker and Gyohten 1992, 81). With help from international financial markets, however, their strategy broke an intractable deadlock.

Nevertheless, the US balance of payments was slow to improve after the Smithsonian Agreement, and the US Treasury concluded that a larger exchange rate change was needed. It negotiated a second devaluation of the dollar in February 1973. By that time, however, foreign exchange markets had little confidence in the sustainability of pegged exchange rates. The pound had been allowed to float in June 1972, the Swiss franc in January 1973, and the yen and lira in February 1973, and speculation against the dollar mounted rapidly after the second devaluation. On 1 March 1973, European central banks, having bought more than $3.6 billion to support the dollar in a single day, withdrew from the foreign exchange market, allowing the dollar to float. The Nth country problem would henceforth be solved by foreign exchange traders.

Adaptations in the 1970s

When they announced the Smithsonian Agreement, the industrial countries made two commitments: to begin a new round of GATT negotiations and to reform the monetary system. They honored the first by starting the Tokyo Round, although they did not complete it until 1979. They honored the second by creating the so-called Committee of Twenty, which then spent two full years drafting an outline for reform of the monetary system.

The Tokyo Round had an ambitious agenda. There were to be more tariff cuts based on a variant of the formula used in the Kennedy Round, another attempt to liberalize agricultural trade, an attack on nontariff

---

35. Solomon (1982) and Paul Volcker (in Volcker and Gyohten 1992) provide detailed accounts of the planning that led to the August decisions and of the negotiations that led thereafter to the Smithsonian Agreement.

barriers, an effort to give "special and differential treatment" to developing countries' exports, and work on codes of conduct to deal with unfair trade practices. When the results of the Tokyo Round are compared with those of the Kennedy Round, they look substantial, but when they are compared with the original objectives, they seem more modest. Average tariff rates on manufactured goods were reduced by about 34 percent (a figure close to the one for the Kennedy Round), but strict use of the new tariff-cutting formula would have led to larger reductions. The Tokyo Round failed to resolve the disagreement between the United States and Europe about agricultural trade, displeased developing countries because it did not fulfill promises to them, and it failed to halt the proliferation of nontariff barriers such as "voluntary" export restrictions (VERs). It broke new ground, however, by adopting several codes of conduct. One code was meant to enforce more effectively the prohibition against export subsidies and extend it to domestic subsidies that resemble export subsidies. Another was meant to eliminate discrimination against foreigners in public-sector procurement and involved an important departure from the unconditional MFN principle. A government subscribing to the code may still discriminate against suppliers from countries that do not subscribe to the code.

Although the Tokyo Round did not meet all its objectives, it was a huge success compared with the Committee of Twenty, which did not meet any of its objectives. It was supposed to design a system of "stable but adjustable exchange rates" and make that system more "symmetric" than the one that had developed in the 1950s and 1960s. The attempt to combine stability with adjustability was probably doomed from the start because of the increase in capital mobility that had contributed to the collapse of the Bretton Woods regime.[36]

The attempt to build a more symmetric system was bedeviled by disagreement about the meaning of symmetry. Seen from the US standpoint, the earlier system was asymmetric because it had deprived the United States of the freedom to alter exchange rates when needed; having been the advocate of exchange rate stability when the Bretton Woods system was being designed, the United States was now the advocate of flexibility. Seen from the European standpoint, the earlier system was asymmetric because it had allowed the United States to postpone balance of payments adjustment by accumulating reserve-currency debt to the rest of the world.[37] The debate was overtaken by events, however, when the govern-

---

36. Memories are short. After the 1992 EMS crisis, the Committee of Governors of the EC Central Banks and the Monetary Committee both suggested that more timely exchange rate realignments could combine adjustability with stability; see Eichengreen (1993).

37. Williamson (1977) casts the disagreement itself in a more symmetric way. The desire of the United States for more freedom to change its exchange rate reflected its belief that surplus countries had *wanted* to accumulate dollars and had opposed an exchange rate realignment to

ments of the industrial countries came to agree that they could not to return to pegged exchange rates, and they turned instead to the task of amending the IMF Articles of Agreement in order to legitimize floating rates, redefine the obligations of member governments, and recast the role of the IMF itself.

The Second Amendment was approved in 1976 and took effect in 1978. It used artful language to mask disagreements about the direction in which the monetary system should evolve. Under the new version of Article IV, members would "collaborate with the Fund and with other members to assure orderly exchange arrangements and to promote a stable system of exchange rates." (The odd location of the word "stable" masked the disagreement between France, which favored a system of stable rates, and the United States, which favored floating rates.) Under the new version, moreover, a government merely had to notify the IMF of the "exchange arrangements" it would apply rather than adopt a fixed parity for its currency. The exchange arrangements themselves could include:

> (i) the maintenance by a member of a value for its currency in terms of the Special Drawing Right or another denominator, other than gold, selected by the member, or (ii) cooperative arrangements by which members maintain the value of their currencies in relation to the value of the currency or currencies of other members, or (iii) other exchange arrangements of a member's choice. (Article IV)

But the Fund was supposed to exercise "firm surveillance" over exchange rate policies and to adopt "specific principles" for its members' guidance.

The revision of the Articles of Agreement thus diluted the obligations of governments, but the change in language was more dramatic than the change in practice. The IMF did not have much influence over exchange rate policies under the old regime, and the growth of international capital markets would have reduced the future importance of access to its resources even without the shift to floating exchange rates. (The last large drawings on the Fund by industrial countries were made by Italy and the United Kingdom in 1976. The United States made a small drawing in 1978.)

Furthermore, the major industrial countries were developing new ways of dealing with their common concerns. The first economic summit took place at Rambouillet in 1975 and paved the way for the agreement on amending the IMF Articles of Agreement. The London Summit, two years later, produced agreement on growth targets for Germany, Japan, and the United States. The Bonn Summit of 1978 replaced that agreement on targets with explicit commitments regarding policy instruments—commitments by Germany and Japan to fiscal expansion in exchange for a

---

eliminate the US deficit. He also argues that European views were heavily influenced by the events of 1971–73; European central banks bought large quantities of dollars on the eve of the 1971 crisis, and they bought even larger quantities in 1972 and 1973, under the Smithsonian Agreement, when the US money supply was growing very rapidly.

commitment by the United States to reform its energy policies. There is disagreement about the degree to which the summit process actually affected policy decisions, and the fiscal commitments made at the Bonn Summit are still blamed in Germany for the subsequent acceleration of inflation, a view that conveniently ignores the effects of the increase in the price of oil brought on in 1979 by the Iranian revolution.[38] Nevertheless, studies of the summit process argue convincingly that it can focus attention on the need for making policy changes, provide opportunities for making them, and foster the formation of domestic coalitions favoring the changes (see Putnam and Henning 1989; Holtham 1989).

Proposals to increase the IMF's influence often suggest that policy coordination be lodged within the IMF. But there is no easy way of reconciling the decision-making processes of the IMF, in which all of its members take part, with the need to hold down the number of countries involved in policy coordination. The durability of the summit process and the frequency of the lower-level meetings among representatives of the summit countries reflect the importance that those countries attach to homogeneity and to the interdependence of their national policies.

Although high capital mobility might have made it impossible for the Committee of Twenty to design a viable system of "stable but adjustable" exchange rates, the actual acceptance of floating exchange rates was more closely linked to the effects of the oil-price increase triggered by the Yom Kippur War of 1973. Its price-raising and income-reducing effects help to explain the depth of the 1974–75 recession and the stagflation that followed. It also sowed the seeds of problems that emerged in the 1980s—high long-term unemployment in Europe, the ballooning of budget deficits that immobilized fiscal policies, and the debt crisis that began in 1982.

As the oil-exporting countries, especially those of the Middle East, could not spend all of their oil revenues, they ran current account surpluses, and the oil-importing countries as a group therefore had to run a deficit. But the subsequent recession in the industrial countries shifted most of the deficit to the developing countries, and they began to borrow heavily (figure 1). The excess revenues of the oil-exporting countries were "recycled" by the industrial countries' banks to finance the payments deficits of the developing countries. There were at first modest efforts to recycle some of the excess revenues through the IMF, but they were abandoned when it became clear that the banks would do the job. Hence, the claims of the banks on developing countries mounted rapidly in the 1970s and the early 1980s (table 5).

---

38. von Furstenberg and Daniels (1992) try to measure actual performance against summit commitments and find that the record is rather poor. But their results are necessarily sensitive to the ways in which they quantify policy commitments, and they fail to distinguish between commitments concerning policy instruments, which are controllable in principle, and those concerning policy targets, which may not be controllable.

Figure 1 Current account balances, 1973–90

billions of dollars

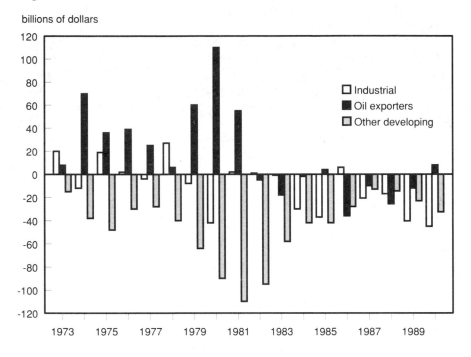

The oil-price increase of 1973 had another effect. It encouraged the developing countries to demand a New International Economic Order (NIEO) that would redistribute income and power in the world economy. The initial success of the Organization of Petroleum Exporting Countries (OPEC) in improving its members' terms of trade and gaining influence in international organizations, including the IMF, "crystallized the concept of strength through collective action and 'solidarity rather than charity.' The developing countries also seemed to infer from the OPEC experience that their commodity exports, which had been traditionally viewed as a sign of weakness, could be turned instead into weapons of collective action" (Bhagwati 1977).

The NIEO agenda included familiar proposals for stabilizing commodity prices, increasing the flow of development assistance, and granting debt relief to low-income countries, but it made many new proposals. It called for a shift in the locus of manufacturing to the developing countries, a shift in the balance of power between host-country governments and foreign firms exploiting their natural resources, the use of revenues from deep-sea mining to finance economic development, and a larger role for developing countries in the governance of the IMF and World Bank.

Many of these demands were endorsed by the UN General Assembly and UNCTAD, but few of them got much further. The members of OPEC

Table 5 Developing countries' debt, 1973–91 (billions of dollars)

	1973	1976	1979	1982	1985	1988	1991[a]
Total outstanding	130.2	228.1	504.7	780.9	953.8	1,161.8	1,284.1
By maturity							
Short-term	18.4[b]	33.2[b]	88.1[b]	146.1	137.7	156.8	164.0
Long-term	111.8	194.9	416.6	634.7	816.1	1,004.8	1,120.1
By creditor							
Official agencies	51.0	82.4	163.5	239.7	342.4	485.5	590.9
Commercial banks	31.1	73.9	208.5	390.1	452.5	484.2	473.6
Others	48.1	71.8	132.7	151.1	158.9	192.1	219.6

a. Estimated.
b. Allocation by type of creditor approximated.

Source: International Monetary Fund, *World Economic Outlook* (various issues). Data for 1973 and 1976 cover all developing countries except certain oil exporters; subsequent data cover all net-debtor developing countries.

had bargaining power—or seemed to have it at the time. Other developing countries did not. And OPEC members were not greatly interested in lending their bargaining power to others. Nevertheless, the controversy over the NIEO served as another important reminder of the changes taking place in the world economy—the strains produced by the increase in the number of participants and their heterogeneity and the resulting challenge to the basic consensus that had produced the Bretton Woods system.

Adaptations in the 1980s

As the end of history approaches, or, at least, the end of this history, it becomes tempting to chronicle events rather than trying to interpret those with long-term implications. Otherwise, readers may wonder why nothing is said about events they remember most clearly or those involving issues in which they are most interested.

There were, of course, dramatic events at both ends of the 1980s: the debt crisis at the start and the collapse of the Soviet empire at the end, and the EMS was born at the start and came near to perishing at the end. Along the way, moreover, the Plaza and Louvre agreements altered exchange rate arrangements among the key currencies, and the Uruguay Round extended the GATT system to international trade in services and agreed to establish a World Trade Organization (WTO) as the new institutional home for the GATT, with better procedures for settling trade policy disputes. At the same time, the North American Free Trade Agreement (NAFTA) raised questions about the direction of future trade liberalization, suggesting that regional bargains might replace global GATT rounds, and trends in US trade policies raised questions about the US commitment to the GATT system. Finally, developing countries become partners, not petitioners, in making decisions affecting the future of the trading system.

When examining the earlier history of the Bretton Woods system, it made sense to focus mainly on relations among governments. When looking at recent developments, it is important to focus on relations between governments and markets. Deregulation accelerated in the 1980s, increasing the impact of private-sector decisions on the world economy. Key decisions by governments, individually and collectively, represented responses to issues raised by the globalization of financial markets, the migration of manufacturing to developing countries resulting in part from the spread of foreign direct investment, and the rapid growth of international trade in services. Furthermore, decisions that governments once took individually had now to be taken collectively. The protection of intellectual property was an important and difficult issue in the Uruguay Round. The prudential supervision of large banks was the main issue on the agenda at the BIS, where central bankers wrote common rules to measure capital adequacy.[39] The need for international cooperation on environmental issues was addressed comprehensively at the Rio Conference.

We look first at the ways in which the issues of the 1980s affected the IMF and Bank, turn next to their impact on exchange rate arrangements, and conclude with their influence on the GATT and national trade policies.

Debt Crisis and the Role of the IMF

The debt crisis started with Mexico in 1982 and spread quickly to other borrowing countries, especially in Latin America.[40] Some accounts of the crisis maintain that banks knew all along that they would run into trouble but had fed this possibility into their calculations. The earlier history of international debt would have led any prudent banker to do that. But three phenomena cause us to question this hypothesis. First, the lending that began in the 1970s was sustained by the entry of additional banks, not an ongoing buildup of claims by the banks that started the process; hence, no individual bank could regulate the risks it faced merely by controlling the volume of its own claims.[41] Second, it is hard to believe that banks could

---

39. On this and related issues, see Kapstein (1994).

40. It is ironic that the crisis began with Mexico, an oil exporter, when much of the lending that led to the crisis represented intermediation between oil exporters and oil importers, but Mexico had borrowed heavily in the expectation of rising oil revenues. The account of the crisis given here draws on Kenen (1992); for other interpretations, see Sachs (1989), Cooper (1992), Cline (1994), Kapstein (1994), and Krugman (1994); on the role of the IMF, see the papers by Jeffrey Sachs and Guillermo Ortiz in Gwin and Feinberg (1989).

41. The importance of this phenomenon is underscored by the problem that faced the banks and debtor countries when they began to sort out the problem: they had first to determine the size of the debt owed by each debtor country.

have forecast the changes in the global economic environment that occurred at the start of the 1980s, including the sudden shift in US monetary policy in October 1979, the depth of the subsequent recession in the industrial countries, and the large effect of the recession on the export earnings of the debtor countries. Third, the spread of the crisis from country to country, when banks halted their lending completely, suggests that the banks were taken by surprise and revised their plans abruptly. We are sympathetic to the suggestion made by Guttentag and Herring (1986) that the banks suffered from disaster myopia—the tendency to underestimate the risk of a rare calamity.[42]

The banks had protected themselves from two of the three risks facing them. The deposits of the oil-exporting countries were denominated mainly in dollars, so the banks made most of their own loans in dollars, protecting themselves from exchange rate risk. Interest rates on most of the loans were tied to the London Interbank Offer Rate (LIBOR), the interest rate paid on most of the deposits, protecting them from interest rate risk. But the banks were exposed to default risk, and their way of minimizing interest rate risk raised their vulnerability to default risk by linking the debtors' debt-service payments to rather volatile interest rates. Furthermore, the link to LIBOR, combined with the debtors' dependence on export earnings from products with cyclically sensitive prices, made it likely that many debtor countries would prosper or suffer together, reducing the protection usually afforded by diversification.

The international financial community responded rapidly to the crisis. Central banks and other official institutions made large short-term loans to Mexico, pending the completion of its negotiations with the IMF. The IMF itself told the commercial banks that it would not approve a drawing by Mexico unless the banks rescheduled Mexico's debt and made new loans to Mexico to help it meet its interest payments. The Fund thus worked to coordinate a concerted response to the crisis, and even before that task was completed, the arrangements made for Mexico became a model for dealing with other countries' problems. By the end of 1983, the banks had reached agreements with 18 debtor countries, rescheduling $35 billion of debt and granting $14 billion of additional credit, and there was a huge increase in the use of IMF resources (table 6).

How can a debtor solve its problem by going deeper into debt? In imprecise but helpful terms, an insolvent debtor must pursue a debt-reducing strategy, but an illiquid debtor should pursue a debt-raising strategy so as to make its interest payments and defend its creditworthiness. Projections made at the time supported the debt-raising strategy.

---

42. But we cannot dismiss the explanation advanced by Dooley (1993) that the banks expected their governments to bail them out if they had trouble. That expectation was not totally unjustified, as the banks had been encouraged to recycle the OPEC surplus, a task from which the governments withdrew as soon as the banks took it on.

Table 6 Drawings on IMF facilities, years ending 30 April (millions of SDRs)

Year	Total	Reserve tranche	Compensatory financing facility[a]	Conditional Total	Conditional Ordinary resources[b]	Borrowed resources[c]	Borrowed as percentage of total
1975	5,103	982	18	4,103	1,604	2,499	49.0
1976	6,591	1,324	832	4,435	469	3,966	60.2
1977	4,910	161	1,753	2,997	2,560	437	8.9
1978	2,503	136	322	2,045	2,045	0	0
1979	3,720	2,480	512	727	727	0	0
1980	2,433	223	889	1,321	819	502	20.6
1981	4,860	474	784	3,602	2,086	1,516	31.2
1982	8,041	1,080	1,635	5,326	2,110	3,216	40.0
1983	11,392	1,134	4,092	6,165	3,025	3,141	27.6
1984	11,518	1,354	1,282	8,882	3,763	5,119	44.4
1985	6,289	229	1,248	4,812	2,250	2,562	40.7
1986	4,101	160	601	3,339	1,878	1,461	35.6
1987	3,685	516	593	2,575	1,687	888	24.1
1988	4,152	35	1,544	2,573	868	1,705	41.1
1989	2,541	413	238	1,890	1,736	154	6.1

SDRs = Special Drawing Rights
a. Includes the buffer stock and cereals facilities.
b. Includes the Extended Fund Facility (EFF).
c. Includes the oil and supplementary financing facility and drawings under the enlarged access policy.

Source: International Monetary Fund, *Annual Reports,* various years. Detail may not add to total because of rounding.

They said that some of the debtors could return to creditworthiness in fewer than five years if the world economy grew steadily, interest rates fell, and there were no large changes in exchange rates or the price of oil.[43] The projections were not far wrong in their assumptions about the world economy, but they underestimated the internal problem many debtor countries faced—the problems involved in raising the real resources they needed for making their debt-service payments rather than those involved in transferring real resources to their foreign creditors.[44]

The first official acknowledgment of the need to revise the initial diagnosis and, therefore, to modify the debt strategy came in 1985, when James Baker, the US secretary of the treasury, urged the debtor countries to follow financial and structural policies aimed at fostering growth together with balance of payments adjustment, asked the IMF and World Bank to support those policies by structural adjustment lending, and asked the commercial banks to increase their own lending. The IMF and World Bank continued to build up their claims on the debtor countries, but the banks' response was more selective; they built up their claims on some countries, but used a number of techniques to cut back their claims on others.[45] This shift to a debt-reducing strategy was blessed formally by the IMF in 1988, although it cautioned against any transfer of risk from private creditors to official institutions. In 1989, moreover, Nicholas Brady, the new US secretary of the treasury, called for "measures to accelerate sharply the pace of debt reduction and pass the benefits directly to the debtor countries." He asked the IMF and World Bank to make financial resources available to debtor countries that wanted to collateralize debt-for-bond swaps, replenish reserves used for cash buybacks, or earmark funds to underwrite future interest payments. Thereafter, several developing countries had help from the Fund and Bank in making debt-reducing agreements with their creditors.

How did the debt crisis affect the Bretton Woods Institutions? Let us look at the role of the IMF through the eyes of a participant in the Bretton Woods Conference of 1944. The IMF was meant to provide short-term

---

43. These are reviewed retrospectively in Cline (1994).

44. Furthermore, the devaluations frequently required to make external transfers complicated the internal problem. They raised the domestic-currency cost of debt-service payments, adding to the debtors' budget deficits. Such deficits, moreover, had to be monetized because the debt problem itself made foreign borrowing impossible and capital flight made domestic borrowing difficult, and the higher inflation rates resulting from monetization nullified the trade balance effects of the devaluations (see, e.g., Reisen 1989).

45. Some sold off their claims at substantial discounts in the secondary market that developed in the wake of the debt crisis. Others took advantage of arrangements proposed by the debtor countries themselves. Chile offered debt-equity swaps to promote foreign direct investment; Bolivia bought back half of its debt for cash at a price close to the one quoted in the secondary market; Argentina, Brazil, and Mexico funded some of their debt into bonds.

balance of payments credit, which is what it did at the start of the debt crisis. A Bretton Woods participant might have been surprised by the comprehensive nature of the policy conditions attached to the use of IMF credit, but this practice was not new, nor were the conditions more onerous than those faced by Britain and Italy in the 1970s.[46]

But the role of the IMF changed gradually thereafter, and the World Bank was also affected. Both began to engage in new forms of lending. The IMF moved from short-term to medium-term lending, and the nature of conditionality changed: instead of insisting primarily on changes in macroeconomic policies aimed at rather rapid external adjustment, it began to insist on changes in microeconomic policies aimed at extensive domestic reforms. This practice began before the debt crisis, with the creation of the Extended Fund Facility (EFF) in 1974, but had been relatively rare. The World Bank moved from project lending, with disbursements tied to actual spending on the corresponding project, to various forms of structural adjustment lending, with an urgent emphasis on rapid disbursement. It became harder to insist that the IMF is still a monetary institution, not a development institution, and should not therefore be combined with the World Bank.

In the 1940s, the problem of postwar reconstruction was met by creating new programs and institutions to meet specific needs, and they were separately funded. In the 1980s, the debt problem was met by making ad hoc changes in the policies and missions of the Bretton Woods Institutions. In the process, moreover, there was a very large transfer of risk from private creditors to official institutions, despite the IMF's earlier warning against it. Between 1982 and 1991, the share of commercial banks in total claims on the developing countries fell from 50 percent to 37 percent while the share of official institutions rose from 31 to 46 percent (table 5).[47] The conversion of the Bretton Woods Institutions into instruments for crisis management was carried further in the early 1990s, when they had to take the lead in financing and managing the economic transformation of Eastern Europe and of the former Soviet Union. Lacking the will to fund that task through their own national budgets, the United States and its partners looked again to the IMF and World Bank, which had again to modify their policies and practices. The IMF's decision in March 1994 to

---

46. There might have been surprise, moreover, at the extent to which the Fund relied on borrowing, not its own resources, to finance its activities and at the flexibility it showed in going beyond the strict quota-based limits on lending to individual members. The extent of IMF reliance on borrowed resources is shown in table 6.

47. The same thing would have happened under the proposal that one of us made to establish a new institution to buy the banks' claims at a discount and issues its own obligations to pay for them (Kenen 1990). But the new institution would have been designed expressly to assume the risks involved; they would not have been shifted to the Fund and Bank.

accept the very weak promises made by Russia is the latest step in a long and troubling process.

It is easy to understand why the IMF is widely viewed as a development institution. It had no role in the making of the Plaza and Louvre agreements, which altered the exchange rate arrangements of the major countries, and it plays only a limited role in their regular consultations.

Exchange Rate Arrangements

At the start of the 1980s, the Reagan administration announced that the United States would no longer intervene on foreign exchange markets. During the next few years, however, the dollar appreciated hugely, and the United States began to run large current account deficits. The Congress responded in much the same way that it did at the end of the 1960s—by drafting legislation to roll back imports—and the administration responded in turn by seeking once again to bring down the dollar. In September 1985, it assembled the finance ministers and central bank governors of the Group of Five (G-5) countries—France, Germany, Japan, the United Kingdom, and the United States—at the Plaza Hotel in New York, where they agreed on joint intervention to achieve what they called in their communiqué "some further orderly appreciation of the main non-dollar currencies."[48]

The dollar depreciated sharply after the Plaza Agreement and continued to decline in 1986 (figure 2). In fact, the size of the decline caused the Japanese authorities to intervene in support of the dollar. The United States was not willing to join in, however, until Japan adopted a fiscal policy package aimed at stimulating the Japanese economy and thus reducing Japan's current account surplus. Once that had happened, another communiqué was issued. In February 1987, meeting at the Louvre in Paris, the governments expressed satisfaction with the exchange rate changes that had followed the Plaza Agreement, declared that exchange rates were now consistent with the economic fundamentals, and thus "agreed to cooperate closely to foster stability of exchange rates around current levels."

But they did not cooperate closely enough. In October 1987, US Secretary of the Treasury James Baker criticized the Bundesbank publicly for a small increase in interest rates, saying that it was inconsistent with the understandings implicit in the Louvre Accord. The uncertainty generated by this dispute was one proximate cause of the 1987 stock market collapse, which led to a further depreciation of the dollar. Thereafter, officials were more circumspect in their statements about exchange rates. Nevertheless,

---

48. For a detailed account of this and subsequent events, see Funabashi (1988); for a more thorough treatment of US exchange rate policy, see Destler and Henning (1989); and for a more recent critique, see Frankel (1994).

Figure 2a Deutsche mark exchange rate

US cents per DM

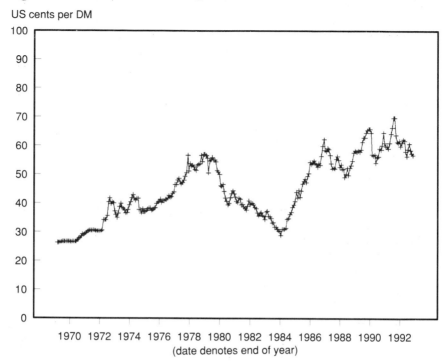

(date denotes end of year)

Figure 2b Yen exchange rate

US cents per 100 yen

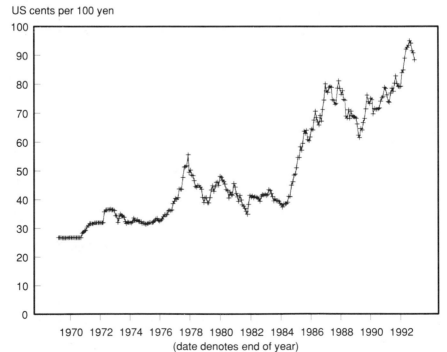

(date denotes end of year)

they continued to engage in concerted intervention to limit exchange rate changes.

Advocates of intensive exchange rate management greeted the Plaza and Louvre agreements as a fundamental change in the exchange rate regime and called on governments to go further—to commit themselves publicly to target zones defended by interest rate policies and intervention (Williamson and Miller 1987; Bergsten 1988; Kenen 1988). They cited the results of new research on the effectiveness of intervention and noted that foreign exchange markets have shown a wary respect for the ability of governments to influence exchange rates.[49] This phenomenon has survived the reassessment of exchange rate management touched off by the EMS crises of 1992 and 1993: when trade negotiations between Japan and the United States broke down in February 1994, the yen appreciated sharply, reflecting rumors that the United States might seek to engineer an appreciation to put pressure on Japan.

Another, more fundamental change in exchange rate arrangements and policies occurred in the 1980s. It began in Western Europe with the transformation of the EMS from a system of pegged but adjustable exchange rates into a system of rigidly fixed rates, was reflected in stabilization programs adopted in Latin America and in Central and Eastern Europe, and has strongly influenced thinking in the IMF.

Under the influence of Nurkse (1945), Meade (1951), and others, the exchange rate was viewed for much of the postwar period as a policy instrument to be used for balance of payments adjustment and thus for reconciling external and internal balance. As attention shifted in the 1970s to the importance of fighting inflation and the need for central banks to acquire credibility, an earlier view reemerged. Exchange rate pegging came to be seen as a device for conferring credibility on domestic policies. This became the focus of European policies, especially those of France and Italy, and the same policy was pursued by a variety of developing countries.

Along with the belief that a pegged exchange rate would enhance the credibility of domestic policy, a second factor worked to increase the rigidity of pegged exchange rates. The relaxation of capital controls made it harder for governments to devalue without exciting the markets. This problem was particularly severe in the context of the European Monetary System, where realignments have to be preceded by international consultations, and it is hard to prevent news of the authorities' intentions from leaking out. In an environment of high capital mobility, governments resist even contemplating a devaluation for fear of precipitating a crisis.

---

49. On the effectiveness of intervention, see Dominguez and Frankel (1994) and Catti, Galli, and Rebecchini (1994); on the markets' view of intervention, see Kenen (1988) and Frankel (1994).

The evolution of the EMS further illustrates the point. There had been frequent exchange rate realignments in the early years of the EMS, but following the adoption of the Single European Act in 1986, which mandated the removal of member countries' residual capital controls, that was no longer possible. There were no realignments from January 1987 until September 1992, when the effects of German reunification and the policies it produced were combined with doubts about the outlook for the Maastricht Treaty, triggering massive speculation against the lira and the pound. It is too early to assess the long-run effects of that crisis and the one that followed in 1993. It is worth noting, however, that France continued stubbornly to defend the franc, even after the widening of the EMS bands gave it the room to reduce French interest rates and permit the franc to depreciate.

Trade Policies and the GATT

Turning finally to trade policies in the 1980s, three developments demand attention. Although the decision to start the Uruguay Round involved an explicit commitment to further liberalization, the main trend in trade policy during the decade took some countries in the opposite direction. Responding to allegations of dumping, the illegal use of export subsidies, and other "unfair" trade practices, the United States and the European Community erected additional nontariff barriers. The number of export-restraining arrangements more than doubled from 1987 and 1989, and many of the new nontariff barriers were aimed at developing countries and at Central and Eastern Europe (tables 7 and 8). Ironically, the targets of those barriers were moving rapidly to liberalize their trade regimes. The Uruguay Round, moreover, proved to be the longest and most difficult of all GATT rounds, partly because of the many issues it faced and partly because it involved a very large number of countries.

The complex agenda of the Uruguay Round afforded opportunities for cross-issue bargaining, but that was not the rationale for taking on so many issues. The agenda was set by the United States, in an effort to forge a new domestic coalition favoring further liberalization. The effects of previous rounds, the appreciation of the dollar in the early 1980s, and increasingly keen competition from Japan and other Asian countries had undermined the old coalition. It was hard to find an American manufacturer, let alone a labor union, that favored freer trade. Even the multinational firms that need open markets at home and abroad to operate efficiently were reluctant to speak up for freer trade. Therefore, the Reagan administration sought to recruit new supporters. It promised to fulfill the pledge made two decades earlier to defend the interests of American farmers against the effects of Europe's agricultural policies.[50] It promised

---

50. When the promise was first made, however, the concerns of American farmers were different from what they were to be in the 1980s. Their early concerns focused on the

Table 7 Export-restraining arrangements, 1987 and 1989

Category	1987	1989
Total number in effect	135	289
By protected market		
United States	48	69
European Community[a]	69	173
Japan	6	13
All other countries	12	34
By restrained exporter		
Japan	25	70
Other industrial countries	23	57
Developing countries	66	121
Eastern Europe	20	41

a. Includes arrangements initiated by individual EC countries (which rose from 20 in 1987 to 96 in 1989).

Source: International Monetary Fund, *Issues and Developments in International Trade Policy*, 1992, table A8; excludes MFA arrangements.

to extend the GATT to international trade in services in order to recruit support from the financial community. And it promised to obtain better protection for intellectual property, ranging from patents on pharmaceuticals to computer software. At the same time, it sought to quell opposition by acting or threatening to act unilaterally against countries with "unfair" trade practices.

The United States also had to deal with opposition abroad. The European Community was far from enthusiastic about a new round of global negotiations, partly because of its preoccupation with the completion of its own internal market. Developing countries were apprehensive about the inclusion of services, trade-related investment measures, and intellectual property. But these reservations and apprehensions were overcome by recognition of the need to prevent the United States from turning away from the GATT system. We will not know for some time whether the game was worth the candle—not even after Washington and Tokyo have worked their way out of their current confrontation and the US Congress has endorsed the outcome of the Uruguay Round.

---

restrictive effects of the CAP, which reduced US agricultural exports to Europe. In the 1980s, they focused on the third-market effects of the CAP because the Community was subsidizing exports of farm products in order to dispose of the surpluses generated by the CAP.

Table 8   Imports by major industrial countries in selected product groups covered by nontariff barriers, 1990

Product group	Percentages of imports from:		
	Developed countries	Developing countries	Eastern Europe and USSR
Food	41.8	28.7	56.7
Iron and steel	56.8	40.6	67.1
Fuels	23.8	12.6	43.8
Textiles	17.0	61.6	69.3
Clothing	27.6	71.6	75.1
Vehicles	58.6	0.7	11.1
All imports[a]	17.1	19.9	30.4

a. Includes products not listed above.

Source: International Monetary Fund, *Issues and Developments in International Trade Policy*, 1992, table A7; uses "broad" group of nontariff barriers and covers Australia, Austria, Canada, the EC, Finland, Japan, New Zealand, Norway, Sweden, Switzerland, and the United States.

Conclusion

We have not reached the end of history, not even the end of the history we were asked to write. We have not discussed the outcome of the Uruguay Round, the negotiation and ratification of NAFTA, the formation of regional arrangements in Latin America and Asia, or the economic transformation of Central and Eastern Europe. We have not analyzed the EMS crises of 1992–93, despite the intriguing parallels with the dollar crises of 1971–73 and the lessons to be drawn for the future of the international monetary system. We have two excuses: our paper is too long, and the events are too recent.

We have laid great stress on the contribution of institutions to postwar growth performance. But how can we really know that the institutions mattered, as opposed to other factors on which we have touched that also affected economic outcomes? Some evidence is provided by comparisons across time and space. Thus, we have provided comparisons with the aftermath of World War I, when institutional arrangements and economic outcomes were very different. Comparisons can also be made across countries that participated to different degrees in the international arrangements of the Bretton Woods system.[51]

---

51. One of us has analyzed the connections between growth and institutional arrangements such as the EPU, the European Coal and Steel Community, EEC membership, and IMF Article VIII status using a panel data set of industrial countries after World War II (Eichengreen and Vazquez 1994).

In emphasizing the salutary influence of international institutions, it is important to resist the temptation to write a Whig history of the postwar world. Not all postwar institutions were optimally structured at the start. Not all the problems that they would confront were anticipated by the framers of the Bretton Woods agreement. There was a significant role for historical contingency in the postwar evolution of the world economy. But this is merely another reason why, as we have argued, the adaptability of the postwar institutions held the key to their success.

Our account has devoted considerable attention to the role and policies of the United States. This does not imply tacit endorsement of the hegemonic-stability view that international regimes cannot outlive their leaders. We find that the United States played a more decisive role in the design of postwar international institutions and in the early attempts to adapt them than in their subsequent operation. A number of those institutions, the GATT prominent among them, continued to function successfully despite the absence of consistent, forward-looking US leadership to guide the evolution of international economic relations. Procedures and understandings (institutions with a little "i") embodied in formal structures (institutions with a capital "I") can sustain the momentum of international collaboration even when a leading country is unprepared to provide the necessary guidance and the conditions for collective leadership remain underdeveloped.

Two further themes run through our account. The first is that the ability of governments to manage change internationally has depended importantly on their ability to manage it domestically. This seemingly trite proposition has important implications. After World War II, domestic interest groups in each industrial country reached an accommodation concerning the distribution of the national income and the structure of the economy. Having achieved agreement at home in ways that were broadly compatible across countries, governments could enter credibly into international commitments. They could commit to the creation of a set of international economic institutions with which all could live, and the credibility of their international commitments was buttressed by domestic stability and support. The consequent growth of international transactions fed back to the domestic economy, reinforcing support for the international system. Domestic institutions, in the sense of rules and understandings, provided support for their international counterparts, and vice versa.

Starting in the 1970s, partly as a consequence of the very success of the Bretton Woods system, the situation began to change. Different domestic arrangements became more difficult to sustain as economies became more open to trade and factor flows. The growing amplitude of the business cycle, slower economic growth, and wider income inequality frayed the social fabric. Countries moved in different directions—some toward more generous income support and labor-market regulation and others, such as the United Kingdom and the United States, toward less generous and less interventionist programs. These strains on domestic institutions complicated efforts to reform international arrangements, and the consequences undermined the effectiveness of existing international institutions. Trade liberalization progressed more slowly because of this failure of institutional adaptation and because the domestic adjustments required by liberalization were more difficult to make when economies were growing less rapidly. (It might have halted completely if the United States had not forged a new domestic coalition favoring liberalization by putting trade in services on the GATT agenda.) Mobilizing resources to deal with problems such as the economic transition of Eastern Europe and the former Soviet Union was rendered more difficult by the stagnation of real incomes in the industrial countries.

Our second theme is that these difficulties have been significantly exacerbated by the great gap in the original Bretton Woods system: the lack of a coherent approach to economic development. Krueger (1993) shows that there are, even now, serious inefficiencies and inconsistencies in the trade, aid, and other policies of the industrial countries. As the developing countries have become participants rather than petitioners in the international system, their different priorities have complicated efforts to reform the system, a fact evident in the SDR negotiation of the 1960s and again in the Uruguay Round. Liberalization in the developing world may attenuate conflicts insofar as domestic objectives come to converge with those of the developed world, but it will not reconcile the very different priorities of producers and consumers of primary products or intellectual property, nor will it solve the large-number problem that has bedeviled the GATT and similarly threatens its successor, the WTO.

Large-number problems can be solved in different ways. Regional groupings provide one solution, whose attractions are already evident. Mere proximity, however, does not always create a commonality of interests, and the quest for deeper integration may lead instead to a second solution—namely, functional rather than regional groups. But functional groups, like regional groups, tend to discriminate against outsiders and close off opportunities for cross-issue bargaining. This is a reason for shunning them or, at least, ensuring their compatibility with a third potential solution: adapting and strengthening the global institutional framework and insisting that both regional and functional negotiations take place within that framework.

As the number and the diversity of significant players continue to grow in the international arena, the need for rules of the road to frame the conduct of domestic policies and international negotiations becomes more pressing. The problems of commitment and coordination that provided the motivation for establishing and adapting the Bretton Woods system need to be addressed anew. While specific proposals are not our charge— other authors at this conference have that responsibility—our historical survey highlights the importance of strengthening the Bretton Woods institutions if the next half century of economic progress is to be as successful as the last.

References

Abramovitz, Moses. 1986. "Catching Up, Forging Ahead, and Falling Behind." *Journal of Economic History* 46: 385–406.

Artis, Michael, and Sylvia Ostry. 1986. *International Economic Policy Coordination.* London: Royal Institute of International Affairs.

Baumol, William J., Sue Anne Batey Blackman, and Edward N. Wolff. 1989. *Productivity and American Leadership.* Cambridge, MA: MIT Press.

Bergsten, C. Fred. 1988. *America in the World Economy: A Strategy for the 1990s.* Washington: Institute for International Economics.

Bhagwati, Jagdish N. 1977. "Introduction." In Bhagwati, *The New International Economic Order: The North-South Debate.* Cambridge, MA: MIT Press.

Bordo, Michael D. 1993. "The Bretton Woods International Monetary System: A Historical Overview." In Michael D. Bordo and Barry Eichengreen, *A Retrospective on the Bretton Woods System.* Chicago: University of Chicago Press.

Catti, Pietro, Giampaolo Galli, and Salvatore Rebecchini. 1994. "Concerted Intervention and the Dollar: An Analysis of Daily Data." In Peter B. Kenen, Francesco Papadia, and Fabrizio Saccomanni, *The International Monetary System.* Cambridge, UK: Cambridge University Press (forthcoming).

Cline, William R. 1994. *International Debt Reexamined.* Washington: Institute for International Economics (forthcoming).

Cooper, Richard N. 1968. *The Economics of Interdependence.* New York: McGraw-Hill.

Cooper, Richard N. 1971. *Exchange Rate Devaluation in Developing Countries.* Essays in International Finance 86. Princeton: International Finance Section, Princeton University.

Cooper, Richard N. 1992. *Economic Stabilization and Debt in Developing Countries.* Cambridge, MA: MIT Press.

Crafts, N. F. R. 1992. "Institutions and Economic Growth: Recent British Experience in an International Context." *Western European Politics* 15: 16–38.

Destler, I. M., and C. Randall Henning. 1989. *Dollar Politics: Exchange Rate Policymaking in the United States.* Washington: Institute for International Economics.

Dominguez, Kathryn, and Jeffrey A. Frankel. 1994. *Does Foreign Exchange Intervention Work?* Washington: Institute for International Economics.

Dooley, Michael. 1993. "A Retrospective on the Debt Crisis." In Peter B. Kenen, *Understanding Interdependence.* Princeton: Princeton University Press (forthcoming).

Eichengreen, Barry. 1992. *Golden Fetters: The Gold Standard and the Great Depression, 1919–1939.* New York: Oxford University Press.

Eichengreen, Barry. 1993. "The Crisis in the EMS and the Transition to EMU: An Interim Assessment." *Economic Policy Issues In Financial Integration,* Helsinki: University of Helsinki.

Eichengreen, Barry. 1994a. "Institutional Prerequisites for Economic Growth: Europe After World War II." *European Economic Review* (forthcoming).

Eichengreen, Barry. 1994b. "Mainsprings of Postwar Europe's Growth and Recovery." In Barry Eichengreen, *Europe's Postwar Recovery.* Cambridge, UK: Cambridge University Press (forthcoming).

Eichengreen, Barry, and Pablo Vazquez. 1994. "Institutions and Economic Growth in Postwar Europe: An Empirical Investigation." Unpublished manuscript, University of California at Berkeley.

Frankel, Jeffrey A. 1994. "The Making of Exchange Rate Policy in the 1980s." In Martin Feldstein, *American Economic Policy in the 1980s.* Chicago: National Bureau of Economic Research.

Funabashi, Yoichi. 1988. *Managing the Dollar: From the Plaza to the Louvre*. Washington: Institute for International Economics.

Furstenberg, George M. von, and Joseph P. Daniels. 1992. *Economic Summit Declarations, 1975–1989: Examining the Written Record of International Cooperation*. Princeton Studies in International Finance 72. Princeton: International Finance Section, Princeton University.

Giovannini, Alberto. 1993. "Bretton Woods and Its Precursors: Rules versus Discretion in the History of International Monetary Regimes." In Michael D. Bordo and Barry Eichengreen, *A Retrospective on the Bretton Woods System*. Chicago: University of Chicago Press.

Guttentag, Jack M., and Richard Herring. 1986. *Disaster Myopia in International Banking*. Essays in International Finance 164, Princeton: International Finance Section, Princeton University.

Gwin, Catherine, and Richard E. Feinberg, eds. 1989. *The International Monetary Fund in a Multipolar World: Pulling Together*. Washington: Overseas Development Council.

Hogan, Michael J. 1977. *Informal Entente: The Private Structure of Cooperation in Anglo-American Economic Diplomacy, 1918–1928*. Columbia, MO: University of Missouri Press.

Hogan, Michael J. 1987. *The Marshall Plan: America, Britain and the Reconstruction of Western Europe, 1947–1952*. Cambridge, UK: Cambridge University Press.

Holtham, Gerald. 1989. "German Macroeconomic Policy and the 1978 Bonn Summit." In Richard N. Cooper et al., *Can Nations Agree?* Washington: Brookings Institution.

Ikenberry, G. John. 1993. "The Political Origins of Bretton Woods." In Michael D. Bordo and Barry Eichengreen, *A Retrospective on the Bretton Woods System*. Chicago: University of Chicago Press.

Kaplan, Jacob, and Gunther Schleiminger. 1989. *The European Payments Union*. Oxford: Clarendon Press.

Kapstein, Ethan B. 1994. *Governing the Global Economy: International Finance and the State*. Cambridge, MA: Harvard University Press (forthcoming).

Kenen, Peter B. 1986. *Financing, Adjustment, and the International Monetary Fund*. Washington: Brookings Institution.

Kenen, Peter B. 1988. *Managing Exchange Rates*. London: The Royal Institute of International Affairs.

Kenen, Peter B. 1990. "Organizing Debt Relief: The Need for a New Institution." *Journal of Economic Perspectives* 4, 8-18.

Kenen, Peter B. 1992. "Third World Debt." In Peter Newman et al., *The New Palgrave Dictionary of Money and Finance*. New York: Stockton Press.

Kenwood, A. G., and A .L. Lougheed. 1971. *The Growth of the International Economy, 1820–1960*. London: Allen & Unwin.

Kindleberger, Charles P. 1973. *The World in Depression, 1929–39*. Berkeley, CA: University of California Press.

Krasner, Stephen D., ed. 1983. *International Regimes*. Ithaca, NY, and London: Cornell University Press.

Krueger, Anne O. 1993. *Economic Policies at Cross-Purposes*. Washington: Brookings Institution.

Krugman, Paul. 1994. "LDC Debt Policy." In Martin Feldstein, *American Economic Policy in the 1980s*, Chicago: University of Chicago Press.

McKinnon, Ronald I. 1993. "International Money in Historical Perspective." *Journal of Economic Literature* 31: 1–44.

Meade, James E. 1951. *The Balance of Payments*. London: Oxford University Press.

North, Douglass C. 1993. "Institutions and Credible Commitment." *Journal of Institutional and Theoretical Economics* 149: 11–23.

Nurkse, Ragnar. 1945. *Conditions of International Monetary Equilibrium*. Essays in International Finance 4. Princeton: International Finance Section, Princeton University.

O'Dell, John S. 1989. "From London to Bretton Woods: Roots of Economic Diplomacy." *Journal of Public Policy* 8: 287–316.

Putnam, Robert D., and C. Randall Henning. 1989. "The Bonn Summit of 1978: A Case Study of Coordination." In Richard N. Cooper et al., *Can Nations Agree?* Washington: Brookings Institution.

Reisen, Helmut. 1989. *Public Debt, External Competitiveness, and Fiscal Discipline in Developing Countries.* Princeton Studies in International Finance 66. Princeton: International Finance Section, Princeton University.

Reynolds, Lloyd G. 1985. *Economic Growth in the Third World, 1850–1980.* New Haven, CT: Yale University Press.

Sachs, Jeffrey, ed. 1989. *Developing Country Debt and Economic Performance.* Cambridge, MA: MIT Press.

Seidman, Joel. 1953. *American Labor from Defense to Reconversion,* Chicago: University of Chicago Press.

Solomon, Robert. 1982. *The International Monetary System, 1945–1981.* New York: Harper & Row.

Triffin, Robert. 1957. *Europe and the Money Muddle.* New Haven, CT: Yale University Press.

Triffin, Robert. 1960. *Gold and the Dollar Crisis.* New Haven, CT: Yale University Press.

van der Wee, Herman. 1986. *Prosperity and Upheaval: The World Economy 1945–1980.* New York: Viking.

Volcker, Paul, and Toyoo Gyohten. 1992. *Changing Fortunes.* New York: Times Books.

Williamson, John. 1977. *The Failure of World Monetary Reform, 1971–1974.* New York: New York University Press.

Williamson, John, and Marcus H. Miller. 1987. *Targets and Indicators: A Blueprint for the International Coordination of Economic Policies.* Washington: Institute for International Economics.

Winham, Gilbert. 1986. *International Trade and the Tokyo Round Negotiation.* Princeton: Princeton University Press.

Zacchia, Carlo. 1976. "International Trade and Capital Movements 1920–1970." In Carlo Cipolla, *The Fontana Economic History of Europe, Volume 5, Part 2: The Twentieth Century,* London: Fontana, 509–602.

Comment

ROBERT O. KEOHANE

This paper presents a magisterial survey, in a remarkably short compass, of the management of the world economy during the last half century. Its principal themes are that policy coordination, particularly during the first 25 years after World War II, was remarkably effective, that the international institutions through which such coordination occurred have been quite adaptable, and that United States' capability and willingness to provide side payments were crucial to those institutions' success. In my judgment, this is quite an accurate set of generalizations, but we must recognize that the process in retrospect looks a great deal smoother than it did to participants at the time. The international regimes that evolved after World War II were by no means fully anticipated in 1944. Indeed, with the beginning of the Cold War in 1947, both the expectations of policymakers and the bargains entered into by governments changed.

During the past 20 years, political scientists have explored this history and have come to conclusions similar to those of Eichengreen and Kenen. We have stressed what is implicit in this paper but is more remarkable to a "dismal science" accustomed to linking international relations with war: the peacefulness of what Joseph Nye and I called complex interdependence, in which nongovernmental as well as governmental actors deal with each other on a variety of issues but do not resort to force or the threat of force in these relationships (Keohane and Nye 1977). Historically, complex interdependence is rare. Yet since 1947 it has been extended from the Atlantic area to the islands of the Pacific Rim, and it seems to be outliving

Robert O. Keohane is Stanfield Professor of International Peace, Harvard University.

the end of the Cold War. In these areas, the dogs of war are not barking in the night, and we should note this fact.

But there is a dog not barking in this paper: the Cold War itself. The beginnings of the Cold War in 1947 reoriented American foreign policy and profoundly changed the relationship between the United States and Europe, and soon thereafter, the relationship between the United States and Japan. Alliances provide incentives to cooperate (Gowa 1993). The Cold War was therefore one of the props of the Bretton Woods system, along with the capability and willingness of the United States to provide side payments. Indeed, the willingness of the United States to help other democracies and the willingness of the countries of Europe and the Pacific Rim to defer to the United States are both hard to imagine in the absence of the Cold War.

To American capacity and willingness to make side payments, Eichengreen and Kenen add two other factors strengthening postwar institutions: the small number of countries involved and the closed nature of domestic economies. Requiring agreement from only a few countries surely facilitated cooperation (Oye 1986). And in the early years, the relative closure of domestic economies probably made international economic management easier. However, as Stephan Haggard indicated in the discussion of this paper, the dramatic increases in economic openness of the last 50 years have created political constituencies for continued liberalism that are much more powerful than those that existed in 1944. Hence liberalization has taken on a powerful dynamic of its own (Keohane and Milner 1994).

In my view, Eichengreen and Kenen should have emphasized at the beginning of their paper another crucial factor in the strengthening of international institutions: the prevalence of pluralist democracies in the strong economies of North America and Europe, partially imitated by Japan. As they point out later in the paper, these political institutions incorporated a consensus in favor of liberal capitalism, full employment, and the welfare state. Hence, the successful international economic institutions of the half century since Bretton Woods have been built on a foundation of compatible domestic politics.

Not surprisingly, the greatest vulnerabilities of the Bretton Woods regimes also involved domestic politics: as the authors point out, governments came under pressure from those interests adversely affected by international competition. As they say: "The ability of governments to manage change internationally has depended importantly on their ability to manage it domestically." This major theme of the conclusion of this fine paper could well be stressed more in its introductory section. Fuller recognition of the importance of this political clash of interests to international economic regimes would reinforce the argument that liberalization attained a self-sustaining dynamic in societies where exports and international investment grew rapidly, thus generating demands for continued, or even greater, openness (Milner 1987).

Like other institutions, international institutions—once they are well-established—take on lives of their own. They are initiated by governments and ultimately can be reined in by governments, but the costs of drastically changing them, or cutting off their funding, may become very large. The institutions' rules shape expectations, exemplify commitments that are costly to break, reduce the transaction costs of making further agreements, and help governments monitor their partners' actions (Keohane 1984). International institutions can only be understood in terms of state power and state interests. How else could we explain the underdevelopment of development institutions as opposed to the trade and finance institutions so central to the richest, most powerful countries? But once established, the institutions acquire their own significance. In his paper for this conference, Fred Bergsten points out that international institutions sometimes disappear, but he has trouble finding examples of significant institutions that did so. Like the March of Dimes, which survived the discovery by Doctors Salk and Sabin of vaccines for polio, the European Community, the Bretton Woods institutions, and even NATO remain robust, even after the end of the Cold War that helped to spawn them.

Internationalization and Domestic Politics

There would be little point in adding either detail or political science jargon to the broad portrait that Eichengreen and Kenen paint. Furthermore, the comparative advantage of political science lies in the murky present, where our interpretations cannot be refuted either by the axiomatic simplifications of economists or the grubby resort to facts of the historians! I therefore want to focus on a point the authors make and extend it into territory they did not explore. The authors say:

> When examining the earlier history of the Bretton Woods system, it made sense to focus mainly on relations among governments. When looking at recent developments, it is important to focus on relations between governments and markets.

Eichengreen and Kenen are pointing here to a phenomenon that has been referred to as internationalization. It is widely recognized, both by policymakers and pundits, that international competition has become more intense and that the world economy is exerting strong impacts on the economies even of large countries such as the United States. National economies by and large have become more integrated into the world economy: their imports and exports of goods, services, and capital and their openness to price signals from the international economy have grown, a result in part of policy changes but also reflecting systemic changes that no country can fully ignore.

As internationalization has occurred, governments' relationships with markets have, as Eichengreen and Kenen point out, become more important. But markets are deeply embedded in domestic politics: interest groups and voters respond first of all to "the economy, stupid." Hence, insofar as markets affect governments, they do so largely through domestic politics. Not only does effective management of the world economy depend on domestic politics; domestic politics is deeply affected by changes in international markets.

It is chiefly up to economists to identify how the links between the global economy and national economies are forged. For my purposes, the point is that international economics increasingly shapes domestic politics. Analysts of domestic politics will increasingly have to regard changes in the world economy as fundamental to their subject matter. It would be difficult, for example, to understand the stagnation of real wages in the United States during the last 20 years—a fundamental political as well as economic fact—without locating the United States in the world economy. Nor could one understand the imbalance between Japanese export industries and its distributional system—or the political pressures that this creates—without understanding Japan's location in the world economy and the strategies of its government and firms for economic advance within it. Real or imagined concerns about international competitiveness even affect such apparently domestic policies as health care.

This is not to say that changes in the world economy dictate changes in national policies, much less that these policies are converging rapidly. For example, the United States has relied heavily on macroeconomic policy whereas Japan's policy under the Liberal Democratic Party (LDP) involved promoting exports by advanced industrial groups while protecting politically privileged domestic sectors such as agriculture and construction. Furthermore, actual policies result from a combination of international forces and domestic political institutions: the responsiveness of LDP politicians to concentrated interest groups rather than to the interests of Japanese consumers was conditioned, as Frances Rosenbluth (1994) has shown, by an electoral system that featured multimember districts and the single, nontransferable vote. I am not advocating international economic determinism. On the contrary, I simply want to emphasize that the importance of government-market relations implies that domestic politics is also central to the world political economy—not only as a cause but also as an effect, in part, of internationalization.

A particularly important way in which internationalization has affected domestic politics is by creating new political coalitions or sustaining old ones. In the advanced capitalist countries, liberal political coalitions have been predominant over the past half century. The consistency of policy that Eichengreen and Kenen chronicle reflects, therefore, a consistency in interests and in the social and economic groups that hold those interests. But changes can also occur.

In work for a project on the domestic political effects of internationalization (Keohane and Milner 1994), Rosenbluth has shown how the growth of export and multinational ties has changed the interests of business in Japan. No longer are the large, internationally oriented firms willing to tolerate high levels of protection for other domestic actors, and no longer do they see the benefits of paying huge campaign contributions to the once-dominant Liberal Democratic Party. The preferences and political behavior of firms in Japan have changed due to their internationalization. In China, as Susan Shirk (1994) has argued, internationalization helped create a group of actors with whom Deng Xiaoping could develop an alliance to oppose the "Communist coalition." This group of agricultural producers, light industry, coastal provinces, and consumers benefited from the opening of China's economy and became the political linchpin in Deng's strategy to unseat the ruling Communist coalition and begin economic reforms.

The interaction between the world economy and domestic politics clearly runs both ways. Publics, elites, and governments react to others' actions and to changes in the costs and benefits of alternative courses of action. Internationalization is hardly an apolitical process characterized simply by adaptation to technologically driven change. Competition and political struggle take place among powerful states with different interests, between sectors within economies, and between governments and multinational enterprises. The resulting struggles are exemplified by the disputes over exchange rates and the role of the dollar in the 1960s, discussed by Eichengreen and Kenen, as well as by the Uruguay Round. As always in the world economy, interests and power are crucial to the outcomes that we observe.

Conclusion

In these comments, I have tried modestly to extend the excellent analysis of Eichengreen and Kenen by pointing out the significance of the Cold War and especially the self-reinforcing dynamic of liberalization that the creation of the Bretton Woods institutions set in motion. Internationalization has deeply affected the interests of firms and individuals—first within the major democracies and later around the world. Domestic politics and international economic relations can only be understood in their symbiotic relationship to one another. Domestic political coalitions are crucial to the postwar international political economy, and changes in those coalitions, which can certainly be prompted by internationalization, can fundamentally change governments' policies and international institutions. No country and no international institution is immune to the impact of the world economy, as the collapse of socialist systems suggests.

In the wake of the unexpected events of the past decade, political scientists are chastened creatures, wary of prediction. The safest prediction is that change in the 1990s and into the next century is unlikely to follow a linear pattern. Liberalization and democratization are not necessarily the wave of the future, and history has not come to an end. Modern capitalism has always developed unevenly, and its gale force winds of "creative destruction," in Joseph Schumpeter's phrase, have always generated political resistance. "The bourgeoisie," said Karl Marx and Friedrich Engels, "cannot exist without constantly revolutionizing the instruments of production, and therefore the relations of production, and with them the whole relations of society" (Feuer, 1959, 10). Both Marx and one of his greatest critics thought that, in Schumpeter's words, the "very success" of the capitalist system "undermines the social institutions which protect it, and 'inevitably' creates conditions in which it will not be able to live" (Schumpeter 1950, 91). Capitalism may be more resilient than Marx and Schumpeter thought, but recent experience in the former Soviet Union suggests that its ability to destroy established social institutions has not diminished.

As we think about the international institutions of the next century, we had better not get too lost in specific proposals for incremental tinkering with the institutions now in place. The global economic forces unleashed by liberalizing political institutions are having profound and far-reaching effects on domestic politics, many of which may be as poorly anticipated as the collapse of state socialism was. We may only be living in the eye of the storm.

References

Feuer, Lewis, ed. 1959. *Marx and Engels: Basic Writings on Politics and Philosophy.* New York: Doubleday Anchor.

Gowa, Joanne. 1993. *Allies, Adversaries and International Trade.* Princeton, NJ: Princeton University Press.

Keohane, Robert O. 1984. *After Hegemony: Cooperation and Discord in the World Political Economy.* Princeton, NJ: Princeton University Press.

Keohane, Robert O., and Helen V. Milner, eds. 1994. "Internationalization and Domestic Politics." Unpublished papers for a collective project. Harvard University.

Keohane, Robert O., and Joseph S. Nye, Jr. 1977. *Power and Interdependence: World Politics in Transition.* Boston: Little, Brown.

Milner, Helen V. *Resisting Protectionism.* 1987. Princeton, NJ: Princeton University Press.

Oye, Kenneth A., ed. 1986. *Cooperation Under Anarchy.* Princeton, NJ: Princeton University Press.

Rosenbluth, Frances. 1994. "Internationalization and Electoral Politics in Japan." Unpublished paper for Keohane and Milner (1994).

Schumpeter, Joseph A. 1950. *Capitalism, Socialism and Democracy.* New York: Harper's.

Shirk, Susan L. 1994. "Opening China to the World Economy: Communist Institutions and Foreign Economic Policy Reforms." Unpublished paper for Keohane and Milner (1994).

Comment

RICHARD PORTES

Robert Keohane has given an Olsonian thesis to explain the drop in growth rates in the latter half of the period we are considering: the accretion of international institutions, which now exert their deadening hand and which we don't know how to cast off. Perhaps the conference participants can tell us how to get out of this Olsonian trap.

The Eichengreen-Kenen paper is indeed a masterful survey, but it is not only that. There are interpretations, some of them quite contentious. My comparative advantage on this panel is in political economy. I won't try to speak as an international macroeconomist, partly because the paper doesn't primarily deal with the straight international macro issues, and where it does—on money and debt—I agree almost completely with the authors.

The key political economy themes focus on institutions and rules. I think that is the right perspective in which to try to interpret the period: the social compact and the distributional settlement; the difference between the first and second halves of the period; and the role of the United States, the World Bank, and the less developed countries. To this list, I would add the EMS and EMU. Finally, I will try to suggest a new, somewhat different, forward-looking perspective on these issues, going from commitment, credibility, and coordination to subsidiarity.

I do not disagree with the authors about what is to be explained: the golden age of growth and why it ended. But some recent research suggests rather more continuity in growth over the entire postwar period—and,

Richard Portes is Director of the Centre for Economic Policy Research in London.

indeed, over the past century and a half—than this paper implies. There-fore, the paper risks explaining a different outcome—one in the opposite direction—than the actual experience of 1945–70 suggests. In any case, even those data suggest that the phenomenon was mainly European, just as the rise in unemployment of the subsequent period has been mainly a European phenomenon.

If there is a growth bonus to be explained, the Bretton Woods institutions' role as conservator of rules could well be valid. But we need more proof than is provided. As the authors point out, there is a reciprocal relationship between those institutions and their functioning, on the one hand, and the stability and growth observed in the first half of the period, on the other. But they do not specify that simultaneous interaction in any great detail, nor provide us with identifying restrictions. Were the rules necessary or indeed useful? Martin Feldstein, for example, (1988) has argued consistently that countries are unwilling to subordinate their per-ceived national interests to international cooperation and that we there-fore shouldn't even try to make them do so. But there need not be any sacrifice. Individuals and countries with very different preferences can trade quite profitably with each other; so can nations cooperatively reconcile their policy stances with mutual benefit, even if their inflation-unemployment trade-offs differ greatly.

The emphasis of domestic politics on "putting your own house in order," which has dominated the past 15 years, suggests that there is no convincing justification for coordination. But that is not necessarily true. There is a strong case for coordination when there are spillovers, when there are economies of scale, and when there are public goods at issue.

But the Bretton Woods institutions did not organize that kind of coordi-nation. It is not clear, therefore, that the coordination theme appears in the Bretton Woods institutions in that sense. Putting your own house in order is clearly not a sufficient point of departure for dealing with trade relation-ships. But is the fully multilateral framework that Bretton Woods repre-sented a necessary condition for such coordination? Consider that the framework for the 1870–1913 period grew out of a bilateral British-French agreement. This may suggest regionalism as an alternative solution. One might even consider the counterfactual hypothesis that there might have been more regional institutions if Bretton Woods had never been and that this might have been a good thing. Perhaps the world economy would have grown more slowly in the first half of the period, or perhaps the world could have avoided the bad times of the second half of the period. This hypothesis is not irrelevant to some of the decisions of institutional design that face us now.

The paper interprets the IMF and the EPU as "a commitment technol-ogy" and a coordination mechanism. It considers how they worked and why countries committed to them. The authors reject the hypothesis that the IMF was effective primarily due to its enforcement of rules against beggar-thy-neighbor devaluations. They also do not believe that the IMF was able to offer sufficient pecuniary incentives to induce commitment. They are then reduced, it seems to me, to invoking the idea of the IMF as a seal of approval on national policies, especially because of its positive effect on international capital markets. But the importance of these markets to national policymakers seems to me a relatively recent phenomenon that does not explain the emphasis countries put on coordination and the role of the Bretton Woods institutions immediately after the war.

The authors then discuss the EPU, which presided over a coordinated scrapping of restrictions on trade, and which they say favored investment based on comparative advantage. But there is a suggestion in the paper, which I think unfounded, that governments were guiding this investment in the direction of comparative advantage for export promotion. I don't see the evidence to support this view. Again, with respect to the EPU, the authors say this was superior to convertibility as a commitment technology and that convertibility would have been easier to reverse than the EPU commitment. That seems to me not in accord with the recent analysis favoring convertibility over a payments union structure for the economies of transition in Eastern Europe and the former Soviet Union. In fact, the emphasis in this region is on moving quickly to convertibility because this gives credibility to domestic economic policies. Yet this is precisely the opposite of what the paper is arguing for the earlier period.

Let us turn to the distributional settlement of the social compact that was, according to the authors, the basis for the political agreement to Bretton Woods. They say, "The ability of governments to manage change internationally has depended importantly on their ability to manage it domestically." I am not clear whether that is Reaganomics, Clintonomics, or some other perspective on the relationship between domestic political economy and the international scene, but I find it hard to recognize in the history of the period. This point seems to need more convincing evidence to support it.

Again, there is a problem of time sequence that makes this a difficult story to tell. This distributional settlement must have preceded or accompanied the emphasis on full employment and the welfare state. That settlement was supposed to induce the body politic to accept the international commitments of Bretton Woods. This conclusion is especially problematic if, as another part of the paper suggested, indeed it was Marshall Plan aid that was essential for reaching the distributional settlement. If that is the case, it is only the EPU—the latest of those international commitments—that might fit the story. But Britain supposedly was among the most reluctant to open up, and the EPU was a key part of that process. If it was the social compact in Britain that brought Britain to accept the EPU and that process, why did the electorate more or less simultaneously throw out the government?

The next question is, what was the precise nature of the deal in this political economy story—was it that labor would accept low real wages while the entrepreneurs would invest? There is no evidence to support the view that either labor or business made any exceptional compact in that respect, nor that entrepreneurs in particular invested more than their animal spirits and profitability criteria would otherwise have justified.

I also find very difficult to understand the suggestion that the similarity across countries on this social agreement was important in achieving the postwar settlement. The authors argue that having achieved agreement at home in ways that were "broadly compatible" across countries, governments could enter credibly into international commitments. What does this mean? In what ways were British socialism, German *ordnungspolitik*, the US market economy, the Swedish welfare state, and Austrian corporatism compatible—and how did that matter in terms of reaching international consensus?

I turn now to the difference between the first and second halves of the period. Despite the disclaimer that the authors would not try to impose upon us a hegemonic stability theory, that does seem to me to be their central conclusion. Nor am I convinced by their interpretation of the second half of the period, because the United States still can get its way in many important respects. At least, that is the European perception. For example, in regard to Russia and the IMF: which country has been driving that process and which has gotten its way? American dominance is also apparent in the World Bank's shift to supporting the private sector and even imposing that as the primary obligation of the European Bank for Reconstruction and Development (EBRD) and in regard to the EU-US deal that was finally struck to complete the Uruguay Round. All other participants in that process turned out, in the end game, to be peripheral. The ideological shift toward "put your own house in order," though led by the United States, was partly a response to the failures of international coordination in the 1970s.

Regarding the role of the World Bank, the authors are puzzled that there was no agency with comprehensive responsibility for development, which would include a whole range of issues: international capital flows, debt, commodity prices. There is a very simple explanation. These are essentially distributional issues at the international level. We have neither criteria nor a consensus for distributional settlements at the international level. There was never a consensus, for example, on any of the "global solutions" proposed to deal with the debt problem of the 1980s, just as there had been none in the 1930s.

Regarding EMS and EMU, I find convincing the analogies the authors have drawn between the breakdown of Bretton Woods and the breakdown of the EMS. Nevertheless, that does not speak at all to the issue of whether there should be a common currency in Europe or for some subset of the European countries. The failure of fixed exchange rates says nothing about the viability or desirability of a common currency. I would also stress something that has been illuminated by the collapse of the EMS: the conflict between French dirigisme and what the French themselves would call Anglo-Saxon *libre échangisme*. We *libre échangistes* have a hard time these days with our French friends. There are broader and longer term implications of that difference of viewpoint both for tensions within the European Union and for the relationship between the European Union and the rest of the world. This relationship will doubtless affect some of the issues of international coordination we are discussing.

Finally "subsidiarity": the standard paradigm we have been using for international economic interaction has outlived its usefulness. It is past its "sell by" date. By that, I do not mean merely that the Mundell Fleming model is 30 years old, nor that the theory of optimum currency areas is not the right framework for assessing whether Europe or some subset of European countries should have a common currency. We need to be able to answer much more convincingly than those domestic policymakers and constituencies who say it is enough to put your own house in order. We must lay out the justification for international cooperation and policy coordination case by case. There are convincing theoretical justifications, even for going so far as central enforcement of binding rules. On the other hand, there are also clear arguments from public economics for local decision making: there is more transparency, better access to information at the local level, and much more responsiveness to individuals and organizational preferences. There are trade-offs to be made, and this has been thought through in some detail in discussions about subsidiarity. Such trade-offs provide the basis for a framework in which one can consider macroeconomic issues, trade issues, and the issues of global institutional design that we are now confronting.

References

Feldstein, Martin. 1988. "Distinguished Lecture on Economics in Government: Thinking about International Economic Coordination." *Journal of Economic Perspectives* 2, no. 2 (spring): 3–13.

Comment

EMILE VAN LENNEP

I have had the privilege to be very close to many of the events relevant to this discussion over the 50 years since Bretton Woods, both as a national official, as chairman of the Monetary Committee of the Common Market and of Working Party 3 of OECD, and as secretary general of OECD. Like a few present at the conference, I attended all the governors meetings of the IMF, from 1952 on, with one exception, when my wife was very ill. So I am indeed very interested in the issues raised at this conference.

I think the authors' paper is comprehensive. They very rightly make the interesting distinction between institutions with a small "i" and Institutions with a capital "I". It is very important to understand the basis for international cooperation and the framework within which it functioned after the war and, in my opinion, should continue to function. In other words, the nations agreed on the institutions with the small "i" that constitute the economic order: free movement of goods and services, labor, and capital through competition, welfare, and growth.

Both nationally and internationally, the market economy cannot function in a vacuum; it requires an institutional framework of rules, rights, and obligations, and there have to be institutions ensuring the application and enforcement of these rules. The Institutions (with the capital "I") created among the Western nations were a basic element of the international economic order: they functioned as custodians of these rules of the game with their independent secretariats—an important element one

Emile van Lennep is minister of state of the Netherlands and a past secretary general of the Organization for Economic Cooperation and Development (1969–84).

sometimes forgets. These secretariats were different from that of the Council for Mutual Economic Assistance, which was a political instrument. In the Bretton Woods institutions, all participating countries were confident that their fundamental interests were being taken into account and that no one power, big or small, dominated. Along with the independence of the institutions, the system's multilateralism was another basic reason for the success of the postwar world.

It is true that the term "Bretton Woods system" is a bit ambiguous. I agree with Fred Bergsten that we should look not only at the IMF and the World Bank; international cooperation on economic matters goes much deeper. Indeed, after the war the Bretton Woods system became part of an overall United Nations system. After the war, the United Nations focused first on regional cooperation: the European Commission for Europe, the Commission for Latin America, the Commission for Asia, and so on. These commissions never functioned in a fundamentally important way. Then the United Nations organized functionally. Besides the Bretton Woods institutions, there were UN institutions for agriculture and science, for instance. Its leaders also thought there should be an Economic and Social Council (ECOSOC) that would serve as a partner of the Security Council and that this council would provide a forum for the world to discuss and decide how the world economy should function. We all know, however, that ECOSOC does not play a role at all, nor did it ever. Neither developed nor developing countries used it, and it has no credibility as an institution.

Therefore, real cooperation took place elsewhere: first in the Bretton Woods institutions on financial, monetary, and economic affairs and, second, among the industrialized countries in first the OEEC and later in the OECD. The OECD hardly figures anywhere in the papers in this volume. I understand why: there is no literature on it. There is literature on the EPU, which the Eichengreen-Kenen paper cites, but none on the OECD. I wrote my memoirs, which naturally include a little piece of history on OECD, and I hope this will help fill the gap and encourage other conferences to consider the OECD's work.

Apart from the global organizations, there is also a large number of regional groupings with widely differing ambitions, ranging from full economic integration with primarily political objectives (the European Union) to more limited cooperation on trade or other issues related to geographic proximity. I agree with the authors of the paper when they argue that both regional and functional negotiations should take place within the global institutional framework.

In this context, I should like to put forward the following additional points for discussion:

- The multilateral system (the economic institution with a small "i") is in danger of being eroded by bilateralism and regionalism.

- The multilateral institutions (with the capital "I") are undermined or downgraded by the largest nations through increasingly unilateral action, bilateral consultations, or groupings such as the Group of Seven (G-7) that act outside the Institutions.

- National economic policymaking requires a careful day-to-day balancing of sectoral and other interests in a coherent overall national policy by governments. International cooperation, particularly in specialized institutions and institutions with a limited mandate, risks contributing to an international strengthening of sectoral interests or approaches. In my opinion, the functional UN specialized agencies, including the Bretton Woods Institutions, inadequately contribute to the needed "horizontalization" of the vital issues confronting the international community.

Let me elaborate on each of these three points. First, the erosion of the multilateral economic system is a serious question. Most people seem to believe that with the completion of the Uruguay Round and the establishment of the WTO the multilateral trading system will be secured. I disagree. Neither the GATT nor the new WTO will be able to roll back the tendency toward regionalism, which is rapidly accelerating throughout the whole world.

Regional cooperation on trade and payments can contribute to multilateralism if it leads to more trade in the world as a whole through more competition. Every economist knows, however, that regional preferential trade systems can lead to trade diversion, in particular if the economies are complementary. The balance of creation and diversion is crucial.

The European Union, in particular after expanding the membership to include the Mediterranean countries and through association agreements, is an example of regional trade arrangements leading partly to trade diversion. The United States, after decades of hostility to regional trade groupings outside the politically motivated European integration, switched to favoring regionalism and itself adopted the goal of regional free trade in the Western Hemisphere and possibly in the Pacific region.

From a global point of view, NAFTA has certainly many positive aspects. However, it cannot be denied that it has a large potential for trade diversion. The present NAFTA is economically less logical than the NAFTA we talked about in the 1970s: the North Atlantic Free Trade Area. But quite apart from the possible effects of trade diversion, the evolution of the multilateral system into a world of trading blocs does not necessarily lead to more open trade worldwide. Blocs are less inhibited about imposing protectionist measures than are individual countries.

In the monetary field, the European Community has been developing strong monetary cooperation since its inception. As far as I can remember, Europeans have always aimed at reconciling closer regional monetary cooperation with the global monetary system. In recent years, tensions unavoidably grew between the two: the overriding priority of fixed nominal exchange rates in Europe is not necessarily beneficial to the smooth functioning of the world's monetary system. On the other hand, the present European program of convergence of budgetary and monetary policies does not conflict with the interest of other countries—on the contrary. Global institutions must continually scrutinize all measures of liberalization of trade and payments and all processes of imposing more discipline within regional arrangements—be it the European Union or NAFTA—to assess their compatibility with the principles of the open multilateral system.

In the 1950s, the IMF mistakenly thought the EPU a heresy, in conflict with the multilateral monetary system. In fact, it was an unavoidable, collective European discrimination against the dollar with policies successfully aiming at restoring nondiscrimination and convertibility. Now, in the 1990s, the IMF should get more involved, in an impartial, discreet way, in the exchange rate policies of the EMS as well as balance of payments financing—issues that often are wrongly treated as purely internal European matters.

Second, the multilateral institutions are being eroded from several sides. The European countries and Japan in many ways have become economically equal partners of the United States. This is the root of the concept of trilateralism—that is, the multilateral system as having three pillars. Unfortunately, this trilateralism has evolved into a sometimes excessive institutionalized bilateralism between the three pillars, even at the highest political level, on issues that are purely global and that involve the vital interests of others.

This trilateralism—or, bilateralism à trois—goes hand in hand with the more general move of big powers away from the rules-based multilateral institutions to small circles, mainly in the form of the G-7. Eichengreen and Kenen seem to be of the opinion that the G-7 process is unavoidable. I have a more reserved opinion. First, a general observation.

During the decades of the Cold War, a remarkable habit of cooperation developed in the Western world. This was certainly based on the common political will to cooperate to build a world economy that would be better than the one between the two world wars; Eichengreen and Kenen refer extensively to this important driving force. But there was also another driving force: the will to resist the growth of Soviet power in Europe and in the world. The consensus in the West on the market economy has been highly successful for the Western world; in recent years it has been equally beneficial—thanks mainly to the Bretton Woods institutions—to large areas of the world as a whole. The end of the Cold War economically signified that the "one world" we dreamt of in the late 1940s finally became reality.

Paradoxically, however, in the early 1990s world political leaders emphasized the need for more regional rather than more global cooperation.

In Europe, a wave of pan-Europeanism called for new European cooperation from the Atlantic to the Urals or beyond. Major problems, such as the drama in Yugoslavia, were called European problems, to be solved by Europe. Regionalism was seen as the key to resisting increasing fragmentation and divisive nationalism.

Of course, proximity should encourage nations to cooperate in promoting peace and stability. Regionalism should not, on the other hand, lead to political isolation or to letting powers outside the region off the hook. This is particularly important for trans-Atlantic relations as well as for the relations with Japan and other Asian powers.

The European Commission has a constant, understandable tendency to identify problems as "European" and to deal with them outside the multilateral system. Unfortunately, with the disappearance of the European superpower, a new "without-America" attitude is translated into pan-Europeanism, and not only in France. The United States, partly as a reaction against inward-looking European attitudes, at the same time is withdrawing into regionalism that could go beyond trade arrangements.

Thus the new regionalism is potentially a threat to the multilateral system, both economically (resulting in trade diversion, discrimination, protection) and politically (undermining the rules-based multilateral institutions through bilateral confrontation between regional organizations or directorates of major powers and through unilateralism).

I mentioned before the two driving forces in the postwar years leading to the habit of cooperation. We are now in a new era in which this habit of cooperation is weakening. International institutions will continue to be important in the coming years. The international cooperation they promote should not only be efficient—that is, there should not be too many people around the table—but also rules-based, representative, credible, and effective.

In the IMF, G-7, G-10, and G-24 each play a role in the consultation, coordination, and decision-making process. In the UN on economic issues, the European Union, the G-77, and sometimes the OECD and other groups play these roles. The post–Cold War era certainly calls for a rethinking of the future role and functioning of some international organizations in the field of security. But in the economic field, there is no need of new institutions—rather, existing ones must be strengthened and the former habit of cooperation must be revived. The effectiveness of the various groups should be judged against the overriding criteria: do they indeed reinforce the multilateral institutions with the small "i" as well as with the capital "I"? I am not sure that the European Union or the G-7 can answer this question in the affirmative generally. They should aim at creating structural links with the Institutions—not only with their secretariats as is often the case, but with the Institutions as intergovernmental bodies.

Finally, the third point I wish to make is that there is a need for "horizontal" international cooperation. International consultation, coordination, and decisions are needed on a great number of issues. The issues requiring horizontal treatment are often interrelated: for example, environment and poverty, population and education, savings ratios and capital inflows, globalization of the economies and migration, commodity prices and debts. National governments must deal with interrelated issues in a coordinated way. In the OECD as well as in a number of regional organizations such as the European Union, many issues can be dealt with within the organization. In the UN system, such issues can be discussed by all nations concerned, but many of the issues are dealt with in separate organizations.

I have a long experience in OECD with the practical difficulties of the "horizontalization" of intergovernmental cooperation. It requires a constant injection of the views of one committee into the discussions of another dealing with, say, trade or environment, or unemployment. The sectoral committee may be competent to address the issue but could benefit from a more balanced, coherent view. Such coordination efforts could also prevent international organizations from linking the wrong issues, such as the alleged social or environmental dumping.

One of the difficulties is that officials of the sectoral committees generally prefer to be among their colleagues, as do treasury officials. But gradually sectoral committee officials realize that if they are not confronted with other internationally relevant views or aspects, their conclusions often lack real influence on government policies. Without horizontalization, international cooperation can be misused to strengthen sectoral lobbies in ways that are perceived to threaten the interests of national governments.

The UN's lack of horizontal coordination is horrifying. Whether the issue is debt, environment, trade, commodities, or development assistance, one sees clearly that the officials responsible for each come from completely separate worlds.

The European Union is illustrative of both successes and failures in horizontalization. Although the organization has the full potential of taking many relevant views into account, the sectors on which the Union has taken over full responsibility—agriculture and trade policy—suffer often from too narrow an approach.

It is, of course, an illusion to think that there could ever be real coordination between the functional organizations and other global and regional organizations. But one can at least expect the leadership and the staffs of the UN organizations to demonstrate a willingness to learn and to cooperate and to avoid an insular attitude based on the fear of an intrusion of other views. With respect to the Bretton Woods institutions, I believe that they would certainly benefit from a more open attitude toward cooperation with other organizations.

Comment

KLAUS ENGELEN

As a German financial journalist who has been covering the Bretton Woods institutions since the end of the 1960s, I have a different perspective on aspects of the international financial institutions (IFIs) that are easily overlooked or in many instances not discussed openly but that go to the core of Germany's role in the Bretton Woods institutions. Specifically, to what extent have one or more countries run the IMF and the European Bank for Reconstruction and Development de facto, on the basis of narrow national interests, while waving the banner of multilateral management and international cooperation? I believe a frank discussion of the behind-the-scenes power play by nations that try to use the IFIs for promoting their own interests should be part of the 50th anniversary review.

The excellent and helpful overview paper by Barry Eichengreen and Peter B. Kenen discusses the difference between "Institutions" with a capital "I" and "institutions" with a small "i." They define the former as the organizations that served as conservators of the rules, conventions, and understandings that structure international economic relations and the latter as the rules and understandings themselves.

When talking about "institutions"—that is, the rules of the game—we should broaden the review by including a second small "i" for the interests—political, economic, financial, and strategic—of an individual member country or groups of member countries of the IFIs.

When assessing the first 50 years of institutions such as the IMF and the World Bank, there should be an open and broad exchange of views—not

---

Klaus Engelen is a financial journalist with Handelsblatt *in Dusseldorf, Germany.*

just by Americans, with a few old British friends in tow, discussing the unique historic achievements mostly among themselves. This volume makes a promising start in that regard, for it includes a broad spectrum of views on the first 50 years after Bretton Woods and the future role of the institutions.

When we recall the key role of the United States in establishing the Bretton Woods institutions, we should not be surprised that American views have prevailed here and at other anniversary conferences. Yet given the different perceptions among donor and receiving countries regarding the record of the Bretton Woods institutions, it seems almost impossible to reach consensus on an assessment of that record.

Mahbub ul Haq argues that the IMF and the World Bank "are no longer institutions of global management, but are primarily institutions to police the developing world, since the industrial world is largely independent of their policy prescriptions and management control." After the decades of North-South struggle in the IMF, the multilateral banks, and the whole UN system, such sour grapes in the birthday wine could be expected.

Yet the strained relations between big and smaller creditor countries and the IFIs have often been overlooked. The Americans—and other shrewd power players in financial diplomacy such as the French and the British—may be surprised to learn of the building anger and frustration in other major creditor nations—Germany in particular—over how the Bretton Woods institutions are run.

Large segments of Germany's political, business, and academic establishment have decried their country's second-tier role in the Bretton Woods institutions and the American and French dominance of those institutions. Germans believe they are the losers of the system—footing the bill without gaining equivalent political clout.

Perhaps it was inevitable that the American-led creation of these institutions as part of a global strategy to build a better world after the horrors of two major wars would have another, less noble purpose: to promote US political and economic interests on a global scale. The Eichengreen-Kenen conclusion that American "side payments" supported US global economic leadership throughout the Cold War lends credence to this view. Yet this criticism from segments of the institutions' membership has actually intensified over the decades. Critics now allege that US global strategists are using their leverage with the international multilateral institutions—not only the IMF and the World Bank but also the important regional development banks—to compensate for the United States' diminishing share in the world economy.

It could be argued that Germany's criticisms overstate the problem and that Germany has not in fact been consigned to a backbench role. After all, Germany, a major exporter, has profited handsomely from the open global economic trading world over the past 50 years. Yet many Germans cannot get over Bonn's series of failures in financial diplomacy.

Germany's problems with the IMF go back to the early 1960s, about 10 years after the Federal Republic became a member. If the key German actors then at the Bundesbank were here today, they would undoubtedly remind us of the pressures for a deutsche mark revaluation during the fixed exchange rate system, which had become flooded with dollars. This pressure culminated in the Smithsonian realignment on 18 December 1971. "At the root of German tensions with the IMF under the old Bretton Woods system of fixed exchange rates in the years leading up to the breakdown of the system was the American attitude of 'benign neglect' toward the external effects of its economic and financial policies," argues Günther Schleiminger, Germany's executive director at the IMF (1968–74) and later managing director of the Bank for International Settlements.

Both Schleiminger and Otmar Emminger, Germany's first IMF executive director, believed that the Germans experienced the toughest conditionality faced by any nation in this century. "Good market principles" were forced upon them; they had little say in the matter. Germany had no role at Bretton Woods, but it nevertheless served American military, professors, government officials, businessmen, and bankers as a proving ground for market economics under the Marshall Plan. This turned out to be fortunate, but that does not diminish the resentment.

According to Schleiminger (Kaplan and Schleiminger 1989), Germany's 1950–51 payments crisis—resolved by a major international rescue operation—had an impact on German attitudes and policy long after the crisis itself. The payments crisis and the stringent conditions attached to the EPU credit forced Germany to cooperate in unprecedented ways. Indeed, the monitoring procedures and restrictive measures were so severe that other countries took pains to avoid similar predicaments. Inside the German government, the payments crisis was instrumental in streamlining decision making and administrative procedures. The burden of international responsibility had been forced on Germany, but the basis was laid for the strengthening of the German currency.

But as the Bundesbank, under the presidency of Wilhelm Vocke, enhanced its independent status by defending the new deutsche mark, and the IMF remained strictly committed to a system of fixed exchange rates and to a US policy later summed up as "the dollar is our currency but your problem," conflict became inevitable.

In the spring of 1957, according to Schleiminger, a confidential report of the Advisory Council to the German Federal Ministry of Economic Affairs endorsed a coordinated realignment of exchange rates. Thereupon, Chancellor Ludwig Erhard sought Vocke's support for the realignment, which would, of course, involve a revaluation of the D-mark. But the central bank was uncompromising. Per Jacobsson, the newly appointed managing director of the IMF, also opposed an upward valuation of the mark and told Vocke so. When Germany finally gave in to American pressure and decided to revalue in March 1961, Otmar Emminger presented the official request. Jacobsson received him with the words: "What have you done, you scoundrel?" Emminger later commented, "In the then existing circumstances, concerted action by all countries concerned was a utopian idea. The process of multilateral exchange rate adjustment, which would indeed have been appropriate as early as 1957, dragged on over a period of ten years and a number of currency crises."

But when, for the first time, German policy collided head-on with both the IMF and the United States, argues Schleiminger, Finance and Economics Minister Karl Schiller forced both of them to bow to global economic realities in the Smithsonian Agreement of December 1971.

Schleiminger believed the IMF lived up fully to its Articles of Agreement, as set forth in Bretton Woods, only for three years, from 1958–61. Before 1958, he argues, the United States excluded the IMF from a role in financing the reconstruction of war-torn Europe; after 1961, the introduction of the General Arrangements to Borrow (GAB) changed the Fund's character. For most of the turbulent period that led to the eventual breakdown of the fixed note Bretton Woods system, Schleiminger says, the IMF treated Germany as something of an outlaw, and this prevailing attitude allowed the United States to continue its policy of benign neglect without being challenged. In Schleiminger's view, the US failure to adhere to the Bretton Woods agreement lay behind the rise of the D-mark vis-à-vis the dollar—with revaluations that brought the mark to 4.00 to the dollar in 1961, to 3.66 in 1969, to 3.22 in 1971, and to 2.90 in 1973.

Prominent developing-country critics of the Bretton Woods institutions, such as Mahbub ul Haq, should recognize that developing countries were not alone in feeling mistreated. A rising monetary power such as Germany can also take umbrage at the policies and processes of these institutions. The rivalries and frictions among the industrialized members should not be underestimated.

I have to concede, of course, that I have used the journalist's prerogative of generalizing and overdramatizing here and there. Here and in several articles in the *International Economy*, I have been somewhat provocative or sarcastic in my treatment of behind-the-scenes politics. Nevertheless, some of the facts about this period have been utterly disturbing.

The 1988 IMF–World Bank annual meeting in Berlin produced the first thorough assessment of Germany's role in the Bretton Woods institutions and in the broader multilateral system. Yet some of Germany's complaints were never addressed: its concern that the US Treasury functioned as a de facto kitchen cabinet, usurping the functions of the Executive Board, and that the IMF served primarily American and French national interests. For instance, Germans objected when Managing Director Michel Camdessus targeted substantial amounts of IMF funds to relieve African problem loans on the French Tresor's books. Similarly, in the Plaza and Louvre accords, the United States mobilized global currency and financial resources to secure a "soft landing" for the dollar and further financing of the huge US "twin" deficits. Furthermore, during the developing-country debt crisis of the 1980s, the Baker and Brady plans were viewed as grand schemes to marshal the resources of other Western governments, commercial banks, and multilateral institutions to provide a safety net for the American banking system and to support American geopolitical interests—particularly evident in efforts to help Mexico.

At the 1988 meeting, one German participant summed up the situation this way: "The Americans have the power, the French get the top jobs, and the Germans and the Japanese come up with the money."

Many things have changed. What the United States could engineer at a time of huge European and Japanese surpluses works no longer. To finance German unity, Germans are practicing Reaganomics on the Rhine— amassing large budget deficits that require outside financing while avoiding tax increases. And the Japanese are no longer buying long-term dollar bonds, having lost more than $300 billion since the mid-1980s on their holdings of dollar securities.

Germans are supplying about half the Western financial assistance for the former Soviet Union and about one-third of Western assistance for the emerging economies in Eastern Europe. They must join the Americans in mobilizing IMF and World Bank resources for the former Eastern bloc countries. Consequently, they have watched a bit helplessly as the IMF has, in Horst Schulmann's words, "lost its monetary character."

So a German might well ask what there is to celebrate at the 50th anniversary of the Bretton Woods institutions. I would nevertheless recommend a more constructive approach: Germans should look for ways to build a domestic consensus on policies for the multilateral institutions. In this regard, questions such as "Who is running these international institutions?" and "Is our country adequately represented in the top positions?" become even more important. Germany's underrepresentation in visible positions within the European Union and the IMF is already a knife that right-wing politicians are sharpening on the election trail.

Having been quite critical of the US role in the Bretton Woods institutions before and after the breakdown of the fixed exchange rate system, I would like to conclude on a conciliatory note. The current US administration appears to be much better aware of the need to decide international economic policy collectively, as well as to fund its implementation collectively. As the recent capital increase and restructuring of the Inter-American Development Bank demonstrated, a German-US partnership can produce results on which it is possible to build domestic consensus and support, of the kind called for by Eichengreen and Kenen.

However, one thing is clear: demonstrating leadership and achieving burden sharing will become more problematic and complex in the years ahead, in particular among the G-7 countries. Hence, the role of the IFIs as intermediaries in this burden sharing will be even more closely scrutinized.

References

Engelen, Klaus. 1988. "Angst and Anger: Why Germans Hate the IMF and the World Bank." *International Economy* (October).

Engelen, Klaus. 1991. "Bonn to Washington: Stop Managing the World by Other People's Money." *International Economy* (October).

Engelen, Klaus. 1994. "Europe's NAFTA Syndrome—That Crowded-Out Feeling in Latin America." *International Economy* (June).

Kaplan, Jacob J., and Günther Schleiminger. 1989. *The European Payments Union: Financial Diplomacy in the 1950s*. Oxford: Clarendon Press.

II

MANAGING THE WORLD ECONOMY

2

Managing the Monetary System

JOHN WILLIAMSON AND C. RANDALL HENNING

In their opening contribution to this volume, Eichengreen and Kenen repeatedly refer to the function of an international regime as being to resolve "commitment and coordination problems." They do not claim that the International Monetary Fund (IMF) has been fulfilling that role in recent years. On the contrary, they remark that "[i]t is easy to understand why the IMF is widely viewed as a development institution," since "it had no role in the making of the Plaza and Louvre agreements. . . ."

We begin by asking what postwar experience has taught us about the form that an international monetary regime should take. In particular, is it desirable to have agreed rules of the game to resolve commitment and coordination problems, or does it suffice to allow changes in exchange rates to reconcile the uncoordinated? The answers we give to those questions suggest the outlines of a desirable regime: no one familiar with our previous work will be surprised to learn that the resulting proposals involve target zones for exchange rates as a first step toward an ultimate comprehensive regime based on the 1987 Williamson-Miller "blueprint for policy coordination." Next we discuss the best institutional locus for such a regime, and identify the IMF as the preferred location. We suggest activating the ministerial-level council, provided for in the IMF Articles of Agreement, to replace the Interim Committee and to oversee the im-

John Williamson is senior fellow and C. Randall Henning is research associate at the Institute for International Economics. The authors would like to thank C. Fred Bergsten, Benjamin J. Cohen, Richard N. Cooper, Jeffrey A. Frankel, Morris Goldstein, Peter B. Kenen, John S. Odell, Shijuro Ogata, Jacques J. Polak, Niels Thygesen, and other participants at the Institute conference for comments on previous drafts.

plementation and administration of the new regime by the Group of Seven (G-7) finance ministers and central bank governors. In offering these proposals, including our recommended division of labor between governments and central banks, we draw on the experience of the institutions of the European Monetary System (EMS) and the suggestions for advancing G-7 cooperation offered by Henning (1994).

What Have We Learned?

Does the monetary system need to be managed at all, or could floating exchange rates and high capital mobility allow it to work perfectly well by itself if only the politicians would leave it alone? This is not a rhetorical question: it is the thesis argued by Corden (1983), embraced by the first Reagan administration with its rhetoric about the need for each country to put its own house in order, and indeed largely followed by the Group of Five (G-5) from 1981 to 1985.

This thesis would be convincing if markets behaved in the way described in the textbooks, with exchange rates determined by private agents whose rational expectations lead them to discount the expected future fundamentals appropriately, and if governments behaved as they were assumed to in the pre–public choice economics literature, so as to maximize the well-being of their citizens. But many of us have become increasingly skeptical over the years about both of these propositions. One has to doubt the degree of rationality embodied in the process of exchange rate determination unless one is prepared to dismiss some recent econometric results, such as the famous finding by Meese and Rogoff (1983) that a random walk outperformed any of the exchange rate models over time horizons of less than a year, not to mention the overwhelming evidence provided *inter alia* by Krugman (1985) and Marris (1985) that the dollar suffered a speculative bubble in the mid-1980s. Our worst fears now appear to have been confirmed by a new paper of Andrew Rose (1994), which finds only weak effects of the monetary fundamentals (and, for that matter, capital mobility) on exchange rate volatility, in contrast to a strong and highly significant link between the existence and width of an official exchange rate band and the degree of volatility. Limiting exchange rate variations does not shift noise from the exchange market to some other market (like the bond market) as traditional models assumed; rather, it mainly diminishes the noise in the system (Artis and Taylor 1989). So the first reason for seeking a managed regime is to compensate for badly behaved markets.

The second reason is to restrain badly behaved governments. It transpired, for example, that "putting its house in order" allowed the United States to accept a dangerously large fiscal deficit, a vastly overvalued dollar, and an exploding current account deficit. As Destler and Henning

(1989) have documented (and Eichengreen and Kenen reiterate), these outcomes led the US Congress to react with a raft of protectionist proposals, which were headed off by international cooperation to depreciate the dollar. The experiment of laissez-faire in macroeconomic policies was a failure so unambiguous that it was abandoned at the very start of the second Reagan administration.[1]

The Tokyo summit of 1986 gave the impression of wanting to develop a system of policy coordination based on a set of "indicators" to replace the laissez-faire that had failed. The Williamson-Miller blueprint was in fact a response to that quest, which also led to the Louvre Accord with its undeclared "reference ranges" (a synonym for target zones) the next year. However, the effort never got much further, and global cooperation has remained episodic, with its main achievement having been to limit the misalignments resulting from changes in nominal exchange rates. Policy coordination played no obvious role in the restoration of fiscal discipline in the United States; it did not prevent the yen from becoming undervalued again in 1989–92; it did nothing to curb the late-1980s asset price bubble in Japan;[2] and it was not used to combat European reluctance to respond to the differential shock of German reunification with the differ-

---

1. In view of this decisive official rejection, it is surprising that the estimate by Oudiz and Sachs (1984) of the size of the potential gains from policy coordination over this period was so small (varying from 0.17 percent of GDP for the United States to 1 percent of GDP for Japan, or some $60 billion per year in total). A subsequent exercise by Sachs and McKibbin (1985) came to rather larger estimates of the benefits, with the interesting twist that the biggest beneficiaries of better policy coordination would have been the heavily indebted developing countries (which would have benefited from lower interest rates in the absence of the competitive appreciation involved in the United States disinflating through monetary restriction alone) rather than those countries whose policies were coordinated. However, the methodology these researchers employed assumes that the macroeconomic policies pursued were in fact motivated by the search for a Nash equilibrium by policymakers who believed (correctly) that the world was as described by the model used in the simulation, which we find an even more improbable characterization of Beryl Sprinkel and Margaret Thatcher than of the models involved. Specifically, because Beryl Sprinkel (who served as undersecretary of the treasury during the first Reagan administration) behaved as though he did not care about the US current account deficit, the calculation assumed it did not matter; if instead one believes that it did, then a policy regime that would have prevented such a large deficit would have had markedly larger benefits than those calculated by this approach.

2. But we reject the charge that, by inducing low interest rates to prevent the dollar from plunging too far, policy coordination *caused* the asset price bubble. On the contrary, from 1988 onward a tightening of monetary policy was desirable in Japan for international reasons (to prevent the weakening of the yen that actually occurred) as well as for domestic reasons. This step was delayed until mid-1989 not out of deference to the United States, which did not maintain political pressure on Japan for low interest rates at that time, but because the Japanese authorities themselves wanted to continue reducing budget deficits and to avoid placing further upward pressure on the yen (Henning 1994, chapter 6). Earlier tightening of monetary policy would have contributed to international adjustment and might also have pricked the asset price bubble.

entiated policies that were needed. Policy coordination to address some of those problems would have improved the conjunctural management of the world economy.

Where there was an attempt to do more was within the EMS. Indeed, an attempt was made from 1987 on to operate the Exchange Rate Mechanism (ERM) as a fixed exchange rate system. That attempt broke down in 1992–93, with the forced withdrawal of first the lira and then the pound, and ultimately a widening of the margins to 15 percent, a range larger than had ever been contemplated by the advocates of target zones.

The reasons for the collapse of the ERM differed by country. Excessive inflation had made the lira and the peseta overvalued. The pound was overvalued because when it belatedly joined the ERM the British government decided for its own reasons to pick a central rate that all the available evidence showed to overvalue the currency. The Irish punt became overvalued when the pound was devalued. France needed lower interest rates than Germany because it had not experienced a comparable increase in spending as a result of German unification and the resulting increase in the German budget deficit. The collapse of the ERM showed once again that it is not possible to hold exchange rates fixed in the face of differential inflation and large, nationally differentiated real shocks.[3]

Thus both fixed and floating exchange rates have been tried again in recent years, and both have once again been found wanting. This failure would indeed be serious if Eichengreen (1994) were right in claiming that capital mobility has hollowed out the range of exchange rate options and forced a simple choice between reconciling uncoordinated national policies through floating exchange rates and renouncing independent national monetary policies. The competing view argued by Williamson (1993) is that what capital mobility in fact requires is that exchange rate management follow two "golden rules": namely, that the authorities avoid getting locked into defense of a disequilibrium exchange rate, and that parities never be changed by more than the width of the band. These rules preclude use of the exchange rate as a nominal anchor, on the lines attempted in the EMS, since that presupposes a willingness to defend the exchange rate even if it has become a disequilibrium rate.

What the golden rules do not preclude is a decision to pursue an active exchange rate policy devoted to avoiding misalignments. Wide bands

---

3. It will be evident that we judge speculative pressures to have arisen because market operators perceived that a one-way option had been created by the defense of rates that were out of line with the fundamentals. This is in the spirit of the modeling of speculative attacks by Krugman (1979) rather than the notion of a self-fulfilling crisis modeled by Obstfeld (1986 and 1994). Ingenious as those models are, Obstfeld provides no evidence that speculators have ever attacked a rate that was not in some important respect out of line with the fundamentals. (On the contrary, his 1994 paper makes it very clear that the Swedish krona was overvalued before it was floated in November 1992.)

whose central rates crawl to avoid being outdated by differential inflation or real shocks, as envisaged in the target zone proposal (Bergsten and Williamson 1983; Williamson 1985a), could become vulnerable to speculative attack only under two circumstances: if estimates of the fundamental equilibrium exchange rates (FEERs) on which the central rates would be based were off base by more than the margin and the market realized that before the authorities, or if self-fulfilling speculative attacks were staged against currencies whose value was not out of line with the fundamentals. We have already commented on the lack of empirical support for the theory of the self-fulfilling speculative attack (note 4). And although we would not claim that the state of the art of estimating FEERs permits them to be pinned down precisely, we would judge that they are unlikely to be wrong by more than 10 percent (see Williamson 1994a for support for that view). It follows that the demise of the narrow-band ERM does nothing to undermine confidence in the feasibility of operating a system of target zones: indeed, the latter was specifically designed to avoid giving rise to the type of situation that caused the ERM crises.

A second major conclusion we would draw from experience is that exchange rate management alone is not enough. Consider the current account deficit that emerged during the first Reagan administration, of which as much as two-thirds is estimated to have been due to the Reagan budget deficit and fiscal tightening in other countries (Helkie and Hooper 1988, 49). Thus even complete success in preventing the dollar from rising more than was justified by the fundamentals would not have avoided the dangerous current account imbalances. At the same time, as Dornbusch (1987) has pointed out, an attempt to prevent the dollar's appreciation by monetary expansion would have been a cure worse than the disease, since it would have reignited the inflation that had just been so painfully brought under control.

The moral is that exchange rate management may need to be accompanied by supportive fiscal policies. The implication that this requires some measure of agreement on fiscal policy appeared to have been accepted at the Tokyo summit, since the fiscal deficit was one of the indicators included on the list endorsed by the summit. It is a conclusion that has also emerged from the literature that has attempted to simulate the effect of operating alternative international monetary regimes (see, e.g., Williamson and Miller 1987, appendix C; Frenkel et al. 1990). The conclusion nonetheless continues to be dismissed as politically infeasible. We would therefore point out that the United States has for some years been engaged in a search for institutional fixes intended to tie the hands of the federal government with respect to fiscal policy, while the countries of the European Union agreed in the Maastricht Treaty to bind their governments by fiscal constraints. Another potential way of imposing such constraints on governments would be to incorporate appropriate rules in a policy regime to which countries would commit themselves through an international agreement.

The third lesson we would draw from postwar history concerns the danger that misalignments and severe macroeconomic and payments imbalances will jeopardize liberal trade and capital flows. Bergsten (1973 and 1981) has long argued that large currency overvaluations provoke protectionist pressures,[4] and this contention has received empirical support from the work of Enzo Grilli (1988). Today there is dangerously widespread concern in industrial countries at the possible loss of jobs from the migration of manufacturing industries to low-income countries. The most obvious way of meeting that concern without threatening the prospects for the low-income countries to achieve export-led growth would be for all countries to agree on a regime for setting current account targets that would obligate newly industrializing countries to match their export growth with increasing imports, rather than follow the Japan-Taiwan pattern of building up excessive trade surpluses. (Since it is in their national interest to make high-yield investments at home rather than low-yield investments abroad, the option the newly industrializing countries are being asked to abandon is not worth much to them.)

Similarly, the developing-country debt crisis demonstrated the threat to the international capital market posed by allowing large current account imbalances to emerge just because they can be financed easily, rather than disciplining imbalances by concerns about sustainability. It seems difficult to believe that any set of current account targets negotiated in the 1970s would have endorsed the large deficits in middle-income countries that cumulatively precipitated the debt crisis.

The cyclical nature of US international monetary policy has contributed to the emergence of large imbalances. Over the decades, US policy has swung from neglect of the balance of payments and/or the exchange rate, toward activism, and then back toward neglect (Cohen 1983; Bergsten 1986; Henning 1987). The organization of private preferences and policymaking institutions creates the latitude for this policy pattern. An international monetary regime could help to stabilize the policies of what is still the most important single participating country.

Designing a New Regime

Of the international monetary regimes that the world has so far experienced, there is no question that the Bretton Woods system in its brief heyday, from about 1959 to 1968, performed best. The 1960s were a golden age in terms of the speed and wide distribution of economic growth, with low inflation and an absence of massive cumulative, crisis-threatening imbalances. The major factors behind this success were surely exogenous

---

4. It is also highly plausible that undervaluations have less impact in weakening protectionism.

to the international monetary system—the opportunities for catch-up growth in Europe and Japan, the scope for exploiting the easy first stage of import substitution in developing countries, the low inherited rate of inflation, the leadership of the United States, and the absence of major shocks. Nevertheless, we would argue that the existence of a set of rules of the game for macroeconomic policy that produced broad consistency between the policies of different countries was also significant (Williamson 1985b). Specifically, the obligation to seek payments balance on the basis of stable, near-equilibrium exchange rates helped to desynchronize the business cycle, to make countries (with the possible exception of the United States) worry about payments deficits before they had built up such large cumulative debt overhangs as to imperil future prosperity, and to provide an environment conducive to the rapid expansion of trade and thus the generalization of world prosperity.

Thus the Bretton Woods system worked like a charm for a decade or so, but unfortunately it was not robust. As Eichengreen and Kenen recall, Robert Triffin (1960) had warned early on about the inherent instability of a system that relied for an expansion of liquidity on US deficits that were bound to undermine confidence in the convertibility of the dollar into gold. Inflation, although low, was allowed to drift upward, since the gold base that was supposed to restrain this development was gradually allowed to become a dead letter as part of the effort to contain the Triffin dilemma.

Above all, the feasibility of an adjustable-peg exchange rate system with narrow bands was progressively undermined by the reemergence of international capital mobility. With renewed capital mobility, governments increasingly succumbed to a commitment-credibility trap: in an effort to preempt a run on the currency, ministers would declare themselves implacably opposed to changing the parity; this in turn limited their policy options, preventing modest adjustments in parities that could have prevented a subsequent blowout in the foreign-exchange markets. This commitment-credibility trap contributed to the brittle character of the Bretton Woods parities.

Domestic political opposition on the part of powerful interest groups also caused governments to delay realignments, to the detriment of the regime. In Japan and Germany, for example, export lobbies blocked and delayed revaluations, creating chronic trade surpluses for these countries. Prospective realignments provoked intensive lobbying and taxed governments' ability to manage coalitions for policy change. The political invective generated by changes in parities acted as a strong incentive for governments to avoid discussing them as long as possible, rendering currencies vulnerable to speculation. Domestic interest group pressure and the commitment-credibility trap thus conspired to persuade governments to adhere tenaciously to parities that were becoming unsustainable.

As Eichengreen and Kenen recount, governments were unable to reach agreement on reform of the regime. Special Drawing Rights (SDRs) were introduced in 1970 as an attempt to address the Triffin dilemma. However, governments did not make the other repairs and renovations—notably the creation of a regime of limited flexibility of exchange rates—that would have been needed to adapt the Bretton Woods system to a changed world. So, in the early 1970s, the regime collapsed.

The main change in the world that would compel any revived regime to differ from that of Bretton Woods is the emergence of a high degree of capital mobility. This not only requires that exchange rate management be conducted on the basis of wide and crawling target zones rather than narrow bands, as discussed above, but it also means that the chance to gain any leverage over the policies of highly creditworthy countries through management of the stock of world reserves has vanished. The proposals developed in the Committee of Twenty in 1972–74, which were centered on the idea of managing the stock of reserves, are thus a dead letter.[5]

With that as background, we turn to a detailed presentation of our proposals. In the remainder of this section we describe what we would regard as the ideal system, which is a somewhat modified version of the Williamson-Miller blueprint, and we outline its advantages. In the next section, which deals with problems of implementation, we discuss how a system of target zones might be a practical first step.

The Blueprint

The blueprint is conventional in assuming that a high level of activity (implying also a high rate of growth[6] and a high level of employment) is good and that inflation is bad, and increasingly so as it rises. The blueprint also assumes that it is desirable to place some limits on current account imbalances. The ideal is not necessarily a zero balance, but imbalances should at a minimum be kept within a range that will not raise questions about the sustainability of financing.

Trade-offs between these objectives must be faced. In particular, lowering inflation generally requires some temporary slack in the economy. Higher activity tends both to increase inflation and to worsen the current account. A more competitive exchange rate, designed to improve the

---

5. We would support a resumption of SDR allocations in order to enable the less creditworthy countries to achieve a prudent buildup of reserves through time without having to make a resource transfer to the rest of the world, but this is not a topic of any great monetary significance.

6. At least, there is a one-to-one correspondence between the level of activity (output on a proportion of potential output) and the growth rate if the growth of supply-side potential is exogenous. This is a reasonable assumption for the short run, but not for the long run.

current account at a given level of activity, tends to increase inflationary pressure.

The blueprint uses a medium-term framework to resolve these trade-offs. Each of the participating governments—assumed to be the members of the G-7—would be expected to have an estimate of the natural rate of unemployment for its economy. These estimates should be continuously monitored for realism by the staff of the IMF, which would be charged with servicing the policy coordination process. All significant countries, not just those involved in the policy coordination process, would also select a current account target, which would need to be consistent with the expected saving-investment balance and therefore with medium-run fiscal intentions. Where a government had no precise view on what current account balance was appropriate, one could take the middle of the range that was judged to be sustainable in the light of past experience as the provisional target.[7] The secretariat would then have to appraise the realism and mutual consistency of the various targets. If an inconsistency emerged, a formula would have to be developed to reduce target surpluses to a uniform level consistent with the aggregate of target deficits.[8] Finally, one would need to check that the estimated natural rates of unemployment were consistent with the current balance targets. (To the extent that a more positive current balance implies a more competitive exchange rate and thus lower real wages, it would tend to raise the natural rate if wage earners have a target real wage: see Barrell and Wren-Lewis 1989.)

Each country would commit itself to a macroeconomic strategy designed to lead, in the medium term, to simultaneous internal balance, defined as unemployment at the natural rate and minimal inflation, and external balance, defined as achieving the target current account balance. Since exchange rates affect trade only with long lags, this implies a commitment that during the intervening adjustment period the exchange rate will be held close to the level (or, strictly speaking, the trajectory) needed to reconcile internal and external balance in the medium term. This exchange rate is the so-called fundamental equilibrium exchange rate (FEER), so termed because it is the exchange rate that implies an absence of "fundamental disequilibrium" in the old Bretton Woods sense (Williamson 1985a). Policy should be directed to keeping exchange rates reasonably close to their FEERs. That is, the exchange rate should be kept within a target zone around its FEER: thus the blueprint incorporates the target zone proposal.

---

7. Whether or not a country has a well-defined view of what it wants its current account target to be, it would be desirable to ensure that the target adjusts toward the realized underlying capital flow, so long as the latter is judged to be sustainable.

8. See Williamson (1994b) for an example of this procedure.

The other intermediate target, in addition to the exchange rate, is the growth rate of nominal domestic demand. The idea of targeting this variable is a slight variation on the proposal to seek a constant growth rate of nominal income (see Gordon 1985; Meade 1984; McCallum 1988; Frankel 1994). It has the advantages of a nominal income target, in terms of providing a constraint on inflation (a nominal anchor) while avoiding the shocks that come from a money supply rule when velocity changes, but is more sophisticated in several dimensions. Specifically, Williamson and Miller suggested a formula designed to keep the economy at steady-state (supply-side growth rate plus acceptable inflation rate) if it is already there, add a term calculated to induce a gradual convergence to the inflation target if inflation starts off too high, add another term designed to reduce any deflationary gap not justified by the need to control inflation, and add also an allowance for any targeted change in the current account balance. This endogenization of the rule would allow rather more effort to combat a recession and rather more accommodation of an inflationary shock than the traditional proposals for nominal income targeting.

There are two reasons for this softening. One is the view that a counter-cyclical policy can be effective in reducing the short-run costs of adverse shocks provided that confidence in the long-term commitment to price stability is maintained. The other is the fear that, if governments are asked to subscribe to excessively harsh rules, they are likely to abandon them just at the time when it is most important to reinforce confidence in their resolve to stick to rules that will reestablish price stability in the medium run.

The reason for targeting the growth of *domestic demand* rather than of *income* is of course to support the process of payments adjustment.

The final element of the blueprint involves translating the implications of the two intermediate targets into rules to guide monetary and fiscal policy. The blueprint envisages three assignment rules to determine which policies should be used to achieve those two intermediate targets.[9] The first states that (sterilized) intervention should be used to try to keep the exchange rate within its target zone. The second specifies that monetary policy, meaning management of short-term interest rates, should normally be used to keep nominal domestic demand growing at the target rate, subject to an override if the exchange rate is threatening to leave its target zone. If this exchange rate override applies to more than one country at the same time, the question arises as to which country should change its interest rate so as to prevent the exchange rate from moving outside its target zone. The natural answer is that the weak-currency country should raise its interest rate if growth of world nominal income is above a target formed by aggregating the national targets, while the strong-currency

---

9. This is where the present version differs from the original Williamson-Miller formulation.

country should reduce its interest rate if growth of world nominal income is below target. The third rule requires that fiscal policy aim to reconcile external balance with full employment in the medium run (the "reverse assignment" of Boughton 1989), but that short-run deviations in the fiscal balance should be accepted if needed to manage demand (the "orthodox assignment"), something that would be especially likely if monetary policy were preempted for exchange rate management.

These rules were designed to secure international consistency of macroeconomic policies. The key to this would be for the participants to agree on a compatible set of current account targets. In a closed system, that would guarantee that exchange rate targets would be consistent and that externally motivated modifications of nominal growth targets would net out. If all countries devoted monetary policy to managing demand growth, then the world level of interest rates would presumptively be appropriate too. However, that presumption would break down if the exchange rate override were applied without a rule to ensure that interest rates were still adjusted in a way that would help to stabilize world demand. It is in this situation that we introduce the rule that replaces the nth currency rule in a manner appropriate to a multipolar world, whereby the onus of changing the interest rate to defend the target zone depends on whether world nominal income growth is too strong or too weak.

Benefits of the Blueprint

So much for description. We now move on to discuss the advantages that we believe this system would offer, and answer some frequent criticisms.

First, the proposals avoid the traditional but totally vacuous call for "better coordination" or "stronger coordination" without spelling out the principles that are to underlie the exercise. On the contrary, the blueprint offers an agreed *policy regime* that would dispense with the need for ad hoc policy coordination. This would avoid limiting action to those (relatively rare) occasions when all parties can expect to benefit immediately as a result of making mutual policy adjustments. The regime would also permit governments to exploit the advantages of precommitment, such as using a credible target zone to get speculators to help stabilize the exchange rate for the reasons first formalized by Paul Krugman (1988).

The relative transparency of such a regime should help the process of democratic monitoring of the coordination process. This in turn should make it more difficult for governments to run aberrant policies, which we would regard as highly desirable.

Some have argued that policy coordination could have negative effects. One famous argument is that of Rogoff (1985), who constructed a model in which policy coordination diminished welfare, since it reduced the cost to the central banks of springing surprise inflations on their long-suffering publics. The domestic demand target incorporated in the blueprint provides an institutional assurance that the greater potency of policy that may result from coordination could not be abused by authorities seeking to maximize their own good rather than that of the public.

A second issue arises from the demonstration by Frankel and Rockett (1988) that coordination among policymakers who use different models might reduce welfare. In an extensive investigation of this topic, Ghosh and Masson (1994) reach very different conclusions. The possibility of welfare losses from coordination is mostly confined to situations in which policymakers have very different views about which model is correct and make no attempt to learn from experience. When the models are similar, coordination yields positive results, unless the models also happen to be wrong. When the models differ drastically, experience will quickly enable governments to learn which model is more nearly correct and adapt their actions accordingly—a process stimulated in part by coordination. Far from rejecting policy coordination, therefore, we believe that the correct conclusion to draw from these studies is that it is fundamentally important to understand the relationship between policy instruments and targets.

It follows that coordination should be limited to that which can be deduced from a robust model and should avoid trying to do too much in the way of fine tuning. We would argue that the blueprint qualifies in this respect. Although no one can claim that macroeconomic theory has put all controversy behind it, the sort of model on which the blueprint is based, combining short-run Keynesianism with a Phillips curve that is vertical in the intermediate run but not a natural constant in the long run, commands a fair measure of consensus on the part of those economists primarily concerned with policy issues.[10] And naturally the blueprint avoids phony prescriptions for controlling inflation, such as the "supply-side" treatment of tax cutting as a panacea and the claim that all could be resolved painlessly by selecting a nominal anchor and making it credible.

A third issue concerns the benefit the blueprint would provide by managing the foreign-exchange market in a way calculated to prevent the misalignments that result both from failing to adjust fixed exchange rates when necessary and from allowing rates to float without any attempt at management. There has been endless debate, to which one of the authors of the present paper has contributed (Williamson 1985a), about the nature of the costs imposed by exchange rate variability, but recent empirical work seems to point to one cost that had not been prominent in previous analyses, namely, an adverse impact on the *level* of investment (see, e.g., Larraín and Vergara 1993). As the new approach to investment theory

---

10. Unhappily, one cannot deny that new classical ideas, which deny the legitimacy of Keynesian analysis even in the short run, have become grotesquely influential among theorists. See Williamson (1994c) for an extended discussion of the theoretical ideas that underlie the blueprint.

developed by Dixit and Pindyck (1994) emphasizes, an investment decision is irreversible and therefore must overcome the option of waiting; the decision whether to invest is not simply a yes-no decision as traditional investment theory assumes. Recognizing the value of this additional option typically raises the rate of return hurdle that an investment has to satisfy. It would seem plausible that a high level of uncertainty about future real exchange rates increases the attractiveness of postponing investment decisions, thereby dampening the (global) rate of investment and thus of growth.

Fourth, the blueprint is designed to secure consistency among the policies of the major countries. As already pointed out, the key to this would be agreement on current account targets. One participant in the conference on which this volume is based held up the prospect that this would in effect turn the IMF Executive Board into a body of world central planners, approving or vetoing every major investment project that a country might want to undertake. That is fantasy. What the international community would have a right to ask of an individual country is that it select a target that poses no sustainability problems, that is consistent with its pattern of capital flows and its medium-term fiscal policy, and that does not involve exporting unemployment to the rest of the world. Such an approach would leave ample scope for countries that found (for example) that they had improved investment prospects, and the ability to tap the international capital market so as to finance additional investment, to seek an increased current account deficit. The basic aim would be to pick a current account target consistent with underlying capital flows rather than force capital flows to fit some planners' target.

One can be sure that German economists and policymakers will worry that a system of policy coordination, and especially one involving exchange rate management, might bring with it the risk of a gradual acceleration of inflation, or of countries being required to import inflation, in the manner that helped bring down the Bretton Woods system in the late 1960s and early 1970s. The blueprint has safeguards against those dangers, in the form of the target for demand growth, and the wide target zones and automatic adjustment of nominal central rates to prevent real central rates from being changed by differential inflation (Williamson and Miller 1987, 52–54).

To what extent would the advice that would have been given by the blueprint in the last five years have addressed the failures of G-7 coordination that were identified earlier?[11] So far as the United States is concerned,

---

11. The judgments presented in this section assume that the agreed FEERs, except for that of the deutsche mark, would have come out in the vicinity of those in the unpublished manuscript of Williamson (1990), a version of which is shortly to be published (Williamson 1994b). The author expressed unease at the level of the mark that resulted from the calculations presented there, which he thought implausibly strong.

it would certainly have prescribed an early start to correcting the budget deficit, during the period of robust growth when tax increases could have been easily absorbed. In the case of Japan, the blueprint would have drawn attention to the need for a more expansionary fiscal policy and to the real depreciation of the yen that occurred in the period 1988–90, the two factors that prompted the damaging reversal of the payments adjustment secured after the Plaza. A tightening of monetary policy to defend the yen would have limited, though it might not have prevented, the asset price bubble that set the stage for the recent recession.

So far as Europe is concerned, the proposed rule for judging the strength of demand would have pointed to the need for restrictive action during both the 1988–89 British boom and the postunification German boom. The strength of sterling at the time of the British boom would have signaled a need for fiscal as well as monetary restraint, which would have enabled sterling to enter the ERM around its estimated FEER of DM2.40 to DM2.60 (Wren-Lewis et al. 1990), rather than at the significantly overvalued rate of DM 2.95, which in due course prompted Black Wednesday (when the pound was taken out of the ERM in September 1992). German unification was a real shock that called for appreciation of the D-mark's FEER or, better still, a wider upside band for the D-mark, as well as monetary and fiscal restraint. Had Europe still found itself in deep recession (a recession whose depth was in fact due to the failure to adjust exchange rates and allow different interest rates despite the massive nationally differentiated real shock of German unification), the blueprint would have called for monetary expansion rather than condoning real short-term interest rates of 3 percent and more during the trough of a severe recession.

Problems of Implementation

We turn our attention now to the institutional and political modalities of implementing target zones and the blueprint. We start with a discussion of the problems of creating such a regime. We then examine the possibilities of starting the move back to a structured international monetary system by introducing target zones for exchange rates. We conclude by discussing specific decision-making functions that would be needed under the blueprint and where they might be located organizationally.

Regime Creation

The blueprint is designed to be a *symmetrical* regime. It does not rely on the dominance of a single state, in the way that the gold standard rested on British dominance and the Bretton Woods regime arguably relied on

American influence. In this respect, implementation and operation of the blueprint would be a historical novelty.

One of the functions that hegemony serves is to resolve the problem of which state or states will adjust their economic policies to maintain the regime. The hegemon targets its macroeconomic policies toward its domestic requirements, sometimes amended to incorporate systemic considerations, while secondary states take their cue from the policies of the hegemon. If the maintenance of fixed parities imposes high political costs—when the hegemon is pursuing inflationary policies, for example—secondary states are tempted to opt out of the regime. Whether they adhere or opt out, conflicts over policy adjustment are relatively simple: the fact of hegemony imposes a take-it-or-leave-it choice on secondary powers.

Under the bargain embodied in the blueprint, however, there is no presumption about the identity of the country that has to adjust its policies.[12] Although the US dollar would still play a larger role as a reserve currency, vehicle currency, and investment currency than others, no particular currency would serve as the nominal anchor. All participants would adjust policies according to the rules. Unless and until the United States is willing to accept the implied constraints on policy, in fact, the major European countries and Japan will not accept the bargain and the blueprint will be a nonstarter.

We recognize that formal rules cannot fully arbitrate international disputes over who should bear the economic and political costs of adjustment: there will always be a need for interpretation, and hence the potential for disagreement. The task of resolving conflicts among the United States, Europe, and Japan may be more complex than in a hegemonic, anchor-currency system. The blueprint will therefore have to find an institutional substitute for the conflict-resolution function performed by hegemony in previous regimes.

Although international regimes are more difficult to create than to maintain (Keohane 1984), and the absence of a dominant power might make it more difficult to achieve reforms now than it was to introduce the Bretton Woods regime or the gold standard, hegemony is not a strictly necessary condition for regime creation. The interwar period had no hegemon, and yet the dilemmas of collective action were overcome on several occasions: substantial international cooperation was restored in the 1920s and in the Tripartite Monetary Agreement of 1936 (Odell 1988; Eichengreen 1989; Oye 1992). Joseph Nye (1990, 87–97) argues that the United States did not possess full hegemony even after World War II and

---

12. Indeed, the presumption is that all of the participants would at one time or another be expected to make policy adjustments that would be politically unwelcome in the short term. The fact that each country would receive benefits in terms of policy adjustments on the part of others is what would be expected to make these adjustments politically palatable.

that the Bretton Woods regime benefited from the Cold War rivalry with the Soviet Union. Moreover, whereas many economists have interpreted the EMS as simply a reflection of German hegemony, Henning (1994) has argued that it rests not so much on German dominance within Europe as on the inherent desirability of price stability, the credibility of German policy, and the consistency over time of the bargain that Germany offered its European partners.

The reason for believing it to be worthwhile to pursue the blueprint without a hegemon is that the alternative is unsatisfactory, as argued earlier in this paper. If and when the key leaders in the key countries become convinced not merely that experience under the current non-system is unsatisfactory but also that an attractive alternative exists, the hope would be that they would take the same sort of initiative that Helmut Schmidt and Valéry Giscard d'Estaing did in 1978, with the same intention of binding their successors. Once established, a regime such as the blueprint, which does not rest on the dominance of a single state, would not be as vulnerable to subsequent changes in the underlying power structure of member states as the Bretton Woods system was.

What would seem more critical for establishing a regime like the blueprint is a domestic political environment conducive to the policy adjustments it calls for. The fiscal rule is the toughest domestic political test for the blueprint. The experience with American fiscal deficits during the Vietnam War and again in the 1980s, and with German fiscal deficits during the 1990s, suggests that fiscal policy is the Achilles' heel of exchange rate stabilization. The fiscal rule is all the more important because, as noted earlier, econometric evidence shows that the largest gains flowing from implementation of the blueprint would come precisely from implementation of the fiscal rule.

However, such a rule would appear to be very much in line with the revealed desire of many politicians to have their hands tied on macroeconomic policy. In the United States, a long string of fiscal deficits has persuaded the Congress to try to limit its own flexibility through the Gramm-Rudman targets and restrictive rules in the 1990 budget agreement. These deficits also have fueled a movement for a balanced budget amendment to the US Constitution. During the 1980s, 32 state legislatures passed resolutions calling for a constitutional convention to draft a federal balanced budget amendment. In 1994, a majority of the US House of Representatives supported such an amendment and a simple majority of the Senate voted for it. Because constitutional amendments require supermajorities of two-thirds in both houses before submission to state legislatures, this measure has not yet been adopted, but it will undoubtedly continue to be raised in the future.

The countries of the European Union have agreed in the Maastricht Treaty to bind their governments to budget deficits not exceeding 3 percent of GDP and ratios of government debt to GDP of no more than 60 percent. Although the language of the treaty tended to soften these constraints, the German Constitutional Court has strengthened them by its 1993 decision on the treaty. These rules are important criteria for membership in the prospective monetary union.

The fiscal rules in the blueprint would therefore respond to the revealed desire to restrain fiscal options. Moreover, whereas most of the current proposals for tying the hands of government on fiscal policy are arbitrary, the rules proposed in the blueprint make greater economic sense and should thus be more defensible politically.

In addition to favorable domestic political conditions, at least a minimal consensus on analytical economics would be required for international economic cooperation. The degree of consensus required depends on the scope of cooperation. Episodic macroeconomic policy coordination can be achieved without agreement on means-ends relationships, as episodes like the Bonn summit of 1978, the Plaza Agreement, and the Louvre Accord clearly demonstrate.[13] Target zones would require somewhat more analytical consensus. The systematic cooperation embodied in the blueprint requires even broader agreement on the basic analytical questions, just as effective international action to contain epidemics required scientific agreement on the medical issues involved (Cooper 1989).

Of course, such consensus does not have to be complete, and we believe that a fair measure of consensus among economists already exists. Moreover, the blueprint would require agreement only among those governments that adhered to it: a meaningful trilateral regime could be operated among the United States, Germany, and Japan, without the full agreement of other countries.

Target Zones as a First Step

One way of building up the necessary degree of consensus might be to implement target zones as a first step toward the blueprint. Past international monetary regimes have focused primarily on exchange rate obligations rather than on comprehensive policy coordination. Today there seems to be an upwelling of support for restoring exchange rate obligations in the form of the sort of loose target zones that constitute one of the central features of the blueprint (Camdessus 1994; Bretton Woods Commission 1994). Since there is as yet no sign of a comparable acceptance of the logic of the rest of the blueprint, it is natural to consider the merits of adopting target zones as a first step.

---

13. For example, asked by one of the authors whether the Plaza Agreement represented a resolution of the strong differences over economic analysis that had prevailed between the first Reagan administration and the European and Japanese governments, an architect of that accord responded, "No, we just agreed not to let those differences get in the way."

Indeed, the United States, Germany, and Japan have for some time been limiting exchange rate fluctuations within broad ranges, and there currently appears to be substantial agreement on desirable exchange rates within the G-3. Thus, instituting wide-banded target zones would amount only to a formalization of what has already been tacitly agreed. The reason that the G-3 have abandoned floating in all but name is that the market has repeatedly pushed exchange rates to levels that threatened to create misalignments, leading the G-3 to intervene. Until the summer of 1994 these interventions were remarkably successful, and even as of this writing (in July 1994) it looks as though vigorous jawboning may have prevented the dollar from moving outside its notional target zone. Incidentally, one advantage of formalizing the target zones is that, since the dollar would not have reached the bottom of its target zone in May-July 1994 (assuming central rates of ¥105 and DM1.60, as seemed to be the consensus, and bands of 10 percent), the markets would not have perceived the dollar's weakness as a "dollar crisis."

However, some officials appear to believe that formal target zones would have invited a real dollar crisis, in the form of a speculative attack on the margins, which they would have been powerless to resist in an era when a trillion dollars a day is traded on the foreign-exchange markets. To worry about that, one has to be able to convince oneself that the speculators who drove the yen above 95 to the dollar could have expected to find someone willing to buy their yen from them at such a rate. Surely the central banks could have been relied on not to do this and thus validate the speculation, for they would have had no obligation to buy yen at an overvalued rate comparable to the obligation to buy the local currency at what had become overvalued rates that gave rise to the terminal crises of the Bretton Woods system and the narrow-band ERM. The fact that a trillion dollars a day crosses the exchanges is irrelevant; what matters is whether the owners of some of those dollars are prepared to lose money in the cause of validating a speculative attack. Until someone provides a convincing answer as to who will lose their money in such a bad cause, the presumption remains that central banks will have no difficulty in defending the margins provided they can be sure that when the rate hits the margin it will indeed have overshot equilibrium. A wide target zone whose central rate is consistently updated to offset differential inflation and adjusted to counter real shocks guarantees that presumption.

Target zones by themselves would largely deal with the problem of badly behaved markets, notably the propensity of the foreign-exchange market to generate misalignments, which we argued above provided one of the two general reasons for seeking a monetary regime. Target zones would, however, be largely irrelevant in disciplining bad behavior by governments. Thus a target zone system could be expected to work well as long as the governments of the major countries choose to conduct their policies according to mainstream recommendations. If the regime confronts a government bent on errant macroeconomic policies, as has happened from time to time in the past, perhaps the best reaction would be to allow the resulting exchange rate movements to go temporarily beyond the zone limits. By employing these "soft margins," the regime (rules, norms, and decision-making bodies and procedures) could survive until a change in government brought a more compatible set of policies.[14]

Once target zones are in operation, exchange rate movements would doubtless soon raise the question of the distribution of policy adjustments needed to defend the zones among participating countries. As long as the need is confined to foreign-exchange intervention, this challenge can be met relatively easily. Once adjustments in monetary and fiscal policy are required, however, the governments and central banks will have to come to agreement on the deeper conflicts that the blueprint is designed to adjudicate. Any target zone regime will eventually have to confront the questions of internal and external balance addressed in the blueprint. Implementing target zones first, however, would be a useful way to focus the attention of governments and central banks on finding solutions to the analytical and political problems posed by policy coordination, and would allow rules to be built up over time on the basis of the evolution of case law rather than requiring ex ante adherence to an abstract blueprint.

One may draw an analogy to the European Union's process of monetary integration. During the first several years of the European Monetary System, central banks and governments chose frequent realignments rather than the severe adjustments of monetary policy that would have been required, especially in some high-inflation countries, to defend the margins. However, as time went by, European governments decided gradually to tighten their coordination of macroeconomic policy while also liberalizing capital controls. When they agreed at Maastricht to form a monetary union by the end of the decade, they pledged not only close coordination of monetary policy but also a convergence of fiscal policy to achieve the single currency. Although the 1992–93 crisis within the ERM has brought into question the Europeans' ability to achieve this progressive tightening of coordination, much greater exchange rate stability than the new wide bands formally allow has been maintained. The crucial point is that exchange rate stabilization has helped to crystallize the debate about policy coordination and stimulate the search for solutions in a useful way, which, despite differences at the G-7 level, might be replicable globally.

We strongly urge that, as the IMF staff seeks principles to govern the distribution of the burden of adjustment, they consider the approach laid out in the blueprint. If that advice is found useful over time, then it might

---

14. The shift to wide bands within the ERM represents a similar, in principle temporary, accommodation of the macroeconomic policies pursued in Germany in the wake of unification and the decisions of the European partners not to change their central rates.

be natural to move a step further and adopt a "proto-blueprint," under which the IMF staff would calculate the intermediate targets and policy responses that the blueprint would imply and present these to the G-7 for consideration. The G-7 would then discuss them in detail, but without being formally obligated to implement the policies indicated.

Instituting this proto-blueprint would serve several purposes. First, it would enable the governments to test the G-7 decision-making mechanisms for administering the blueprint and the international consensus on the analytical economics. Disagreements over economic issues could identify areas of research to be conducted before the blueprint is formally adopted. Second, it would give governments a realistic sense of the policy changes required under the blueprint. Third, the proto-blueprint would demonstrate the potential benefits of policy coordination in the most concrete fashion to national policymakers. It would highlight the policy changes on the part of other governments that will benefit each one's own economy. Equally important, it would identify how international negotiations and the Fund staff can strengthen those bureaucracies and officials pressing for policy reform at the national level.

In this way the G-7 governments could assess the domestic political costs of making policy adjustments, weigh these against the benefits, and determine the political palatability of the blueprint. As an intermediate step, they might treat the recommendations of the blueprint as presumptive guidelines rather than formal obligations. In due course they could decide on a timetable to adopt the blueprint formally and the institutional modalities.

The proto-blueprint exercise would be greatly assisted by the fact that four of the present G-7 members are already subject to the macroeconomic surveillance program conducted within the EU Council of Ministers. Governments present a convergence program designed to meet the objectives set out in the Maastricht Treaty. The Council of Ministers reviews progress in the implementation of the plan and progress toward meeting the convergence criteria. The council has sharply rebuked member governments that are not living up to their commitments embodied in the plan. Note that the EU surveillance mechanism is much stronger than the proto-blueprint in requiring actual policy adjustments to meet the targets.

Institutional Architecture

Assuming that the governments reach an accord to implement target zones or the blueprint, what institutional form should the management of the new regime take? A fundamental problem in institutional design is to find a balance between representing a broad set of countries, to underpin legitimacy, and small-group decision making, to achieve efficiency. To strike this balance, we recommend employing the International Monetary

Fund and its staff as the context within which decisions are made by the G-7 meetings of finance ministers and central bank governors and by a Committee of Central Banks.

The IMF is the most satisfactory forum within which to manage a new international monetary regime for several reasons. Using the IMF would permit a natural integration of the decisions by participants in the regime with those of nonparticipants (e.g., with respect to the selection of current account targets). The Fund could provide a channel whereby the interests of nonparticipants in the decisions of the participants could be brought to bear. Finally, the IMF already has available the sort of robust bureaucracy of economists, analysts, and technicians that would be needed to support the regime.

On the other hand, it would be unrealistic to expect that the G-7 countries would allow the detailed negotiations on establishing intermediate targets for exchange rates and rates of demand growth, let alone those on the policy changes needed to achieve those intermediate targets, to be largely determined by countries outside the regime. A large group, moreover, would undermine secrecy needed in making sensitive decisions.

We would therefore retain the G-7 finance ministers and central bank governors as the first forum in which the major issues in the implementation and administration of target zones and the blueprint are negotiated and discussed. A principal advantage of keeping the G-7 at the center of international monetary management is that it would build on an existing institution. All of the countries that are crucial to the success of the regime are included within the G-7.[15] Decisions within the G-7 should continue to be made by consensus.

We recommend, however, that the finance ministers and central bank governors draw more fully on the resources of the Fund staff by giving them the responsibility of preparing discussion papers and decision memoranda for the G-7 meetings along with the staffs of the national finance ministries and central banks. The managing director of the IMF, who presently participates in the portion of the meetings devoted to multilateral surveillance, should be included in the whole of the meeting. He or she would thus participate in the discussion of current account targets, target zones, and adjustments in monetary and fiscal policy needed to defend them and could thereby bring the concerns of the remaining members of the IMF to the table. The G-7 ministers should meet at least quarterly, as they do now, with their deputies meeting as often as necessary.

---

15. These seven countries would be the ideal domain for the blueprint, and we assume their adherence for purposes of the following discussion. Any member of the G-7 that did not adhere to the new regime could still join the deliberations of the body as a potential or aspiring participant. This would parallel the procedure under the EMS, where the ministers of countries that are not full members of the ERM participate in meetings of the Ecofin Council along with the full participants.

Among the most important tasks of the G-7 would be to establish the targets for the current account balances of the participants in the target zone regime, to establish the FEERs, and to realign target zones in response to real shocks or new evidence about the need for a payments adjustment. If the G-7 eventually adopted the blueprint regime, this body would also have the task of establishing the targets for nominal demand growth and identifying the needed fiscal adjustments on the part of participants. If the G-7 governments were to agree to the imposition of sanctions for violating the rules of the regime, the G-7 would have to decide if and when to apply them against countries that failed to fulfill their responsibilities.[16]

Before implementing its decisions, the G-7 should seek the approval of the appropriate bodies of the IMF. The G-7 would not be *legally* required to do so. To the contrary, the Articles of Agreement explicitly allow such exchange rate regimes among groups of members, which are obligated only to notify the Fund of changes in their arrangements (Article IV, sections 2a and 2b). The Fund should exercise "firm surveillance" over target zones and the blueprint (Article IV, section 3b), an authority that has not been exercised in the case of the EMS. To faciliate the operation of the regime, and to provide mediation between the participants and nonparticipants, the G-7 should voluntarily submit their regime to IMF surveillance.

As presently constituted, however, the Executive Board would be passing judgment on decisions taken by officials who are much more senior than the Fund executive directors. It would be desirable, therefore, to constitute the Executive Board at the ministerial level when making important decisions to set up, implement, and operate the regime. Such a body, called the "Council," has been provided for within the Articles of Agreement since the Second Amendment (1978) and could be activated by 85 percent of the voting power within the Fund (Article XII, section 1; schedule D). By including the same finance ministers as within the G-7, the council could consult and confer with those individuals responsible for G-7 decisions.

Further, as Keynes originally proposed, the Executive Board itself should be upgraded by appointing ministerial deputies as executive directors (Finch 1994). Under this change, which could be implemented by each country group, or "constituency," within the Fund, the G-7 deputies would be members of the board, which would oversee international monetary matters under the authority of the council when the ministers are unable to convene. The alternate executive directors, people appointed at roughly the same level as the current executive directors, would carry on the regular business of the Fund.

---

16. Ideally, sanctions would take the form of financial penalties, similar to the negative interest rates on excessive reserve balances proposed by Keynes in 1942, with the revenue applied to worthy international causes, rather than trade restrictions.

Exercising the Fund's powers of surveillance over the exchange rate policies of its members, the council would sanction the new regime and the decisions made within it. The council would examine and discuss the current account targets of both the participants and the nonparticipants in the regime, the target zones for the participating currencies, and adjustments in monetary and fiscal policy needed to sustain them. The council, or the Executive Board meeting under its aegis, would approve realignments, for example.

We would expect that the council and the Executive Board would usually accept the decisions of the G-7, for whom these decisions would be far more consequential than for the nonparticipants. The approval of the Fund bodies, nonetheless, would be substantially more than a rubber stamping of the decisions of the G-7. First, the council and the board could reinforce the majority within the G-7 in exercising peer pressure over miscreants. Second, the G-7 would consult with them through this process, giving the council and the board immediate notice of decisions and the right to cross-examine the representatives of the G-7 countries. Third, the accumulation over time of a record of decisions and advice on the part of the council and the board could contribute to a process of learning. If a particular G-7 government resisted a change in fiscal policy, for example, ongoing discussion within the council would help to crystallize opinion regarding the need for action. And, finally, because the G-7 governments do not quite command a majority of the votes within the IMF, the approval of these bodies would inevitably be more than simply pro forma.

The actual role of the council or Executive Board would depend on the type of G-7 decision being approved. General surveillance over the regime and discussions of macroeconomic policy adjustments required to meet intermediate targets, for example, could be conducted at the ministerial level. A realignment of the target zones, on the other hand, might generate currency speculation and therefore cannot be subject to a substantial delay between the G-7 decision and its implementation by central banks. In this case, the Executive Board, meeting at the level of either the deputy ministers or more likely their alternates based in Washington, could be convened on a few hours' notice to approve the decision.

Activating the council would be a better way to lend institutional support to the new regime than relying on the existing Interim Committee or even a strengthened Interim Committee. The Interim Committee, like the proposed council, meets at the ministerial level and has the same representative configuration as the Executive Board. The Interim Committee, however, possesses no formal powers of decision making. Although it has provided political guidance to the work of the Executive Board, all formal decision-making authority resides in the Executive Board and the Board of Governors. The size of the meetings of the Interim Committee and the length of its deliberations have become disproportionate to the formal powers it wields, and there is growing sentiment that it needs strengthening (Camdessus 1994; Bretton Woods Commission 1994).

The council, on the other hand, would have real decision-making authority within the Fund. It could therefore approve (or reject) decisions made within the G-7 with all the formal surveillance authority of the Fund. The Interim Committee was so named, after all, because it was intended to serve as a bridge to the creation of the council. If the Interim Committee is too weak, it should be replaced (after 20 years!) as originally envisaged.

Within the framework of responsibilities established by governments through decisions of the G-7—notably the targets for the growth of demand—the national central banks should be granted broad, independent authority to manage monetary policy and the monetary regime.[17] (Note that the target for the growth of domestic demand incorporated in the blueprint offers a way of granting independence to central banks without requiring them to ignore everything except price stability.) The central banks, acting together in a Committee of Central Banks that would in turn confer with the G-7, should make the operational decisions about intervention and monetary policy adjustments.

The central banks should also decide, first, on whether to countenance an overshooting of the target zones, within the guidelines established by the G-7; second, on assignment of intervention responsibilities; and third, on extension of credits with which to finance intervention. By their presence in the G-7 meetings as members and through their committee, the governors of the central banks should advise the G-7 on the full range of macroeconomic and monetary issues. The committee, in particular, must warn the G-7 when the fiscal policies of governments make maintenance of the target zones impossible without provoking inflationary or deflationary changes in monetary policies in one or more participating countries. The committee should have the right to initiate consideration of a realignment within the G-7.[18]

---

17. Henning (1994) proposes four principles to guide the institutional architecture of monetary reform and the sharing of authority between governments and central banks within the regime. First, governments should affirm their commitment to central bank independence in making domestic monetary policy and delegate to their central banks the operational management of exchange rate stabilization. Second, governments should retain principal responsibility for the international monetary regime, agreements negotiated therein, and decisions on realignments of parities or adjustments of bands. Third, although tension is inevitable between governments and central banks over the priority to be given to exchange rate stability in the conduct of domestic monetary policy, that conflict can be managed through well-articulated bargains between them governing their prerogatives in external monetary policymaking. Finally, decision making within governments should keep policy well grounded in the interests of the private sector in currency management.

18. This right would represent stronger authority than the central banks have had vis-à-vis Ecofin within the EMS regime.

A further word on the role of the Fund staff is in order. The technical functions to be performed under a target zone regime or the blueprint are manifold. Under the blueprint the list includes determination of the targets for nominal growth in domestic demand; determination of the FEERs, which also requires calculation of saving-investment balances and targets for current account balances and capital flows; assessment of whether world demand is growing too fast or too slowly to achieve the nominal income target for the group, so as to determine the onus for adjusting short-term interest rates when currencies reach the edges of their target zones; translation of the real effective exchange rate that represents fundamental equilibrium into bilateral nominal exchange rates, and periodic revision of the nominal rates in order to maintain the target zones constant in real terms; and analysis of necessary realignments when country-specific real shocks make these necessary. The economic calculations underpinning the operation of the regime must be conducted and revised on a continuous basis, which requires good information about economic conditions and a sizable bureaucracy to process the data and interpret the results. The staff of the IMF was originally designed for precisely such tasks. This assignment would represent a return on the part of the Fund staff to its original postwar mission.

Finally, if the blueprint is to operate effectively, the requisite institutions and policy processes must be put in place at the national level. First, a well-articulated bargain between the government and the central bank within each country regarding prerogatives in external monetary policy is essential. Second, in order to maintain adherence to the regime, national decision-making processes that keep the government grounded in private, societal interests in stabilizing currencies and avoiding misalignments are important (Henning 1994).

The advantages of this institutional infrastructure for target zones and the blueprint are several. First, it builds on existing, functioning institutions such as the G-7 and IMF, and it nudges the Fund back toward its postwar raison d'être of managing the international monetary regime. Second, it balances the need for efficiency in decision making with the need for broader participation to enhance legitimacy. Third, it can be implemented without an arduous and conflict-ridden amendment to the Articles of Agreement of the Fund.

Conclusion

Acceptance of target zones, or even more the blueprint, would imply a surrender of a degree of policy flexibility, or "sovereignty." Why might governments agree to tie their hands in this way? One reason is that in an interdependent world the welfare of each country's own citizens depends intimately on what other governments are doing, and where international spillovers are important it is entirely possible that each country will bene-fit by rules that tie others down in an equivalent way. As Robert Keohane (1984, 257–59) has written, retaining the maximum room for maneuver carries substantial costs in terms of cooperation forgone. A second reason is that tying one's hands permits garnering the benefits of precommit-ment, and subscribing to an international regime should enable commit-ments to be secured while at the same time safeguarding a degree of flexibility to respond to unforeseen circumstances. A third reason is that governments that know what they are doing like to try and bind their successors, which may not be as sensible as they are. There is simply no point in keeping open options that it would be undesirable to exercise.

To illustrate, consider US policymaking during the final days of the Bretton Woods regime. Prior to the switch to floating rates in March 1973, officials of the Nixon administration and the Federal Reserve refused to advocate or to orchestrate a tightening of domestic monetary policy in order to defend the dollar. But the monetary flexibility that the United States insisted on retaining did not benefit the American public. Maintain-ing the fixed rate system demanded not that the United States tighten monetary policy as opposed to keeping it lax, but that the Fed raise interest rates earlier, beginning in 1972, rather than waiting until 1973, after the switch to flexible rates, to make the decisive shift. The United States exploited the flexibility it gained at the cost of the fixed rate regime not to sustain the health of the American economy but to commit a gross error of monetary overexpansion. That mistake fueled US and world inflation, which required a severe recession to correct.

Some critics of target zones and the blueprint argue that these regimes would not have been able to prevent the dramatic increase in US fiscal deficits in the early 1980s under the Reagan administration, the subse-quent appreciation of the dollar, and the deterioration of the current account position. We acknowledge that, given the domestic political cir-cumstances at that time, the mechanisms we propose might not have constrained the United States to moderate its deficits, especially if those mechanisms had been recently instituted rather than having acquired the respect that comes from successful longevity. It does not follow, however, that target zones or the blueprint would not have been a substantial improvement over the flexible rate regime. First, even when renegade governments break international agreements, it is useful to have such agreements in place in order to provide a benchmark for what policy adjustments are needed and to fortify domestic critics of the aberrant policy. Second, even in the case of the Reagan deficits, target zones might have limited the part of the dollar rise that was not due to the fiscal fundamentals. Third, the Reagan deficits represent an extreme case indeed and thus would be an inappropriate test for the usefulness of target zones or the blueprint most of the time. As John Odell suggested in the confer-ence discussion, few would have argued in the mid-1940s that the United

Nations should not have been created because it could not have prevented World War II.

The nonsystem of the past 21 years has not been a great success, to say the least. But in that period we have learned a lot about how to construct a better system, just as the architects of the United Nations learned from the failures of the League of Nations. It is time to try again.

References

Artis, Michael J., and Mark P. Taylor. 1989. *Policy Coordination and Exchange Rate Stabilization.* London: Bank of England.

Barrell, Ray, and Simon Wren-Lewis. 1989. *Fundamental Equilibrium Exchange Rates for the G7.* CEPR Discussion Papers 323. London: Centre for Economic Policy Research.

Bergsten, C. Fred. 1973. "Further Directions for U.S. Trade." *American Journal of Agricultural Economics* (May): 280–88.

Bergsten, C. Fred. 1981. "The Cost of Reaganomics." *Foreign Policy* 44 (Fall).

Bergsten, C. Fred. 1986. "America's Unilateralism." In C. Fred Bergsten, Etienne Davignon, and Isamu Miyazaki, *Conditions for Partnership in International Economic Management.* Report to the Trilateral Commission 32. New York: Trilateral Commission.

Bergsten, C. Fred, and John Williamson. 1983. "Exchange Rates and Trade Policy." In W. R. Cline, *Trade Policy in the 1980s.* Washington: Institute for International Economics.

Boughton, James M. 1989. "Policy Assignment Strategies with Somewhat Flexible Exchange Rates." In M. H. Miller, B. Eichengreen, and R. Portes, *Blueprints for Exchange Rate Management.* London: Centre for Economic Policy Research and Academic Press.

Bretton Woods Commission. 1994. *Bretton Woods: Looking to the Future.* Washington: Bretton Woods Commission.

Camdessus, Michel. 1994. "The IMF at Fifty—An Evolving Role but a Constant Mission." Address to the Institute for International Economics, Washington (7 June).

Cohen, Benjamin J. 1983. "An Explosion in the Kitchen? Economic Relations with Other Advanced Industrial States." In Kenneth A. Oye, Robert J. Lieber, and Donald Rothchild, *Eagle Defiant: United States Foreign Policy in the 1980s.* Boston: Little, Brown.

Cooper, Richard N. 1989. "International Cooperation in Public Health as a Prologue to Macroeconomic Cooperation." In Richard N. Cooper, Barry Eichengreen, Gerald Holtham, Robert D. Putnam, and C. Randall Henning, *Can Nations Agree? Issues in International Economic Cooperation.* Washington: Brookings Institution.

Cooper, Richard N., Barry Eichengreen, Gerald Holtham, Robert D. Putnam, and C. Randall Henning. 1989. *Can Nations Agree? Issues in International Economic Cooperation.* Washington: Brookings Institution.

Corden, W. Max. 1983. "The Logic of the International Monetary Nonsystem." In F. Machlup et al., *Reflections on a Troubled World Economy.* London: Macmillan.

Destler, I. M., and C. Randall Henning. 1989. *Dollar Politics: Exchange Rate Policymaking in the United States.* Washington: Institute for International Economics.

Dixit, Avinash, and Robert Pindyck. 1994. *Investment under Uncertainty.* Princeton, NJ: Princeton University Press.

Dobson, Wendy. 1991. *Economic Policy Coordination: Requiem or Prologue?* POLICY ANALYSES IN INTERNATIONAL ECONOMICS 30. Washington: Institute for International Economics.

Dominguez, Kathryn A., and Jeffrey A. Frankel. 1993. *Does Foreign Exchange Intervention Work?* Washington: Institute for International Economics.

Dornbusch, Rudiger. 1987. "Exchange Rate Economics: 1986." *Economic Journal* (March).

Eichengreen, Barry. 1989. "Hegemonic Stability Theories of the International Monetary System." In Richard N. Cooper, Barry Eichengreen, Gerald Holtham, Robert D. Putnam, and

C. Randall Henning, *Can Nations Agree? Issues in International Economic Cooperation.* Washington: Brookings Institution.

Eichengreen, Barry. 1994. "International Monetary Arrangements for the 21st Century." Paper prepared for the Brookings Institution project on Integrating the World Economy.

Finch, C. David. 1994. "Governance of the International Monetary Fund by Its Members." In Bretton Woods Commission, *Bretton Woods: Looking to the Future.* Washington: Bretton Woods Commission.

Frankel, Jeffrey A. 1994. "The Stability Properties of a Nominal GNP Rule in an Open Economy." *Journal of Money, Credit and Banking* (November).

Frankel, Jeffrey A., and K. E. Rockett. 1988. "International Policy Coordination When Policymakers Do Not Agree on the True Model." *American Economic Review* 78 (June): 318–40.

Frenkel, Jacob A., Morris Goldstein, and Paul R. Masson. 1990. "The Rationale for, and Effects of, International Economic Policy Coordination." In William H. Branson, Jacob A. Frenkel, and Morris Goldstein, *International Policy Coordination and Exchange Rate Fluctuations.* Chicago: University of Chicago Press for the National Bureau of Economic Research.

Ghosh, Atish R., and Paul R. Masson. 1994. *Economic Cooperation in an Uncertain World.* Cambridge, MA: Basil Blackwell.

Gordon, Robert J. 1985. "The Conduct of Domestic Monetary Policy." In A. Ando, E. Egudi, R. Farmer, and Y. Suzuki, *Monetary Policy in Our Times.* Cambridge, MA: MIT Press.

Grilli, Enzo. 1988. "Macroeconomic Determinants of Trade Protection." *The World Economy* 11 (September): 313–26.

Gros, Daniel, and Niels Thygesen. 1992. *European Monetary Integration: From the European Monetary System towards Monetary Union.* Brussels: Centre for Economic Policy Studies.

Helkie, William L., and Peter Hooper. 1988. "An Empirical Analysis of the External Deficit, 1980–86." In R. C. Bryant, G. Holtham, and P. Hooper, *External Deficits and the Dollar.* Washington: Brookings Institution.

Henning, C. Randall. 1987. *Macroeconomic Diplomacy in the 1980s: Domestic Politics and International Conflict among the United States, Japan, and Europe.* Atlantic Paper No. 65. London: Croom Helm for the Atlantic Institute for International Affairs.

Henning, C. Randall. 1994. *Currencies and Politics in the United States, Germany, and Japan.* Washington: Institute for International Economics.

Henning, C. Randall, and I. M. Destler. 1988. "From Neglect to Activism: American Politics and the 1985 Plaza Accord." *Journal of Public Policy* 8 (June-December): 317–33.

Kenen, Peter B. 1988. *Managing Exchange Rates.* London: Royal Institute for International Affairs.

Kenen, Peter B. 1992. *EMU after Maastricht.* Washington: Group of Thirty.

Keohane, Robert O. 1984. *After Hegemony: Cooperation and Discord in the World Political Economy.* Princeton, NJ: Princeton University Press.

Krugman, Paul R. 1979. "A Model of Balance-of-Payments Crises." *Journal of Money, Credit, and Banking* 11: 311–25.

Krugman, Paul R. 1985. "Is the Strong Dollar Sustainable?" In *The US Dollar: Prospects and Policy Options.* Kansas City: Federal Reserve Bank of Kansas City.

Krugman, Paul R. 1988. "Target Zones and Exchange Rate Dynamics." NBER Working Paper 2481. Cambridge, MA: National Bureau of Economic Research.

Larraín, Felipe, and R. Vergara. 1993. In L. Servén and A. Solimano, *Striving for Growth after Adjustment: The Role of Capital Formation.* Washington: World Bank.

Marris, Stephen. 1985. *Deficits and the Dollar: The World Economy at Risk.* POLICY ANALYSES IN INTERNATIONAL ECONOMICS 14. Washington: Institute for International Economics.

McCallum, Bennett T. 1988. "Robustness Properties of a Rule for Monetary Policy." Carnegie-Rochester Conference Series on Public Policy (Autumn).

McKibbin, Warwick J., and Jeffrey D. Sachs. 1991. *Global Linkages: Macroeconomic Interdependence and Cooperation in the World Economy.* Washington: Brookings Institution.

Meade, James E. 1984. "A New Keynesian Bretton Woods." *Three Banks Review* (June).

Meese, Richard A., and Kenneth Rogoff. 1983. "Empirical Exchange Rate Models of the 1970s: Do They Fit Out of Sample?" *Journal of International Economics* (February).

Nye, Joseph N. 1990. *Bound to Lead: The Changing Nature of American Power.* New York: Basic Books.

Obstfeld, Maurice. 1986. "Rational and Self-Fulfilling Balance-of-Payments Crises." *American Economic Review* 76: 72–81.

Obstfeld, Maurice. 1994. *The Logic of Currency Crises.* NBER Working Papers 4640. Cambridge, MA: National Bureau of Economic Research.

Odell, John S. 1988. "From London to Bretton Woods: Sources of Change in Bargaining Strategies and Outcomes." *Journal of Public Policy* 8 (July-December): 287–315.

Oudiz, Gilles, and Jeffrey Sachs. 1984. "Macroeconomic Policy Coordination Among the Industrialized Economies." *Brookings Papers on Economic Activity* 1.

Oye, Kenneth. 1992. *Economic Discrimination and Political Exchange: World Political Economy in the 1930s and 1980s.* Princeton, NJ: Princeton University Press.

Putnam, Robert D., and C. Randall Henning. 1989. "The Bonn Summit of 1978: A Case Study in Coordination." In Richard N. Cooper, Barry Eichengreen, Gerald Holtham, Robert D. Putnam, and C. Randall Henning, *Can Nations Agree? Issues in International Economic Cooperation.* Washington: Brookings Institution.

Rogoff, Kenneth. 1985. "Can International Monetary Policy Cooperation be Counterproductive?" *Journal of International Economics* (May): 199–218.

Rose, Andrew K. 1994. "Exchange-Rate Volatility, Monetary Policy, and Capital Mobility: Empirical Evidence on the Holy Trinity." University of California, Berkeley. Photocopy.

Sachs, Jeffrey D., and Warwick J. McKibbin. 1985. "Macroeconomic Policies in the OECD and LDC External Adjustment." NBER Working Papers 1255. Cambridge, MA: National Bureau of Economic Research.

Triffin, Robert. 1960. *Gold and Dollar Crises.* New Haven, CT: Yale University Press.

Williamson, John. 1985a. *The Exchange Rate System,* rev. ed. POLICY ANALYSES IN INTERNATIONAL ECONOMICS 5. Washington: Institute for International Economics.

Williamson, John. 1985b. "On the System in Bretton Woods." *American Economic Review* (May).

Williamson, John. 1990. "Equilibrium Exchange Rates: An Update." Washington: Institute for International Economics. Photocopy.

Williamson, John. 1993. "Exchange-Rate Management." *Economic Journal* 103 (January): 188–97.

Williamson, John. 1994a. *Essays on the Estimation of Equilibrium Exchange Rates.* Washington: Institute for International Economics.

Williamson, John, 1994b. "Estimates of FEERs." In John Williamson, ed., *Essays on the Estimation of Equilibrium Exchange Rates.* Washington: Institute for International Economics.

Williamson, John. 1994c. "The Theory Behind the Blueprint." *British Review of Economic Issues* 16 (June): 1–22.

Williamson, John, and Marcus H. Miller. 1987. *Targets and Indicators: A Blueprint for the International Coordination of Economic Policy.* POLICY ANALYSES IN INTERNATIONAL ECONOMICS 22. Washington: Institute for International Economics.

Wren-Lewis, Simon, Peter Westaway, Soterios Soteri, and Ray Barrell. 1990. *Choosing the Rate: An Analysis of the Optimum Level of Entry for Sterling into the ERM.* NIESR Discussion Papers (February).

Comment

RICHARD N. COOPER

I am broadly sympathetic with this paper. The authors believe that financial markets can misbehave and that that misbehavior can have unwanted effects on the real economy. The paper is mildly Keynesian in character in the sense that it allows for a nonvertical short-run Phillips curve, which is supported by all the evidence. The authors lean against inflation without, however, extolling universal price stability under all circumstances. They have a bias in favor of international economic cooperation. I share all of those views, so that in the universe of economists I find myself quite close to these two. Furthermore, the paper is very well put together. Its proposals have been carefully thought out, including the institutional aspects as well as how the mechanism of their proposal would work.

Having said all that, however, I find the proposal unacceptable. It has two fatal weaknesses. The first, which is acknowledged up front in the paper, is that it requires national current account targets. They are at the center of the proposal, the starting point for everything else. Yet I see no basis for establishing such targets in today's world. And without them the proposal falls, since they are the basis for determining the fundamental equilibrium exchange rates (FEERs). Under the proposed procedures, current account targets would be advanced by each country and then examined for consistency (that is a necessary part of the scheme). Then, if necessary, the targets would be changed (if I understand the proposal

Richard Cooper is Maurits C. Boas Professor of International Economics at Harvard University. He was previously under secretary of state for economic affairs (1977–81) and chairman, Federal Reserve Bank of Boston (1990–92).

correctly) by the Executive Board of the International Monetary Fund, which gives that body extraordinary authority. Let me illustrate, by way of some examples, what I think the problems are.

If we had to set targets, what should Japan's surplus be today? Many people, including me, believe Japan's surplus is too high. But "too high" is not good enough for this proposal. We have to decide how much too high. What should it be? A lot of Japanese officials believe that the Japanese saving rate will decline sharply with the aging of the population, which is expected to take place over the next ten to twenty years. Therefore Japan needs an exceptionally high rate of saving now to anticipate this later decline. I have a completely different hypothesis. Japanese saving rates will decline, not with the aging of the population, but with the dying off of the old population. I believe much consumption behavior is habitual, rather than oriented to the life cycle, and therefore a high national saving rate is not necessary at present. The difference could be quantitatively important. Which of us is right? Only time will tell. But to implement the Williamson-Henning proposal we would have to decide who is right, more or less, or reach a compromise between those two views about savings formation, and perhaps others as well.

What should Canada's surplus be? Canada is a rich country by world standards, not far behind the United States. On classical grounds it should run a current account surplus. Yet Canada has had a deficit in most years of its existence since 1867, leaving aside the two world wars and a few aberrant years in the 1980s. What is the basis for deciding what Canada's surplus should be? Canada has been a net importing country, even though it is wealthy, because it is really a developing country, short of capital relative to complementary factors of production.

Should Brazil be assigned a surplus or a deficit? Assuming we can decide that question, we still have to decide a magnitude. Brazil's position has shifted from deficit to surplus and back several times during the past decade. Perhaps, then, the target should be put at zero. But maybe those recent fluctuations were aberrant, related to the debt crisis, and Brazil should again have a deficit, as it did in the 1970s. How are we to know? Large investment projects, appropriately financed in part in the international capital market, would imply a deterioration in the current account surplus or an enlargement of the deficit. Some countries would have to be on the other side, running larger surpluses to finance Brazil's larger deficit. That would require approval, if I understand it correctly, by the Executive Board of the International Monetary Fund before big projects could go forward.

In the mid-1970s the Organization for Economic Cooperation and Development undertook to try to set current account targets following the first oil shock because of concern that the oil-importing countries would try individually to reduce the inevitable deficits too quickly and put contractionary pressure on the world economy. That short-term effort failed, although my impression is that the fact of the discussion was useful, even though they failed to reach targets. Ted Truman of the Federal Reserve has reminded me that there was a similar exercise associated with the Smithsonian Agreement in late 1971, which also failed to reach targets.

In pointing to the difficulty of setting comprehensive targets I do not mean to exclude the possibility of making qualitative judgments from time to time about the appropriateness of countries' surpluses or deficits. But the proposal before us requires much more than that occasional judgment about whether a position is too big or too small. It requires us to agree on particular numbers. I see neither a practical nor a normative basis for doing that.

The second fatal weakness gets into the realm of political philosophy. Taxation and government expenditure are right at the heart of democratic government. Williamson and Henning do not take tax and spending authority completely away from national governments, but they would very sharply constrain it. National legislatures are mentioned only once in the paper. The authors seek, in effect, a much more sophisticated and internationalized version of the balanced budget amendment (which has been under discussion in the United States and recently again failed to pass the Congress), preferably by treaty, but if necessary by executive agreement instead.

This would mark a major inroad into the authority of parliaments. Now, democracies are not noted for their efficiency at anything. But they have one outstanding advantage, which is that the people choose their representatives, and when they suffer the mistakes they have no one else to blame. Williamson and Henning would take that away from them. I believe that a system such as they propose, should it somehow be put in place, would not be politically sustainable under democratic government.

Henning in his oral remarks at the conference emphasized the current attraction of apparently arbitrary fiscal rules. But it is worth noting that the budgetary rule now operating in the United States is limited to five years. Unless it is extended, it will lapse after five years, and it could be changed at any time by new legislation. Some kind of rule has been on the books since the modified Gramm-Rudman-Hollings amendment was passed in 1987, but the rules have been changed more often than every five years. That is very different from a treaty, which locks each country into an arrangement with other countries for a much longer time.

The authors talk about aberrant fiscal policy and fiscal adventures, and we all know what they have in mind. Let us ask how their system would have fared had it been in place during the last 15 years. Would it have permitted us to avoid some of the mistakes of the past? If we had had this system in place, would it have inhibited Ronald Reagan's defense buildup and 1981 tax reduction—the sources, along with the tight monetary policy of the period, of the strong overvaluation of the dollar in the mid-1980s? My answer to that question is an unambiguous negative. The first Reagan administration—the administration that mined Nicaragua's harbors in violation of international law and was willing to violate the antiballistic missile treaty by reinterpreting it in a way that was legally indefensible—was antithetical to international cooperation. It had its distinct view about the role of the US government in the world, and about how the economy operated. The Reagan administration's mistake in the fiscal sphere was recognized early on, by the way, but too late to reverse it. We spent the rest of the decade trying to correct it. Nonetheless, I would suggest that a Williamson-Henning regime would not have restrained the first Reagan administration in any way.

It is fashionable now to criticize the German fiscal policy of 1989–90, immediately following German unification. A lot of troubles flow from it. But play the thought experiment of what view we would be taking of Germany's rapid and expensive unification had the August 1991 coup in the Soviet Union succeeded rather than failed. Chancellor Helmut Kohl would be a hailed as a national hero for having moved quickly to seize a tiny window of opportunity to achieve an important and long-standing national objective. That the coup failed gives us all the luxury of criticizing the fiscal complications that this unification created. But again I would suggest that the Williamson-Henning regime would not have inhibited Kohl; indeed, membership in the European Monetary System did not inhibit him at the time.[1]

Finally, think about the oil shocks of the 1970s. These were global shocks, not country-specific ones, and almost all of the major industrial countries are importers of oil. But global shocks can have different effects on the major countries. What should be the current account targets following an oil shock, and what should be the adjustment in the FEERs following such shocks? That is an exercise that we actually went through, and although the discussion was extremely useful in emphasizing the international implications of country-specific actions, it fell far short of the tight regime that Williamson and Henning propose.

I conclude by suggesting that the two large fiscal shocks in the United States and Germany of the past 15 years, both of which resulted in substantial misalignments of exchange rates, would not have been stopped by this regime. But is that too severe a test? I think not. Had it not been for such events, the proposal probably would not have been advanced in the first place. Small variations in exchange rates are allowed within the bands. It is precisely the large misalignments that the proposal is designed

---

1. Many of the fiscal commitments made by Kohl—full pensions to East Germans at a one-to-one exchange rate and no tax increases in the West—were designed to gain approval on both sides of the border for unification by absorption of the five new Länder into the Federal Republic of Germany under the latter's constitution and laws. The alternative, a bilateral negotiation, would have taken far longer. Also, West Germans wanted to stop the heavy east-to-west migration that had begun to take place.

to eliminate, and if it could not have eliminated the important misalignments in our recent experience, we should ask whether the heavy commitments it requires are worthwhile.

Well, if not this system, what? That is a challenging question. I favor collective exchange rate management, and I lean toward what some time ago was called a "braking and smoothing" strategy, under which monetary authorities decide whether market exchange rates as such are disrupting or threatening to disrupt real economic activity. They decide whether to intervene, and preferably they make those decisions in collaboration with authorities in other countries and then intervene collectively. Indeed, that is the kind of system that we have operated. It is decried as ad hoc, but there are lots of things worse than skillfully managed ad hockery.

Finally, just for completeness, I will mention my bold suggestion (which Williamson and Henning dismiss in a sentence) that in the long run, but not for the next few years, we will desire irrevocably fixed exchange rates among the major currencies—in effect, a common currency among the industrialized democracies (see Cooper 1987). Exchange rate movements, dominated as they are by financial transactions, will be seen as increasingly disruptive of real economic activity, especially investment. Irrevocably fixed exchange rates would of course entail a single monetary regime. But I do not believe it would require the strong restraints on national fiscal action that Williamson and Henning require in their framework, and I see that as one of the advantages of irrevocably fixed exchange rates over the blueprint.

Reference

Cooper, Richard N. 1987. "A Monetary System for the Future." Reprinted in R. N. Cooper, *The International Monetary System.* Cambridge, MA: MIT Press.

Comment

SHIJURO OGATA

There are at least three basic understandings about the international monetary system that many of us can share. First, although the current exchange rate regime has been flexible enough to cope with unexpected developments such as oil crises, it cannot escape from two fundamental drawbacks, namely, volatility and misalignment of exchange rates. Second, more stable exchange rates are desirable, but greater exchange rate stability can only be attained through the improvement of international balances, at least among the major currency countries, and not through concerted exchange market intervention alone. Third, the present international monetary system has not been so bad at crisis management, as we witnessed in November 1978, March 1980, September 1985, and February 1987, when the system was able to correct excessive and undesirable moves in exchange rates, but it has not been good at all at crisis prevention. How can we improve crisis prevention? And what lessons can be learned from the successes of previous crisis management and the failures of previous crisis prevention? These are the fundamental questions.

On the basis of these propositions, I would like to comment on the very stimulating paper just presented. My suggestions are not dramatic, but I hope they are realistic and pragmatic.

My first two comments relate to the institutional setup of exchange rate management. First, I support Williamson's and Henning's idea of going back to the IMF and its original function. The G-7 has become an impor-

Shijuro Ogata is senior adviser for Yamaichi Securities Co., Ltd., Tokyo, director of Barclays Bank PLC, and chairman of Barclays Trust and Banking Company (Japan) Limited.

tant group, but it has become excessively political. The monitoring of exchange rates and exchange markets, which must be the concern not only of the seven major industrial countries but of all IMF members, should be handled by an "International Monetary Council," or whatever one chooses to call it—a kind of expanded G-7 within the IMF.

The formation of a small group such as this within the IMF might well be strongly opposed by those members who would be excluded. An answer to this might be to streamline the function of the Interim Committee, to change it from its present function as a speechmaking forum to a more effective executive committee. Even then, some small group of world leaders associated with the IMF, but not necessarily representing member countries, might be needed to prompt effective and timely action from behind the scenes. The advisory committee proposed in the next paragraph might be able to serve such a purpose, and the valuable views expressed in the OECD's Working Party 3 and at meetings of the Bank for International Settlements could be also taken into consideration.

Second, another important problem is how to get the major countries to listen more attentively to enlightened international public opinion. Since the major countries no longer need financial help from the IMF, they are paying increasingly less attention to its views, whether expressed in its annual consultations or in its *World Economic Outlook*. My suggestion is to establish an advisory committee consisting of persons of undisputable international repute, including some from the major countries themselves, and to refer to it any recommendation of critical importance before it is presented to the members in question.

The remainder of my comments address the substance of international economic policy coordination. I have strong reservations about so-called fundamental equilibrium exchange rates (FEERs). There is a basic problem of how to calculate such rates accurately. But even if they could be calculated, the results could be too painful for the countries in question to accept. Current account imbalances cannot be reduced by exchange rate changes alone. If, nevertheless, one tried to calculate the level of exchange rates under which imbalances could be substantially reduced, the resulting rates might be too high or too low to be acceptable to the countries in question.

Another option would be to adopt domestic purchasing power parities as the basis for determining exchange rates. But when there are large differences between market exchange rates in the markets and the rates implied by domestic purchasing power parities, adoption of the latter could actually worsen international imbalances.

In any event, whenever one uses theoretically calculated exchange rates, whether they are FEERs or rates based on purchasing power parities, there is a basic problem of how to bring market rates in line with the calculated rates. Fairly often the G-7 only approved the current level and did not suggest any other level. It is true that market rates are not always desirable, yet it is hardly realistic to aim at "desirable" rates when these are far away from the rates currently prevailing.

My suggestion under these circumstances is very modest. International cooperation should be strengthened so as to prevent "undesirable" exchange rates rather than to seek, prematurely, "desirable" exchange rates. By "undesirable" I mean levels of exchange rates or a direction of exchange rate movement that would enlarge already existing international imbalances.

I do not mean by this that we should sit back until exchange rates reach such undesirable levels or move in such undesirable directions. Given the previous failures of crisis prevention, I would urge strengthening surveillance over the performance of major currency countries, with special attention to their external balances, exchange rates, and macroeconomic policies.

There are two additional points. First, although the Williamson-Miller blueprint is designed not to rely on the dominance of a single state, it must be admitted that the US dollar retains and will continue to retain a special position in the international monetary system, because of the sheer size of US economy and the existence of large and efficient US financial markets. I do not see any need to change that situation by deliberate means. Because of the dollar's special position, if the US authorities indicate their greater concern about exchange rates and their greater willingness to share exchange risks if necessary, that will enhance the credibility of any international attempt to secure greater exchange rate stability.

Second, in this kind of international exercise one cannot expect any leadership role from Japan, particularly given Japan's current domestic political instability. Once such an exercise is launched internationally, it may be possible to obtain wide support among the Japanese because of their serious concern about exchange rate instability. It would probably be much easier than to secure a national consensus on Japan's role in international peacekeeping operations.

Comment

NIELS THYGESEN

John Williamson and Randall Henning have prepared a rich paper on international monetary coordination: they present both the main argument why management of the international monetary system is desirable and some rather detailed prescriptions for the implementation of their proposals. It is easier to agree with their case for international monetary management, based on the double need to dampen badly functioning financial markets and to constrain strongly deviant government behavior, than with their prescriptions. The latter, not surprisingly, are based on the so-called blueprint that one of the authors published (with Marcus H. Miller) in 1987 as an extension of his earlier proposal for exchange rate target zones. It is a pleasure to pay tribute to John Williamson for consistency and clarity in his advocacy of a proposal that has raised the level of analysis of global as well as regional monetary arrangements, even if it has failed so far to persuade policymakers. In the present version the blueprint has been refined on a couple of minor points, while the international institutional framework within which it could be implemented is treated in greater depth than before.

Virtues and Weaknesses of the Blueprint

The blueprint aims at improving international macroeconomic management by coordination of exchange rates and national budgetary policies in

Niels Thygesen is senior research fellow at the Economic Policy Research Unit of the Copenhagen School of Business and professor at the University of Copenhagen.

order to improve performance with respect to internal and external balance, the latter represented by a sustainable current account balance. This proposal would have much to recommend it in economic logic, if it could be assumed that knowledge of how economies operate and interact were sufficiently accurate, and that governments were able to make commitments with respect to their budgetary policies.

Richard Cooper's comment explains in some detail why our empirical knowledge is insufficient to give a definite current account target the pivotal role it takes on in the blueprint. In a world of fully mobile capital, the notion of what is a sustainable current account position becomes very vague. Even if a number were to be picked somewhat arbitrarily from the range of possible values, there would be considerable uncertainty in determining the combinations of real exchange rate and budgetary positions that could achieve it. It is valuable that the effort be made, and as carefully as possible, but there can be few illusions even among the most confident model builders that the results will convince policymakers. There are too many uncertainties, and too many dimensions to the coordination problem, for the prescriptions to correct more than the most glaring international imbalances. Despite the relative success of the ad hoc efforts in the 1980s, first in bringing down the US dollar in an orderly way through the Plaza Agreement and then in dampening the fluctuations over the last seven to eight years in the main currency relationships following the Louvre Accord, the efforts did not visibly go beyond occasional interventions and announcements, as the authors themselves are the first to admit.

The other assumption, namely, the ability and hence willingness of governments to commit themselves to internationally constructive budgetary actions, even when they know quite well what these are, is also questionable. Two examples from the past decade and a half—the surges in the US budget deficit in the first half of the 1980s and the explosion in the German public deficit following reunification—show why this is so. Promises to consolidate public finances, even when underpinned by detailed agreements with the legislature, as was done in the United States in the Gramm-Rudman-Hollings Act and the 1990 long-term budgetary agreement between President George Bush and Congress, could not be implemented according to even the most generous interpretation of international understandings. Japan may claim to be a partial exception to the rule, having on several occasions since 1986–87 adjusted budgetary policy in ways consistent with Group of Seven (G-7) recommendations.

The European Experience in Policy Coordination

With both of these central assumptions in question, it is not so surprising that the G-7 countries have confined themselves to ad hoc efforts to dampen exchange rate fluctuations. What is more surprising is the failure of the member states of the European Communities (now the European Union) to move in the direction of comprehensive policy coordination along the lines of the blueprint. One would expect both of the above assumptions to hold up better in the regional context. With fairly stable exchange rates within the region, particularly as the 1980s progressed and the European Monetary System (EMS) firmed up, and hence less uncertainty about cross-border transmission effects of domestic policy changes in the global system, the analytical case for budgetary policy coordination should be stronger. Furthermore, with so many policy areas regarded as a common concern to the EU member states, the scope for constructive bargains on adjustments in national budgetary policies should, in principle, be much wider. The reasons why these opportunities have not been realized may contain useful lessons for the design of an improved management of the international monetary system. Since my mandate, in contrast to those of my two fellow discussants, is restricted to discussing the relevance of the European experience, I shall, in the rest of my comments, concentrate on that task.

The Early EMS

There is a certain nostalgia—implicit rather than openly expressed—in the Williamson-Henning paper for the early days of the EMS when intra-European exchange rates were realigned quite regularly. Many, like John Williamson, saw the early (i.e., 1979–83) EMS as a definite improvement over the Bretton Woods system in several respects. It provided for collective decision making on realignments while avoiding the rigidity of nominal exchange rates. At times, particularly when a country sought a devaluation, participation in the system visibly facilitated deindexation and domestic budgetary consolidation in an internationally appropriate manner. France in 1982–83 is the prime example, but there were others.

The early EMS was a defensive mechanism set up to ensure that exchange rate changes, which had been relied upon excessively in the 1970s, would be pushed more into the background. The system was not initially set up to promote strong convergence in terms of inflation, but only to limit the scope for divergence; discipline was not a key concept at the time, even though it soon became clear that the appearance of symmetry—the use of a divergence indicator to help determine which country should adjust interest rates in order to stay within the fluctuation margins—was not a feature of the system in reality.

After March 1983 the system became more asymmetric, not because of any desire by Germany to impose its policies on the rest, but because most of the other European countries developed a consensus around policies of disinflation and budgetary consolidation, which permitted a gradual convergence toward the low and falling inflation rates then prevailing in Germany and the Netherlands.

The EMS participants were quite successful in improving their performance and cohesiveness in the face of basically common external shocks in the early 1980s—the second oil-price hike and the gyrations of the dollar—relative to the results of the 1970s, but they had almost no success in redistributing demand between countries by policy instruments other than realignments. Arguably they got the policy mix wrong, as everybody was consolidating budget deficits from 1983 onward; even the Bundesbank was at times critical of the tightness of German budgetary policy. But at the time budgetary orthodoxy took precedence over demand management, and the authority—in place since 1974—for making collective recommendations through the Council of Ministers and prepared by the European Commission remained almost unused.

Are there any lessons from the early EMS experience for the design of a future reform of the international monetary system? It would appear that the Europeans did begin a process of convergence and indirect coordination, even though they limited their rule book, or policy regime, to exchange rate cooperation. This was an achievement, given that the starting conditions for the EMS were unpropitious, with high and divergent inflation rates making occasional exchange rate changes necessary to prevent substantial misalignments. When these changes had to occur, it was fairly obvious what needed to be done. This is rather different from the situation prevailing in the global economy toward the mid-1990s, when inflation rates are roughly similar in the major countries and the case for stable exchange rates is stronger than it was for the EMS participants in the beginning. But the latter succeeded in using the realignments as a useful trigger for domestic policy adjustments. They were also able to rely in crisis periods on capital controls to gain time to design these adjustments. Europe managed a fixed but adjustable exchange rate system reasonably well about a decade ago, but that is not a reliable pointer to an international system, where the challenges are different.

The Tight EMS and Its Demise

In the mid-1980s the Europeans took a different course in policy coordination from that recommended by Williamson and Henning. Market integration for goods and services was deepened through the Single Market, and factor mobility was enhanced. These initiatives would have been hard to devise without the limited monetary integration achieved in the EMS; they in turn raised the incentive to develop the system further. For that purpose institutional reform leading toward Economic and Monetary Union (EMU) with a single currency was on the agenda from 1986 on. Since such a reform takes a long time to negotiate and then implement, the participants endowed themselves beginning in 1987 with reinforced defenses to keep the EMS in place during a lengthy transition with increasingly mobile capital.

For nearly five years the package known as the Basel-Nyborg Agreement did operate quite smoothly. Fluctuations inside the margins were the first buffer when a disturbance hit a currency, to be followed up by a judicious mixture of foreign-exchange interventions and relative adjustments of short-term interest rates. If this combination of efforts proved inadequate, a realignment could on rare occasions be resorted to. The central rate was then allowed to change by at most twice the width of the band, to minimize jumps in market exchange rates. As long as these principles were adhered to, market participants could be sure that no gains could be expected from taking open positions in EMS currencies.

All of this could be said to be in the spirit of increasingly tight international policy coordination of the type envisaged by Williamson and Henning, although with little emphasis on budgetary policy. But two factors made the EMS an uneasy compromise in the transition to EMU: the system became overly rigid, and financial liberalization had more destabilizing implications for exchange rates than had originally been understood. These two explanations are well set out in both official and academic contributions (Group of Deputies of the Group of Ten 1993, Eichengreen and Wyplosz 1993), although after the event.

Excessive rigidity was observed also in the global system toward the end of the Bretton Woods era. The United States then objected to finding itself in a position where it could not devalue its currency. Germany following unification felt it needed some real appreciation of its currency, but could not obtain it. Upward adjustment of the German price level was so strenuously resisted by the Bundesbank that companion efforts became too much for some of the weaker EMS currencies, and sterling and the lira left the regime. Market participants anticipated that other countries would also break out and cut interest rates. Governments finally took the unexpected step of widening the EMS fluctuation margins very considerably (to ±15 percent) on 1 August 1993.

It was not anticipated that international financial integration would undermine in this way the ambition of the EMS participants to maintain stable exchange rates between themselves. Initially the removal of capital controls—now completed by 11 of the present 12 member states—was seen as complementary to increasingly tight monetary integration. Liberalization at first reinforced the credibility of the commitment to the EMS regime. The philosophy was that governments, by subjecting their policies to the judgment of international financial markets, would increase the pressure on themselves to conduct eventually consistent policies; the EMS would, despite its tightly managed nature, become a "market-led system," to use the term of Padoa-Schioppa and Saccomanni in their paper in this volume. Markets clearly took the prospect of EMU with a single currency seriously when it emerged in the surprisingly swift negotiation phase of 1989–91. Interest rates converged at both the short and the long end despite the tensions introduced by German reunification and the large budget deficits that so preoccupy policymakers in several European countries.

This confidence evaporated as the prospects for EMU weakened in 1992: the Maastricht Treaty was rejected in a referendum in Denmark, and a similar outcome loomed in France. This exposed those participants who had converged the least and for whom the fading of EMU was the most dangerous. Once two of them had exited, it became very difficult to contain pressures against the others. The emphasis among market participants shifted from analyses of past performance to perceived differences in future policies, notably as impatience with recession could be expected to impose itself at different times in the remaining EMS countries according to domestic political debates and timetables. If the mood of market participants shifts in this direction, participation in an EMS-like arrangement requires more than commitment and a good past record—a ban on the discussion of alternative policies would also be helpful.

The Present EMS: Target, but No Zone?

Since by 1993 the option of accelerating movement toward EMU was no longer available in view of the elaborate, gradualist procedures of the Maastricht Treaty, the decision later by the EC finance ministers on 1 August 1993 was logical: to widen fluctuation margins so as to create sufficient exchange rate uncertainty to make speculation against the remaining central rate unattractive. The strategy appears to have succeeded so far; over the first year since the introduction of the wide margins, most of the eight currencies linked to the deutsche mark in the EMS have returned to their previous narrow margins. Inflation rates are clustered in the 2 to 3 percent range, and long-term interest rates have on the whole remained close together for seven of the nine currencies in the EMS—although with some widening of differentials with respect to German rates during the period of rising bond rates since February 1994—indicating that financial markets expect convergent inflation performance and stable exchange rates in the longer run.

A major question mark over this unintended new form of transition is whether the wide margins provide a sufficiently constraining framework to allow a significant number of countries to enter the final stage of EMU according to the Maastricht timetable, that is, before the end of the 1990s. There is no formal requirement to reintroduce the narrow margins as a step toward EMU, but there is a concern, particularly if the transition is lengthy (and it may take another four years) that some participants will find irresistible the pressure to avail themselves of the freedom of action that the wide margins have left. If participants were to use the wide margins rather fully, or even seek changes in central rates, plans for EMU would retreat further in the future. The attitude toward the present regime—which could be labeled "exchange rate targets without a zone" (since the zone is so wide)—is therefore mixed: satisfaction with short-term stability, but doubts about long-term robustness, if required to survive.

Economic and Monetary Union

There is a fourth version of European monetary arrangements, which cannot yet contain any lessons for the international monetary system, since it exists only on the drawing board: the provisions for the final stage of EMU. From the viewpoint of the blueprint the EMU strategy is radically different. The emphasis in EMU is on transgressing the international coordination framework in the monetary area by moving to irrevocably fixed exchange rates among participants, and subsequently ("as soon as possible" according to official statements) to a single currency. This jump to a national model will necessarily be an important qualitative one, regardless of how closely the participating central banks have cooperated during the transition. Because this step, by removing fully the scope for national monetary policies and exchange rate changes among those who choose to join, is so momentous, there was no appetite for setting up a tight machinery for coordinating national budgetary policies. In any case, monetary union indirectly imposes tighter limits on the sustainability of national budgetary policies; with inflation and devaluation ruled out as options, the long-term budgetary constraints will become more visible.

The Maastricht Treaty was not, however, fully convinced of the long-term rationality of governments. It also had to take into account that the member states had started the EMU process from widely different budgetary positions. The treaty set down reference values for government deficits and debt (both as proportions to GDP) that reflected average behavior by the member states at the time the treaty was drafted in 1990. In order to qualify for the final stage of EMU, countries must not stray far or permanently from the deficit norm of 3 percent of GDP, and they should keep their debt dynamics under control, aiming to approach the norm for the debt ratio of 60 percent at an appropriate rate. The collective monitoring of these indicators by the Council of Ministers will be underpinned by modest financial sanctions after the start of full EMU; these are a less serious sanction than possible exclusion during the transition, but still an interesting new departure in an international regime, which is rightly picked up in the Williamson-Henning paper.

The budgetary provisions of the treaty have been criticized as arbitrary and possibly superfluous. They are interesting in the global context, not least because they are less ambitious than prescriptions for genuine macroeconomic coordination. The Maastricht criteria are meant only to discourage strongly deviant behavior, while leaving discretion to national governments as long as they maintain their deficits within a normal range of no more than, say, 3 to 4 percent of GDP. It is interesting that this was seen as adequate for macroeconomic management in EMU.

Lessons for the International Monetary System

What lessons does the European experience offer for the issues of global monetary management addressed in the Williamson-Henning analysis? This question is complicated by the several stages (the discussion above identified four) through which monetary integration in Europe has gone in only the past 15 years.

The first stage was the EMS of 1979–83. In this stage exchange rates were realigned rather frequently, but crucial initial steps in domestic adjustments were made, often using the occasion of a realignment. The difficulty in using this early experience as a global model is the change in the financial environment. Today's capital markets would not wait for governments to undertake the fairly sizable realignments observed in that period; they would have forced them about, and probably enlarged them. But the need for realignments today in the global system is less evident than it was in Europe in the early 1980s. This model seems to provide the least relevant lesson.

The second stage, the hardening of the EMS over the decade from the end of the large realignments in 1983 to the partial suspension of rates in 1993, provides mainly a negative lesson. It proved in the end very difficult to defend narrow margins, as they invited speculative attacks as the credibility of exchange rate commitments became questionable either because of the buildup of misalignments or because of anticipated future shifts in domestic policy which would undermine a fixed exchange rate. The system was particularly vulnerable after German reunification, which was a large, asymmetric shock. Since the global economy is likely to witness more asymmetric shocks than are the EU countries, it would be hazardous to aim for the high degree of exchange rate rigidity observed in the EMS in this period. This model is therefore also less than fully relevant to the global system.

Almost by default, the EMS ended up with the present regime, the crucial element of which is the central rates, their margins having become so wide that they may never be tested. Have the Europeans finally opted for the target zone idea, or even the blueprint, since they now also pay more attention to the correction of national budgetary imbalances? This is the question put by US advocates of the target zone proposal, including the hosts of this conference.

It would not be correct to regard the present loose version of the EMS as a trial run of the blueprint. The aim of the present regime is to preserve as much as possible the public good, very important for advanced integration of markets, of exchange rate stability while keeping the option of moving to full EMU alive through more emphasis on medium-term budgetary consolidation. The aims are different, as are the methods: more emphasis on tight monetary coordination, less on the use of budgetary policies for international stabilization purposes.

The fourth and final stage of EMU exists so far only in the minds of those who prepared it. Irrevocably fixed exchange rates and a single currency, combined with substantial national budgetary autonomy, will require a long gestation period to get near the global monetary reform agenda. The case for moving toward a single currency for the world's major regions can be made, but it is weaker than that for EMU, where the economies involved are more likely to be affected by symmetric shocks and where reactions to them are more likely to be similar. With a politically set objective to move toward a single currency and a complete pooling of monetary sovereignty in a common and independent central bank, with price stability as the primary objective, much of the ambiguity of international policy coordination of both targets and instruments disappears. Nonmonetary policies become more transparent in their design and effects; finally, it may suffice to constrain medium-term deviant national budgetary policies, without coordinating them on an ongoing basis, which may be regarded as too intrusive.

In short, the lessons from the European experience are not easy to apply to plans for the future international monetary system. The most appropriate model may be the early EMS, but that arrangement had to devote more attention to managing realignments of currencies, in view of the divergences that then existed, than should be necessary. The narrow-margin, tightly managed, but still adjustable EMS of the second phase may seem more appropriate to today's problems, but the markets lost confidence in it. This experience would probably be repeated at the global level if a similar system were put into place, given the strong incentives for speculative attacks triggered by different policy arrangements and interpretations of them in the United States, Japan, and Europe.

The present EMS, with its declared central rate within very wide margins, may therefore merit closer attention as a model, but at the global level it would be met with the objection that any proposed constellation of central rates would be open to much argument. In Europe, in contrast, the central rates that survive have been tested by markets and found acceptable by governments. Those who appear, like Williamson and Henning, to believe that current exchange rates in the global system are not very far from the fundamental equilibrium exchange rates of the blueprint face a major challenge in persuading policymakers of the correctness of this view and of the gains from embodying it in a declared grid of central rates for the world's major currencies. If such a system could be put in place, it might well prove robust, even though it would fall well short of the blueprint.

This comment has not addressed the institutional framework within which the blueprint could best be implemented. These issues can only be resolved once it is clear what is to be coordinated in the international monetary system and according to what principles. Europeans have made some progress with institutional issues, and the considerations are well discussed in the Williamson-Henning paper. If one wants to go as far as the EU member states in pooling monetary sovereignty, an international treaty would be necessary. However, for the more modest suggestion in this comment that announcement of a grid of central rates would be the most constructive initial step, informing the IMF of the decision and the underlying agreement among the participating central banks, with an invitation to the IMF to monitor the initial stages, could be enough.

The European experience and the elaborate European blueprint that is the Maastricht Treaty provide some interesting pointers as to how the division of responsibilities between governments and central banks could be organized. The Williamson-Henning paper correctly interprets this as an arrangement in which central banks become fully in charge of implementing policy once central rates have been agreed by governments. Whether the central bankers should have any formal authority to suggest realignments, as is hinted in the paper, seems to me doubtful. If central rates are established within a wide target zone, it would not make sense to make small and regular changes in them. And large changes—which one hopes could be avoided—should be the responsibility of governments. They might prefer not to have any semipublic advice on that decision.

References

Eichengreen, Barry, and Charles Wyplosz. 1993. *The Unstable EMS*. Brookings Papers on Economic Activity 1. Washington: Brookings Institution.

Group of Deputies of the Group of Ten. 1993. *International Capital Movement and Foreign Exchange Markets: A Report to the Ministers and Governments*. Rome.

Williamson, John, with Marcus H. Miller. 1987. *Targets and Indicators: A Blueprint for the International Coordination of Economic Policy*. POLICY ANALYSES IN INTERNATIONAL ECONOMICS 22. Washington: Institute for International Economics.

3

Managing the Trading System: The World Trade Organization and the Post–Uruguay Round GATT Agenda

JOHN H. JACKSON

The Uruguay Round Achievements: A Watershed for Trade Policy?

The Uruguay Round, the eighth round of broad trade negotiations under the auspices of the General Agreement on Tariffs and Trade (GATT), is clearly the most extensive yet undertaken by the GATT system, and possibly by any similar body in history. The goals of the September 1986 ministerial meeting at Punta del Este, Uruguay, which set forth the agenda for the round, were extremely ambitious. If only half those objectives had been achieved, the Uruguay Round would still be the most extensive and successful trade negotiation ever. In fact, despite the many years of delay and negotiating impasses, the Uruguay Round has achieved considerably more than half its objectives. As an example of the magnitude of the effort, it was reported that the Final Act signed in Marrakesh, Morocco, on 15 April, 1994 weighed 385 pounds and included over 22,000 pages! Just the basic texts reproduced as part of the Final Act totaled 424 pages.

It is interesting to consider the Uruguay Round outcome in light of the objectives formally stated at Punta del Este. Those objectives shifted somewhat over the seven-year negotiating period. From the beginning, a most important objective of the round was to extend the rule-based discipline of GATT treaties to three new subject areas: trade in services, trade in agricultural products, and protection of intellectual property. Of these, only

John H. Jackson is Hessel E. Yntema Professor of Law at the University of Michigan School of Law. He was formerly (1973–74) general counsel to the US Trade Representative.

services and intellectual property were truly new territory for the GATT. The GATT had always formally applied to agricultural trade, but for a variety of reasons agriculture had escaped the GATT discipline in practice. Attempts to bring agriculture into the GATT fold had failed in the two previous negotiating rounds: the Kennedy Round of 1962–67 and the Tokyo Round of 1973–79. In addition, the Punta del Este declaration gave priority to the negotiation of new rules governing subsidies, changes in dispute settlement procedures, new attention to the problems of textile trade, and further elaboration of rules relating to product standards. A number of other issues were also targeted for attention.

The result fulfills the ministers' original intentions to a remarkable degree, although with some gaps. An additional important result, the charter establishing a World Trade Organization (WTO), stemmed from a proposal that emerged only after the 1986 conference. If there is satisfactory implementation of the agreement, the Uruguay Round will have made important achievements in the following 11 areas.

Services. The services agreement, known formally as the General Agreement on Trade in Services (GATS), is a major new chapter in GATT history. Although in some ways seriously flawed, this text now offers an overall umbrella concept for trade in services to which, it is hoped, an ongoing negotiating process will provide additional detail, probably over at least a 50-year period. In this respect the structure of the new WTO (see below) is vital.

Intellectual Property. The agreement on trade-related intellectual properties (TRIPs) is a splendid new achievement. It brings considerable new international rule-based discipline to the level of protection accorded patents, copyrights, trade secrets, and similar intellectual properties, even though some specialists and interest groups appeared disappointed by certain gaps in the text.

Agriculture. The results of the round in agriculture are in many respects meager, certainly as measured against the aspirations expressed at Punta del Este (and in the United States). Nevertheless there is now, for the first time, some realistic expectation of discipline in the form of rules over agriculture trade (especially in the areas of subsidies and border restrictions). As with most other subjects of the Uruguay Round, further attention will be needed over the years and decades ahead, but the Uruguay Round has achieved an important start.

Subsidies and Countervailing Duties. The results of the round include a new subsidies "code," again not without flaw, but with an overall conceptual approach that much improves on the Tokyo Round code. Worries here focus on the ambiguity of several exceptions clauses that could lead to abuse.

Textiles. Textiles are covered in the Uruguay Round in the form of an agreement to phase out, over the course of a decade, the special textile regime known as the Multi-Fiber Arrangement, which has always been an embarrassment to the GATT. Again, many feel the textile agreement is flawed—the phaseout is considered either too slow or too fast—but the direction seems right.

Standards. Trade rules for product standards have been further addressed, building on the accomplishment of the Tokyo Round code. It has become obvious that questions involving standards are much more complex than many had thought, and there are some fundamental policy differences, such as the clash of environmental interests with trade policy goals. The Uruguay Round text provides the next group of improvements, although more attention will be needed.

Safeguards. One of the major failures of the Tokyo Round was its inability to achieve an agreement on safeguards and escape clause measures. In this respect the Uruguay Round succeeded where the Tokyo Round had failed, and a very impressive and ambitious safeguards code is part of the round's results. It not only provides guidelines and criteria for normal use of the escape clause but establishes a rule against the use of voluntary export restraints of various kinds. If this agreement is satisfactorily implemented, it could be an impressive addition to world trading discipline.

Market Access. The Uruguay Round results include impressive advances in those issues grouped under the rubric of "market access," including a reduction in the use of quotas (and a shift of quotas to tariffs), as well as very substantial tariff cutting (some say the most of any round to date). Some of the most substantial tariff cutting has been on the part of developing countries, but in addition there have been some important advances in reducing tariffs in certain sectors to zero.

Developing Country Integration. As a result of the Uruguay Round, developing countries are more fully integrated into the GATT/WTO system than before. The agreement includes a requirement that all countries, including developing countries, have tariff and services schedules, and constraints are placed on certain exceptions for developing countries. This measure could be one of the most important features of the Uruguay Round result, bringing a discipline to at least the newly industrializing countries (NICs).

Dispute Settlement. One of the many achievements of the GATT, despite the institutional deficiencies ("birth defects") under which it has had to operate since its founding, has been the development over four decades of a reasonably sophisticated dispute settlement process. However, a certain number of flaws in those procedures have been widely recognized. The Uruguay Round agreement, for the first time, establishes an overall unified system of dispute settlement procedures for all portions of the agreement, and a legal text (rather than just customary practice) to serve as the basis for carrying out those procedures. The new procedures include measures to avoid the blocking that occurred under previous consensus decision-making rules, and a new appellate procedure to substitute for some of the old procedures that were vulnerable to blocking.

The WTO Charter. One of the interesting achievements of the Uruguay Round is the development of an institutional charter for a new World Trade Organization. This organization will help facilitate international cooperation in trade and economic relations and will fundamentally change the GATT system to accommodate the vast new terrain of trade competence thrust on the trading system by the Uruguay Round. Some have even said that the creation of the WTO may be the most important result of the Uruguay Round.

The Charter of the World Trade Organization
Genesis of the WTO

It is well known that the GATT was never intended to be an organization. It was negotiated in 1947–48, while negotiators were preparing the charter for a proposed International Trade Organization (ITO). The GATT was to be a multilateral trade and tariff agreement, which would depend for its organizational context and secretariat services on the ITO. The ITO never came into being because the US Congress in the late 1940s declined to approve it. The GATT, however, was negotiated under advance authority granted to the president in the 1945 extension of the Reciprocal Trade Agreements Act (the first such act had been passed in 1934). Compounding the anomalies of that period, the GATT 1947 treaty instrument was applied only "provisionally." At the time, it was contemplated that the GATT would be applied for several years until the ITO came into force, and then would be put under the umbrella of, and brought into conformity with, the ITO charter. However, because the ITO was never brought into being, the GATT itself gradually became the focus for international governmental cooperation on trade matters.

Despite this inauspicious beginning, the GATT has been remarkably successful over its nearly five decades of existence. Its success is partly due to its ingenious and pragmatic leadership, particularly in its early years, as the GATT struggled to fill the gap left by the failure of the ITO. As the decades passed, it was recognized that the GATT system was being increasingly challenged by the changing conditions of international economic activity, including the greater interdependence of national economies and the growth of trade in services. Concern developed that the GATT was too handicapped to play the role of the necessary "third leg" of the Bretton Woods system, complementing the International Monetary Fund (IMF) and the World Bank. Its problems and "birth defects" included:

- its provisional application and grandfather rights exceptions;
- ambiguity about the powers of the Contracting Parties (the countries that were signatories to the agreement) to make certain decisions;

- ambiguity regarding the waiver authority and risks of misuse;

- its murky legal status, which led to misunderstanding on the part of the public, the media, and even government officials;

- defects in the dispute settlement procedures;

- a general lack of institutional provisions, which made constant improvisation necessary.

In December 1991 the Uruguay Round negotiators, led by GATT Director-General Arthur Dunkel, prepared and released a draft text of treaty clauses covering the entire set of negotiation results up to that point, with indications of work yet to do. This was an important project with many implications. Included in this draft was, for the first time, a tentative draft of a new charter for a Multilateral Trade Organization, or MTO. This draft had a number of flaws, which some governments recognized, but through hard work the negotiators were able to revise the draft and iron out the flaws. In the December 1993 draft the new organization was retitled the World Trade Organization.

What Is the WTO?

With the new WTO Charter, the Uruguay Round agreement, when implemented, should provide a better institutional structure to fill the gap left in the Bretton Woods structure. Several general characteristics are noteworthy.

First, the charter for the WTO can be described as a "mini-charter." The organization it establishes is not an ITO; rather, the charter is limited to setting up the institutional and procedural structure that will facilitate and in some cases be necessary for effective implementation of the substantive rules negotiated in the Uruguay Round. The WTO Charter itself is thus entirely institutional and procedural, but it does incorporate, in its annexes, the substantive agreements resulting from the Uruguay Round.

Second, the WTO essentially will continue the GATT institutional ideas and many of its practices, but in a form that should be better understood by the public, media, government officials, and lawyers. To some small extent, the WTO overcomes a number of the GATT's birth defects. Article XVI, section I of the charter expressly states the intention to be guided by GATT "decisions, procedures and customary practices" to the extent feasible. The practice of consensus is better defined and for the first time becomes a legal procedure in some important decisions, rather than just a practice.

Third, the WTO structure offers some important advantages for assisting the effective implementation of the Uruguay Round. For example, a new "GATT 1994" is created to supersede the old "GATT 1947." This procedure avoids the constraints of the amending clause of the old GATT, which might make it quite difficult to bring the Uruguay Round agreement into legal force. At the same time, the WTO ties together the various texts developed in the Uruguay Round and reinforces the idea of the negotiators that countries accepting the Uruguay Round must accept the entire package (with a few exceptions). No longer will the Tokyo Round approach of side codes, derisorily termed "GATT à la carte," be the norm.

The WTO Charter establishes for the first time the basic, explicit legal authority for a secretariat, a director general, and other institutions such as the General Council. It does this in a manner similar to many other international organizations, and it obliges nations to avoid interfering with the officials of the organization.

Another important aspect of the WTO structure is that it facilitates the extension of the GATT institutional structure to the new subjects negotiated in the Uruguay Round, particularly services and intellectual property. Without some kind of legal mechanism such as the WTO, this would have been quite difficult to do, since the GATT itself only applies to goods. The new structure separates the institutional concepts from the substantive rules. The GATT 1994 will remain a substantive agreement (with many of the amendments and improvements developed throughout its history, including in the Uruguay Round). The WTO has a broader context. Similarly, the WTO will be able to apply a unified dispute settlement mechanism and the Trade Policy Review Mechanism (TPRM) to all of the subjects of the Uruguay Round, for all nations that become members.

Fourth, the WTO Charter offers considerably better opportunities for the future evolution and development of the institutional structure for international trade cooperation. Even though the WTO Charter is minimalist, the fact that there is provision for explicit legal status and the traditional organizational structure helps in this regard. Since the WTO focuses on the institutional side, it also offers more flexibility for future inclusion of new negotiated rules or measures to help nations face the constantly emerging problems of world economics.

The Legal Structure of the Uruguay Round Results

The WTO charter itself is confined to institutional measures, but four important annexes to it contain hundreds of pages of substantive rules. The annex structure is important; the different annexes have different purposes and different legal impacts.

Annex 1 contains the large texts, termed "multilateral agreements," that constitute the bulk of the round's results. All these are "mandatory" in the sense that they impose binding obligations on all members of the WTO. This reinforces the single-package idea of the negotiators, departing from the Tokyo Round approach of "pick and choose" side texts. The annex 1 texts include:

- Annex 1A: This contains the GATT 1994, the revised and all-inclusive GATT agreement with its ancillary agreements, and the vast schedules of tariff concessions that make up the bulk of the pages in the official treaty text. The schedules for each of the major trading countries—the United States, Japan, and the European Union—each constitute a volume of printed tariff listings.

- Annex 1B: This contains the GATS (the services agreement) and also incorporates a series of schedules of concessions.

- Annex 1C: This contains the TRIPs (intellectual property) agreement.

Annex 2 contains the dispute settlement rules, which are obligatory for all members, and which form (for the first time) a unitary dispute settlement mechanism covering all the agreements listed in annexes 1, 2, and 4 (i.e., all but the TPRM procedures).

Annex 3 contains the TPRM procedures, under which the WTO will review and report on the overall trade policies of each member country on a periodic and regular basis. The approach is not supposed to be legalistic, and questions of consistency with WTO and annex obligations are not the focus; rather the focus is on the general impact of the trade policies, both on the country being examined and on its trading partners.

Annex 4 contains four "plurilateral agreements," acceptance of which is optional. This is a slight departure from the single-package ideal, but the agreements included tend either to be targeted to a few industrial countries or to be hortatory in nature without real legal impact. Clearly this annex, which may be added to, leaves open some important flexibility for the organization to evolve and redirect its attention and institutional support to new subjects that may emerge as important during the next few decades. The agreements currently included in Annex 4 are:

- the Agreement on Trade in Civil Aircraft

- the Agreement on Government Procurement

- the International Dairy Agreement

- the International Bovine Meat Agreement

As already mentioned, Annex 1A contains the GATT 1994, which is essentially the old GATT as it has been modified by amendments and many of the Tokyo Round codes as updated in the Uruguay Round, as well as some new Uruguay Round agreements. Thus, appended to the GATT 1994 are such agreements as:

- the Agreement on Agriculture

- the Agreement on Sanitary and Phytosanitary Measures

- the Agreement on Textiles and Clothing

- the Agreement on Technical Barriers to Trade

- the Agreement on Trade-Related Investment Measures

- the Agreement on Antidumping

- the Agreement on Valuation

- the Agreement on Preshipment Inspection

- the Agreement on Rules of Origin

- the Agreement on Import Licensing

- the Agreement on Subsidies and Countervailing Measures

- the Agreement on Safeguards

In addition, the GATT 1994 contains a series of "understandings" that further modify the GATT, as well as some ministerial "decisions and declarations."

Two of the agreements that are now part of GATT 1994 concern what are probably the most contentious of the "rules of conduct" clauses of the GATT, namely, those on antidumping and on subsidies and countervailing duties. Another concerns product standards (technical barriers), also addressed in the sanitary and phytosanitary agreement. The legal relationship of these various GATT additions to the core GATT agreement itself is not always clear.

As impressive as the Uruguay Round results are, there clearly are a number of issues left over that the WTO system will need to address in coming years, in addition to overseeing a satisfactory implementation of the Uruguay Round results themselves. The descriptions above hint at some of these leftover issues, and others can be named. Together these include:

- enhancing and extending liberalization of trade in agricultural products;

- future extensive negotiations on services;

- further elaboration of the rules on subsidies;

- further market access efforts;

- greater integration of developing countries as well as monitoring of the WTO and GATT rules to ensure fair treatment of those countries;

- attention to the problems of antidumping rules and the risks they raise for undermining some of the Uruguay Round results;

- the problem of integrating economies in transition (China, Russia, etc.) into the WTO system.

Decision Making in the WTO

The governing structure of the WTO follows the GATT 1947 model in some respects, but departs from it substantially in others. At the top there is a "Ministerial Conference," which is held not less than every two years. Next there are not one but four "Councils." These include a General Council, which seems to have overall supervising authority, can carry out many of the functions of the Ministerial Conference between sessions of the latter, and presumably meets at least as often as the GATT 1947 Council (monthly with exceptions). In addition, however, there is a council for each of the Annex 1 agreements, thus:

- a Council for Trade in Goods

- a Council for Trade in Services

- a Council for Trade-Related Aspects of Intellectual Property Rights

There is also established a Dispute Settlement Body (DSB) to supervise and implement the dispute settlement rules in Annex 2, but the General Council is also authorized to perform the DSB's tasks. Likewise there is a TPRM Body for the TPRM.

It has been alleged that the WTO Charter is an important intrusion on national sovereignty. Apart from the general problems of how to define "sovereignty" in a world that is increasingly interdependent, the WTO contains an elaborate matrix of decision-making procedures bounded by important constraints. Basically there are five different techniques for making decisions or formulating new or amended rules of trade policy in the WTO: amendments to the agreements, decisions on various matters, "interpretations," waivers, and finally, the negotiation of new agreements.

A careful examination of the WTO Charter suggests that, apart from the addition of many new subjects to the substantive annexes, the WTO has no more real power than what the GATT itself possessed under the previous agreements. This may seem surprising, but in fact the GATT treaty text contained language that was quite ambiguous and could have been misused (but fortunately was not) to provide rather extensive powers. For example, in Article XXV of the GATT the Contracting Parties, acting by majority vote, were given the authority to take joint action "with a view to facilitating the operation and furthering the objectives of this agreement." This is very broad and ambiguous language. Under the WTO Charter, considerably more attention has been given to the question of decision making in a number of different contexts, and certain restraints have been added, such as increasing the voting requirements for certain actions to three-fourths of the members (e.g., for many waivers and for formal interpretations) there is also a provision in the amending clauses that a country will not be bound by an amendment passed over its opposition if the amendment would "alter the rights and obligations of the members." Likewise, the waiver authority is more constrained and will be harder to abuse. Furthermore, formal "interpretations . . . shall not be used in a manner that would undermine the amendment provisions." Thus there are more legal grounds than under GATT 1947 to challenge any overreaching on the part of the system's institutions. The protections of national sovereignty built into the WTO Charter rules on decision making are substantially enhanced.

The Uruguay Round and GATT/WTO Dispute Settlement Procedures

One of the many achievements of the GATT, despite its "birth defects," has been the development of a reasonably sophisticated dispute settlement process. The original GATT treaty contained very little about dispute settlement, although it did specifically provide (in Articles XXII and XXIII) for consultation and then submission of issues to the contracting parties. As time went on, however, practice began to evolve toward a rule-oriented system. For example, in the late 1950s the practice was introduced of setting up panels of individuals to make determinations and findings and recommend them to the contracting parties. Before that, disputes had then been considered in much broader working parties comprising representatives of governments.

During the next several decades the contracting parties utilized the panel process more and more. Increasingly, the reports began to focus on more precise and concrete questions of violations of treaty obligations. At the end of the Tokyo Round in 1979, the contracting parties adopted an understanding on dispute settlement that embraced some of these concepts and formalized the practice concerning dispute settlement procedures that had developed.

In the 1980s dispute settlement panels were for the first time assisted by a legal section of the GATT. The panels' reports became much more precise and better reasoned. Many countries, including the United States (which has been the most frequent single applicant in dispute settlement procedures in the GATT), found it useful to take issues to panels as part of their broader approach to trade diplomacy.

However, as might be expected given the history of the GATT, a number of defects and problems remained. Some of these were gradually overcome through practice. But the Uruguay Round December 1993 draft presented a major new text concerning dispute settlement procedures, the "Understanding on Rules and Procedures Governing the Settlement of Disputes." The new text solves many, but not all, of the issues that have plagued the GATT dispute settlement system. It accomplishes the following:

- It establishes a unified dispute settlement system for all parts of the GATT/WTO system, including the new subjects of services and intellectual property. Thus, controversies over which procedure to use will not occur.

- It reaffirms the right of a complaining government to have a panel process initiated, preventing blocking at that stage.

- It ingeniously establishes a new appellate procedure that will substitute for some of the process of council approval of a panel report. Thus, a panel report will automatically be deemed adopted by the council unless it is appealed by one of the parties to the dispute. If appealed, the dispute will go to an appellate panel. After the appellate body has ruled, its report will go to the council, but in this case it will be deemed adopted unless there is a consensus *against* adoption, and presumably that negative consensus can be defeated by any major objector. Thus the presumption under previous procedures is reversed, with the ultimate result that the appellate report will come into force as a matter of international law in virtually every case.

The WTO as a Bretton Woods Partner

The combination of events and institutional developments of the last few years—the North American Free Trade Agreement (NAFTA), the evolution of the European Union toward deeper and broader integration, and the extraordinarily elaborate Uruguay Round results, as well as developments in China and Eastern Europe—probably amount to the most profound change in international economic relations institutions and structures since the origin of the Bretton Woods system itself. Inevitably, of course, this raises the question of the role of the new WTO in the "new Bretton Woods system," as a partner to the IMF and the World Bank.

It is therefore significant that for the first time we will have an explicit treaty-charter agreement establishing an international organization for trade, which can take its place beside the other Bretton Woods organizations. This may seem a mere formalism, but it can have importance in orienting public and official perceptions and understandings. It could have a healthy influence in increasing the prestige of the trade organization and treaty system, and clearly that is one of the hoped-for results. No longer will government officials or the press have to run through the slalom of legal obstacles that the previous system posed, with its provisional application and its convoluted multiple dispute settlement procedures, as well as the difficult web of treaties that applied. The new structure carries forward much of the complexity of the old, but the new WTO Charter should be considerably better understood by all. Furthermore, there are at least some indications in this structure of the need for the organization to pay attention to its public image. The success of an organization with such a potentially profound impact on economic affairs, touching many lives and national aspirations, requires giving some attention to how it is understood by public constituencies in different cultures and economic systems.

An important defect of the Bretton Woods system up to now, lacking the international trade organization that was part of its original design, was what many perceived as its lack of "coherence." This meant the lack of appropriate coordination and discussion between officials of national governments and international organizations who concentrated on monetary and lending questions, on the one hand, and those involved in the somewhat "messier" problems of trade in goods (involving many different interest groups and other political and economic forces), on the other. One of the purposes of the new WTO will clearly be to assist in providing this coherence, partly by establishing a high profile, understandability, and prestige for the WTO itself and for its own officials and those assigned by national governments to deal with it. If the new arrangements are managed appropriately, there should be a considerably greater interchange among the three Bretton Woods institutions, possibly through certain joint committees, or at least through greater attention to such issues as how trade matters affect balance of payments and other monetary questions and, vice versa, how monetary affairs, including exchange rate changes, can have great effects on trade policy.

Indeed, in recent years and even recent weeks a number of circumstances have poignantly demonstrated the importance of the connection between monetary and trade policy. The bilateral trade tensions between the United States and Japan and the ensuing dramatic exchange rate shifts are one such example. The desires and advantages of some of the newly privatizing or "marketizing" economies (Russia and other former Soviet republics, China, and others) also amply demonstrate this link, as economists and policymakers stress the need for floating exchange rates in order for trade relations to be successful.

Even the original GATT recognized the monetary-trade link in several of its articles. Countries that were Contracting Parties but not members of the IMF had an obligation under the GATT to enter into some sort of monetary framework agreement. Likewise, the GATT included provisions for trade measures linked to balance of payment difficulties.

A number of issues that are left over for future work will have important implications for the work of the World Bank and possibly the Fund. For example, antidumping and subsidy rules have often been contentious. Apparently recommendations have occasionally been made to developing countries to use these rules in a way that would seem less than optimal. It is hoped that the new institutional structure will create an environment of better coordination and mutual understanding between trade specialists and monetary specialists.

Likewise agriculture and food policy deserve much more attention, as do policies relating to commodities and commodity agreements. All of these can be substantially affected by monetary movements, particularly in some smaller countries.

Dispute resolution procedures are an important attribute of an international treaty regime. Indeed they are looked upon as essential to implementing treaty obligations in a manner that gives them the credibility they need to operate successfully in international economic relations. It is inevitable that some monetary issues will find their way into some disputes resolved through these procedures.

Other monetary and financial links to trade policy include:

- the effects of exchange rate shifts on trade rules regarding financial services;

- methods of financial adjustment costs caused by liberalizing new trade rules;

- questions about whether and when trade barriers and other distorting measures (such as subsidies) affect exchange rates or inhibit the ability of the monetary system to adjust;

- the question of the responsibility of a balance of payments global surplus country to contribute to "rebalancing";

- the question of the use of trade measures to offset balance of payments difficulties;

- calculations of antidumping margins and subsidy impacts in the context of exchange rate shifts;

- effects of debt on trade and monetary imbalances (and vice versa).

Regulating International Economic Behavior: Future Directions of the WTO System

The Interface Problem

Many rules of the trading system attempt to minimize government measures that interfere with or distort free markets. The GATT, of course, was largely based upon free market principles. It is not surprising, therefore, that it is often difficult to apply the GATT's trading rules to nonmarket economies. But even among the Western industrial market economies, despite their similarities, there are wide differences in the degree of government involvement in the economy and in the forms of regulation or ownership of various industrial and other economic segments. As world economic interdependence has increased, it has become more difficult to manage relationships among economies where such differences are encountered. The problem is analogous to the difficulties involved in trying to get two computers of different designs to work together. Just as one needs some kind of interface mechanism to allow computers to exchange data, so in international economic relations, and particularly in trade relations, some interface mechanism may be necessary to allow different economic systems to trade with each other harmoniously.

For example, part of the definition of dumping is selling for export at below-cost prices. But in nonmarket economies are there meaningful costs and prices? In the case of subsidies, it may be easy to identify cash payments to an exporter, but myriad other government policies also affect the competitiveness of a business. If the goal is really to achieve a level playing field, does that imply that all governments must adopt uniform policies? If not, how will it be possible to analyze the effect of different policies? Besides, isn't trade to some degree based precisely on the *differences* between countries? As the subject of "unfair" practices develops, however, it becomes clear that it reaches deeply into matters of domestic concern to governments, so that questions of unfairness become more controversial. For example, governments that grant subsidies typically feel that they are an essential and praiseworthy tool, useful in correcting income disparities or in helping disadvantaged groups or regions. It is argued that dumping, although a form of price discrimination, actually has beneficial effects on world and national prosperity, encouraging competition. The rules for responding to some unfair trade practices allow the use of import restrictions such as added duties (and, in dumping and countervailing duty cases, even quantitative restrictions), which can be anticompetitive and detrimental to world welfare. The exporting nations that are the targets of these actions feel bitterness toward these restrictions on their trade, and they argue that the rules on unfair trade are being manipulated by special interests for effectively protectionist reasons.

The interface problem and the difficulties of defining what is or is not unfair may arise in the context of two economies that differ only slightly in their acceptance of basic free market economic principles. Even in such cases, differences in the ways the two economies operate over the course of a business cycle may create situations that one or the other considers unfair, even though these differences may not have resulted from any consciously unfair policies or practices. For example, differences in debt-equity ratios between corporations in the two countries have an effect on marginal cost, which can affect incentives to produce, especially during an economic downturn. Likewise, differences regarding worker "tenure"— that is, the degree to which employment is regarded as "permanent," and thus the degree to which labor is a fixed cost—can affect the marginal cost calculation. (Firms generally have an incentive to sell at any price that exceeds short-term variable costs, since fixed costs have to be paid anyway. This can induce pricing "below average cost".)

This discussion is only illustrative of a much broader application of the interface concept. Many other cross-country differences in economic structure can have a variety of consequences that cause trade tensions and thus suggest a need for interface mechanisms. These can include:

- differences in banking and monetary institutions (e.g., the degree of independence of the central bank);
- differences in the structure of retail sales markets;
- differences in views, laws, and institutions relating to competition and antitrust policies.

There are no easy answers to these problems. Indeed, they are much more complicated than even the foregoing discussion indicates. For example, whatever general rules may exist, it is argued that special considerations should apply to developing countries. In addition, it must be recognized that economic structural characteristics vary from sector to sector within a country, and that advantages that tilt one way for one sector might tilt in the opposite direction for another sector. Furthermore, these differences may alter across time, and the direction of the tilt might reverse.

Market and Government "Failure" in an Interdependent World

"Economic interdependence" is a term commonly used today to describe the developing conditions of international economic relations. Manifestations of the galloping pace of new economic linkages are everywhere: enterprises must cope with competition and developments from abroad; national governments find it increasingly difficult to regulate their economies; democratic political leaders find it hard to fulfill election promises and to satisfy constituencies because of forces beyond their control; resentment against foreign competition and influences stirs the electorate and could even endanger democratic governments.

Since the 1940s world economic relations have been guided but not governed by a set of institutions nobly put in place by visionary leaders during the years immediately after World War II: the Bretton Woods system (the IMF, the World Bank, and the GATT), the United Nations complex of organizations and agencies, the Organization for Economic Cooperation and Development, and others. Since then many thousands of treaty instruments and organizations have been designed for commodity regulation, transport regulation, taxation, and many other subjects. The 1948 draft ITO charter failed, but the GATT uneasily took its place. A number of regional trade arrangements have also developed. Yet the operation of this system has not kept pace with actual economic changes.

As the decades passed, leaders discovered that trends were hard to control without important multilateral coordination, whether informal (such as in the G-7) or formal (through the web of bilateral, regional, and multilateral treaties). The seventh major GATT trade negotiation—the Tokyo Round of the 1970s—was an ambitious effort to develop more rules for the trading system, and the eighth—the Uruguay Round—has been an even more ambitious attempt to enlarge and improve the system, so that complex and multilayered new subjects such as trade in services and trade-related intellectual property will be covered.

Various suggestions for priority attention after the Uruguay Round have already been made, with environment and trade concerns often topping the list, and competition policy not far behind. These subjects in particular have been perplexing informed participants in the world economic system. Although intense exploration of the relationship between environmental protection policies and trade rules and policies is relatively new, already within the last few years this exploration has led down intricate paths with many twists and turns. These issues are intertwined with many issues of government, such as:

- questions of rule making at the international level, and whether such rules adequately consider some of the scientific and moral concerns involved in the subjects that are now being linked to trade;

- questions of international dispute settlement procedures and to what extent they adequately consider opposing policy goals, or provide for appropriate advocacy from interested authorities and citizen groups;

- questions of whether international procedures adequately incorporate democratic processes, including transparency and the right to be heard;

- the relation of international rules to domestic constitutional and other laws;

- the operation and procedures of national constitutional bodies and how these promote or inhibit international cooperation;

- the activity of interest groups, both those with broad concerns and those more oriented to specific interests or single issues, and how this activity relates to international institutions and procedures.

The WTO Agenda after the Uruguay Round

Although it is environmental issues that have suddenly pushed the frontiers of thinking about these various problems (and others), this thinking can be viewed as a forerunner of comparable activity concerning a number of different "regulatory issues," including:

- competition policy

- labor standards

- commodity agreements and regulation

- product standards (food, pharmaceuticals, product safety, etc.)

- insurance

- banking and fiduciary institutions

- investment protection

- securities regulation and institutions

- government procurement procedures and preferences

- shipping and transport (including air transport)

- intellectual property protection and regulation

- taxation

Many of the regulatory "interdependence" questions faced in these various and seemingly disparate subjects are similar. Among these questions are, for example:

- problems of regulatory competition, in which governments lower their standards of regulation in order to attract economic activity within their borders (sometimes called the "race to the bottom" or, in the United States, the "Delaware corporation" problem, alluding to the legal headquartering of many corporations in that state);

- procedural requirements, "due process," avoiding abuse of power and process, and, as previously mentioned, democratic principles including transparency;

- questions of subsidiarity, or the appropriate allocation of regulatory powers among national government bodies, subnational bodies, and international bodies (to some extent the currently criticized concept of "sovereignty" relates to these questions);

- how to manage the transnational problems and tensions that arise in the context of these different regulatory goals and procedures; various ideas include harmonization, reciprocity, the use of interface mechanisms, cooperation agreements (at least for procedure), and extraterritorial unilateral measures.

Fundamental differences among societies and governmental structures obviously affect some if not all of these questions. For example, when a society's economy is organized according to market principles, many of these questions, particularly as to competition policy, will be answered differently than in a nonmarket economy.

Likewise, the governmental and institutional structures of a society, such as the degree to which a government is democratic, the amount of protection of human rights, the amount of social cohesion within the society, the degree of corruption in the government or in nongovernmental structures, and the presence or absence of hierarchies and elites in the society, all relate to these various questions. These differences among societies make it very difficult to achieve the degree of international cooperation and coordination of economic regulation that would otherwise be possible and that is increasingly essential in the face of interdependence. The advocacy of the environmentalist movement during the debate over the NAFTA with respect to the efforts at coordination represented in the NAFTA draft agreement are a particularly interesting example of these problems. The NAFTA also demonstrates how deep into national sovereignty some international regulatory treaty clauses will go.

Various theories and models of economics can help us in understanding these problems. Obviously, the doctrines of comparative advantage are relevant. So also is the "prisoner's dilemma," which suggests the need often for cooperation among actors (governments or otherwise). Public choice theory, a subject of increasing attention, sheds interesting light on how governments actually go about regulating the economy.

Various Responses

Clearly there are a number of different ways to approach the issue. We can group them roughly under the following headings: unilateral, bilateral, regional, and multilateral. Running through all of these levels are several general questions, such as the following:

- Should cooperative approaches be basically voluntary, or should they be binding under international law? If binding, should there be sanctions for violations?

- Should the emphasis on cooperation be procedural, or should it relate more substantively to the rules being applied?

- With respect to substantive rules, should the approach be that of national treatment (nondiscrimination between domestic and imported goods) or most-favored nation (nondiscrimination among imported goods and exporting countries), or should there be some sort of minimum standards as the basis of a rule to apply?

Unilateral Approaches

One response to the problem has been for a nation (such as the United States) to attempt to apply its own policy rules and principles to private or governmental actors operating outside its borders. Such "extraterritorial reach" has occurred in the application of US antitrust law to foreign-based cartels and other types of collusion, in certain US environmental statutes (such as the well-known recent case of the tuna embargo), and in such statutes as Section 301 of the US trade laws. There is no question that some of these unilateral US actions have been effective. There is also no question that many of these unilateral actions have evoked great criticism from trading partners, and in some cases retaliation (for example, in the form of "clawback statutes" designed to negate treble or other damages awarded in antitrust cases, and in the form of retaliatory trade actions). The degree to which such unilateral action will continue to be successful is a matter of debate, as is the extent to which it is appropriate for a large power like the United States to take such action. The answers are seldom a simple yes or no, but rather somewhere in between.

Bilateral Approaches

Sometimes two countries or groups of countries enter into bilateral agreements such as the US-EC Cooperation Agreement on antitrust matters. It appears that so far most of these agreements have been procedural in nature.

Another bilateral approach is that of the US-Japan Structural Impediments Initiative, which consisted of in-depth discussions (with much focus on competition policies) about societal structures that impede trade. Likewise, a plethora of other bilateral discussions and pressures have been tried in the US-Japan relationship.

Regional Approaches

A slightly broader approach is to act through regional agreements. Clearly the treaty rules of the European Union go very far indeed in trying to harmonize and rationalize policy within that group of countries. Certain bilateral or trilateral free trade agreements such as the US-Canada Free Trade Agreement and the NAFTA have some similar measures.

Regional approaches can constructively contribute to international economic relations by allowing smaller groupings of economies to establish deeper cooperation than that likely to gain broad multilateral agreement among over a hundred nations. Regional approaches can also be used to tailor rules more specifically to regional needs, and they can provide a bench test for experimentation that might influence later multilateral efforts at cooperation. For example, the relatively deep cooperation and harmonization of hundreds of economic problems within the European Union is a rich lode of experience that can often be instructive for broader multilateral negotiations.

The danger, of course, is that of developing tensions between regional blocs. Another problem is that important trading relationships (like the US-Japan or the Canada-Japan relationship) are often not embraced within an adequate regional treaty framework, while less important ones are. Therefore it is important that a credible and effective multilateral mediator, able to apply multilateral rules, be available to inhibit dangerous temptations in regional blocs.

Multilateral Approaches

Over the decades since World War II there have been a number of multilateral efforts to develop some harmonization or cooperative rules for various regulatory policies. In particular the Organization for Economic Cooperation and Development, the United Nations, and UN Conference on Trade and Development have worked on a variety of proposals and voluntary rule guidelines, particularly concerning competition policy. Finally of course, the GATT with its uneasy origins, and now the WTO, must be considered an important alternative or (more likely) complementary approach.

Conclusions

The subject we are addressing is part of a vastly broader question of how governments can regulate economic behavior that crosses borders in the interdependent world economy that we face now and in the future. A series of perplexing institutional questions, as well as other policy questions, are part of this general subject. Approaches can be considered in different groupings, such as unilateral actions, bilateral activity, and regional and multilateral activity and institutions. The new WTO Charter and dispute settlement procedures offer an important step forward for the multilateral institutions related to international economic matters. Certainly, these institutions should be part of an overall framework for trying to address the questions of trade frictions, interface, and market failure, and for some international relationships they should be the principal part. Whether the multilateral system can successfully serve as the principal vehicle for dealing with these problems, however, remains at issue. A certain degree of evolution and experimentation seems inevitable, suggesting a need for empirical study and pragmatic approaches to the many policy issues involved, while continuing to advance the notion of a rule-oriented system as central to the needed interface mechanism.

References

The reader may find it useful to consult some of the following works by this author.

Jackson, John H. 1967. "The General Agreement on Tariffs and Trade in United States Domestic Law." *Michigan Law Review* 66: 249.

Jackson, John H. 1969. *World Trade and the Law of GATT: A Legal Analysis of the General Agreement on Tariffs and Trade.* Charlottesville, VA: Bobbs Merrill.

Jackson, John H. 1986. *Legal Problems of International Economic Relations.* 2nd ed. St. Paul, MN: West Publishing.

Jackson, John H. 1987. "United States of America." In Francis G. Jacobs and Shelley Roberts, *The Effect of Treaties in Domestic Law.* London: Sweet & Maxwell (7 U.K. Comp. L. Series 141).

Jackson, John H. 1989. *The World Trading System: Law and Policy of International Economic Relations.* Cambridge, MA: MIT Press.

Jackson, John H. 1990. *Restructuring the GATT System.* London: Royal Institute for International Affairs.

Jackson, John H. 1992. "Status of Treaties in Domestic Legal Systems: A Policy Analysis." *American Journal of International Law* 86: 310.

Jackson, John H. 1992. "World Trade Rules and Environmental Policies: Congruence or Conflict?" *Washington & Lee Law Review* 49: 1227.

Jackson, John H. 1993. "Regional Trade Blocs and GATT." *World Economy* 16: 121.

Jackson, John H. 1994. "Alternative Approaches for Implementing Competition Rules in International Economic Relations." *Aussenwirtschaft—Swiss Review of International Economic Relations* no. 2/94 (forthcoming).

Jackson, John H. 1994. Testimony prepared for a US Senate Committee on Foreign Relations hearing on "The World Trade Organization and U.S. Sovereignty" (14 June).

Jackson, John H. 1994. Testimony prepared for a US Senate Finance Committee hearing on "Uruguay Round Legislation" (23 March).

Jackson, John H. 1994. "The Uruguay Round Results—Strengthening Cooperative Mechanisms for an Interdependent World." *Common Market Law Review* (forthcoming).

Comment

ALAN WM. WOLFF

The Uruguay Round agreement began to become a reality just four days before this conference. The negotiators in Geneva thought that they had something real in hand when they wrapped up in Geneva on 15 December, or when the Final Act was signed in Marrakesh on 15 April. But in fact it was only when the trade subcommittee of the House Ways and Means Committee began its nonmarkup markup—that odd, Alice-in-Wonderland process that the US government has twisted itself into for consideration of trade agreements nowadays—that one could say that the words began to become reality for the United States.

The tenor of discussion on Capitol Hill is rather curious, because there are no strong opponents to the Uruguay Round; to my knowledge, no one of any significance—no industry, union, or sector—is flatly opposed to this set of agreements. The textile industry is in fact not opposing the agreement, and even though the International Ladies Garment Workers, the Amalgamated Clothing and Textile Workers, and the AFL-CIO are not happy with the outcome of the round, and indeed are critical of it, they are not working on the Hill to oppose it.

On the other hand, neither is anyone thrilled with the outcome of the Uruguay Round. To be sure, there is a group of boosters who are working for its passage, but they do so without a sense that it is vitally important to their own commercial interests. Rather they are for it because they believe, as American business believes, that the world will be a better place if the

Alan Wm. Wolff is managing partner of the Washington office of the law firm of Dewey Ballantine. He was formerly (1977–79) deputy US special representative for trade negotiations.

Uruguay Round agreements go into effect—they have bought into Fred Bergsten's bicycle theory, that continued progress in trade liberalization is needed just to keep existing arrangements from keeling over.

So where does the controversy arise? In fact it arises in three areas that are not directly related to the substance of most of the sectoral issues. One of these, as John Jackson mentioned and to which I will return, is sovereignty. Another concern is budgetary, as some in this country are wondering where we will find the money to replace the tariff revenues that we stand to lose under the agreement. It is one of the strengths of past reciprocal trade agreements that tariff cutting was never considered a budget issue until this year. But now it is a budget issue, and it will not be an easy one: the US government will have to come up with $14 billion over five years, or $40 billion over ten years, or else pass a congressional waiver—and that requires 60 senators.

Authority to undertake future negotiations will be an issue. There is interest in reaching agreement on matters concerning labor, the environment, and human rights. In this context, the establishment of a World Trade Organization (WTO) is clearly a major achievement, at least potentially. I strongly agree with John Jackson that we needed formality. Those of us who are either children or grandchildren of Bretton Woods wanted to see the trade element of the international economic system become formal, and it is becoming formal. Beyond the emotional satisfaction one draws from that fact, it is a substantive benefit that most of the countries now signing up for membership will have to choose the *prix fixe* menu rather than order à la carte.

On the matter of sovereignty: one always loses some sovereignty in any international agreement. That's the nature of the process. But the amount of sovereignty that the participating countries lose in the Uruguay Round agreement is not unacceptable, and I think that those who are posing this argument will be overcome.

The Dunkel draft that was the starting point of negotiations in December had some unacceptable provisions in it, as Jackson has pointed out. Allowing the substantive rules of a charter to be amended by majority vote would not have been acceptable if the results had been binding on individual members. The absence of a standard of review was very important for the dispute settlement process, and such a standard has been added. Thus, the key issues that would have aroused fatal opposition to the agreement have been successfully addressed.

There are in my view five concerns with the WTO. The first involves dispute settlement. On this I disagree somewhat with what John Jackson has said. What was done in dispute settlement is what I would have done if I had continued in government. The United States was trying to put into place automatic procedures to allow it to pull away the foundations of the European Union's Common Agricultural Policy. We had lost several cases in this area, or rather we had won them but failed to get the judgments implemented. The United States attributed that failure to the defects in the litigative system. But in my view our problem did not lie with a defective litigative system; our goals could only be achieved through negotiation. Perhaps I see it that way because over the years I have tended to approach these issues less as a lawyer and more as a negotiator. Nevertheless, whether dispute settlement works is going to be the litmus test of whether the WTO is seen as a success or a failure.

What are the problem areas? There are fewer substantive rules than one would like. The area of private restraints of trade and anticompetitive practices is not covered by the GATT. The "peace clause" in agriculture and the phase-ins of developing country obligations are going to cause difficulties. There is the lack of a doctrine of judicial restraint. In our judicial system, courts have a reason not to go beyond their authority. They have a long tradition of judicial restraint, and there is a series of checks and balances built in. What are the checks and balances in the GATT/WTO system? An activist secretariat—and there have been examples of panel cases that have gone in a direction more of legislation than of adjudication—can expand countries' obligations. That could discredit the system. The environmentalists have made much of the lack of transparency. It does tend to discredit the system when some people can go into a room and come back out a while later with an answer, and one cannot tell what questions were raised and what arguments were made.

A second issue is the inadequacy of support for litigation. Gary Hufbauer argued this from a US point of view, but it applies to the European Commission as well. Both the US government and the European Commission have limited resources to dedicate to support of the international litigation system, and this could cause the system to be discredited quickly. There are several possible solutions. Increasing the staff is an obvious one; others might be private participation in the panel process, greater transparency, an independent institutionalized review of whether the panel process is working, and congressional approval of changes in law and settled practice.

Beyond dispute settlement, there are several things that the WTO does not cover. It is in the nature of international agreements that they are never adequate. For every new issue that is covered, there is always something else just as important that is not. The major uncovered area that I see looming is private restraints of trade. There are many areas in which these occur; for example, Canada and Japan do not trade in steel products. It is one of those little oddities in international trade. The Canadians have shipped steel to Japan twice in the last decade or so. Once they apologized because it was an error, and the second time it was a diverted shipment. It is not that there is a government quota—it just is one of those things one comes across that will someday have to be addressed.

Industrial targeting, or industrial policy, is clearly going to be an issue. There are others: labor, the environment, human rights, the unfinished business of financial services, investment, the accession of China and Russia. The trade specialist would like to hope that some of these issues really will not be allowed to intrude, but in fact, since America will not bend in its moral values, as Henry Kissinger discovered and has now enshrined in his book *Diplomacy*, they are going to be a feature of the trade scene, and they are not going to leave.

A third area, and perhaps the one on which my views will find the least agreement around this table, is the loss of US unilateralism. I think US unilateralism has been a wonderful thing. The *Financial Times* has not yet come out strongly in favor of it, but there's always hope. Beginning in 1971 with President Nixon's import surcharge and the negotiations that followed, which led to the Tokyo Round in 1985, and continuing with Reagan's unilateralism in the guise of section 301, which led to the Uruguay Round, the United States has been the foremost driving force for trade liberalization just by threatening to act unilaterally. Others don't like it, but it brings them to the table. We need it for market-opening pressure.

My fourth concern involves what John Jackson called the interface mechanism. Jackson mentioned this in this paper; countervailing duties and other interface mechanisms have just been weakened because of "green-lighting"—we can get into that later. This means that there are permitted subsidies if one gives them the right name—a horrible concept. Antidumping is a major and very important interface mechanism, and it has been weakened. When there are closed economies, there will be dumping. Jackson argues that some of the practices that are labeled as dumping may not have had that intent. But the motive, in my view, is wholly irrelevant—it's the effect that counts. It is not the unfairness that one should be concerned about; it is the trade distortion, the inefficient allocation of resources and the unacceptable consequences of that misallocation in our own market.

Finally, my fifth concern is with the clause in the WTO agreement that states that "each member shall ensure the conformity of its laws, regulations, and administrative procedures with its obligations in the annex agreements." This clause is a sleeper. Some people in Washington or Brussels or Tokyo or elsewhere may wake up and discover that they have to do a lot more thinking about the rules and regulations they adopt. They will find there are many matters formerly considered wholly domestic that must now be looked upon with an eye to the views of officials in foreign capitals and international civil servants in Geneva.

In conclusion, the success of the WTO is not a foregone conclusion. It will take an enormous amount of effort. I don't think any government has thought very deeply about how it is going to make this institution work, and work successfully. The expectations are in fact very high, and it will take a lot of careful thinking by people like John Jackson to make the WTO a success.

Comment

KENNETH A. OYE

As John Jackson has observed, the World Trade Organization and the GATT 1994 will strengthen multilateral trade law. The Uruguay Round agreement reduces tariffs, limits voluntary export restraints and orderly marketing agreements, and limits reliance on countervailing duties in dumping cases. It sets forth frameworks on agriculture, services, and intellectual property rights. It legitimates discussions of the relationship between trade and environmental and labor standards. Most significant, it strengthens the rule of law in trade by establishing binding dispute resolution procedures.

But the legally oriented, rules-based approach to trade relations embodied by the new GATT may have opportunity costs. Adherence to formal nondiscriminatory rules precludes reliance on ad hoc bilateral and regional bargaining. The stronger dispute resolution mechanisms at the heart of the new GATT may limit recourse to the forms of trade pressure that opened markets during the 1980s and 1990s.

In recent years bilateral, regional, and multilateral approaches to trade liberalization have been quite complementary. To modify a favorite metaphor, the multilateral trade bicycle has moved forward, propelled by the pumping of discriminatory bilateral and regional legs. We may now, however, be entering a period where these approaches may be increasingly in tension with each other. Ironically, the crowning achievement of the new GATT, the mandatory dispute resolution mechanism, may

Kenneth A. Oye is director of the Center for International Studies at the Massachusetts Institute of Technology.

weaken the discriminatory legs that have been responsible for much recent movement toward liberalization.

Past Discriminatory Liberalization?

Over the last decade, bilateral and regional negotiations have been stepping stones rather than stopping points for trade liberalization. By bartering preferential market access for preferential market access, countries reduced barriers to trade, albeit on bilateral and regional terms. The market-oriented, sector-specific (MOSS) talks and the Structural Impediments Initiative eased direct and indirect barriers to trade between the United States and Japan. Section 301 and Title VII actions poked and prodded Japan, Korea, Taiwan, and some Latin American countries toward liberalization. The European single market initiative, the Canadian-American bilateral free trade agreement, and its successor the North American Free Trade Agreement substantially reduced barriers to trade among contracting parties without substantially raising barriers against others.

Consider how the discriminatory exchange of market access for market access can promote liberalization. By offsetting domestic biases toward protection and other forms of regulation, discriminatory international bargaining strategies have served as a force for economic liberalization.

In the absence of external pressure, domestic equilibrium outcomes tend to be biased toward protection. Sector-specific protection provides concentrated economic rents for import-competing industries. By contrast, the costs of protection to export-oriented groups and consumers are relatively diffuse. From the perspective of an exporter, any specific import-restricting measure may invite retaliation, slice into the export earnings of potential customers abroad, and raise the price of exports abroad by strengthening the national currency. But these costs tend to be distributed across many exporters. From the perspective of a consumer, any specific import-restricting measure will raise prices slightly, but these costs, too, are widely spread. As a consequence, import-competing groups have a clear and concentrated interest in lobbying for protection, while export-oriented groups and consumers have a more diffuse interest in lobbying against it.

International discriminatory bargaining strategies can partly offset domestic biases toward protection by broadening antiprotectionist coalitions. When nations barter market access for market access on a sector-by-sector basis, export-oriented firms develop a material and tangible interest in lobbying against protection. In fact, nations rely on bilateral and regional bargaining strategies in order to mobilize export-oriented groups and firms within their negotiating partners.

In my study of trade in the 1930s and the 1980s (Oye 1993), I found that economic discrimination often yielded liberalizing outcomes by mobilizing export-oriented interests in the battle against protection. Even during the 1930s, the spread of bilateral commercial policy throughout the British Empire, continental Europe, and Latin America inadvertently drove a wedge between export-oriented and import-competing sectors in the United States. As a result, an unconditionally protectionist American policy gave way to a policy of reciprocity. In the late 1970s and the mid-1980s, Indonesia enlisted British engineering firms and China used American farmers to influence the size of textile quotas. During the 1980s, tacit American bilateralism helped enlist export-oriented firms in Japan in the battle against Japanese agricultural protection. Time after time, external economic discrimination has helped enlist the formerly disinterested in antiprotectionist coalitions.

These findings on the effectiveness of bilateralism in the past are consistent with a study by the Institute for International Economics on Section 301 actions, the most controversial of American experiments in explicitly discriminatory bilateral approaches to managing market access. Thomas Bayard and Kimberly Elliott (1992) found that bilateral market-opening measures were reasonably successful. They examined all 89 applications of Section 301 between 1975 and 1992 and found that 36 cases had succeeded, 31 had failed, and 22 were incomplete or indeterminate. The US Trade Representative has been more aggressive against Japan than against the Europeans, with Japan the most frequent target of complaints initiated by the agency itself. And the success rate varied markedly across targets. Bayard and Elliott found success rates of 75 percent against Japan, 40 percent against the European Community, and 82 percent against Korea and Taiwan. Section 301 cases were more effective against target countries that were highly dependent on trade with the United States than against targets that were not. Finally, Section 301 cases were far more effective when directed against border measures than when they were directed against other trade practices.

During the spring of 1994, bilateral bargaining helped open Japanese markets. After the United States and Japan failed to reach agreement on implementation of the Framework Agreement, a series of American threats was followed by a series of Japanese market-opening measures. In late February and early March, the Clinton administration threatened to impose sanctions to punish Japan for violating the 1989 telecommunications agreement. In mid-March, the Nippon Idou Tsushin Corporation (IDO) agreed to open 159 new base stations for Motorola cellular phones. The official US response to these developments was jubilant. President Clinton declared that "this is a big win for everyone." Trade Representative Mickey Kantor called the telecommunications deal a "first step forward" on the broader agenda, since in it Japan accepted indicators of progress that it has resisted in other forums. US Ambassador to Japan Walter F. Mondale said, "I think there is a roadmap here that's helped," and declared that the cellular telephone agreement demonstrated the value of getting the government involved in prodding the private sector to cooperate in opening markets. That same month, the Japanese government and Japanese corporations took further liberalizing steps. Vice Minister of Transport Mukaiyama granted "type designation approval" for imports of Jeep Cherokees, and the Toyota Corporation announced it would increase its purchases of imported automobile parts.

In addition to promoting openness directly, discriminatory bargaining may have also served as a midwife and model for the GATT. By the end of 1993, the bilaterals, the NAFTA, and the Asia Pacific Economic Cooperation forum after its November meeting in Seattle had created plausible alternatives to the GATT. As one European trade negotiator observed, the existence of such an alternative helped break the Franco-German-American deadlock that had blocked agreement on the Uruguay Round. Many innovative features of bilateral and regional agreements were incorporated into the GATT 1994 and the WTO. Provisions for liberalization of services and for protection of intellectual property rights are found in both the NAFTA and the GATT 1994. Furthermore, the bilateral dispute resolution mechanism in the Canada-US trade agreement was a model for the NAFTA and for GATT 94. In retrospect, the bilateral and regional initiatives of the past decade strengthened the multilateral GATT initiative.

Future Nondiscriminatory Defense of the Status Quo?

As John Jackson suggested in his remarks, the immediate effect of the Uruguay Round will be to strengthen the rule of law in world trade. More precisely, the substantive liberalizing provisions of the new GATT will now be interpreted through mandatory dispute resolution procedures. But this may be only part of the story. Over the long term, the WTO and the GATT 1994 may maintain the status quo at the expense of reducing but not eliminating pressure for further liberalization.

There is a tension between, on the one hand, reliance on nondiscriminatory multilateral trade laws as codified and exemplified by the GATT 1994 and the WTO, and on the other, reliance on discriminatory bilateral and regional bargaining strategies of the sort discussed above. I would argue that this tension should be resolved decisively in favor of the rule of law if the GATT 1994 had adequately addressed critical substantive trade issues. But in the rush to complete the agreement by the end of 1993, negotiators stepped around many important but contentious issues. The new GATT defines "binding," "mandatory," and "multilateral" frameworks on services, agriculture, and intellectual property rights. But these frameworks have yet to be filled out. There is much hard work to be done because the hard issues were deferred. For example, Jackson characterized the agricultural section as meager, albeit important, start. Provisions for trade in services and for intellectual property rights are more fully developed than provisions for agriculture, but even these frameworks are not final agreements. The GATT also considers an important set of emerging issues, namely, the controversial connections among environment, labor standards, and trade. But it does so in a nonbinding "optional," "plurilateral" Annex 4. And the new GATT does not adequately address domestic regulatory harmonization and competition policy, the issues that have been so much in contention in bilateral and regional discussions. Yet without recourse to bilateral means, it seems unlikely that endogenous biases toward maintaining protectionist regulations can be overcome.

The Dispute Settlement Understanding requires members to use the dispute settlement mechanism when they seek redress of a violation of one of the agreements or nullification or impairment of the benefits of the agreements. The automatic nature of the new procedures will vastly improve the enforcement of the substantive provisions in each of the agreements. No country will be able to block the adoption of panel reports. Members will be required to implement obligations promptly or be subject to retaliation.

Will the United States have to change the way it does business in trade negotiations because of the new dispute settlement procedures? There is disagreement on this point. In private discussions, Japanese trade officials have suggested that Japan could use the new mandatory dispute settlement procedures to counter US invocation of Section 301 and US imposition of countervailing duties. They maintain that the agreement clearly provides Japan with the substantive grounds and procedures to outlaw these American practices. But this leaves open the question of whether it would be wise for Japan to utilize mandatory dispute settlement procedures against American countervailing duties or Section 301 measures.

Not surprisingly, the Japanese view is not consistent with interpretations by officials of the US government. According to the International Trade Administration:

> The only required changes to Section 301 concern minor adjustment of time frames for special 301 (intellectual property rights) and subsidies investigations. The U.S. will continue to be able to use Section 301 to enforce our rights. Section 301 also will be available for actions not covered by Uruguay Round disciplines. (US Department of Commerce 1994)

The rub here is that the United States does not appear to be free to threaten to reduce terms of access in areas treated by the new GATT to achieve greater market access in areas that are *not* covered by the new GATT. And this has been American practice in the past.

The crucial support for the GATT tendered by House Majority Leader Richard A. Gephardt (D-MO) and other NAFTA opponents rests on their interpretations of these issues. It is unclear at this time whether implementing legislation will be consistent with the GATT. On 15 April Gephardt hailed the signing of the Uruguay Round agreement, but he warned that the United States must take steps to "retain the basic framework of U.S. trade law." He explained:

> That means ensuring that we write the implementing bill to ensure that our dumping and countervailing duty laws enforce our rights and allow us to fight predatory trading practices. It means that we must ensure that our [Section] 301 law . . . really works.

Gephardt said that the United States must not allow other countries to compete in global trade by "degrading" the environment or limiting worker standards. He also said that Japan "got a free ride" in many ways because many of its market barriers will not be removed under the agreement.

If resistance to the GATT builds, then ambivalent supporters will be able to gut the GATT through the implementing bill while adhering to their commitments to support ratification. Disagreements over the interpretation of GATT 1994 and the WTO are unlikely to block American ratification. However, interpretative ambiguities may well be "resolved" in the American context through the insertion of clarifying language in implementing legislation. These interpretive ambiguities are ultimately likely to be resolved in the international context through the decisions of panels that will be convened to wade through precisely these points as part of the newly established dispute resolution process.

Conclusions and a Caveat

Should the GATT 1994 and the WTO emerge from the Congress unscathed, what are the prospects for further trade liberalization? The Uruguay Round agreement is likely to reduce but not eliminate pressure for further liberalization. Neither nondiscriminatory multilateral rules nor bilateral bargaining, taken independently, are the most powerful forces for liberalization and deregulation. Over the long term, the diffusion of ideas, the impact of market-driven shifts in exchange rates, and fundamental concerns over productivity and growth are more consequential sources of pressure for reducing protection and easing regulations. For example, the ideal of liberalization, the bitter costs of yen appreciation, and the desire to cut the costs of intermediate products for Japanese firms were what drove the June 1994 report of the Japanese prime minister's task force on eliminating regulations and anticompetitive practices responsible for the gap between international and domestic Japanese prices. But in these areas, as in early discussions of protection, endogenous biases toward stasis can be strong. Even in an era of dispute resolution under law and generalized sentiment for indirect protection through regulation, there may still be a significant role for the old-fashioned politics of preference. Discriminatory threats, crass and irritating though they may be, may be needed to create concentrated interests in the struggle against regulation as well as protection.

References

Bayard, Thomas O., and Kimberly Ann Elliott. 1992. " 'Aggressive Unilateralism' and Section 301: Market opening or Market closing?" *World Economy* 15, no. 6 (November).

Oye, Kenneth A. 1993. *Economic Discrimination and Political Exchange: World Political Economy in the 1930s and 1980s*. Princeton, NJ: Princeton University Press.

US Department of Commerce, International Trade Administration. 1994. "Dispute Settlement Understanding" (11 January).

Comment

MARTIN WOLF

John Jackson has provided a typically lucid and erudite account of the Uruguay Round in general and the World Trade Organization (WTO) in particular. It would be both foolish and redundant to add my mite to his discussion of these topics. What I have to say is instead largely complementary to Jackson's paper, although it covers some of the same ground as his penultimate section, on issues to be dealt with in the future.

The present discussion considers five questions:

- where the world should be going;
- why it will prove difficult to stay the course;
- where the world is already;
- what the next steps should be;
- what big questions must be addressed.

Where the World Should Be Going

The end of the Cold War and the triumph of the market paradigm create a unique opportunity to integrate the entire world economy, via the market. This is also a desirable objective, conducive to increased prosperity throughout the world.

Martin Wolf is associate editor and chief economics leader writer at the Financial Times *of London.*

In suggesting this I am relying on certain fundamental propositions about the nature of international economic relations, namely, that:

- In trade the prosperity of others enhances one's own—this is a win-win game.
- The gain from trade is imports, with exports the cost of acquiring those imports.
- The principal gain from trade liberalization is the opening of one's own market, not those of others.

These are the abiding principles of international trade theory. They are, of course, controversial, not merely among self-proclaimed "practical people" but even among professional economists. But they seem to me well-founded, both in theory and practice. They do, of course, also have implications for what trade policy is all about. It is not about reconciling fundamental conflicts of interest among rationally self-seeking states. It is more about dissuading states from actions that hurt their own citizens more than they hurt others. The aim of international trade policy is, therefore, to help states act in their own individual interest, thereby also acting in the interest of all.

Today's world makes it possible to envisage worldwide application of these liberal principles. That is the opportunity that was partly seized in the completion of the Uruguay Round. This success needs to be built upon in the years ahead.

Why It Will Prove Difficult to Sustain That Course

There are at least four closely connected reasons why it will be difficult to exploit the opportunities available to us:

- changes in patterns of global comparative advantage;
- the increasing internationalization of economies;
- changes in the lineup of big players;
- the end of the Cold War.

Consider each of these in turn.

It was only about 40 years ago that a division of labor started to emerge within manufactures between rich and poor countries. It has proceeded apace, stripping advanced industrial countries of their comparative advantage in more labor-intensive manufactures and also, to an extent, in physical capital–intensive (but less skill-intensive) areas of manufacturing, such as shipbuilding, automobile assembly, and production of steel. While the question remains controversial, this development may well be one of the reasons for the decline of male unskilled and semiskilled employment (as well as of the relative wages of such men) in virtually all advanced countries. The questions to be asked are, first, whether these countries will remain liberal in the face of this development; and second, how they can manage the social problems this development portends.

This changing pattern of trade is closely related to the internationalization of economies. Trade is no longer a marginal force, even in the largest economies. No country, however big, can ignore the consequences of international trade. Trade is indeed at the heart of domestic politics, as it is of international relations.

A list of the leading industrial economies of 80 years ago would, with the exception of Japan and, to a lesser extent, Italy, consist of the same countries as today; only the ranks would be different. Ranked by gross national product, the United States would have been first 80 years ago, with a share of world gross output roughly the same as it has now; Germany would have been second, not third; France fourth, not fifth; and the United Kingdom third, not sixth. Russia would probably have been fifth. Given the great upheavals of this century, this is a remarkably unchanging picture.

Japan's onset has been the harbinger of fundamental change. East Asia now accounts for about 20 percent of global gross product (measured at market exchange rates). Its share seems bound to rise sharply over the next half century, to surpass each of North America and Europe, and perhaps both taken together. In the process, China seems certain to become a great economic power. India, too, may manage a takeoff into sustained rapid growth.

Finally, the end of the Cold War has deprived the advanced industrial countries of their strategic glue. Habits of cooperation can rapidly disappear in the presence of niggling trade disputes. Already American authors write of Japan as if it were the new evil empire. Can effective common institutions be sustained in the absence of a common enemy?

The end of the Cold War, the growth of trade, and the scale of social, economic, and political differences among major participants, along with their growing number, will create great difficulty in coping with trade adjustment and managing the trading system. It is worth remembering also that the arrival of each new economic power—Germany, the United States, and Japan—over the past 120 years has led to vast strain, not excluding war.

Where the World Is Now

Given all these difficulties, the completion of the Uruguay Round was not just a great but an essential achievement. It has also been quite a surprising one. I, for one, had not expected it to be completed, either when it started or in 1990, although I did become more optimistic after the European Community (as it then was called) finally decided to attempt some reform of its ludicrous Common Agricultural Policy.

As Jackson's paper makes clear, if ratified, this agreement will make a great difference to the scope and legal rigor of the trading system. Even though incomplete in important respects, it represents a remarkable achievement in global economic cooperation. Three features of the Uruguay Round outcome seem particularly important:

- the inclusion of agriculture, textiles and clothing, and services;
- the integrated and more powerful dispute settlement mechanism;
- the trade policy review mechanism.

The completed Uruguay Round provides a platform on which can be built the liberal global economy I outlined above.

It is particularly remarkable that the rules of the General Agreement on Tariffs and Trade have been revitalized 20 years after the Bretton Woods exchange rate rules collapsed. This was also necessary. The international monetary system could, with floating exchange rates, fall back on the market, but the rules of the GATT embody the market.

The achievement underlines something else. Unglamorous though it is, the GATT has, in many respects, been the most successful of the economic institutions created after World War II. The reason is that its effectiveness depends on the role it has played in influencing the domestic policies and politics of the Contracting Parties. As that name for its members shows, the GATT embodies an international legal system, one that works by being incorporated into the domestic laws of members. In a world of nation-states, this—not the size of its buildings, nor of its staff, nor of its financial resources—is what determines an international institution's power.

What the Next Steps Should Be

For all its achievements, the Uruguay Round is not the end of trade policy history. So what comes next?

- The results of the round must be ratified and effectively implemented.
- The WTO must be established.
- China, Russia, and a number of smaller countries must all become members.
- Further liberalization must be undertaken, particularly of agriculture and services. Ideally, tariff peaks should also be lowered.

- The new issues of environment, labor standards, and competition must either be contained (in the case of the first two) or incorporated (in the case of the last).

This is a heavy agenda, and one that raises some fundamental issues. Three in particular deserve comment.

First, what remains of the liberalization agenda is itself important. This is particularly true of services and of agriculture, for in both of these what has been achieved so far looks rather modest.

The second is that how soon and how China is incorporated also matters. Ideally, China would be a founding member of the WTO, but not as a state-trading country. It should be required to make specific commitments to move along the path of economic liberalization, with a country-specific discriminatory safeguard clause in effect until it has completed most of that journey. This demands, above all, that China's protection should be largely through tariffs and that exchange restrictions on current account should also be eliminated.

Third, two of the new issues placed by the United States on the WTO agenda have worrying implications. These are the environment and labor standards, both of which can readily become excuses for increased protection. In both these areas perhaps what is most needed is good old-fashioned humility on the part of the advanced industrial countries, who seem to believe that, being themselves without sin, they are entitled to throw not just the first, but all the stones.

Some of the "environmental" concerns of the United States relate in fact not to the environment, but to animal rights. This is evidently true of the desire to protect dolphins from the nets of Mexican fishermen. But it is not obvious why everyone should share these US values. Hindus might as reasonably object to US treatment of cows.

There is, it appears, only one environmental issue that is both global and, if the prophets of doom are correct, potentially cataclysmic. This is global warming. Yet even today, according to World Bank statistics, some two-thirds of greenhouse gases are emitted by industrial countries (with the proportion of the cumulative emission up to this point far larger than that). Emissions per capita from industrial countries are about 10 times as great as from developing countries. This is a grotesque imbalance in the use of what environmentalists judge a valuable but unpriced global resource. How dare the United States, which refuses to impose even a reasonable level of taxation upon the use of gasoline, complain so self-righteously about Mexican fishermen's killing of dolphins, as if this were a central issue? Are developing countries to be compelled to preserve their forests to absorb the carbon dioxide that industrial countries keep emitting? Physicians, first heal yourselves.

Equally hypocritical is the stance of labor standards. That this is an area where the United States and France agree is disturbing enough in itself. It is worth remembering that today's major industrial countries also limited the effectiveness of trade union organization during what economists call the capital-widening phase of economic development, which is when workers are pulled into the industrial labor force from farms (or, in the case of the United States, also from abroad). They were right to do so, because the interests of employees are not those of the labor force as a whole. Pushing up the wages (or improving the working conditions) of already privileged workers in the export-oriented industries of developing countries could blight the prospects of far more people than would be helped. Even child labor is not necessarily undesirable, given the alternatives. It is certainly unacceptable to deprive families of income without being prepared to make up that loss.

Trade policy could too easily become a cheap way to bully developing countries into adopting standards that are inappropriate or inequitable. Worse, it could be a way for advanced countries to justify their own protection. Neither alternative should be acceptable, and neither must be accepted.

What Big Questions Must Be Addressed?

Looking forward to the next half century, we see that the institutional framework for the trading system is well established and the requirements for its successful functioning are largely understood, both in theory and practice. But this does not mean that the challenges it faces will be overcome with any ease. Above all, there remain a number of fundamental questions to be addressed.

Nondiscrimination versus Discrimination

The GATT's fundamental principle was and supposedly still is nondiscrimination. With the growth of regional trading arrangements, the vitality of this principle has been seriously eroded. The growth of such discriminatory arrangements creates predictable problems. Those who are excluded feel insecure or threatened. There is greater room for quasi-imperial domination of weak countries by powerful preference givers. There is more uncertainty about future market access. Trade also becomes more bureaucratically complex, particularly as rules of origin—inescapable in free trade areas—become more prevalent.

The ill effects of discrimination can be contained, but only inside a strong global framework. Such a framework is necessary in any case, since almost half of world trade is interregional (the bulk of intraregional trade is within Europe). Furthermore, much of the trade with the greatest potential for generating economic benefits must be interregional, because it has been the most restricted in the past.

Globalism versus Regionalism

It seems an iron rule that successful economies do not discriminate, while flops form trade blocs. That is why the shift of the United States from nondiscrimination to regionalism in the 1980s was so revealing of its changing image of itself.

A deliberate focusing of trade on neighbors is not self-evidently sensible. Since trade tends naturally to be concentrated on neighbors, it is far from obvious why that tendency should be reinforced. One reason is that it may be easier to obtain reciprocal commitments to liberalize from neighbors. Another is that the costs of trade diversion are smaller and the benefits of secure market access larger if discriminatory liberalization is with countries with which one should be trading a great deal in any case. That is particularly true for small neighbors of giants, such as Canada or Austria. But the best reason for discrimination is political. It is a way to cement a closer political relationship.

An alternative to regional discrimination is an open arrangement, available to any country, wherever located, that is willing to make the necessary commitments. The GATT is a mutual disarmament treaty for mercantilists. A free trade area is a kind of zero option, something countries seem able to accept. A free trade area open to any country prepared to accept its rules may be the best way to marry discrimination with global liberalization.

To be more precise, why should the European Union now be contemplating free trade with Russia, just because they may soon share a border, but not with the United States, Canada, Australia, or New Zealand? This idea seems ridiculous.

The question of how to sustain global institutions in the teeth of discriminatory regionalism is made more important by the growing role of Asia, which is not—and seems unlikely ever to become—a discriminatory trading bloc. It is, instead, the area of the world with the fastest growing intraregional trade, although this is being generated by liberalization on a most-favored nation basis. If this Asian orientation does not change, then the global trading system matters not only for its decisive influence upon interregional trade, but also because it regulates the trading policies of countries within the fastest growing region of the world economy, including their policies toward one another.

Diversity versus Harmonization

The increasing salience of trade within domestic economies and politics increases demands for "fairness," which usually turns out to mean harmonization of regulatory regimes (as in labor standards and the environment, discussed above). But the growing diversity of the participants in international trade also makes such harmonization both less reasonable and less feasible.

Arguments can be advanced for harmonization. But they are not as strong as proponents tend to think. Diversity, including regulatory diversity, is the principal source of the gains from trade. If, for example, one country is prepared to tolerate a form of local pollution that other countries dislike, moving the polluting activities from the latter to the former will result in an all-round improvement in economic welfare.

At the same time, regionalism combined with harmonization, as in the European Union, has a tendency to engender increased economic rigidity, which in turn generates protectionist pressure. It would be natural to try to foist such rigidities on other, poorer countries. If, for example, Portugal is prevented from exploiting its comparative advantage within the European Union, it will feel entitled either to demand protection against outsiders who are not similarly burdened, or to insist that outsiders bear comparable burdens. Neither alternative seems acceptable.

The Market versus Sovereignty

Markets are global and individualistic. Politics are collective and, particularly in democracies, redistributive. Politicians and those who seek favors from them often justify the interventions they propose by reference to the view that trade is war.

The main purpose of the international trade regime is to protect the market from the free play of politics. Given its origin in the 1930s, this should be perfectly obvious. Nor should it be objectionable. Domestic constitutions, with their entrenched rights and divisions of power, serve the same purpose. Even the notion of representation is a restriction on democracy, which could instead be implemented through referenda. Moreover, in the case of international trade, by restricting one's own country's freedom of maneuver, one simultaneously restricts that of other countries. How else can a degree of predictability be introduced into the laws and regulations that govern the global economy?

Yet the tensions remain, as the debate in the United States on ratification of the WTO shows. As economies become more open to one another, the debate is also likely to become noisier. A particularly significant source of tension is what trade threatens to do to the post–World War II distributional settlement within the advanced industrial countries. As unemployment soars and/or the relative wages of the unskilled fall, trade receives part of the blame, making it more difficult to sustain the coalition in favor of liberalism. Already in the United States the trade union movement, for example, has shifted decisively away from its earlier support.

Multilateralism versus Unilateralism

Finally, there is the tension between the desire of the United States for freedom of unilateral action and the health of the multilateral system. Many Americans argue that one reason the Uruguay Round succeeded is that other countries fear American unilateralism. They are not wrong. But those countries now expect the unilateralism to be contained. If it is not, they are likely to conclude that, at least in this fundamental respect, the round was a failure. If so, the WTO itself will lose most of its credibility.

It is important for the United States also to recognize that the beneficial effects of unilateral pressure for market opening were smaller than often supposed. In the course of the 1980s and early 1990s, in particular, markets have largely opened because of unilateral liberalization by developing and former communist countries. These countries have, in fact, shown a more sophisticated appreciation of the economics of trade than the advanced industrial countries, obsessed as the latter are with a mercantilist desire to obtain export markets. It is this process that most needs to be nurtured if markets are to remain open worldwide. It is not helped by actions that suggest that advanced industrial countries doubt the benefits of their liberalism for themselves.

Conclusion

The world enjoys a great opportunity in the conclusion of the Uruguay Round. Whether or not it is fully exploited will continue to depend on how the advanced industrial countries behave. There are strong pressures upon them to draw back, and there are difficult issues to resolve, but there are also powerful reasons for them to engage ever more fully in a dynamic world economy. By concluding the Uruguay Round, they have made a choice. What matters now is to ensure that they do not change their minds.

4

Managing Development and Transition

NICOLÁS ARDITO-BARLETTA

In the 50 years since Bretton Woods, the world has reached substantial consensus on the necessary, but not sufficient, requirements for economic growth and human development in the developing and now in the transitional economies. This paper summarizes lessons we have learned about economic development since Bretton Woods. These lessons have important implications for international management of the transition: that is, how nations and international institutions coordinate trade policies, facilitate financial and technology transfers, deal with global problems such as population growth and the environment, and how they gear international financial organizations—including the International Monetary Fund, the World Bank, and the regional development banks—toward a role as catalytic agents and engines for orderly development.

In broadest terms, development experience shows a need for international rules that are firm enough to avoid disparities and frustrations but flexible enough to accommodate creative initiatives in individual countries and to encourage many and varied economic linkages in the world community. When managed well, the development process requires searching for common ground and complementary opportunities, and it promotes respect for basic moral standards in a world of diversity, freedom, and competition. It also requires different approaches to address the

Nicolás Ardito-Barletta is chairman and director general of the International Center for Economic Growth, Panama, and former president of Panama (1984–85) and vice president for the Latin American and Caribbean Region, the World Bank (1978–84).

distinct development problems of countries and regions at different stages of development.

The overriding lesson of history is that human freedom and development are achieved by building a community with interlocking purposes and associations. We economists like to call that community "the marketplace"—be it local, regional, or global—where goods and services are exchanged. But our understanding of development must be broader, looking beyond the economic and material to encompass other things we value, such as the common habitat.

Development should empower both people and nations. Within a framework of rules and common interests, development focuses on building the capacity, structures, institutions, and sense of purpose to widen horizons; to share, negotiate, and achieve; and to face crises constructively. Development is a profoundly moral and human objective, one that will always challenge people to realize both freedom and community—individually, nationally, and globally. Pope John XXIII captured the essence of this challenge when he said that "development is the name of peace."

International institutions can best promote this broad mission through rules, legal institutions, and organizations that reconcile the objectives of countries and regions at different stages of development. These institutions should foster communications, guide economic activities among developed countries, and build linkages and mutually beneficial economic exchanges between developed, transitional, and developing economies. Since private economic activity on all sides is the decisive engine moving the global economy, international and national governance systems must strengthen guidelines that orient private activity toward reinforcing objectives. International cooperation on development should help integrate developing and transition economies to the world economy in ways that will sustain their development.

The end of the Cold War and the collapse of most communist, highly centralized economies have greatly expanded the consensus that market and market-oriented economies are the best instruments to pursue economic growth and improve human welfare. Both developing countries and economies in transition from socialism are moving rapidly to more decentralized systems. Most are attempting to increase their linkages with the international economy. Many of the challenges they face are similar, but there are also differences.

The former socialist economies must create legal institutions, including private property and related rules of the game, for the functioning of a market economy and of decentralized political systems. In contrast, most developing countries need to reform existing institutions, improve their human resources, and apply economic policies of opening and decentralization more consistently.

The Emerging Consensus on Growth and Development

The main determinants of national development are internal to each country. In an increasingly interdependent world, national development is also influenced by the state of the world economy, trade arrangements, and international financial flows.

National Development

Before proceeding to the history of international development cooperation since Bretton Woods, I will summarize the consensus that has emerged regarding economic development. The so-called Washington consensus on economic policies for growth and development—the view commonly associated with the Bretton Woods institutions—reflects a broad professional agreement among economists, policymakers, and many leadership groups that has widened over time. It begins with the view that decentralized, market-driven or market-oriented economies are the best performers in terms of production and economic growth, economic efficiency, and flexibility and adaptability to change in the international situation caused by economic cycles and by secular changes in technology, information, relative prices, factor mobility, and consumer preferences. Differences arise regarding the desirable degree of government intervention to correct market failures, take advantage of externalities, or achieve specific welfare and noneconomic objectives. That is why I refer to both market and market-oriented economies. But these differences are secondary to the basic proposition of the market as the best organizer of daily economic decisions by millions of economic agents engaged in myriad economic activities. The results of the daily initiatives of people freely pursuing their own interests greatly surpass the results of centralized government control. We must begin with the obvious.

There is also recognition that selective state interventions, frequently identified with East Asian experience, are not easy to implement optimally, both for technical as well as political and administrative reasons. Nevertheless, such interventions can be feasible and useful to correct market failures, take advantage of externalities, and provide strategic guidelines that permit maximization of both social and private returns to investment. They are also essential to transfer resources for alleviating poverty and to foster development of human capital. Successful state intervention is the result of enlightened leadership and of competent, modern, professional bureaucracies. However, they contribute to growth only when they foster saving, investment, exports, productivity, and high social returns to investment.

The optimal functioning of the market also depends on orderly governance. Sound economic policies, human and physical infrastructure, institutions that provide rules for orderly activity with safeguards for people and property, knowledge and technology, and stable political institutions empower nation-states to achieve sustainable growth and human development.

Let me elaborate on some of these matters:

Macroeconomic policy must provide a stable framework for the real economy. Sound fiscal and monetary policies are needed to avoid inflation and to provide positive real interest rates, a competitive exchange rate, and a well-functioning financial system to intermediate between savers and investors.

Microeconomic policy must allow price flexibility and adaptability so people can take advantage of new opportunities and exploit disequilibria in the marketplace. It must also ensure low transaction costs by supplying inexpensive government services and a well-functioning legal system to define and protect property rights and economic exchange. The equalization of social and private rates of return on investment can best be accomplished in an open, competitive, and flexible environment where an outward trade orientation plays a critical role. Export-led growth is the most effective way of expanding markets and achieving productivity gains.

Distributional issues are best handled by transfers through the national budget. Providing for human development, basic needs, and basic infrastructure requires a high level of public investment or the investment of public funds channeled through private institutions. Social safety nets must be structured in ways that do not distort the relative prices of factors of production.

Poverty alleviation remains a permanent challenge. But there is now an emerging consensus that it has to be addressed by (1) investment in education, health, nutrition, low-income housing, communications, and information; (2) employment generation through economic growth; (3) support of small enterprise development through credits, technical assistance, the provision of information, and clear, secure property rights; and (4) the provision of efficient public or private safety nets.

It is not my purpose to discuss areas of disagreement about emphasis or detail; I want merely to underline the powerful change that has taken place. Developing countries increasingly have recognized they cannot control and guide the economy by price and credit controls, regulations, generic government interventions, the creation of state enterprises, and irresponsible fiscal and monetary policies. Economic policy tools must be used to support a decentralized, outwardly oriented market economy. Governments must still govern the economy, but not through direct controls and interventions. It is also necessary, however, to deliver public services to the poor and to involve the poor in decisions on how best to invest in these programs. Such empowerment remains at the core of the search for programs to combat poverty.

There is a long-standing consensus regarding the need for human and physical infrastructure. The international development banks have made a distinguished contribution in this area, but there is an ongoing need for improvement. Technical criteria for effective and efficient allocation of these investment resources are well-developed, but developing countries need to further develop the institutional capacity to prepare, evaluate, budget, implement, and maintain infrastructure projects. There is an emerging recognition that private entities can provide, manage, and even finance such projects.

The modernization of public administration in developing countries, key to responding to the change in economic orientation and to improving public-service delivery, remains one of the high priorities of national development. The effective delivery of well-structured public investment programs is part of this modernization.

There is a growing recognition that the "rules of the game"—that is, the institutional framework—are critical for a well-functioning market or market-oriented economy. Property rights, contract guarantees, commercial codes, antitrust legislation, financial systems, and social security are indispensable to this framework, as is a well-functioning judicial system. It makes a tremendous difference whether the rules apply equally to all or whether they favor "rent-seeking" groups in ways that create inflexibilities and discrepancies between social and private rates of return on investment. A competitive, open society cannot be consistently structured along hierarchical lines, with rules established by different groups with political power. The costs of economic activities increase manyfold when rules and regulations permit favoritism, occasion arbitrariness and corruption, or when they are frequently changed by the changing governments. Restrictions on market entry or exit, price and profit administration, and investment and output controls all hinder efficient economic activity.

Knowledge and technology are the basis of productivity increases, and developing countries gain a good deal by applying knowledge and technology developed in the more advanced countries. However, they must create the capacity to adapt this technology as well as create their own; they need trained people, organizations such as universities and think tanks, and a national culture that emphasizes assimilation of new knowledge. International trade and investment carried out by private agents remain the main channels for technology transfer. In some specific areas, such as agriculture, where social rates of return to research and development are higher than private rates of return, publicly sponsored international research and knowledge transfers by groups such as those international research institutions supported by the Consultative Group on International Agricultural Research have produced useful and dramatic results. In addition, international regulation for the protection of intellectual property has been negotiated in the Uruguay Round of trade negotiations. A beginning has been made for the international governance of private transfers of intellectual property rights.

Finally, the political system has to provide predictability, accountability, participation, and a set of parameters within which policy may fluctuate, generating confidence sufficient for investment, trade, and economic activity.

Yet even though there is a recognizable degree of consensus on the broad parameters of the "promised land," we are still learning how to get from here to there. The task is made more complex in part because transition and developing nations have different starting points and levels of development. Developing countries today have private and public economic activity and institutions that are consistent with a "mixed" economic organization. Their development challenge is how to stabilize and adjust the economy to achieve higher and more efficient sustainable growth. They need appropriate market and outward-oriented policies, deregulation and modernization of institutions, human resource development, and macroeconomic policies that foster stability. On the other hand, transition economies, which are creating institutions completely different in function from those of the past 50 years, have different needs: a public-sector financial system based on taxation, a private economy, private financial markets, and reoriented trade patterns, to name a few. The well-being of most of their populations depends upon the success of their political and economic transition.

Even though excellent research has been done on the appropriate sequencing of adjustment and policy reform based on successful country experiences, management of transition is as much an art as a science. Too many complex variables are involved related to the political processes of countries, the position of powerful interest groups, the national knowledge and awareness about the mechanics of economics, and development leading to "local ownership" of ideas on growth and human development and policies to achieve them.

The International Setting

Obviously, the growth in production and trade of the countries of the Organization for Economic Cooperation and Development, which comprise 80 percent of the world's total output and trade, significantly influence the performance of developing countries. Development will be stronger and more sustained if the OECD countries maintain dynamic growth, stable prices, more open trade, and a multilateral policy supportive of capital and technology transfers to developing countries. These actions help not only the less developed world, in which the majority of mankind live, but also is in the rich countries' own interest. Expansion of world markets is the surest way of sustaining growth, productivity increases, division of labor, specialization of functions, and human development. Although trade competition from less developed countries' exports does pose a growing challenge to the OECD countries, the gains from trade for both developed and developing countries are greater than the cost of adjustment to new market realities.

From the perspective of developing countries, successful outward trade orientation implies diversified exports. Trade relations based on import of industrial and capital goods by developing countries in exchange for exports of primary goods and raw materials does not represent a growth-promoting trade-off. Several developing countries, such as the Asian newly industrializing economies, have achieved successful outward trade orientation, without policies discriminating against exports, by encouraging exports of manufactured and processed goods through stimulation of foreign investment, training of professionals and skilled labor, and development of foreign markets. Such policies permitted NIEs to diversify exports.

The interdependence created by the international economy is affecting governments' ability to set policies independently of their neighbors. The globalization of trade and finance makes industry and capital more mobile among countries, restricting governments' ability to tax and regulate without loss of international competitive capacity. As a result, countries are having to implement similar policies to avoid losing a competitive edge. The information and communications revolution is also opening frontiers that are beyond governmental control and is increasing the fluidity of international economic transactions (Mathews 1993).

Scientific and technological change continues to be a major international factor. The application of new knowledge and technology to production, to markets, and to the creation of new and cheaper goods causes continuous changes in consumer preferences, diversifies trade patterns, affects the competitive capacity of countries, and influences the allocation of inputs, especially job creation.

Perhaps it can be said that these trends increase the volume of tradeable goods in relation to nontradeables for most economies around the world, which is also an indication of greater economic interdependence. The scientific and technological revolution also favors decentralized, market economies, which allow the necessary flexibility, adaptability, fluidity, and creativity to shift between different modes of production, markets, and production opportunities.

In international finance, the communications, technological, and institutional revolution has facilitated high volumes of financial flows that are beyond the control of central banks. This has occurred not only in developed countries, but more recently in developing countries as well. After the unprecedented recycling of petrodollars during the 1970s and early 1980s, a cataclysmic aberration that led to the debt crisis, and adjustment, Asian and Latin American countries that have sustained appropriate balance of payments, financial, and fiscal policies have recently witnessed large financial inflows. The implications of this trend for countries and for international financial institutions (IFIs) will be reviewed later in this paper.

International capital movements and their impact on balance of payments and investment levels continue to be a critical issue for developing countries. The international community needs to continue developing mechanisms that will provide developing countries and transition economies access to external finance. There are still profound discrepancies in development levels, which affect countries' capacities to benefit from the international financial and investment markets. For example, the sub-Saharan African countries' combination of development problems, discussed later in this paper, put them in a separate category with special implications for the quality and quantity of international cooperation needed.

The World Bank and regional banks lend significant long-term financial resources for development. The full implications of the role of those transfers are considered later. Yet despite significant increases in lending, in recent years net transfers are often negative, creating a temporary burden on countries already struggling to cope with external debt service and growth. Even though the worst aspects of the debt crisis are over, the sizable remaining debt should receive careful attention over the next decade and beyond to ensure that it will not again become an obstacle to developing countries' growth.

Population growth and the protection of the ecological environment also have major implications for the progress of developing countries. With a world population of more than 5 billion people, moving to 8 to 10 billion over the next 60 years, there is a well-recognized pressure on natural nonrenewable resources and on the world's forests. To ensure sustainable development, national and international development managers must keep in mind the need to reduce population growth rates and establish mechanisms and incentives to protect the natural environment.

Although the world economy as a whole, especially the OECD countries, is growing slowly, there are great opportunities and challenges in the next decade. On the one hand, there is great convergence in political attitudes and professional knowledge favoring the creation of market or market-oriented economies and recognizing the importance of human development. On the other hand, the world faces the challenge of recovering growth while expanding trade, strengthening international coordination while private activity increases and diversifies, and sustaining efforts to incorporate the developing countries and transition economies into the global economy.

Development Lessons from the Bretton Woods Era

In development terms, the postwar world was made up of industrialized countries, what later became the OECD group, some of them recovering from the devastation of war; a rapidly forming block of socialist nations; an emerging group of former colonial countries in Africa and Asia; and in Latin America, a group of 130-year-old nations that combined European and indigenous cultures.

A combination of technical, political, and ideological factors in the wake of the interwar period, and especially the Great Depression, led developing countries toward inward-looking import substitution coupled with an increased emphasis on the public sector as producer and regulator of the private economy. Governments increasingly regulated and intervened in trade, the financial system, prices, agriculture, manufacture, labor markets. Such intervention was in part a reaction to the business-cycle fluctuations that precipitated the depression of the 1930s and the resulting financial vulnerabilities of these countries. Socialism (of the Fabian, European and Marxist-Leninist genre) had a heavy influence. Very liberal interpretation of Keynesian theories led developing countries to consider fiscal deficit financing as adequate for employment generation and growth, regardless of the level of use of installed capacity. Infant-industry protection and terms-of-trade arguments influenced the movement toward inward-looking, import-substituting growth strategies.

The new, former colonial countries were reacting against anything resembling the imperial power. At the same time, a residue of mercantilist and clientelist practices and favoritism remained. The new industrialization and regulatory policies made economic and political sense to powerful interest groups of the right (business groups) and of the left (labor and farmer unions) that were strongly steeped in the tradition of extracting rents from government regulation of markets and economic activity.

As a result, the public share of economic activity grew steadily through the 1950–80 period in most developing countries. Developing countries traded raw materials, food, and agricultural products for manufactured and capital goods from developed countries. Financial transfers to developing nations from developed countries with capital surpluses took place mostly through private foreign direct investment in import-substituting industries or in raw material and agricultural exporting industries and through lending by national development agencies, the World Bank, and later the regional banks for public investment projects. The private foreign purchase of financial instruments issued by developing countries had stopped during the Great Depression.

Developing countries derived other lessons from postwar events. Both the experience of European reconstruction and development models of the Harrod-Domar variety pointed in the direction of investment in physical capital as the key to sustained growth. The Marshall Plan pointed the way to international capital transfers as the necessary complement to domestic savings in order to increase investment levels and growth in developing countries. As communism became an international threat to the United States and its Western allies, the issue of development of the low-income countries would become not only a moral commitment, but also a strategic priority in the Cold War. Financial aid and technical assistance became the main instruments of foreign development policy. The developed world also considered trade, but mostly concerned itself with reducing price and volume fluctuations for major internationally traded commodities.

Foreign aid was channeled through bilateral national programs and through multilateral institutions, mainly the World Bank and the regional banks. However, bilateral programs generally proved to be more subject to political considerations than were multilateral aid programs, where decision criteria tended to be based more on the projects' technical merit. Bilateral aid programs normally responded to annual or biannual congressional appropriations and thus funding levels for these programs oscillated, to the detriment of the recipient countries and their long-term development goals. Loans for such programs were committed as quickly as possible, with a long list of conditions to be satisfied before implementation. As a result, implementation of many projects was delayed and often bogged down. The regional banks took longer to prepare and negotiate their projects than did bilateral aid agencies, requiring mostly special management strengthening conditions for implementation. Such special project administration units did not become permanent institutional improvements in the countries. While the World Bank traditionally also took longer to prepare and negotiate projects than did bilateral agencies (because it insisted on stricter technical and institution building standards as preconditions for commitment), project disbursement and execution was usually relatively fast.

Aid Programs of the 1950s to the 1970s

The World Bank set the pattern for multilateral development lending institutions. It moved from reconstruction finance to development finance and technical assistance, and it concentrated lending mostly on physical infrastructure projects. The Bank evaluated the creditworthiness of borrowing countries and established high technical standards for project evaluation and execution, as well as for institutional improvements of the local entities carrying out the projects, in order to protect its own creditworthiness in world financial markets.

Donor countries also supported project financing because international procurement of capital goods for the projects opened outlets for new exports. Recipient countries found long-term project financing useful to build much-needed infrastructure.

Given the Bank's low lending levels and the increasing political and social problems of developing countries, pressures increased to create regional banks: in Latin America, where the Inter-American Development Bank (IDB) and the Alliance for Progress became specific answers to the emerging problems of the region; in Africa, where postcolonial sensitivities made it necessary to create a fully African owned African Development Bank; and in Asia, where the Vietnam War provided the impetus to put in practice the notion, earlier conceived at the United Nations, of an Asian Development Bank. In this case, the ADB more closely resembled the structure of the World Bank due to US and Japanese influence (Webb 1994).

The emergence of regional institutions was accompanied by diversification in lending patterns and types of funding. Besides regular lending supported by financial intermediation in world capital markets, the development banks initiated concessional lending supported by special donor-country funding, such as that of the International Development Association (IDA) at the World Bank and the Social Development Fund at the IDB. Some financing of private projects was initiated, especially by the International Finance Corporation (IFC) and by lending to central banks or development banks, which in turn lent to private enterprise. All the institutions became financial intermediaries for long-term project loans, using government guarantees, technical assistance, and close supervision of their loans to reduce risks and borrowing costs and to increase the flow of funds (Webb 1994). Most lending to developing countries was to governments and public enterprises because they provided government guarantees.

International lending for development was viewed at the macro level as a way of transferring resources through long-term debt to increase the level of national investment and to support the balance of payments of developing countries. At the micro level, it was viewed as a way of helping to create the national infrastructure (physical, human and financial) for development and for technology transfer. As knowledge and experience accumulated in the 1960s about the relationship between production and productivity as functions of the inputs of physical and human capital, labor, and technology, the development banks diversified their lending to include social development projects (in water, sanitation, education, low-income housing, etc.), agriculture, and other noninfrastructure areas. Poverty alleviation became a central concern of IDB lending in the 1960s and World Bank lending in the 1970s. The main criteria were a project's ability to increase productive capacity among the poor and to make the means of production available to them through credit, infrastructure, and technical assistance.

In the 1970s, the World Bank also rapidly increased the level of lending to developing countries, thereafter lending more than all the regional development banks combined. It also strengthened its development and policy research capacity dramatically, becoming by far the major center for development knowledge.

Up to the mid-1970s, most countries had very little use for macroeconomic policy instruments (Little 1993). Exchange rates were fixed relative to several of the main hard currencies. Import controls were part of the import substitution policies. Reserves were normally kept low and were not built up with favorable movements in the terms of trade. Fiscal policy consisted in deciding how much of the government deficit would be financed domestically because this would determine the increase in the quantity of money and inflation. Monetary policy was used mainly to keep interest rates low, producing an excess demand for credit and allowing governments to direct credit to priority sectors, which they defined. When a balance of payments crisis ensued, the IMF was called in at the last minute, and short-term policy corrections, including devaluations, were agreed upon in exchange for temporary financial support from the Fund.

Developing countries began to emphasize trade for development in the 1960s. As the OECD countries moved toward freer trade arrangements through the Kennedy Round of trade negotiations, the developing countries, through the UN Committee on Trade and Development (UNCTAD), began to look for preferential trade arrangements. These were obtained through the Generalized System of Preferences, by which developed countries gave developing countries nonreciprocal trade concessions. However, developed-country nontariff barriers made many such preferences ineffective.

There was also emphasis on inward-looking regional integration schemes, especially in Latin America, following the example of the European Community, and in the French and British Commonwealth countries. The East Asian countries, pressed by a difficult political situation with China and Vietnam, began to follow development patterns more similar to Japan's—emphasizing market-oriented, export-led growth.

At the time, policymakers did not understand that import taxes (high tariffs) were both a tax on consumers and on exportables, reducing the incentives to export. Hence, they believed inward-looking import substitution policies were consistent with export promotion. It was not clearly understood, either, that high tariff walls encouraged rent-seeking groups to obtain additional discretionary government subsidies and supports that, in effect, increased the costs of production across the board. These policies, combined with overvalued currencies, were a strong deterrent to nontraditional exports.

Until the first oil price shock in December 1973, a sufficient number of countries with sound fiscal policies as well as import substitution policies were posting high growth rates. But as the size of their public sectors grew, so did the amount of regulation and the pressures to run large fiscal deficits. In effect, many countries in Latin America, South Asia, and Africa lost the flexibility needed to adapt to changes in international economic circumstances. The East Asian economies with their outward orientation were an exception. At the same time, the Bretton Woods system was changing swiftly, with increasing levels of international inflation and the devaluation of the dollar. The regulated international system was giving way to changing international economic realities. The regulated and centrally controlled developing economies would have to adapt as well.

The External Debt Crisis

The recycling of petrodollars allowed the developing world to borrow heavily between 1974 and 1982. The amount of financial transfers made through private banks at flexible interest rates with short grace and loan periods was many times the total, long-term development lending and aid from multilateral and bilateral development organizations. This factor, combined with international stagflation and strong commodity price fluctuations, created a period of economic and financial volatility for the developing world greater than any since the Great Depression. The crisis was aggravated by the collapse of private-bank lending after Mexico suspended external debt service in 1982.

In this period, developing countries' experiences varied a great deal. Those that did not become heavily indebted and had export-oriented policies and prudent fiscal and monetary policies came through the crisis relatively well. On the other extreme, those countries with high debt ratios, high fiscal deficits, loose monetary policies, and inflexible export capacity due largely to inward-looking development strategies had major recessions followed by long periods of stagnation and a reduction in living standards that required restructuring of their economies. Those that invested wisely used borrowed petrodollars to improve their infrastructure. But many made poor investments and amassed large amounts of debt to pay for current public expenditures and debt service, to finance imported consumer goods, and to line the pockets of corrupt officials.

The developing countries, by and large, were not structurally prepared to assimilate such large amounts of external financial resources so quickly, nor could they handle the fast-changing international economic situation. Even countries such as Chile, Peru, Argentina, and Uruguay, which in 1978–83 were reducing inflation and opening their trade and financial systems, had to partially or completely postpone or abort their efforts due in part to the difficult international economic fluctuations.

The combination in 1981–85 of large external debt, high interest rates prompted by OECD countries' disinflation policies, and adverse terms of trade caused the developing countries to increase their already-large external debt by approximately one-third.

One aspect that the crisis highlighted was that economic controls and regulations and inappropriate macroeconomic policies had worsened the situation of many developing countries by inducing capital flight. The balance of payments crisis and the fiscal situation were aggravated both by heavy borrowing and capital flight.

Guided by their stockholders, the Bretton Woods institutions and the regional development banks initiated a variety of approaches to stabilize the situation in developing countries and to contribute to the stability of the international banking system. The development banks, worried about having negative transfer problems with developing countries that were no longer able to disburse standard project loans, devised sectoral, program, and adjustment lending mechanisms to support developing countries in the transition. These loans provided balance of payments and budget support for global or sectoral programs in exchange for the application of specific macroeconomic or sectoral policies for stabilization and readjustment.

Project lending complemented domestic capital formation by direct financing of infrastructure projects—such as hydroelectric dams, irrigation systems, roads, and education—and through indirect mechanisms such as credit for private agriculture or industry. The conditionality for such lending evolved to include project preparation and evaluation, procurement and contracting mechanisms, administrative capacity and institution building, as well as some sectoral policies regarding utility pricing, marketing, technical assistance, and credit conditions. Disbursements were made as projects achieved specific advances.

Until 1980, those were the characteristics of development lending. The new sectoral and program lending went beyond that to incorporate quick disbursement loans, which are implemented by tranching disbursements as governments put in place the required sectoral and macroeconomic policies. The development banks had avoided such lending because of its inherent technical, administrative, and political difficulties. With nearly insolvent countries and international private banks on the verge of being unable to comply with the regulations of developed countries' central banks, the debt crisis motivated the World Bank and the regional banks to extend added support to developing countries and the international banking system at a moment of extraordinary international and national financial stress.

The massive nature of the external debt problem has also forced the redefinition of the IMF's standby agreements in support of stabilization policies. Previously, such programs tended to be geared to the short run. The massive balance of payments and fiscal deficits of indebted countries have made it necessary to introduce more gradual, medium-term stabilization programs that dovetail with structural adjustment programs.

The whole issue of sequencing of macro and micro policies, demand management, and supply response instrumentation has been more thoroughly researched since the debt crisis, and new modalities of policy implementation are emerging (Edwards 1992). There are complex technical issues related to IFI-provided capital inflows, which may alter the desirable real exchange rate and fiscal adjustment necessary to reorient economic activity. There are also issues of political viability of stabilization and adjustment policies if the social costs of adjustment grow too high or if recovery and job creation are not evident before the next government elections. The IMF's new, more gradual approach of providing external financial support at increasingly reduced levels while the borrower implements policies to deal with its deficits and disequilibria is the essence of conditionality. Conditionality works best when it is country specific, taking into account local political and economic realities and the capacity of governments to perform.

In the mid 1980s, it was recognized that the external debt problem affected the whole international community and that the developing countries, the private international banks of developed nations, and the adjustment policies of OECD countries were all closely interrelated. That recognition led countries and institutions to identify cooperation formulas with these elements:

- Developing countries stabilize and adjust their economies and restructure their external debt.

- The international financial community, IFIs, and private and central banks of OECD countries provide additional financing and restructure debt at closer to market value.

- OECD countries maintain growth with stability that enables them to absorb more developing-country exports.

The success of those coordinated efforts has varied by country but by and large they have mitigated the immediate, dangerous effects of the debt crisis and permitted renewed growth in most developing countries outside sub-Saharan Africa. Part of the external debt has been discounted, and the rest has been restructured. This coordination would not have been possible without the support of the OECD countries. They have done it unilaterally, through the United States' Baker and Brady Plans, as well as in coordination with the Paris Club and the Group of Seven nations, which also participated in implementation of the Brady Plan.

The New Development Management Equation

The salient reality of the last decade is that with the debt crisis and the collapse of the socialist bloc more than 80 countries have had major short-term emergencies and development problems. As a result, the Bretton Woods institutions and the regional banks have been stretched to their utmost capacities to coordinate support programs together with donor countries and private entities such as commercial banks. The capacity of the IFIs to provide leadership and coordination needs to be sustained.

Three development management aspects emerging from the experience of the 1980s deserve special consideration:

- the transition and developing countries' management of the transition from crisis to stability and adjustment;

- IFIs' management in support of developing countries and in their coordination among themselves;

- coordination among the developing countries, the international private banking community, and the IFIs to handle the external debt problem and sustain financial transfers to developing countries.

Countries' Management of Transition

The greater the debt ratio, the fiscal and balance of payments deficits, and the inflexibility of the state-regulated economy and the lower the country's ability to diversify exports, the more complex policy management has been for developing countries. Reduced imports have produced economic stagnation, higher unemployment, lower social standards, and more difficult fiscal constraints. The political management of policy reform has been difficult and prolonged at best, testing countries' institutional and organizational fabric. Successful management of the transition, whether in democratic or more centralized governments, has required a combination of strong political leadership, competent and coherent technical teams, close work and coordination with the various sectors of society affected by the adjustment, and a sustained information and learning process on the part of the public at large and leadership groups within each country. Successful policies—those that fairly distribute the costs of adjustment across society—also garner credibility for the governments that enacted them (Williamson 1993). Chile, Mexico, Costa Rica, and Argentina are concrete examples of successful adjustment in the Western Hemisphere. A wealth of experience has emerged about the optimal, least expensive, and most politically viable sequence of policy actions (Edwards 1992; Nelson 1994).

In countries with successful adjustment programs, fiscal deficits have been controlled by traditional means—reducing expenditures, raising revenues, and restructuring debt—and also by large-scale privatization of state enterprises. The proceeds from privatization have been used to reduce debt and to increase public investment in infrastructure and poverty alleviation. They have also helped reduce balance of payments deficits. These balances have improved with the turnarounds in the trade accounts but also with debt service reduction, repatriation of flight capital, and new foreign private financial flows. Competitive real exchange rates, lower inflation, positive real interest rates, reestablishment of capital markets, and clear rules for capital movements have contributed to improve the capital account. Trade-opening policies are helping to increase and diversify exports, improve efficiency and productivity, and reorient productive investment. The initial increase in imports improved capital formation and technology transfer but also affected noncompetitive manufacturing sectors. Production and investment are also benefiting from greater relative price flexibility. In most cases, structural adjustment is taking longer than most people expected. But economic inefficiencies brought on by decades of policies that hindered job creation and human capital formation take time to reverse. Concern for poverty alleviation and employment generation has increased as adjustment advances. Programs to improve such situations reduce social costs and improve political viability.

Since 1989, the transition economies of the former socialist bloc have gone through dramatic and sudden changes in political and economic structure. They have had to put in place a private, market-oriented economy with the appropriate institutional structure without falling into the trap of irresponsible macroeconomic policies and inconsistent microeconomic policies and while avoiding the collapse of production, exports, and employment. The collapse of the Soviet export market has aggravated the transition problems in Central and Eastern European countries. Some countries in the region have tried the "big-bang" approach; others have tried "gradualist" approaches. In both cases, there have been early successes and failures. Here again, we see that the careful combination of political will and power, technically competent professional teams, negotiated agreements with affected groups, as well as appropriate social safety nets are some of the necessary ingredients for success. The process remains more an art than a science, and it has to be locally owned.

Sub-Saharan African countries are in a class of their own. In general, they register lower levels of economic development and less political and institutional cohesiveness. They have large (relative to GDP) external debts and a prolonged deterioration of living standards. Early attempts at stabilization and adjustment have not been successful because social costs remained too high for too long, eroding the consensus necessary for sustained policies. The private sector of African economies is usually not developed enough to respond quickly with additional saving, investment, and exports. The stabilization and structural adjustment process is necessarily long-term in this region: market integration has to be strengthened, private sectors have to be developed, and basic institutions consolidated. These efforts must be accompanied by strong and sustained actions to improve human development, the formation of professional and entrepreneurial teams, and technical assistance programs to rural and urban small enterprise development (Jaycox 1993; Sirleaf with Fuma and Adei 1993).

The development challenge has been made both easier and more difficult by the collapse of the communist world and the expanded number of transitional economies—easier because of the international consensus regarding the effectiveness of market economies in addressing development needs and more difficult because the socialist bloc requires scarce financial, technical, human, and institutional resources, and supplying them strains the patience and resilience of peoples, nations, institutions, and the international governance system beyond any prior experience.

Management by the IFIs

The IFIs have adapted to the new development realities and have shown a capacity for international leadership of the process. There have been failures; sometimes they have aggravated the internal problems of developing countries. At other times, the IFIs have sought instant results without paying sufficient attention to the political, institutional, and social capacity of the countries to respond. On occasion, their technical analyses and prescriptions have not taken a sufficiently long-run view of the adjustment process. Other times, they have tended to impose solutions on countries without taking local professional expertise into consideration. But by and large, the IFIs have performed well, skillfully coordinating support for developing countries and former socialist countries undergoing different types of transitions.

In the process, the IMF has adopted a more medium-term, flexible set of parameters to support stabilization policies, and the World Bank has increasingly coupled lending with sectoral and macroeconomic policy considerations to support structural adjustment. The regional banks have remained more project-oriented and have increased coordination with the World Bank and the IMF. Areas of responsibility between the IMF, the World Bank, and the regional banks now overlap. IFI coordination has become necessary and helpful to avoid acting at cross-purposes.

The salient fact is that the IFIs have been there with the institutional, financial and technical capacity to play a larger role than before. As a result, a world economy altered by expanding and diversified activities of countries and private agents is finding new answers to guide unfolding change and development.

Developing Countries, IFIs, and the Private International Financial Community

The coordination and negotiations engendered by the debt crisis have put countries back on the road toward further development, have allowed commercial banks to salvage their internal situations and reposition their businesses, and have provided the IFIs with an expanded role monitoring developing countries' growth.

By improving their economic policies, many Latin American and Asian countries have attracted large flows of funds. Their emerging capital markets have benefited from intermediation with country debt paper and from the creation of financial instruments with international acceptability. It remains to be seen how volatile those flows may be and how much additional equity investment they generate in these countries. On the other hand, many developing countries, including those of Sub-Saharan Africa, do not yet have access to the private capital markets of the world and depend completely on financial transfers from IFIs and bilateral aid programs loans.

The World Bank and regional development banks have been cofinancing projects with private financial sources for a long time. Since the debt crisis began, international banks have sought their information, coordination, and conditionality guidance. Most of the large banks that are still financing developing-country projects have also sharpened their risk assessment capabilities.

There is more that can be done to expand the range of options for transferring capital to developing countries through equity investment and lending. At the country level, the critical ingredient is macroeconomic policies that foster stability and openness, development of capital markets, and linkages with international financial markets. At the international level, the World Bank and regional banks can continue transferring considerable resources for development to public and private projects and perhaps exercise a leading role as coordinators of external support for development, while providing country information based on their monitoring of economic performance. The central objective would be to supervise the orderly development of the international financial markets and thus avoid the wide fluctuations in financial flows and resource transfers that led to the 1974–82 crisis. The flexibility, diversity, and effectiveness of the financial markets could be enhanced by strengthening the coordination and supervision relationships of the IFIs, the private financial organizations, and the countries. The IFIs can provide increased technical assistance to strengthen the effectiveness and stability of local capital markets. They can also modify their provisions for supporting countries experiencing large capital outflows. Freer local and international capital markets also require improved regulations that will strengthen their stability and predictability.

Development and Global Trade Growth

International commercial expansion, so necessary to increase global economic growth, will require a concerted and sustained effort to continue reducing trade barriers in both developed and developing countries. The umbrella provided by the recently concluded Uruguay Round needs to be expanded and diversified. It needs to be a parameter within which emerging regional markets in Europe, North America, and Asia may be organized as forces for trade creation rather than trade diversion. The new World Trade Organization (WTO) ought to become a forum for strengthened trade governance and negotiations.

Improving the Management of Development and Transition

I started by defining development as the empowerment of people to achieve development and of nation-states to enable this development by providing the policy framework, institutional base, governance system, physical infrastructure, and human resources needed to pursue economic and development objectives in a sustainable way. The international environment was also included to underline the components in trade, technology, and finance needed for growth.

The IFIs should provide a range of development support services to developing countries. I propose evolution and diversification of their mission, not radical change. These changes should be consistent with the increased reliance on private economic activity in the developing world. My recommendations along these lines are of two types: country-specific and issue-specific.

The Country Focus

Because most of the development effort comes from the countries themselves, it is crucial that external finance, technical assistance, and policy guidance be channeled in such a way as to be "owned" in the country. Strategies, policies, and programs of a given developing-country government should be defined jointly to ensure both political and technical viability. The local government may also need support in "selling" the program to local interest groups. This dialogue is an exercise both in persuasion and in helping participants track results and is especially critical at the beginning of a new government, as it defines its political and development agenda. Commitments have to be made in ways that do not preempt the governments in the eyes of its public before it is ready to tackle particular constituencies affected by each policy adjustment. The local government must have the political elbow room necessary to negotiate difficult policy adjustments with those who may be winners and losers in the process. The IFIs should coordinate among themselves and with the new government the approach to be followed during the life of the administration and set up a joint task force that would follow up with negotiation and execution.

Obviously, the complexity of the program will vary with the degree of stabilization, adjustment, and ongoing development required. The IFIs must consider both the "continuity" factors that go from one administration to the other as well as the "correction" factors that the new government wants to introduce. The IFIs should be prepared with a medium-term package of investment projects, potential sector and adjustment programs, technical assistance and training, development strategy and policy analysis. Slices of that package should be introduced at the beginning of each new government and during the execution of the jointly defined cooperation program.

When the development trajectory of a given country is relatively good, then project and sectoral financing with institutional and capacity-building components and normal policy dialogue is most important. When the country is in a critical transition situation, then the full range of support mechanisms have to be brought into the picture. These programs should help the country define an internally viable and consistent package of domestic actions, supported by external finance and technical cooperation, that will bring the country back to a "normal" development path— one in which domestic saving and investment, increased production, productivity, and exports are sufficient to maintain dynamic and sustainable growth and human development.

Program and structural adjustment lending will remain a critical and useful cooperation tool over the long term. The experience of recent years shows that carefully structured and negotiated structural adjustment can ease the domestic costs of adjustment and improve the political viability of the adjustment process.

This process must persevere despite the resistance of major groups in society who are not completely persuaded of the "goodness" of the policy change, especially when they have to pay the early cost. Explaining the vision, the strategy, the program, and the action and having participatory negotiations are essential to convincing these groups about the new development direction. A ratification of the new policies through elections is a critical component. The support of the development banks needs to be steady and flexible to accommodate unanticipated changes in pace and substance.

The transition cannot be deemed a success until the benefits of the new framework are evident to a majority of the population and leadership groups. When this happens, the public learns much about the necessary conditions, rules, and policies for their national and human development. This new awareness that a higher and better plateau of national organization has been reached gives longer-term stability to the new policy framework.

With respect to transitional economies of the former socialist bloc, the new institutional framework to support a market economy is as important as a stable macroeconomic policy framework. Although the work of the IMF and the World Bank in Eastern Europe deserves high praise, there have been criticisms of insufficient support to privatization and to institution building (Mizsei 1993).

Given the trend toward more decentralized market economies, the IFIs need to target their support to the production of public goods, to break specific bottlenecks, to cover important areas temporarily left untouched by private and local activity, and to bridge gaps.

The support umbrella IFIs provide can and should be coordinated. If the recipient's most relevant tasks are developmental in nature—structural adjustment and medium-term infrastructure building—then either the World Bank or the corresponding regional bank should take the lead, supported by the IMF and other development institutions. Because regional banks often have a larger presence than the World Bank in smaller countries, they are better positioned to take the lead in those cases. If the most relevant problems are in the realm of macroeconomic policy and urgent financial imbalances, than the IMF, closely supported by the World Bank and the corresponding regional bank, should be at the forefront.

One of the most important ingredients to securing local ownership of development is to have local professionals and institutions participate in the production of the analysis and recommendations and in the communication of concepts and guidelines to local leadership and the public at large. The IFIs have extensive research and technical assistance programs that can be partially shared with local think tanks and other nongovernmental organizations. At the same time, the IFIs can learn more about the local circumstances, values, and constraints through the local institutions that may modify their universal technical conclusions.

Building local capacity that eventually makes the external programs unnecessary should be a major long-term goal. This graduation should not be based only on generic criteria such as per capita income but should more broadly be based on whether the country has healthy economic indicators, is maintaining a development policy framework, is building its institutions and training its people, is bringing in foreign capital and technology and is producing exports.

Through a series of strategic retreats, the development institutions should gradually withdraw to a monitoring and coordinating role as local institutions and private international mechanisms take over the bulk of development-oriented transactions and the developing country fends for itself.

The Issue Focus

It is not productive to view development on the basis of single issues that appear to be the most salient constraint at a given time—whether it be poverty alleviation, environmental protection, or infrastructure. The broader perspective is more important, emphasizing the viability of national development, opportunity, and links to the international economy. Attention to single issues can only be meaningfully understood within that context.

In that spirit, I review several important development issues—finance and resource transfers, project financing, poverty alleviation, institution building, financing of private activity, knowledge and technical assistance, protection of the environment—and close with brief comments on coordination among the IFIs.

External Resource Transfers

Experience has demonstrated that external resource transfers can support national development if the appropriate policy framework is in place (Lele and Nabi 1991). Without such a framework, excessive external resources create an excuse for not adopting the policies that increase local saving, investment, and exports. Wide fluctuations in the level of external financial support can also be damaging to development. At present, the developing countries often face negative net transfer of resources. Positive net transfers from the development banks must be maintained to support the policy framework and capital formation.

The external debt crisis has been largely resolved, but the debt remains. Debt reduction and restructuring programs have helped reduce the debt-ratio indicators and the impact of debt service on recovery. As the growth of high debt countries is sustained, the relative debt burden will decrease. Trade in much more diversified debt instruments and privatization of public enterprises has helped countries improve debt management. Lower interest rates have made a most significant contribution. But with further economic fluctuations, debt service could again affect the net transfer of resources to developing countries. To sustain growth, it may be necessary for pending debt to be restructured again, and the IFIs could again play a useful coordinating role.

The external debt situation of Sub-Saharan African countries needs to be treated differently. The development tasks of those countries are formidable, and external debt service remains a major constraint to recovery. Perhaps a mechanism of debt reduction tied to adjustment policy implementation can be devised to lighten the debt burden as those economies are positioned for new growth.

Concessional financing provided by the World Bank and regional banks will remain an important contribution to capital formation and development activities of the poorest countries for the foreseeable future. Besides the concessional aspects of longer maturity and grace periods and lower interest rates, such lending should continue to be accompanied by the various types of conditionality useful to improve policies, institutions, and training of professionals.

The external financing complements domestic investment, but its contribution to technology transfer is far more significant. The accompanying package of project knowledge, administrative skills, institution-building components, training, and policy advice tends to be even more significant in the long run. The conditionality for project, sectoral, and program lending should continue incorporating those elements.

Project Financing

Many developing countries need to continue improving project evaluation and execution in their public-sector investment programs. The lack of stable, professional civil services with up-to-date training in these areas is a major obstacle to such improvement. In many countries, this lack is due to national governance systems that still depend on "patronage politics" to sustain part of its political base. In others, lack of recurrent training in public administration erodes and makes obsolete the installed professional capacity. The long-standing efforts of international agencies to help upgrade the civil service must continue.

Project financing was the early contribution of development banks to national development, and it remains a critical element. Taking into account the specific needs of each country, it can perhaps be generalized that project investment should concentrate on infrastructure (both physical and human), on poverty alleviation, and on critical development sectors such as agriculture, the financial and capital markets, export sectors particular to each country, and improvements in the institutional framework and governance structures. The last two are recent additions to the array of sectors amenable to external development projects and are further discussed below.

Experience has shown that complicated projects, including those with too many components, such as the World Bank rural development project of the 1970s, are beyond the capacity of most countries. Care must be exercised to avoid such complex projects.

Human Development and Poverty Alleviation

Much can be done to improve human development and alleviate poverty around the world. The channeling of resources to effective programs that contribute to that objective will remain a public responsibility, even though at times it can be done through private channels. The development institutions can make a long-term substantial contribution in this direction by empowering people to assume responsibility for their development. Loans for education, health, nutrition, sound water, and low-income housing would best achieve this objective. The training of local professionals dedicated to implementing poverty reduction programs should be a priority of IFI loans in this area. Administrative organizations devised for such programs should incorporate "client-supplier" feedback mechanisms (Castañeda 1992).

Policy advice and conditionality should stress quantitative and qualitative changes in public-sector budgets to increase allocation of resources to human development programs and reduce allocations to nondevelopment activities such as the growth of bureaucracies or of military expenditures.

Institutions and Governance

In the early days, bilateral development agencies paid more attention to lending for institutional framework and governance structures than did the World Bank and regional banks, which had to protect their portfolios by financing projects whose payoff was more tangible. But experience has shown that sustainable development needs a sustained policy framework. It therefore makes economic sense to introduce loans and technical assistance to build institutional and governance capacity. A priority area for most developing countries is orientation of public administration away from production enterprises and excessive regulation and paperwork and toward development of human capacity, physical infrastructure, and effective judicial systems. Sector loans and technical assistance would help achieve that objective. Techniques to package training, technical assistance, and reorganization within a loan have to be developed further. It is not an easy matter, since it touches upon issues previously considered the sovereign rights of nations.

Financing of Private Economic Activity

Since private economic activity is becoming the central actor in the development process, the World Bank and regional banks need to establish new mechanisms to provide badly needed long-term financial support to critical private economic activities such as utilities and infrastructure, private development banks, small and medium-sized enterprises, and recently privatized enterprises. This implies not only increasing cofinancing of project and sector loans between the IFIs and private financial sources, but also strengthening the IFC and similar financial corporations in regional banks, as well as changing the focus of the banks toward lending to private activities. For this purpose, the banks could lend up to perhaps 10 percent of their portfolio to strategically selected private economic activities. They could also allocate a percentage of their net returns to their financial corporations for the same purpose (Ryrie 1993; IDB 1993).

Equally important is the policy advice and conditionality regarding the appropriate policy framework, institutions, and regulations necessary to enhance the development of private economic activity.

Production of Knowledge and Technical Assistance

In effect, these are two separate issues. The World Bank, IMF, and to a lesser extent the regional development banks have become the leading producers of development knowledge and policy. That knowledge can be enriched further by increasing joint research efforts with developing- and developed-country academic communities and can be used more effectively by sharing it more widely with the policymakers in developing and transition economies. The key IMF, World Bank, and regional bank publications should be made more available to universities and think tanks worldwide.

In addition, the increased level of technical assistance attached to development bank loans should be geared toward increasing local ownership of that technology. This can be accomplished by creating joint teams of local and external talent and by including meaningful training components in technical assistance projects. The IFIs already incorporate some of those components in their programs. Additional steps in that direction should be encouraged.

Protection of the Environment

The IFIs can continue to make a significant contribution in this area. Besides including project components for environmental protection, they can increase technical assistance to show how economic policy in general and fiscal incentives in particular may be used to induce businesses and human beings to maintain and improve the ecological environment (Panayotou 1993).

Implications for the World Bank and Regional Development Banks

Much has been said and written about the reorganizations, mergers or modernization of the Bretton Woods institutions and the regional development banks. I will not dwell in great detail on the range of options others have explored (Wapenhans 1993; Naim 1993). Many of them have merits, and the governing bodies of those organizations have to analyze them carefully.

I would merely like to recognize that those international organizations have made a considerable contribution to development in its national and international context. The traditions, relationships, mechanisms, and methodologies already established have much value, resilience, and flexibility. They should continue evolving as development requirements evolve and need not be subjected to major surgery, destruction, and revision.

The role of the development banks can be strengthened through several of the actions suggested above. Government guarantees that underwrite them have been critical to the success of their financial intermediation. Continued effectiveness will depend both on sustaining their professional quality and on the volume of resources they can continue to apply. To increase the IFIs' financing capacity, especially if donor-country legislatures decrease the supply of callable capital, a small change in the gearing ratio can be considered.

Closing Remarks

The Bretton Woods system as such stopped functioning in the 1970s. But the Bretton Woods institutions have continued making an important contribution to international and national development by evolving as circumstances changed and by diversifying the services they provided for development.

As sources of development finance, knowledge and technical assistance, and international coordinators and mediators, the Bretton Woods institutions and the regional development banks have no historical parallel. They enjoy a well-earned prestige. They have the institutional strength and flexibility to adapt their services to the new development concepts they have helped to promote and enjoy increasing international acceptance.

The trend toward a more open international economy continues. Private activity is increasingly the engine of change and integration, both at the national and international level. Market-driven and market-oriented economies are for now the choice of most countries. Consequently, the development banks can now be more effective than before, supporting growth and human development in developing countries and contributing to their full incorporation into a more integrated world economy. In a world of diversity, freedom, and competition, development banks can play a major role in finding common ground between developing and developed countries and in creating complementary development opportunities.

References

Castañeda, Tarsicio. 1992. *Combating Poverty: Innovative Social Reforms in Chile During the 1980s.* International Center for Economic Growth (ICEG) publication. San Francisco: ICS Press.

Edwards, Sebastian. 1992. *The Sequencing of Structural Adjustment and Stabilization.* ICEG Occasional Paper No. 34. San Francisco: ICS Press.

Inter-American Development Bank (IDB). 1993. *Multilateral Assistance for the Private Sector.* Prepared by the High Level Advisory Group on Private Sector Development. Washington (March).

Jaycox, Edward. 1993. *Capacity Building: The Missing Link.* American Institute (May).

Lele, Uma, and Ijaz Nabi. 1991. *Transitions in Development: The Role of AID and Commercial Flows.* ICEG publication. San Francisco: ICS Press.

Little, I. M. D. 1993. "Macroeconomic Analysis and the Developing Countries; 1979-90." ICEG Occasional Paper No. 41. San Francisco: ICS Press.

Mathews, Jessica. 1993. "The Changing Nature of National Sovereignty: Some Implications for the World Bank." Washington: World Resources Institute.

Mizsei, Kohman. 1993. *The Role of the Bretton Woods Institutions in the Transforming Economies.* Paper for the Committee on the Future of Bretton Woods Institutions. Washington.

Naim, Moises. 1993. *The World Bank: Its Role, Governance and Organizational Culture.* Paper for the Committee on the Future of Bretton Woods Institutions. Washington.

Nelson, Joan, ed. 1994. *A Precarious Balance: An Overview of Democracy and Economic Reforms in Eastern Europe and Latin America.* International Center for Economic Growth and Overseas Development Council publication. San Francisco: ICS Press.

Panayotou, Theodore. 1993. *Green Markets: The Economics of Sustainable Development.* International Center for Economic Growth and Harvard Institute of International Development publications. San Francisco: ICS Press.

Ryrie, William. 1993. *Reshaping the Development Task in a World of Market Economies.* Paper prepared for the Committee on the Future of the Bretton Woods Institutions. Washington.

Sirleaf, Ellen Johnson, J. S. A. Fuma, and S. Adei. 1993. "Long-Term Development Capacity in Sub-Saharan Africa." Paper for the Committee on the Future of Bretton Woods Institutions. Washington.

Wapenhans, William. 1993. *Efficiency and Effectiveness: Is the World Bank Group Prepared for the Task Ahead?* Internal Working Paper. Washington: World Bank.

Webb, Richard. 1994. "The Evolution of the Multilateral Development Banks." Conference sponsored by the Group of 24, Cartagena, April.

Williamson, John, ed. 1993. *The Political Economy of Policy Reform*. Washington: Institute for International Economics.

Comment

MAREK DĄBROWSKI

Managing the Transition Process in Postcommunist Economies

In 1989 the former communist countries embarked on the transition from a centrally planned command economy to a market economy. In parallel with this economic transformation, they began to transform their political systems from more or less repressive dictatorships into Western-style democratic regimes. The transition to democracy and the market is a new and very important phenomenon both in the economic and in the political sphere, with similar processes taking place simultaneously in Latin America and Asia.

The Economic and Political Importance of the Former Communist Countries

Compared with Latin America and Southeast Asia, the former communist countries, even if one includes Russia and the other former Soviet states, represent a relatively small fraction of world output and an even smaller fraction of world trade. This group of national economies has now and probably will have for years to come a rather limited *direct* impact on the world economy. Perhaps only China, with its enormous population and

Marek Dąbrowski, former first deputy minister of finance in Poland (1989–90), is vice chairman of the board at the Center for Social and Economic Research in Warsaw and chairman of the Council of Ownership Changes under the prime minister of the Republic of Poland.

rapidly growing economy, can influence global economic trends to any serious extent. Nevertheless, the future of economic transformation in the former communist world is of crucial importance for the rest of the world for at least two reasons.

First, one can observe a very close relationship between the progress of the economic transition, on the one hand, and the stability of these young democratic regimes and the Western orientation of their foreign and security policies, on the other. It is no surprise that the so-called Visegrad group of countries (the Czech Republic, Hungary, Poland, and Slovakia), together with Slovenia and the Baltic states, represent the most stable democratic order in the region and display a strong determination to join both NATO and the European Union. Meanwhile those countries such as Ukraine that have failed to make serious and comprehensive economic reforms now face a very uncertain political future and can be seen as potential sources of regional and global destabilization. From this point of view, the prospects of economic transformation in the larger former communist countries that have nuclear weapons—Russia, Ukraine, Kazakhstan, and Belarus—can have serious implications for global security.

Second, the economic and political situation in the former communist countries is important to the prospects for regional cooperation and integration, especially in Europe. If the economic and political transformation in the Visegrad group and the Baltic countries is successful, they will join the European Union at the beginning of the next century, significantly enlarging its territory and potential.

The Features of the Postcommunist Transformation

The new democratic governments in the former communist bloc inherited a range of serious economic problems, which determine the policy agenda of the transition.

First, the total or almost total nationalization of the economy left a very limited role for private saving and implied either explicit prohibition of or serious restrictions on private economic activity. Making matters worse, the official systems of education and propaganda in all the former communist countries tried to convince people of the superiority of state (sometimes referred to as "social" or "all-national") over private ownership. This indoctrination lasted more than 40 years in Central and Eastern Europe (including the Baltic republics) and more than 70 years in the other parts of the former Soviet Union.

Second, the former communist countries inherited huge structural distortions stemming from monopolization, economic autarky, administrative price regulation, and centralized investment decisions. The former communist economies were strongly oriented to domestic and regional markets (the latter through the Council for Mutual Economic Assistance [CMEA]) and were more or less separated from other markets by currency inconvertibility, price controls, trade restrictions, and the state monopoly in foreign trade.

Third, domestic and external macroeconomic disequilibrium prevailed and was especially strong in the last years of the communist regimes, during which they lost their capacity to control economic and social life. Only the former Czechoslovakia, Hungary, and the former German Democratic Republic avoided dramatic macroeconomic crises, but even in these countries (and especially in Hungary) the degree of macroeconomic stability was far from Western standards. Domestic disequilibrium manifested itself in the form of a rising budget deficit and monetary expansion, difficulties in controlling wages, and other serious problems, leading to high inflation either in repressed form (a "shortage economy," to use Janos Kornai's terminology) or in open form. The external imbalances usually led to growing foreign debt.

Some have claimed that the agenda of the economies in transition does not differ very much from the policy reforms adopted in the last 10 to 15 years by many middle-income developing countries (such as Chile, Mexico, Argentina, Peru, Egypt, and India) and after World War II by some of the developed countries (e.g., Germany and Japan). That assessment, however, neglects the size and complexity of the problems inherited by the former communist countries.

The reconstruction program undertaken in postwar Germany under Ludwig Erhard, although comprehensive and complex, involved only the reintroduction of a stable currency and market regulation after some 10 years of a fascist command economy and war. The economy was never nationalized, and all basic legal market institutions survived, having been only partly suspended during the war.

Most of the developing countries that sought to change their economic systems had to contend with high inflation or hyperinflation and had to liberalize economies that were overregulated and closed to external competition. Some of them had accumulated a lot of structural distortions. However, these distortions were in no case as dramatic as those inherited by the former communist countries, especially in the former Soviet Union. Some developing countries had also to privatize their economies, but all of them, including Chile after Allende, undertook their reforms from a starting point of private-sector domination of the economy. Chile's transition was probably the most comprehensive and radical outside the former communist bloc. But even the Chilean transformation of the 1970s and 1980s seems less difficult and dramatic than what has been necessary in Eastern Europe and the former Soviet Union.

The enormous difficulty and complexity of the transition process in the former communist countries determines the usefulness of different possible strategies of economic transformation. It also presents a new challenge for Western governments and international financial institutions in terms of financial and technical assistance.

Transformation Strategies and Their Effectiveness

More than 30 countries in Europe and Asia are involved in the transition from communism. With the exception of Cuba and North Korea, there are virtually no classic communist economies left. That does not mean, however, that all the transition countries have already completed the journey—or even most of it—from a socialist economic system to a market economy. Indeed, some of the post-Soviet states, such as Ukraine, Belarus, and the states of Central Asia, have not yet made an unequivocal strategic decision to move in this direction. They are either looking for a third way or even trying to preserve what remains of the communist system in politics and the economy (e.g., partial price controls, export controls, and a central role for state ownership).

With respect to the speed, comprehensiveness, and radicalism of the economic transformation up to now, one can classify the countries of Central and Eastern Europe and the former Soviet Union[1] into five broad categories:

- countries that embarked on a very radical, once-for-all transformation of the economic system, made possible through the "importation" of a stable currency and of most economic institutions from the outside, practically overnight (the only country in this category is the former German Democratic Republic, which experienced such a transformation in mid-1990);

- countries that embarked on a radical path of transformation consisting in macroeconomic stabilization and an extensive domestic and external liberalization of the economy, followed (generally with some delay due to the need to draft appropriate legislation and set up monitoring institutions) by the launching of privatization (in this group are Poland in 1989–91, the former Czechoslovakia in early 1991, Albania in 1992–93, and Estonia and Latvia in 1992–93);

- countries that embarked on a gradual or partial transformation consisting in a number of significant, sometimes even very radical changes,

---

1. I exclude China and Vietnam from this classification. In these countries radical pro-market economic changes have taken place while communist parties continue their repressive political dictatorship. Both countries seem to present more analogies with the countries of Southeast Asia than with the former Soviet Union or Eastern Europe.

which, however, did not make up a comprehensive package and generally do not ensure elementary balance in the economy (typical examples are Romania and Russia);

- countries that undertook no significant systemic changes and made little progress toward liberalization and privatization of the economy, leading sooner (Ukraine) or later (Belarus, some Central Asian states) to economic destabilization and high inflation or hyperinflation;

- countries at war, where economic reforms, even if launched (as in Armenia), have been halted, and where war-related expenditures together with the destruction and disorganization of the economy have led to hyperinflation (this group includes Bosnia and Herzegovina, what remains of Yugoslavia, Georgia, Armenia, Azerbaijan, Tadjikistan, and to some extent also Croatia and Moldova).

The categorization proposed here differs significantly from the standard dichotomy between shock therapy and gradualism approaches that was the standard for (sometimes very emotional) discussion two or three years ago. Yet the real picture is even more complicated than what I have described. In practice there are several variants both of the radical scenario and of gradualism. Some cases escapes neat classification. Hungary, for example, was initially considered an example of gradualism to be set in contrast to Poland; now, after four years of transformation, it can be included in the same group with Poland. The case of Slovenia seems basically similar.

In early 1991 Bulgaria carried out a radical Polish-style liberalization and stabilization of the economy; later, however, it slowed the pace of change. So far no large-scale privatization campaign has been started in that country. The pressure of unreformed state enterprises on macroeconomic policy and the weakness of that policy produced a macroeconomic crisis in late 1993 and early 1994. The currency collapsed and inflation jumped to more than 10 percent monthly. Bulgaria is thus gradually sliding into the third group.

Lithuania, whose macroeconomic policy in 1992 was little different from that of Ukraine, has since the spring of 1993 been following its Baltic neighbors. In recent months Yugoslavia and Croatia have taken ambitious anti-inflationary measures.

The progress of economic transformation so far prompts some important practical conclusions First, there is no way to avoid a relatively large output decline, especially of industrial production in the state sector. The degree of inevitability of that decline largely depends on the inherited structural disproportions. Those countries that were not afraid to undertake a radical transition program geared toward stabilization and liberalization, and that decided to privatize relatively quickly and open the economy to foreign capital (the second group in my classification), were the first to arrest the output decline and restore economic growth. Poland is the best example, and been joined in recent months by the Czech Republic, Hungary, Slovenia, and Estonia. Eastern Germany, where economic growth has also returned, can be seen as an exception. The output decline in 1990–92 in the former German Democratic Republic was extremely severe. The reason seems to lie in the uncontrolled rise in the wages paid by eastern German enterprises toward the western German level.

On the other hand, those countries that attempted to maintain previous production levels through subsidies, credit expansion, and protectionism have already recorded more dramatic GDP decreases than those that chose the radical scenario, with no prospects in sight for a return to economic growth. This decline has been accompanied by high inflation or hyperinflation, with all the attendant social costs.

Second, the policy of granting concessions to and bargaining with various pressure groups does not produce the expected political results and does not increase the degree of social acceptance of the changes under way. Here the experience of Russia, Romania, Ukraine, and Lithuania (while the Sajudis movement was in power) is the best proof. On the other hand, where a strong institutional foundation of a market economy has been established, even when the political forces of the ancien régime are returned to power in elections (as has happened in Poland and Hungary) they have had to continue the policy of reform.

Third, the comprehensiveness and appropriate sequence of changes play a decisive role. In particular, effective institutional changes can hardly be introduced when the economy remains in macroeconomic imbalance and closed to external competition. The example of the radical Russian privatization, performed under conditions of high inflation, soft budget constraints for enterprises, and an absence of competition, should be a good lesson to those politicians who would like to postpone the politically difficult tasks of stabilization and deregulation. Formally privatized enterprises that remain dominated by insiders (i.e., under manager and employee ownership), acting in a very "soft" environment, continue to behave like state enterprises. They prefer to bargain with the state rather than compete on international markets. Bulgaria's experience shows the opposite danger: insufficiently rapid progress in privatization undermines the positive results of macroeconomic policy.

Fourth, one should not be afraid of "overshooting" when embarking on a stabilization program or any other component of transformation policy. The practice of postcommunist countries shows that this danger is not likely to materialize. Much more real is the threat of "undershooting" or diluting the program to a degree that makes it ineffective. The ability to act fast and with determination seems to be more important than technical perfection in designing policy instruments. Political consent to reform measures does not usually last long, so it should be used in full. If that opportunity is wasted (as it was in Ukraine when that country gained independence in 1992), the next one may be a long time in coming.

The Role of Western Governments and the International Financial Institutions

One can speak of three types of Western assistance to the former communist countries: financial assistance, technical assistance, and policy conditions accompanying the first two.

Financial assistance includes a variety of forms of support: International Monetary Fund (IMF) and World Bank loans, International Finance Corporation investments, IBRD loans, grants from the European Union (under the PHARE and TACIT programs), initiatives of the G-7 and the G-24, bilateral support, trade credits, debt rescheduling and reduction agreements with the Paris and London clubs, and others. I cannot in this brief comment analyze the composition of this support in detail, but what is obvious is that it differs greatly from country to country. Among the Central and Eastern European countries, Poland, as a leader of the economic and political transformation, has received the most financial assistance. Czechoslovakia and Hungary received considerably less, partly because they did not apply for it. For example, Hungary never asked for debt rescheduling or debt reduction. Bulgaria, despite its launch of a very ambitious program in 1991, was left practically alone, receiving very little financial and other support relatively late. Bulgaria was also hurt not only by the collapse of CMEA trade and the Gulf crisis in 1990–91 but also later by the UN economic sanctions against Yugoslavia.

Among the former Soviet republics, Russia seems to be the unique focus of attention of the G-7 and the G-24 as well as of the Bretton Woods institutions. The other republics receive far less support, partly because they are not prepared to undertake serious reforms (true of Ukraine and Belarus as well as the countries involved in military conflicts), and partly because they are probably seen by the West as politically less important. However, some of the others are implementing ambitious reforms under very uncomfortable external economic conditions (I have in mind both the Baltic states and Kyrgyzstan, which are suffering serious external shocks) and need far more real assistance then they have received so far.

Technical assistance can be provided in two areas: advice on the general concepts of economic reform, and advice on specific technical aspects of the transition process. Most of the reforming countries—including Poland, Czechoslovakia, Bulgaria, Hungary, Russia, and Slovenia—have designed their reforms autonomously with only supplementary support from IMF and World Bank experts. International financial institutions could play a greater role in designing a transition strategy for countries that have delayed reform when the latter do not have enough experts of their own to do the job. Nongovernmental academic experts can also be useful here.

Almost all the former communist countries have sought assistance in solving their specific technical problems. The organization of the central bank, the use of monetary instruments, the organization of capital markets, tax reform and administration, privatization, and the keeping of national statistics are only a few of the areas where help is needed. This kind of assistance is especially important in the former Soviet Union, where few market institutions have survived the communist period. The former Soviet republics must also in many cases build the standard institutions of independent states from the ground up.

The direction and quality of technical assistance given by the international financial institutions have been in general adequate to the nature and scale of the problems of the transition. However, some specific mistakes were made. Probably the most important was the attempt, which continued for some time, to support the ruble zone in the former Soviet Union.

Conditionality is perhaps the most important aspect of external assistance. Relatively few countries enjoy sufficient internal consensus and sufficient determination on the part of the new political elites to make unpopular decisions and avoid populist pressures. Poland was one of these fortunate countries (but only in the first two years of transition); others were Czechoslovakia (and later the Czech Republic), Estonia, and Latvia. In all the other countries a kind of external pressure, coming mainly from IMF conditionality, was and remains very helpful in keeping economic policy (especially its fiscal and monetary components) reasonably on track. Tough external conditionality can only help reformers in the region.

Has IMF played this role forcefully enough? As far as Central and Eastern Europe are concerned, the answer seems to be generally positive. There is greater doubt about the IMF's role in the former Soviet republics. I do not side with those politicians and economists who blame the IMF for demanding too much from the governments and central banks of the post-Soviet states. On the contrary, I think that the IMF was too soft on these countries. This assessment applies especially to the IMF's new financial window, the Systemic Transformation Facility (STF). Even if one accepts the idea of extending the content and conditionality of typical IMF macroeconomic agreements to systemic arrangements, there are serious doubts as to whether all the conditions applied are ambitious enough to make the transition program really effective. With inflation running at 5 to 10 percent per month and budget deficits around 6 to 10 percent of GDP (in countries where most of the fiscal deficit must be monetized because of the lack of financial markets), the macroeconomic environment is not stable enough to support privatization and the other institutional reforms, and there is no guarantee that hyperinflation will be avoided. As I have already argued, this kind of gradualist policy is inefficient, both from the economic and from the political point of view. Support in these circumstances does not help the reformers; on the contrary, it encourages populist forces to increase their demands. Moreover, even these "soft" agreements are not usually fulfilled.

Russia's experience with "first tranche" credit in mid-1992 and the first tranche of the STF in mid-1993 provides the best example. Both agreements were violated by the Russian government and the Russian central bank almost as soon as they were signed. Yet that did not stop the IMF Executive Board from giving Russia the second tranche of the STF in April 1994, again on very weak conditions. Belarus, where STF programs in effect supported nonreform structural policies and very soft macroeconomic policies, is another example of this doubtful practice.

This type of policy can lead only to loss of the IMF's credibility. If there is a political case for giving some special type of financial assistance outside of standard IMF rules, it should be given on a bilateral or plurilateral basis (for example, directly by G-7 governments) rather than through IMF and World Bank channels. That would allow the IMF to preserve its image as a tough institution—an image that seems to be of important international value.

Practical experience shows that a policy of "soft" financial assistance, rather than encouraging the acceleration of reforms, actually supports communist or national-populist forces. Moreover, it hardly seems in keeping with the foreign policies and national security interests of the Western countries to give some of these countries more room for military spending or for engaging in aggressive policies toward their neighbors. Russia is again the best example.

Comment

WILLIAM R. CLINE

With the end of the debt crisis after a dozen years, the international financial system has just completed an expensive and traumatic experiment on the functioning of its policy mechanisms and institutions. It is important to take a proper reading of the results of this experiment.

Debt policy had three goals: to preserve the stability of the international banking and financial systems, to facilitate debtor-country adjustment at minimum cost in terms of human suffering and forgone output, and to reestablish capital-market access as early as possible. Viewed as a whole, the debt strategy succeeded brilliantly on the first and third objectives, but the results on the second were disappointing.

The banking system was in severe jeopardy in 1982. By the late 1980s it was no longer vulnerable. The exposure of the nine largest US banks to the 17 highly indebted Baker Plan countries fell from 194 percent of capital in 1982 to 51 percent by 1992 due to a buildup in capital and the setting aside of loan-loss provisions beginning in 1987.

Capital-market access staged an astonishing recovery, as net capital inflows to Latin America, which had fallen from over $40 billion in 1981 to a plateau of about $10 billion in 1983–89, soared to $22 billion in 1990, $37 billion in 1991, and nearly $60 billion in 1992. Low US interest rates no doubt contributed a push, but it is hard to believe the renewed inflows would have occurred without the improved confidence associated with debt normalization.[1] The inflows were in the form of direct investment, bonds, and other portfolio flows rather than bank lending, but clearly investors gained enough confidence from the way the debt crisis was handled to place their money at risk. The essentially cooperative, market-oriented, quasi-voluntary nature of the evolving debt strategy of the 1980s played a crucial role in achieving this result. In contrast, there had been a

---

William R. Cline is a senior fellow at the Institute for International Economics.

1. The case of Brazil is sometimes cited as a counterexample because a formal Brady deal was not finalized until early 1994. But even there, the largest surge in capital inflows occurred in 1992, coincident with the agreement in principle with the banks.

miserable failure to reestablish capital-market access in the previous debt crisis. After widespread and confrontational defaults in the 1930s, Latin American nations were locked out of the capital markets for four decades.

The record for maintenance of economic growth during the debt crisis of the 1980s was much worse than that for the postcrisis revival of the capital markets. Whereas real GDP in Latin America had grown at an annual average of 6.2 percent in 1967–81, the rate fell to only 1.5 percent in 1982–92 (IMF, *World Economic Outlook*, 1981, 112; 1990, 112; 1993, 131). Deterioration on inflation was even worse, as several countries experienced hyperinflation for the first time in the mid- and late 1980s. Even so, growth in the region climbed back to a respectable 3.2 percent by 1993.

It is unclear whether a different strategy could have achieved better growth results. It is misleading to suggest, as Eichengreen and Portes (1989) seem to do, that the contrast between the 1930s and the 1980s shows Latin America might have done better to remain in default this time around as well. In the 1930s, Latin America was able to enter into the easy, initial phase of import-substituting industrialization, a strategy consistent with the autarkic implications of extended default. By the 1980s, however, that development model had long been exhausted.

Instead, the poor growth record in the 1980s was largely inevitable for two reasons. First, there had been artificially high growth in the late 1970s supported by overborrowing (and overlending), and a sobering aftermath was inescapable. The real problem was debt hangover, not debt overhang. Second, the advent of populist political regimes in many countries in the mid-1980s meant that a period of macroeconomic disarray was practically inevitable, with or without the external debt burden, and that only after a learning process would domestic (especially fiscal) policies be compatible with stable growth. Chile and Colombia were the exceptions that proved the rule.

On balance, the debt strategy may be judged a success. Two reasons for its success stand out: the consistent attempt to formulate the strategy in terms of a coherent analytical framework and the ongoing willingness to shift diagnosis and strategy in the face of new evidence. The initial diagnosis—that the problem was not one of fundamental insolvency and so warranted additional lending—was not far off the mark, considering that even Brady Plan countries eventually received debt forgiveness equivalent to only about 15 percent of total debt (and for the middle-income countries as a whole, the fraction was only 6 percent).[2] The use of the International Monetary Fund to internalize the individual-bank externality associated with the free-rider problem was an astute implementation of the initial strategy.

The shift of emphasis to longer-term structural change and indicative planning for coordinated lending in the Baker Plan was an appropriate

---

2. The reductions were about twice as large for bank claims, but these claims represented only about half of total debt.

midcourse correction. Contrary to the general impression, the banks actually delivered on at least two-thirds of their new-money commitments under that plan. The Baker Plan proved to be all that was needed for Chile and Colombia and, at least on strictly economic grounds, would have been adequate for Mexico and Venezuela if oil prices had not collapsed in 1986. Thus, Mexico lost some $8 billion annually from lower oil prices, whereas its relief from lower interest obligations under Brady forgiveness was only about $1½ billion annually.[3]

More broadly, however, the shift of the strategy to Brady debt reduction again represented a coherent response to new evidence. Large secondary market discounts offered a natural opportunity to shed debt in exchange for increased creditor security. Massive analytical work backed the shift, and although some parts were questionable (the debt overhang and its alleged effect of prospectively taxing investment; see, e.g., Diwan and Rodrik 1992), the transition toward voluntary debt reduction was well-conceived and well-advised.

Indeed, the Brady Plan is a rare example of a major international economic initiative that accomplishes its goals. The plan set out in 1989 to forgive about $70 billion in debt for 39 countries. By now, it has forgiven close to $60 billion for 18 countries, representing 86 percent of the original target for forgiveness and covering a group of countries accounting for over 80 percent of bank debt of the original universe of debtors considered. Capital-market access has been reestablished, as have conditions for stable growth in most of the countries involved. In fact, the favorable results are disproportionate to the modest amount of relief,[4] leading one toward the conclusion that in many cases the reversal of political perceptions was the more important phenomenon rather than the change in the economic burden. J. P. Morgan said that willingness to pay is more important than ability to pay, and lancing the political boil of perceived inequity in the distribution of the burden of adjustment between the banks and the debtors permitted a reversal of unwillingness to pay.

Many will argue that the debt crisis shows the international system is cruelly, if not dangerously, slow to respond to crises. Forgiveness should have been conferred much earlier, and perhaps much more deeply, in this view. But deeper forgiveness would have required the quasi-voluntary remedy to slide into a mandatory framework, with the endless legal

---

3. Indeed, the most rigorous work on Mexico shows that it was the maturity-smoothing rather than interest-reducing content of the Brady deal that contributed the exchange rate confidence and resulting domestic interest-rate reduction vital to the country's turnaround (Claessens, Oks, and van Wijnbergen 1993). The implication is that forgiveness may not have been necessary after the oil price decline and that a multiyear rescheduling agreement (MYRA) might have sufficed.

4. For example, Mexico's $1½ billion annual interest savings is only about two-thirds of 1 percent of GDP and 3 percent of export earnings.

challenges and damage to investor expectations that transformation would have entailed and with the corresponding likely effect of lengthy delay in a return to market access. Earlier forgiveness would have been questionable on the economic merits before the shock of oil price collapse in 1986, risky systemically before the large bank provisionings of 1987, and irrelevant in any event for those Brady countries in which negotiations dragged well into the 1990s despite the availability of the program in 1989 (often because of continued domestic policy disarray). More fundamentally, the central problem was often the need for domestic economic reform, and early forgiveness could have delayed the adoption of reform by giving the false impression that an easy external solution was at hand.

In historical terms, the debt strategy represents a successful international adjustment to a system-threatening crisis. The crucial roles of the International Monetary Fund at first and then the World Bank as well should remind us that these institutions continue to be the front-line defense of the financial system, and that it would be risky to close them down, as some suggest.

The broader lessons include the following. First, market orientation is more likely to succeed than international regulation. Any scheme of mandatory forgiveness unrelated to secondary market prices and the extent of collateral, especially on an undiscriminating global rather than case-by-case basis, would almost certainly have cast a pall on capital markets for years to come and thus been counterproductive for the debtors.

Second, international economic policy has an inescapable political-economy dimension. The political dimensions of the debt crisis, and most especially the domestic political perceptions of what was deemed a fair and acceptable workout, typically dominated economic considerations. The need somehow to address outraged senses of political unfairness, even when the underlying economics are less severe than the rhetoric, is apparent in other issue areas as well, such as the US-Japan trade conflict.

Third, the debt crisis illustrates a process that the system would do well to imitate in other issue areas: the role of intense, ongoing theoretical and analytical work in an effort to rediagnose the problem and reshape international policy.

Fourth, the experience suggests that it is undesirable to stave off one international problem when to do so sows the seeds of another. In retrospect, the official community's encouragement of the handling of adjustment to the oil shocks by petrodollar recycling through syndicated bank lending helped foster overlending and inadequate domestic adjustment in the late 1970s and early 1980s.

Fifth, domestic economic policy is the primary determinant of the outcome, as illustrated by the contrasting results for Chile and Peru (despite the relatively higher initial debt in Chile). Similarly, massive capital flight worsened debt conditions beyond original expectations, even though the actual current account deficits themselves turned out to be relatively close to the early projections, yet capital flight reflects domestic policy rather than external shocks.

Sixth, debtor governments are ill-advised to be indifferent to large external deficits on grounds that they are private rather than the consequence of government fiscal deficits. The experience of such countries as Argentina showed that private debts tend to become socialized, imposing a fiscal domestic transfer problem on the country in addition to an external transfer problem. A corresponding lesson is that debtor governments should send strong signals to the private sector that this socialization will not happen again.

Seventh, there is a need for the IMF and/or World Bank to provide public data and analysis to send signals to the private capital market when a country is beginning to overborrow. The capital markets are prone to wide swings, and private credit rating agencies may not be immune to lobbying by their country clients.

Eighth, it is important to review international mechanisms to guard against moral hazard. In this regard, there is a case for placing a time limit on the Brady Plan. Otherwise, private lenders may have an exaggerated sense of limits to their losses, and borrowing countries may have the impression that if anything goes wrong the debt can enjoy another round of Brady forgiveness. The risk of moral hazard presumably applies to other systemic issues, such as the inadvisability of a one-way bet on exchange rates under a fixed-rate regime.

Finally, market participants should be aware that if there is a repeat of the debt crisis, it could well be more difficult to deal with. The reason is that the new class of creditors is an atomized group of bondholders and other investors instead of a quasi-centralized group of banks acting through syndicates. Such responses as new lending are thus likely to be more difficult to mobilize in any future crisis. Moreover, bondholders are probably under the illusion that they enjoy seniority. This was true in the crisis of the 1980s, but after the conversion of bank claims to securitized Brady bonds, the vast bulk of debt is now in the form of bonds, and seniority is only feasible when it is possible to be senior to something else.

References

Claessens, Stijn, Daniel Oks, and Sweder van Wijnbergen. 1993. *Interest Rates, Growth and External Debt: The Macroeconomic Impact of Mexico's Brady Deal*. Policy Research Working Papers 1147 (June). Washington: World Bank.

Cline, William R. 1994. *International Debt Reexamined*. Washington: Institute for International Economics. Forthcoming.

Diwan, Ishac, and Dani Rodrik. 1992. *External Debt, Adjustment, and Burden Sharing*. Princeton Studies in International Finance no. 73 (November).

Eichengreen, Barry, and Richard Portes. 1989. "Dealing with Debt: the 1930s and the 1980s." In Ishrat Husain and Ishac Diwan, *Dealing with the Debt Crisis*. Washington: World Bank.

Comment

STEPHAN HAGGARD

Despite the supposed decline of the Bretton Woods institutions, their importance to the developing world has increased dramatically since 1944. In the first three decades of the postwar period, the International Monetary Fund and the World Bank gradually reoriented their operations to the developing countries; with the debt crisis and the collapse of commercial lending to the developing world in the 1980s, their role grew rapidly. The General Agreement on Tariffs and Trade also became steadily more important to the newly industrializing countries as their manufactured exports grew and the advanced industrial states became less tolerant of free riders on the global trading system.

As Nicolás Ardito-Barletta has already raised many of the central issues in the relationship between the developing countries and the Bretton Woods institutions, I will confine myself to a brief historical overview that emphasizes the trend he notes toward the increasing incorporation of the developing countries into the international system. That history can be divided into three distinct phases. During the first 15 years the participation of the developing countries in the Bretton Woods institutions was relatively limited. During the 1960s and 1970s the developing countries' participation in the system increased, but politics turned confrontational as the developing countries issued a radical challenge to the Bretton Woods rules. Although that challenge failed to achieve its objectives, the result was a subtle move toward a formally two-tiered regime in which developing countries were officially exempt from most obligations.

Stephen Haggard is professor at the Graduate School of International Relations and Pacific Studies, University of California, San Diego.

The third and current phase is one of more intense involvement of the developing countries with the Bretton Woods regime. In the case of the GATT, this involvement has taken the form of a gradual incorporation of the upper-tier developing countries into the system.[1] In the case of the IMF and the World Bank, that involvement takes the form of increased lending and expanded conditionality, but also greater political conflict. Whereas the gradual incorporation of developing countries in the GATT system is a testimony to the rapid growth in parts of the Third World over the last two decades, the continuing importance of the Bank and the Fund in the affairs of the developing world is evidence that success is far from ubiquitous, and a reminder of daunting development problems that remain unsolved.

Since regionalism has recently received bad press, it is important to remember that the Bretton Woods institutions were, despite their universalist pretensions, basically a North Atlantic regional arrangement; indeed, their origins lie in bilateral cooperation between the United States and Britain during the war. The developing countries did not play much of a role at Bretton Woods or in the birth of the GATT, and this contributed to their belief that the United States and Europe dominated the agenda of these institutions. This was particularly true following the Marshall Plan, which showed the priority that US policy gave to European reconstruction, and the death of the International Trade Organization, which was to have addressed a number of the concerns of developing countries.

Moreover, the developing countries for the most part harbored deep ideological skepticism about the underlying model on which the Bretton Woods institutions were based. This skepticism was not simply the result of nationalism, the lure of Soviet planning, or misguided theories of dependency and unequal exchange; the development policy community itself foresaw a substantial role for the state in the development process and was quite pessimistic about the prospects for developing-country exports or access to commercial finance.

This combination of political and ideological skepticism did not matter much until three developments changed the international politics of North-South relations. The first and most significant was a series of events that extended the Cold War to the Third World. The Korean War and deepening American involvement in Vietnam were extremely important in Asia in this regard, and the rise of Nasserism in Egypt, the Congo crisis, and Fidel Castro's revolution in Cuba changed the international politics of the Middle East, Africa, and the Western Hemisphere, respectively. The effect of these developments was to dramatically increase the political salience of the developing world for both the United States and the Soviet Union, and to increase the importance given to aid to developing coun-

---

1. For a more extended discussion, see Haggard (forthcoming).

tries; the US-led Alliance for Progress of the 1960s, with its roots in the Cuban revolution, was indicative of that trend. Developing countries complained bitterly about the politicization of aid, but it seems clear that in the absence of such politicization, both bilateral and multilateral assistance would have been less.

The second great historical development was the wave of decolonization of the 1960s, particularly in Africa. Decolonization strengthened the nonaligned movement and the Group of 77 and allowed the developing countries to seize control of the agenda of the one-nation, one-vote United Nations.

The belief that the UN organizations could provide the leverage to construct a New International Economic Order (NIEO) would have seemed completely fanciful were it not for a third development. The oil crises of the 1970s gave rise to the illusion that the developing countries in fact had the collective power to lead the construction of new economic regimes for development. OPEC power and the cartelization of other commodities would force a North-South dialogue and a variety of wide-ranging reforms, from preferences to commodity agreements and massive increases in resource transfers.

At one level this belief now seems totally misguided; however, it is now also clear that the developing countries were surprisingly successful in extracting concessions. Part IV of the GATT, the Generalized System of Preferences, and UNCTAD had the effect of transforming expectations concerning the developing countries in the trading system; in effect, the trading system moved toward a two-tiered one in which the developing countries were largely exempt from GATT obligations. Borrowing from the Bank and the Fund was much more limited than it was to become in the crisis-ridden 1980s, but with European reconstruction largely complete by the end of the 1950s, developing countries became the main clients of both institutions. It also became clear that concessionality would have a place in the World Bank system. The creation of the International Development Association (IDA) as a conduit for concessional lending by the World Bank introduced an outright aid component, however modest, into the mission of the Bretton Woods institutions, and the UN family became increasingly preoccupied with development questions.

Despite these important changes, the NIEO agenda vanished without a trace in the 1980s. Again, a combination of political and economic developments changed the nature of North-South relations. The first development was an ideological shift toward the right among the advanced industrial states. This shift included not only the rise of Ronald Reagan and Margaret Thatcher, both of whom were undiplomatically blunt about the Third World's agenda, but also a neoclassical revival within the development policy community itself. Nothing summarizes this shift more clearly than the change in leadership at the Bank from Robert McNamara, with his emphasis on rural development and basic human needs, to A. V.

Clausen, a commercial banker and Reagan appointee, who emphasized the benefits of markets and free trade.

Although the changed ideological milieu cannot be downplayed, two other changes were much more significant for the developing countries' relations with the Bretton Woods institutions. The first was a shift in US trade policy that can be dated quite precisely to the fall of 1985. Facing increasing protectionist pressures from Capitol Hill as a result of the strong dollar, the Reagan administration finally moved to "do something" about trade policy. The Reagan strategy was to counter traditional protectionist pressures through the formulation of a more aggressive bilateral market-opening policy. This strategy is typically associated with an increasingly aggressive stance toward Japan. But the United States was the major absorber of the growing volume of developing country exports as well, in part because the American market was large and open, and in part because of historical ties to the two regions where the export-oriented newly industrializing countries were located: Latin America and East Asia.

Although bilateralism is typically thought of as antithetical to multilateralism, this was not wholly true with respect to the new US strategy. The underlying presumptions of American bilateralism were closely tied to the GATT in two respects. First, the upper-tier developing countries would not be allowed to claim special and differential status or to free ride on the system any longer. This principle of graduation from preferences had been aired during the Tokyo Round and was implicit in the conditional most-favored nation status that characterized the Tokyo Round codes; developing countries (and others) could not benefit from the codes unless they signed and abided by them. Second, American bilateralism provided a means for putting new issues on the agenda that would subsequently be negotiated in the multilateral framework of the GATT. With respect to many of these issues, including trade-related investment measures and intellectual property, developing countries were the principal targets.

The second major economic development of the 1980s was the debt crisis. As William Cline addresses this issue in his comment, I will confine myself to four political observations. First, although the IMF and the World Bank could not ultimately dictate to the unwilling, their power over the policy agenda increased enormously over the decade. That power was tied to the fact that while the two institutions' resources may have been less than adequate from a normative point of view, their relative share of total capital flows to the developing world increased sharply as a result of the decline in commercial lending and foreign direct investment. The advanced industrial states also came to recognize—belatedly in the case of the United States—that the Bretton Woods institutions were absolutely pivotal to managing the debt crisis. The institutions showed a remarkable ability to innovate in response to the demands on their material and technical resources, and a variety of new facilities and funds came on stream, including the Extended Fund, Structural Adjustment, and Extended Structural Adjustment facilities, Structural and Sector Adjustment loans, and replenishments of the IDA. Moreover, the agenda of the institutions widened steadily and substantially, from short-term adjustment measures, designed primarily to reequilibrate the balance of payments, to the presumption of broader structural and institutional reforms.

A second aspect of the influence of the Bretton Woods institutions during the debt crisis was their increasing role in the formation of personal networks and the transmission of policy-relevant knowledge. The influence of the IMF and particularly the World Bank was not limited to policy dialogues undertaken in connection with their lending programs. The Bretton Woods institutions were also a training ground for economists and policymakers, the locus of substantial research on the development process, and the central point of dissemination for what John Williamson has labeled "the Washington consensus."[2]

A third aspect of the debt crisis—and ultimately the most important— was that it contributed to quite profound political changes in the developing countries themselves.[3] The crisis not only discredited particular governments, contributing in some instances to the collapse of authoritarian rule and the transition to democracy, but it also discredited development strategies that had been politically entrenched for long periods of time. New groups emerged, such as exporters, with a strong interest in reform.

The final political aspect of the debt crisis was that it resulted in an even further differentiation of developing countries. The concept of the Third World as a homogeneous bloc was already questionable by 1970; by the end of the 1980s it was totally anachronistic. Countries at different levels of development and in different regional settings had distinctive problems and interests, which shaped their relationships with the Bretton Woods institutions.

In East and Southeast Asia, the turn toward export-oriented growth strategies that had begun in the 1960s in Korea, Taiwan, Hong Kong, and Singapore had spread to the countries of the Association of Southeast Asian Nations and was reaching the point of political irreversibility. These countries continued to draw on the services of the IMF and the World Bank over the 1980s, but with the exception of the Philippines all managed either to avoid debt crises altogether or to adjust largely on their own initiative.

---

2. John Williamson, who coined the term "the Washington consensus" (Williamson 1989, 1) was referring not only to the policy of the US government but also to that of the Bretton Woods institutions.

3. For discussions of the domestic politics of adjustment, see Haggard and Kaufman (1992), Williamson (1993), and Haggard and Webb (1994).

On the other hand, as trading states the Asian countries had become principal targets of US bilateralism. Partly as a result, they had begun to develop a strong interest in the Uruguay Round negotiations, particularly in those issues that promised to discipline the behavior of their major trading partners: subsidies, dumping, textiles, and dispute settlement. The support that these countries lent to the Uruguay Round has been underappreciated but conforms closely to the observation that weak countries have a strong interest in rules that limit the discretion of the strong.

In Latin America, crises generated dramatic reform efforts across the continent, with strong support from the IMF, the World Bank, and the Inter-American Development Bank. The sweeping trade liberalizations associated with the reform process paved the way for a number of important Latin American countries, including particularly Mexico, to join the GATT and to participate actively in the round.

The outstanding question hovering over the region was whether the reforms had been truly consolidated at the domestic level. Electorates had rejected the populist responses to the crisis visible in the early democratic administrations in Argentina, Bolivia, and Peru, and appeared to embrace the reform effort. But recent events in Brazil, Venezuela, and Mexico demonstrate the fragility of domestic support for the reforms, particularly where growth has been slow or erratic. There is a strong residual hostility to the Bretton Woods institutions and the principles on which they rest. The Venezuelan riots of 1989 were associated in the public mind with the launching of an IMF program, and the rebels in the southern Mexican state of Chiapas sought to link their efforts to the passage of the North American Free Trade Agreement.

A third set of developing countries, which might be called the Greater European System, includes the Mediterranean associates and the western tier of Eastern European countries. These countries have been important recipients of both IMF and World Bank assistance. Turkey's development trajectory, for example, resembles in important ways that of the larger Latin American countries, although its debt crisis came earlier; when it initiated an aggressive reform effort in 1980, Turkey became the darling of the multilateral institutions. Both the Bank and the Fund have also stepped aggressively into the formerly socialist countries. However, for these countries the institutions of the European Union are probably as important as the Bretton Woods institutions, not only because trading patterns inevitably center on Europe to a substantial degree, but also because a number of those countries are looking forward to ultimate entry into the Union.

Finally, the countries of Africa and South Asia have a very different relationship to the Bretton Woods family. With the exception of India, which with Brazil led developing country resistance to the Uruguay Round, the GATT is largely irrelevant to these countries. The key institutions are the network of aid donors, which include the Bank and the Fund but also go far beyond them to include the country-specific consortia of major donors and the institutions of the Lomé Convention and the franc zone. Nonetheless, these donors continue to rely heavily on the Bretton Woods institutions for the provision of technical advice and for the monitoring of adjustment programs.

As far ahead as we can see, these countries will remain heavily dependent on international largesse. However, the task that the donors face is becoming even more daunting. Not only do the traditional development problems remain immense, but in a number of the poorest, war-torn countries the central institutions of government themselves are crumbling. It is still unclear how the Bretton Woods and UN institutions will manage these failed states, or the extent to which outside administration can substitute for indigenous ones, but to the extent that the major powers concern themselves with these issues, they will rely heavily on the World Bank and the IMF to assist them.

The broad pattern may now be summarized. On the one hand, we see a gradual incorporation of the upper tier of developing countries into the institutions of the international trading system. Both international pressure and changed interests on the part of the developing countries themselves have fed this development. Those countries graduating into the GATT have, for the most part, also reached the point where they have access to private sources of capital and can gradually be weaned from reliance on the IMF and World Bank; indeed, the international institutions, and particularly the World Bank, should be pressed more aggressively to "graduate" countries and activities that, although successful, are no longer necessary. Upper-tier developing countries should also be tapped more aggressively to increase their contributions.

On the other hand, the international financial institutions continue to have a central role in assisting the debtors, the former socialist countries, and the poorest groups in the middle-income countries who may lack adequate political representation. The World Bank and the IMF are likely also to play a role in reconstructing the failed states of Africa, Haiti, Cambodia, and elsewhere, at least when their civil strife has ended.

Are there gains to be had from consolidating the operations of these institutions? I don't think so. The functions of the two have blurred at the margin, as the IMF recognized that balance of payments adjustment may involve longer-term structural reform and the World Bank recognized that sectoral and project lending would fail if the macroeconomic and broader policy environment was flawed. However, the functions of the two organizations are distinguishable, the creative tension between them has worked well, and they have shown a tremendous capacity to innovate and adapt to changing circumstances. I see no reason why they should be merged.

It does have to be understood and faced squarely, however, that the IMF and the World Bank will not be able to operate solely on the near-commercial criteria that govern the bulk of their operations, nor with the resources presently available to them. The successes of the last two decades in East Asia and the sweeping reforms in Eastern Europe and Latin America should not obscure the profound environmental, social, and economic deterioration that has taken place in other parts of the developing world. The historical record shows that the three Bretton Woods institutions are—whatever their flaws—by far the most efficient international institutions for dealing with these questions; they are as worthy of support now as they were fifty years ago.

References

Haggard, Stephan. *Developing Nations and the Politics of Global Integration.* Washington: Brookings Institution. Forthcoming.

Haggard, Stephan, and Robert R. Kaufman, eds. 1992. *The Politics of Adjustment.* Princeton, NJ: Princeton University Press.

Haggard, Stephan, and Steven B. Webb, eds. 1994. *Voting for Reform: Democracy, Political Liberalization, and Economic Adjustment.* New York: Oxford University Press.

Williamson, John. 1989. *Latin American Adjustment: How Much Has Happened?* Washington: Institute for International Economics.

Williamson, John, ed. 1993. *The Political Economy of Policy Reform.* Washington: Institute for International Economics.

Comment

MOISÉS NAÍM

The G-4 Effect and Other Organizational Factors in the Reform of the IMF and the World Bank

Most of the analyses and proposals prompted by the 50th anniversary of the Bretton Woods institutions center on large, systemic issues of global governance, on the need to respond to new economic and political realities, or on the impact of the policies of the International Monetary Fund and the World Bank. From the search for mechanisms to dampen exchange rate volatility, to proposals to merge the IMF with the World Bank (or even to close them down), to the effects of structural adjustment, the anniversary has stimulated a wide debate on many important issues.

Yet surprisingly little attention has been given to the factors that shape the internal behavior of the Bretton Woods institutions. The way in which these institutions are governed, the mechanisms and processes through which their priorities are chosen and their strategies defined, and the incentives and values that drive their internal culture have received scant attention. In fact, these are generally perceived as very minor, even bureaucratic details. The attractive challenges for most officials and analysts are either to get the policy prescriptions right, or to activate a political process that would lead to the adoption of the systemic changes they favor.

It is, indeed, possible that, as a result of the debates spurred by the anniversary, we will see some major adaptations of the Bretton Woods

Moisés Naím is senior associate at the Carnegie Endowment for International Peace. He has served as executive director at the World Bank and as minister of industry of Venezuela.

institutions to the new economic, political, and technological circumstances of the world. Unfortunately, policy-induced changes in global governance require the agreement of a significant number of countries that often have sharply differing views and priorities. Therefore, regardless of the quality and merit of proposals to radically alter the way in which the international economy is currently governed, the probability that sweeping changes will be adopted is not very high. The mid-1990s finds the world without a rallier of nations that is capable of assembling the international coalition needed to induce the systemic reforms called for by the changes in the international economy that have occurred since the Bretton Woods conference.

Such adaptations will therefore have to be made within the context of the existing institutional framework. From this perspective, gaining a deeper understanding of how the institutions really work and of the factors that influence their performance can provide useful insights into their ability to adapt to the new challenges. It is therefore useful to highlight some of these issues that are often overlooked but that deserve more attention when discussing proposals to reform the world economy.[1]

Strategic Ambiguity

Most recent reviews of the IMF, the World Bank, or the regional development banks have concluded that they suffer from the lack of a precisely defined mission. Changes in the international financial system eroded the raison d'être of the IMF, while the adoption of an ever-expanding definition of the determinants of underdevelopment added to the portfolio of goals that the development banks are expected to address. In recent years the need to assist countries emerging from decades of communism also added to the diversification of the goals of the Fund and the Bank.

The lack of a precise mission has allowed the institutions to adapt quite effectively to changes in their environment. Since their creation, the World Bank and the IMF have reinvented themselves several times in response to new challenges that their founders had not contemplated.[2] The downside of this flexibility is, of course, a significant dose of strategic ambiguity. The combination of a blurred mission, a drastically changing external environment, constantly growing demands, and a problematic governance structure has led to a rapid accumulation of goals. The excessive number of priorities breeds not only goal congestion but strategic confusion. Obviously, these are conditions that would impair effectiveness and efficiency in any organization. Goal congestion is most visible in the development banks—with portfolios of goals that range from the role of women in

---

1. A more detailed analysis of these issues is presented in Naím (1994).

2. See, for example, Bretton Woods Commission (1994) and *The Economist*, 9 July 1994, 69–75.

development to the regulation of telephone companies—but it has also plagued the operations and the organizational effectiveness of the Fund.

Goal congestion derives not only from a blurred, changing mission. It is also the result of the very different expectations that influential constituencies have regarding the fundamental role of these institutions. Take the case of the World Bank, whose problems on this score are found—in more acute forms—in all the other regional development banks. Different audiences and constituencies have conflicting expectations as to what the institution should stand for—what it is supposed to do and how.

While there are many different answers to such questions, they can be generically grouped into four dominant categories or "models" of the World Bank. A very common one emphasizes the primacy of the financial intermediation function of the Bank. It can be labeled the Bank-as-a-bank model. From this perspective, issues such as the Bank's standing in capital markets, its loan-loss provisions, the quality of its portfolio, and the creditworthiness of its clients are of paramount importance. Deterioration in any of these jeopardizes the capacity of the institution to fulfill its other, developmental goals, which, therefore, have to be subordinated to these financial priorities. At the other end of the spectrum is a view of the Bank that, instead of financial intermediation, emphasizes international distributional justice. From this perspective the World Bank is essentially a mechanism for transferring funds from rich to poor countries. It is, in effect, a fund that is periodically filled with money from rich countries, to be disbursed to poor countries, and then replenished again once it is exhausted.

A third, frequently held view emphasizes the "evangelical" role of the Bank. According to this view, the main role of the Bank—especially since policy-based lending was adopted—is to convert borrowing countries' governments to its liberal, "market-friendly" development doctrine. From this perspective, the Bank's combination of knowledge and money provides a powerful lever that can catalyze beneficial changes in the countries that follow its advice. A fourth and in many ways contrasting model holds that, in effect, the Bank is simply another instrument utilized by its more influential shareholders—the United States and the other industrial countries—to advance their own national interests.

All these models are not merely descriptive: they often underlie the expectations and the prescriptions for action advanced by the different internal and external constituencies of the Bank. Such a polarized set of assumptions about the fundamental purpose of the Bank makes it very difficult for the institution to have a sharply focused mission. Furthermore, in the words of one of the Bank's most senior officials:

> These different views are held by the same sets of shareholders; and indeed, often by the same shareholder. Which view predominates depends on the subject and time. An institution that gets such diverse and variable guidance as a steady diet

will have problems in focusing on fewer objectives far greater than those created by
internal constraints. (private communication with the author)

The consequence, of course, is a proliferation of priorities and the need to house under a single corporate roof an organization that has to be able to provide its clients with sound advice about topics ranging from highway maintenance to judicial reform.

Sharply differing assumptions about the fundamental purpose of the institution also affect the strategy making and the organizational functioning of the IMF. Although its charter defines for it a more narrow institutional scope than that of the Bank, in recent years the Fund has also been adding new topics to its agenda. Its ventures into the more qualitative aspects of the budget cuts it often has to recommend have led the IMF to develop an interest in subjects like military expenditures or the environmental consequences of the conditions it imposes on its borrowers.

The propensity of the Bretton Woods institutions both to lack a clear mission and to suffer from goal overload places a heavy burden on their organizational functioning. The inability of their governance systems to provide clearer guidance is an important determinant of these problems.

Conflicted Governance

Ambiguity of mission, goal congestion, and strategic volatility in the Bretton Woods institutions are, to a great extent, the consequence of the way in which decision making at the top of these institutions is organized. In general, once an objective is incorporated as part of the agenda, it becomes almost impossible to remove it. Political factors, organizational inertia, and the governance system of the institutions make it very difficult to shed goals, at least formally.

It is fair to recognize, however, that in the case of the World Bank and the IMF the existing governance system has worked fairly well. It has not replicated some of the sorry experiences of other multilateral institutions, such as several of those in the United Nations system. It has also proved capable of responding to the new demands imposed by the international political and economic environment.

In effect, one can argue that it is almost a miracle that the Bank and the Fund are still recognized, even by their harshest critics, as technically competent organizations. To their credit, over the years they have been capable of attracting and retaining a respected pool of highly talented and skilled professionals. As a general rule, in the World Bank and the IMF, staff recruitment and promotion are determined more by merit than by politics. In many areas, the reports produced in these institutions become indispensable references in any discussion pertaining to their subjects. Furthermore, at a time in which the capacity of the world for effective multilateral action seems to have been impaired by the end of the Cold

War, the Bretton Woods institutions continue to offer a conduit through which international collective action can be reliably channeled.

These unique strengths and values counsel caution in any attempt to reform the institutions. Experience has repeatedly shown that even the most resilient and sturdy of institutions is extremely vulnerable to mistakes made in the course of well-meaning reforms. This caveat notwithstanding, the Fund and the Bank—and to an even larger extent the regional development banks—are, like all institutions, in constant need of organizational repair and maintenance. As noted, their governance system is a strong candidate for attention and reform.

The governance system of a multilateral financial institution typically has a board of governors, composed of ministers or central bank presidents or governors, who delegate responsibility to a full-time board of directors. The overall management responsibility falls on a strong president or chief executive officer. The authority to adopt new strategic initiatives usually rests with the president and his or her top management, even though in some cases such initiatives are taken as a result of the pressures of influential external constituencies. In recent years, legislatures, nongovernmental organizations, and the media have substantially increased their capacity to shape the agenda and even the strategy of the multilateral financial institutions.

The other important element of the governance system of the Bretton Woods institutions is the board of directors of each. While the formal role of the board is quite clear, in practice it is quite complex and ambiguous. The board represents the interests of shareholders and has almost total authority over the affairs of the institutions. Executive directors do not have any management responsibility and are not individually accountable for any specific decision made by the institution. Although the board has to approve every transaction and policy initiative, such initiatives are usually launched by management. Also, while executive directors do not have any day-to-day responsibilities, they work full-time in the institution. And although they are representatives of the governments that appoint them, they are employees paid by the institution.

In all organizations, a tension exists between shareholders or their representatives (i.e., the board of directors) on the one hand, and management on the other. This is true not just of private-sector organizations, but whenever an overseeing body has authority over the group of people who carry out daily management responsibilities. Management tends to want to maximize growth, autonomy, and scope for its operations, whereas the board seeks to minimize risk, exposure, and the need for capital increases. This tension in the relationship can, in fact, be very productive, but if it is excessive, management is usually stifled, and an atmosphere of distrust, resentment, and inefficiency ensues. If, on the other hand, this tension is too weak, organizations tend to develop an operational bias toward the priorities favored by management, sometimes at the expense of shareholders' interests. Striking a healthy balance in the tension between board and management is often an important precondition for the long-term institutional survival of the organization.

In the Bretton Woods institutions, the balance between shareholders and management is particularly fragile. Governors tend to be ministers, who already have such a full agenda that they cannot devote enough of their time, effort, and attention to the supervision and overall management of the institutions. In fact, the issues relating to the institutions typically enter the governors' agenda only when they pertain to their own countries. Partly out of necessity, the governors delegate the monitoring, oversight, and the provision of a sense of direction of the institutions to the midlevel staff in their ministries, and to the executive board member representatives.

The board, in turn, is fraught with conflicts of interest and other structural deficiencies that limit its effectiveness. First, some directors represent borrowing countries, others represent donor countries, and still others represent both borrowing and donor countries. Second, whereas management is typically composed of specialists with many years of experience in the institutions, executive directors are political appointees who rarely stay more than three years in the job. Third, paradoxically even if they are political appointees, executive directors tend to have less access to the higher echelons of their governments than do the top management of the World Bank or the IMF. Fourth, with the growing complexity and diversity of the institutions' agenda, it becomes very difficult for executive directors to exercise effective oversight over all the issues on which they are supposed to make decisions. Very often, this leads to a highly ritualized and symbolic decision-making process, in which management receives very little strategic direction from the board.

Reforming the way in which executive directors are recruited and trained for their jobs, together with a concerted effort to upgrade the way in which the board of directors of the Bretton Woods institutions operate, may end up having more beneficial effects than many of the good ideas about global reform that, unfortunately, have little chance of being implemented.

The G-4 Effect

Institutional performance is affected not only by formal goals and strategies, resources, or organizational design. Organizations also have a tacit, informal, and often hard to discern set of values, rules, habits, and routines that define their functioning and therefore their overall performance. The Bretton Woods institutions are no different. In fact, they have a very strong and deeply ingrained organizational culture, which has provided over the years the glue that unifies and gives coherence to organizations that are constantly subject to strong centrifugal pressures. After all, these are large, complex, highly diversified, and multipurpose organizations with operations all over the world. They are staffed with people from different countries and with different religions, cultures, and technical backgrounds. The institutions also have to reconcile their political character with their technical vocation. Furthermore, as discussed above, they are rarely anchored by a stable and well-defined mission statement. All these characteristics tend to fragment the organizations by department, specialization, and geography, and along many other fault lines.

To compensate for the consequences of this organizational fragmentation, an elaborate set of unwritten rules has emerged over the years to facilitate the integration of the institutions' many disparate parts, cultures, and technical orientations. Yet while it certainly helps to increase corporate cohesion, the strong organizational culture commonly found in the Bretton Woods institutions can also act as a formidable obstacle to change. One important trait of this culture is its inward orientation. The need to balance the strong centrifugal, splintering forces has given rise to equally strong centripetal forces that, for many purposes, make internal constituencies more important than external ones. This inward-oriented organizational culture has its roots in three major factors. First is the extreme job dependence of most of the staff. Second is the lack of competition enjoyed until now by the Bank and the Fund. Third is its budget-driven performance.

In all organizations, employees are critically dependent on their jobs. As a result their behavior at work is strongly influenced by job retention tactics. At the Bretton Woods institutions these tactics are exacerbated by the fact that the institutions tend to offer more advantageous work conditions than can be found elsewhere, or even have a virtual monopsony in certain job categories. A Bangladeshi specialist on central banking or an Argentinean expert on agricultural reform could certainly find other jobs, in their own countries or elsewhere. It is much less certain, however, that those jobs would be as well-paid or as interesting as those they have at the Bank or the Fund. I call this the G-4 effect, alluding to the US visa category that non-US citizens that work in the Bretton Woods institutions have, and that has to be relinquished almost immediately upon termination of employment.

Losing a job is always a traumatic experience. The trauma increases with the length of tenure of the job that is being lost.[3] When the job loss entails not only the instantaneous loss of the G-4 visa but also the loss of the tax-exempt status, the education and health benefits, and the rest of the perquisites enjoyed by employees of the Bretton Woods institutions, it

---

3. The average tenure at the World Bank, for example, is 10 years. Also, a large number of staff are recruited at the midcareer level, when they are in their late thirties and early forties.

becomes an event of catastrophic proportions. This extreme dependency affects all staff equally, not just the non-US employees, and is a pervasive and crucial element of the institutions' culture. The point is that the G-4 effect is a metaphor for an institutional characteristic that makes Bretton Woods staff more dependent on their employment by these specific institutions than is normally the case in other professional organizations where job mobility is less rigid and traumatic.[4]

Therefore, although job retention tactics influence behavior in all organizations, at the Bretton Woods institutions such tactics acquire an importance that overrides all other concerns. The G-4 effect greatly heightens the importance of office politics. It stimulates the emergence of clanlike groups whose members support and promote each other in a muted but intense rivalry with members of other clans. It encourages the building of informal coalitions and mutual support groups, raises the aversion of individuals to taking risks, and increases resistance to organizational change. The sensitivity to unwritten rules of behavior is amplified and the importance of informal but deeply grounded routines, codes, and values creates a very powerful organizational culture. Such culture makes promotion and job stability much more dependent on the person's internal reputation than on the opinions of those outside the organization.

A second important factor that determines this inward-oriented culture is the lack of competition that the Fund and the Bank have traditionally enjoyed. This has allowed the institutions to be relatively aloof from their clients. After all, a client that is not satisfied with the services rendered by the institutions has not had the option of taking its business elsewhere. Furthermore, built into the relationship between the Bretton Woods institutions and their clients is the assumption that governments are reluctant to make the unpopular changes in their policies on which loans are conditioned. This often creates a relationship where governments are expected to complain publicly about the harsh policy measures that the institutions are forcing on them. Frequently, complaints about IMF or Bank policies are expressed even in cases where the staffs know that the client government agrees that the policies imposed by the Fund or the Bank are necessary and will eventually be beneficial. The assumption that this is often the case and the fact that clients have no alternative has historically made it very easy for the staff in the institutions to ignore the complaints of clients.

A third factor underlying this inward orientation is the fact that these are quasi-public institutions and, as such, budget driven. Unlike private

---

4. The G-4 effect varies with nationality and profession. For example, for European and Japanese staff members the pull of the G-4 effect is often less intense than for staff from developing countries. Also, a staff member specializing in finance may have many more equivalent job possibilities outside the Bank than, for example, a specialist on issues of women in development. This naturally influences employees' feelings about job dependency and, in turn, their organizational behavior.

businesses, the Bretton Woods institutions do not depend upon selling a product to the outside world; their budgets determine their output. Under these circumstances the opinion of clients matters much less than the opinion of those in charge of allocating budgets.

The implication of these observations is not that the performance of the Bretton Woods institutions could be improved by changing the visa status of its non-US employees. It is, rather, to use the G-4 effect to highlight the importance of subtle but powerful forces acting within these organizations and that are often ignored when discussing grand plans about the multilateral financial system. In practice, these almost invisible factors often get in the way of such grand designs. The challenge is to alter the more dysfunctional aspects of this culture without losing the advantages derived from the strong sense of attachment, long-term commitment, and institutional loyalty that is common among the staff of the Bretton Woods institutions.

Conclusions

The fact that the 50th anniversary of the Bretton Woods institutions coincides with a time of radical changes in the world order will certainly inspire bold new ideas. New institutions will be proposed, as will drastic redesigns of existing ones. Reality, however, is very likely to foil the adoption of radical changes. Radical change requires a degree of consensus and international leadership that does not currently exist.

This does not mean that major progress cannot be achieved in improving the relevance of the Bretton Woods institutions to new world conditions. Some of the changes may be viewed as too small or "managerial" for a time calling for revolutionary measures. But concentrating on these "small" changes has the advantage that they are much more likely to generate a return. Also, although they are small in comparison to more grandiose ideas, these changes may, in fact, amount to quite a revolution when compared with the current situation. Not enough attention has been paid to these institutional considerations.

We have argued that the low impact that the external environment has had on the Bretton Woods institutions has led to very inward-oriented organizational cultures. Such a culture, in addition to lack of competition, the budget-driven nature of the institutions, and the proliferation of goals and the difficulty of measuring many of them has created an internal environment that discourages the emergence of stronger management practices. It is critical, therefore, that shareholders pay more attention to the workings of these institutions and to long-term institutional objectives. They must not focus only on the occasional emergencies that are too visible or important to avoid.

Finally, it is essential that all of these institutions retain those elements that make them efficient and effective. These include strong technical capacities, the ability to attract and retain highly skilled, competent personnel, and the ability to produce valuable, usable knowledge. At the same time, it is necessary to encourage personnel to forge closer ties with their clients. To achieve this, the Bretton Woods institutions will have to generate new incentives within their organizational cultures that make them more efficient. In this way internal performance will be more linked to output, and inputs less linked to budget reports.

The G-4 effect illustrates the impact that these often-neglected factors have on the Bretton Woods institutions. Articulating a more focused mission, attaining a wider consensus about their precise role, and setting up better governance structures will become urgent priorities for those interested in healthier and more effective Bretton Woods institutions. As the outside world changes, so must these institutions. Only if they do change will they continue to be more successful than any other international organization in providing global public goods that today are as much in undersupply as they were at the end of World War II.

References

Bretton Woods Commission. *Bretton Woods: Looking to the Future.* Washington: Bretton Woods Commission.

Naím, Moisés. 1994. "The World Bank: Its Role, Governance and Organizational Culture." In Bretton Woods Commission, *Bretton Woods: Looking to the Future.* Washington: Bretton Woods Commission.

III

Managing the New International Economic Issues

5

Managing a Market-Led Global Financial System

TOMMASO PADOA-SCHIOPPA AND FABRIZIO SACCOMANNI

L'expérience de chaque homme se recommence. Seules les institutions deviennent plus sages.[1]

H. F. Amiel

The question put to us on this 50th anniversary of the Bretton Woods conference is how the international community should manage financial markets in the next 50 years.[2] Rather than attempt to jump ahead to the year 2044, we have taken a more cautious approach based on the conviction that the roots of the future are planted in the soil of the past, and that the tree they nourish will be shaped by the present environment.

Our analysis and conclusions have of course been influenced by our experience as central bankers and by the fact that our intellectual and professional formation took place when the Bretton Woods system was in full bloom, presiding over a period of strong, noninflationary growth and broad stability in exchange and financial markets. This experience has persuaded us of two things: first, that the governance of the world economy requires an institutional framework, and second, that the post-1973

Tommaso Schioppa is deputy director general, Bank of Italy, and was previously chairman of the Basle Committee on Banking Supervision, Bank for International Settlements. Fabrizio Saccomanni is head of the foreign department, Bank of Italy, and was chairman of the foreign exchange policy subcommittee, European Monetary Institute.

1. "Experience starts over with every individual. Only institutions become wiser."

2. One of the authors was involved in a similar exercise a few years ago, although covering a shorter time horizon (Padoa-Schioppa 1988).

arrangements embodied in the revised charter of the International Monetary Fund (IMF) do not provide such a framework. Indeed, we do not subscribe to the view that the present arrangements are simply an adaptation of the Bretton Woods system, retaining its essential institutional features and fundamental objectives. We shall argue that the emergence of global financial markets has fundamentally altered the reality that the IMF was intended to manage. Promoting exchange rate stability and adjustment is still the IMF's mandate, but the institution no longer has the power to pursue such goals on a global scale.

We would not want, nor do we consider it possible, to return to the old Bretton Woods system. Rather, we think that it is important to analyze the present nature of monetary and financial markets and the policy implications thereof, and to draw from the analysis a *new* set of rules and institutions. We attach a crucial importance to institutional arrangements because we are convinced that, just as domestic financial markets are subject to the rule of law within countries, so international markets cannot be left to operate in a legal and institutional vacuum. The evidence shows that international cooperation of a noninstitutional nature has generally failed to sustain the momentum of its own action beyond the short term, often leading to the undoing of the results achieved. Not surprisingly, we see a clear need for a central banking function emerging from the globalization of currency and financial markets. We are concerned that policy functions in the global financial system either are carried out in an ad hoc manner through sporadic intergovernmental action, are left to the spontaneous initiatives of market participants, or simply do not exist.

This paper is organized as follows: the first section below summarizes our interpretation of the demise of the Bretton Woods system, which we define as a government-led international monetary system (or G-IMS), and the emergence of what we call a market-led international monetary system (or M-IMS). The next section briefly analyzes the implications of the M-IMS for the main policy areas in which central banks are normally involved. Subsequent sections cover the three areas (monetary conditions, payment services, and banking and finance) that compose the M-IMS and for which public functions are necessary; present market developments and policy responses are described. The penultimate section is devoted to the institutional dimension of the M-IMS, and the final section presents some conclusions.

The Legacy of Bretton Woods

Main Features of the G-IMS

Bretton Woods was a system of multilateral institutions and rules designed for nation-states pursuing full employment and economic stabilization in a world with strong political leadership and limited trade and financial integration. The system was intended to provide a response to a long period of economic isolationism that had culminated in a global war.

As the end of the war was nearing, the governments of the winning market-oriented powers, learning from the experience of the 1930s, decided to make a drastic turn toward an open and managed multilateral system, in which trade and monetary relations would be subject to formal rules for exchange rate and trade policies aiming at noninflationary growth in conditions of "economic peace." Aside from the governments' memory of the interwar monetary anarchy, another crucial factor behind Bretton Woods was the conviction, developed in the aftermath of the Great Depression, that governments had the power to enhance national welfare through discretionary policy action.

In the Bretton Woods system, discretionary policy and systemic rules were to interact in such a way as to internalize the externalities produced by the international economic integration that the system was to promote. The two strategic aims of the postwar international economic policy agenda were the promotion of free trade to foster welfare and growth and the pursuit of stable exchange rates. To this end, Bretton Woods established a sort of division of labor: on the one side, *markets* would determine the international allocation of resources, assisted by trade liberalization policies; on the other, *governments* would determine the overall level of domestic activity through active macroeconomic policies. Monetary stability was to be attained through fixed (albeit adjustable) exchange rates in an environment of segmented capital markets.[3]

The new arrangements contained a strong blend of rules and institutions. Exchange rates could be adjusted only in the event of fundamental imbalances and only with the consent of the IMF. Multilateral institutions were to encourage trade expansion, manage and monitor the new exchange rate regime, promote currency convertibility, and extend balance of payments and development assistance to individual countries. In the attempt to reconcile free trade with macroeconomic and financial stability and domestic policy discretion, the system also laid down restrictions on short-term cross-border capital movements. Capital controls were seen as necessary to limit the destabilizing potential of capital flight, which had caused serious disturbances during the interwar period (Nurkse 1944). Thus, free trade was reinstated among nations together with a government-led international monetary system (G-IMS), whose stability was ensured by the preeminent role played by national governments (directly or

---

3. De Cecco (1985) and Panizza (1985) provide evidence that the banking establishments in Britain and the United States were not really happy with this concept and pressured their respective governments to eliminate from the final Bretton Woods agreements all those features of the plans put forward by John Maynard Keynes and Harry Dexter White that might have limited their role in international finance.

through the IMF) and their policy functions in international economic and financial relations.

The G-IMS contained an intrinsic asymmetry: on the one hand, it promoted the internationalization of economic relations through *free trade*; on the other, it aimed to *control finance* within a limited, domestic dimension. Over time, the tension arising from this conflict would jeopardize the survival of the system.

The Rise of International Financial Markets

Until the beginning of the 1960s, domestic financial markets tended to be protected from external competition by capital and exchange restrictions introduced to limit the destabilizing impact of short-term cross-border flows of private capital.[4] As a 1967 study by the Organization for Economic Cooperation and Development (OECD) reported, international capital transactions were still dominated by official operations effected outside of financial markets. Payment and credit facilities based on intergovernmental bilateral arrangements evolved only slowly into multilateral schemes involving the major international commercial banks. Private-sector finance was still dominated by traditional domestic banking activity and was subject to government controls. Securities markets were narrow, and transactions by nonresidents rarely had an impact on domestic markets. Security issues abroad represented only a small additional source of financial support for national markets, where discriminations were applied, notably in Europe, in favor of domestic borrowers, especially national governments.[5]

From a systemic point of view, the segmentation and small size of international financial markets, as well as their limited capacity to process and use information efficiently, helped minimize the risk of foreign-exchange and international payment crises. Under these conditions, the destabilizing potential of news was limited.[6]

---

4. The Organization for Economic Cooperation and Development (1967, 256), noting the widespread persistence of capital controls in all major industrial countries, concluded that "all these controls come down . . . to the search for stability and to the desire to pursue . . . a monetary and financial policy which is independent of external pressures exerted by certain capital movements."

5. See the Joint Economic Committee report of 1964 (US Congress 1964), the Segré Report (European Economic Community Commission 1966), and OECD (1967).

6. As a consequence, it would not be inappropriate to argue that exchange rates during that period were governed more by *real* forces than by expectations prevailing in the international asset markets or by interest rate differentials across countries, as would happen later. The real nature of the exchange rate determination process may have kept the expected volatility of exchange rates at a low level for the whole period considered, thereby reinforcing the stability of exchange rates around the established parities.

The success of Bretton Woods brought about the internationalization of finance. Sustained output growth and free trade after the return to multilateral convertibility in Europe in 1958 stimulated the development of international finance, as market participants increasingly exploited the large arbitrage opportunities created by national restrictions. Capital controls proved only partially effective, as they excluded the multitude of traditional savers and investors from international financial markets, but did not prevent large companies from developing a significant international financial activity by way of commercial credits and trade payment terms. It is through these channels that pressure was exerted on various currencies throughout the early 1960s. International capital movements associated with portfolio and direct investment also started to grow significantly, especially from the United States toward Europe, where economic stabilization and new market opportunities provided good business incentives. US banks borrowed abroad to supply credit to the rapidly growing industrial multinationals, thereby taking on the role of world financial intermediaries.[7] Dollar holdings started to accumulate abroad, and the potential for international speculation against the dollar grew markedly.[8]

The new regulations adopted by the US administration in 1965 to contain that potential through the Voluntary Credit Restraint Program (VCRP) created a loophole in the monetary control exercised by the Federal Reserve (De Cecco 1985) and led US banks to lend money abroad through their offshore branches. Dollar deposits could be shifted on and off domestic bank balance sheets at will through the expanding Eurodollar circuit and could be traded outside the United States, independent of US monetary policy.[9] Thus, the US balance of payments ceased to be the sole channel for supplying international liquidity, and the dollar-deposit multiplier progressively slipped out of Fed control. The emergence of less regulated markets lured world investors with prospects of larger profits and liquidity: international flows of private capital began to pose problems for domestic monetary control in major countries. By the end of the

---

7. Regulations prevented banks from competing domestically for deposits by offering higher interest rates, while the large US financing needs arising from the Vietnam War decreased the funds available in the domestic interbank market for alternative uses.

8. During this period, and especially during the 1970s, international competition among banks began to grow sharply, especially in bidding for large deposits and investment projects. The strength of the large non-US banks and banking systems and their presence in international activity increased significantly.

9. Yeager (1976) reports figures from the Bank for International Settlements that show the net size of the Euromarket (excluding interbank deposits) growing from about $7 billion in 1963 to about $91 billion by the end of 1972 (about 77 percent of these funds were denominated in dollars). At that point, outstanding Eurocurrency deposits, net of double counting, represented 35 percent and 17 percent of the narrow and broad money supply, respectively, in the United States.

1960s, with economic fundamentals in the United States deteriorating sharply and the dollar becoming increasingly overvalued, speculative activity in the foreign-exchange markets reached a level far exceeding the defensive capacity of national monetary authorities. An impressive show of market strength came in 1969 when massive inflows of hot money in Germany severely threatened the Bundesbank's ability to control domestic monetary conditions, eventually leading to the temporary floating of the deutsche mark—an episode that was to leave an indelible mark on German central bankers (Emminger 1977).

The events that led to the final collapse of the Bretton Woods exchange rate and monetary regime in 1971–73 are well known and do not need recalling. However, it is worth emphasizing that, in the end, the mobility of capital worldwide and the impact of international finance on the conduct of monetary policies were to prove Bretton Woods inadequate for a world economy that its rules and institutions had helped to integrate.

The Emergence of the M-IMS

In the years after the collapse of Bretton Woods, and especially in the 1980s, the market-led international monetary system (M-IMS) emerged in its entirety. This was as much the result of exogenous developments in the world economy and in the monetary and financial system as it was the consequence of deliberate policy decisions made by the key countries and approved by the IMF. One such decision was to let the markets handle the recycling of petrodollars after 1974. Another was the failure to cancel newly created Special Drawing Rights (SDRs) in the face of a massive increase in international liquidity during the 1970s. Yet another was the failure to agree on a "substitution account" in the IMF to replace dollars with SDRs in 1979. These events marked the demise of the multilateral management of international liquidity. Following the revolution in communications and information technology, domestic and offshore financial markets were opened and integrated into a single global market, including all the industrial countries as well as a growing number of developing countries (IMF 1991, Goldstein and Mussa 1993).

It has become a commonplace, in which at times we have indulged ourselves, to describe the post–Bretton Woods era as a *nonsystem*. Upon reflection, however, we have come to realize that present arrangements do indeed constitute a system, with its own patterns of economic relationships, mechanisms for international money creation and exchange rate determination, market and policy practices, channels of communication between governments and between participants, and codes of conduct (however informal these might be).

The present system is the converse of the preceding one. Where the fully developed policy mechanisms of the G-IMS were combined with an embryonic market component, the reverse is true in the M-IMS. This was largely the result of a natural long-term natural process driven by people and innovation, one that government restrictions of any sort could hardly impede. It has eroded the effectiveness of the monetary policy functions of domestic central banking, in that it has removed the territorial correspondence between financial markets and central banks' jurisdiction. At the same time, the traditional distinctions between banks and nonbanks (Golembe and Mingo 1985) were blurred by financial liberalization and innovation, thus weakening another pillar (the special nature of banks) upon which central banks' monetary policy functions were based (Corrigan 1982). To secure financial stability, central banks have to face this double challenge.

Narrowing the wide *institutional gap* between the global nature of the M-IMS and the domestic charter of central banks is the major problem facing any attempt to reform international monetary and financial relations, and the key task that a "new Bretton Woods" would have to tackle. Whereas the exchange rate rule and the official (as distinguished from market) credit and payment mechanisms during the years of Bretton Woods were broadly sufficient to satisfy policy needs in an environment of highly regulated and segmented domestic financial markets, a more complete set of policy functions is necessary to ensure monetary and financial stability in global financial markets.

The identification of such policy needs and the search for ways in which to meet them today are the object of the following three sections of this paper. They will be devoted to the three areas that constitute modern monetary and financial systems and for which central banks have competence: monetary creation, payment services, and bank intermediation—or, to phrase it in policy terms, monetary and exchange rate policies, payment systems oversight and operations, and banking supervision. Of this triad, which is directly related to the well-known Hicksian triads of functions of money and motives for holding it (Hicks 1967), the Bretton Woods system and the IMF covered only the first element, disregarding the other two. Domestic systems cover them all. Thus, a natural avenue to explore at this stage might be the adaptation of today's financial policy functions to the M-IMS and an evaluation of progress achieved so far through international cooperation in the areas of money, payments, and banking supervision.

Monetary Conditions

Market Developments

Key exchange rates and international liquidity have become essentially market-determined in the M-IMS. A *multicurrency reserve system* developed whereby currencies other than the US dollar increasingly attracted investors, at a time when financial liberalization and new communication technologies were lowering the transaction costs and increasing the speed of transferring funds across currencies. As a result, exchange rate volatility (figures 1 to 3 and table 1) increased dramatically, especially after 1973, while persistent departures of the relevant exchange rates from their equilibrium level emerged and widened.

International liquidity expanded at a much more rapid pace than under the G-IMS. In addition to the unprecedented increase caused by the exceptional growth of currency reserves and the large jump in the price of gold (tables 2 and 3), from the 1960s onward international liquidity increasingly reflected the expansion of the Eurocurrency markets. In fact, the market enabled countries to maintain deficit positions by incurring additional liabilities (liability financing) that were much larger and more persistent than would have been possible if they had relied on mobilizing own reserves (asset settlement).

With floating exchange rates and full capital mobility, international monetary conditions have in turn become increasingly dependent on the national monetary policy stance of the major industrial countries and on the lending policies of the major financial intermediaries (banks and securities houses), with the latter being influenced by the former.

After 1973 international monetary conditions were mainly influenced by the expansionary policy stances adopted by the major industrial countries (with the notable exception of Germany) to cope with the recession induced by the oil shock. The turning point occurred in 1979 with the severe tightening of US monetary policy under Federal Reserve Chairman Paul Volcker, to which Japan and the European Community eventually adjusted. Since then the overall stance of monetary policies in the major countries has been generally prudent and aimed at curbing domestic inflationary pressures, particularly those arising from fiscal deficits. As a result, inflation has been declining in the industrial world since the 1980s, and there has been an increasing convergence of inflation rates around low levels.

The anti-inflationary policy stance pursued by major industrial countries was crucial in reestablishing control over international monetary conditions in spite of floating exchange rates and full capital mobility. However, there have been large and abrupt changes in the currency denomination of monetary and financial flows, with important repercussions on the exchange rates and domestic monetary conditions of individual countries. Such changes have at one time or another affected all the major industrial countries since the mid-1980s as the process of liberalization of capital movements and financial integration throughout the world began to accelerate.

The process was associated with a number of factors:

Figure 1 Volatility of nominal exchange rates, deutsche mark–US dollar, 1960–94

Percentage change from previous month

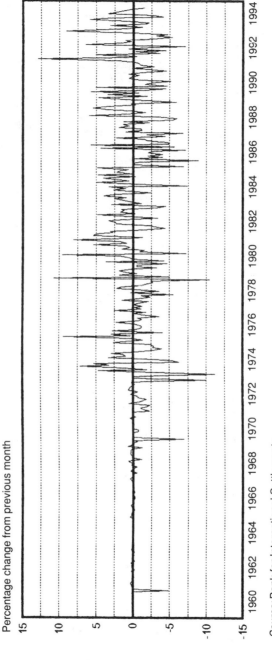

Source: Bank for International Settlements.

Figure 2 Volatility of nominal exchange rates, yen–US dollar, 1960–94

Percentage change from previous month

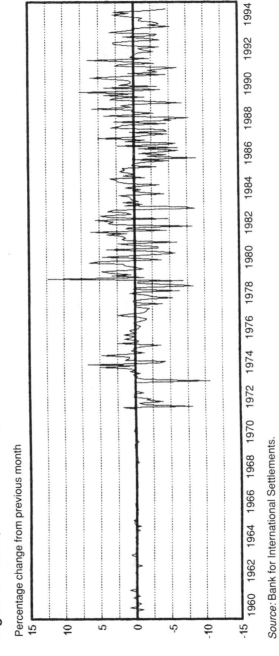

Source: Bank for International Settlements.

Figure 3 Volatility of nominal exchange rates, deutsche mark–yen, 1960–94

Percentage change from previous month

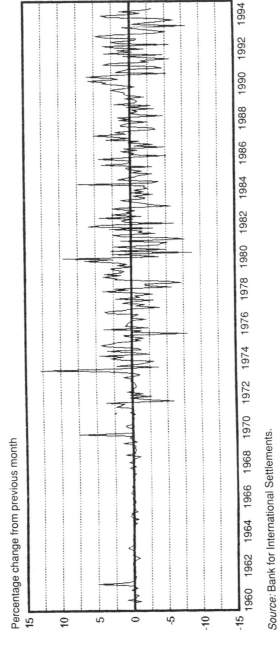

Source: Bank for International Settlements.

Table 1 Relative volatility of nominal exchange rates among the G-3 currencies, 1960–94

Exchange rate	Standard deviation of monthly percentage change			
	1960–71	1972–80	1981–90	1991–94
Deutsche mark–dollar	0.82	3.43	3.39	4.04
Yen–dollar	0.80	3.06	3.52	2.55
Deutsche mark–yen	1.08	3.21	2.68	3.22

Source: Bank for International Settlements.

■ **Internationalization of portfolios.** As the liberalization of capital movements progressed, investors started to look at opportunities offered by financial markets abroad, particularly in fixed-income government bonds, searching for "high coupon" countries.

■ **Banks' decline relative to markets.** With financial liberalization and deregulation and the push to securitization fostered, inter alia, by the debt crisis, banks lost their central role in intermediation; exclusive direct relationships between lenders and borrowers were largely been replaced by price signals as a vehicle for transmitting information.

■ **Financial market determination of exchange rates.** As demand for foreign exchange related to financial transactions (including demand for hedging of foreign-currency risks through forwards, futures, and options) rapidly outgrew that related to trade transactions, exchange rates became increasingly determined as asset prices, quickly reacting to changes in expectations, news, and interest rate differentials, often independently of changes in economic fundamentals.

■ **Market volatility.** As information and communications technology enhanced the speed with which market participants react to news, market price volatility amplified; the transmission velocity of shocks across financial markets and the destabilizing potential of news increased markedly.

■ **Market concentration.** The institutionalization of financial investment management has resulted in a concentration of market activity in the hands of comparatively few financial institutions (banks, securities houses, mutual funds, hedge funds, etc.), all operating simultaneously in foreign-exchange, money, and bond markets, often with highly leveraged positions and using broadly similar "technical analyses" and conventions of behavior.

■ **No insulation, no discipline under floating.** The floating rate system, or the delegation to markets of the determination of exchange rates, perhaps inevitable in an M-IMS with the features just described, has proved incapable not only of insulating countries that are economically

Table 2 International reserves of all countries, 1949–93 (billions of US dollars)

	1949	1959	1969	1979	1989	1993 (November)
Gold[a]	33.00	37.60	38.50	36.40	36.50	32.00
Gold premium	−0.30	0.10	0.20	495.60	381.70	339.20
Currency[b]	10.90	16.20	33.50	281.30	676.10	952.60
IMF[c]	1.70	3.30	6.70	31.90	60.40	65.10
Total	45.30	57.20	78.90	845.20	1,154.70	1,388.90

a. Valued at $35 per ounce.
b. US dollars plus other currencies.
c. SDR reserves plus reserve position in the IMF.

Source: Authors' calculations from data in Triffin (1991) and IMF statistics.

and financially interdependent, but also of consistently exerting market discipline over economic policies.

Although some of these factors have been in operation for a long time, their effects have fully combined only recently, possibly as late as 1990–91, with the completion of the liberalization of capital movements in Europe and the signing of the Treaty on Economic and Monetary Union (EMU; Goldstein et al. 1992, Goldstein and Mussa 1993, Group of 10 1993). This triggered a massive inflow of capital into European bond markets, particularly in high-coupon countries, using savings from all over the world to take part in a "convergence play" that could only be conceived and implemented by professionals. When delays in the ratification process of the EMU treaty made it clear that convergence might not occur after all, the market rediscovered domestic imbalances and policy dilemmas in the high-coupon countries and began to run for cover, closing or hedging open positions, thus precipitating the crisis in the European Monetary System (EMS) in September 1992 and the virtual suspension of the Exchange Rate Mechanism (ERM) in August 1993.

The harsh lesson of the EMS crisis is that the operation of foreign-exchange markets in the new environment may place an additional constraint on monetary authorities in the use of exchange rate policy to complement a stability-oriented monetary policy. Indeed, even a country with good economic fundamentals but without a reputation for being an "inflation fighter," such as France or Ireland, cannot use a stable exchange rate to reinforce an anti-inflationary monetary policy stance if the implied interest rate premium required to keep the exchange rate stable in the absence of such a reputation is perceived to exact an unacceptably high toll in terms of lost output and employment: the very use of a parity peg invites "bets" from the markets, which are able to mobilize unprecedented resources for the purpose. The fact that a country may not be willing to

Table 3 Average year-to-year changes in international reserves of all countries, 1949–93

	1949–59	1959–69	1969–79	1979–89	1989–93
Gold[a]	1.26	0.21	−0.49	−0.02	−2.47
Gold premium	negl.	9.09	22,518.18	−2.09	−2.23
Currency[b]	3.28	9.71	67.24	12.76	8.18
IMF[c]	8.56	9.37	34.19	8.12	1.56
Total	2.14	3.45	88.29	3.33	4.06

negl. = negligible
a. Valued at $35 per ounce.
b. US dollars plus other currencies.
c. SDR reserves plus reserve position in the IMF.

Source: Authors' calculations from data in Triffin (1991) and IMF statistics.

push up interest rates as high as 1,000 percent to defend the parity is then seen as evidence of a policy dilemma, the solution to which can only be the abandonment of the parity. The events within the EMS over the entire period, from the forced floating of the lira and the pound sterling to the eventual widening of the ERM band to 15 percent, provide ample evidence that a "serial killing" attitude did come to dominate from the moment markets became convinced of the unsustainability of the prevailing policy stance (Group of 10 1993).

The protracted turbulence in bond markets around the world that began in February 1994 offers a further and broader example of the functioning of international capital markets in the new environment. Coming at the end of a long period of steady declines in interest rates and sizable capital gains on bonds, the slight tightening of US monetary policy, albeit long awaited, led to the panic selling of government bonds in the United States and everywhere else, totally ignoring the fundamental divergence in cyclical conditions in the United States and Europe. When the long-expected rise in the grossly overbought dollar against the yen failed to materialize, as the US administration was perceived to favor a weaker dollar in its trade dispute with Japan, stop-loss sales in the dollar-yen market combined with profit-taking sales in European bond markets to add to the overall bearish trend. These developments demonstrate the high degree of integration reached by financial markets in the main industrial countries; they have also produced an undesired tightening of monetary policies in Europe and Japan, contrasting with the needs and the policy intentions of these countries. Even in the United States, where some tightening was desired, the rise in long-term interest rates appears inconsistent with the textbook view that early central bank action to nip inflation in the bud lowers inflationary expectations and contributes to the easing of long-term rates. These constraints on the conduct of monetary policy in the new financial environment give the unpleasant impression that the only monetary policy the markets would welcome is one of continuous bold cuts in official interest rates; as a second-best, markets could accept a policy that would increase official rates drastically, so as to generate again expectations of a subsequent decline. Any policy of gradual easing or gradual tightening would be poorly received, because it generates uncertainty, the situation that professional market participants most dislike.

These trends in financial market behavior are likely to continue. Available evidence indicates that international portfolio diversification, with a few exceptions, is still in its infancy (table 4). If the degree of diversification seen in certain advanced countries were to be reached elsewhere, the volume of cross-border flows of savings would rise enormously.[10] Moreover, new countries and new currencies are likely to be added to the list of markets eligible for portfolio diversification: the recent growth in portfolio investment in Latin America and other "emerging markets" is a case in point. In this scenario it would be reasonable to expect a further increase in the institutionalization of savings both in the form of an *increase in the proportion* of savings managed by institutional investors and an *increase in the number* of such investors.[11] It would also be reasonable to expect increasing demand for ways to hedge exchange and interest risks, and therefore strong growth in the market for hedging instruments, especially derivatives.

The main concern for the monetary authorities in the new environment is that the increased volatility of interest and exchange rates may lead to collective slippage toward more accommodating monetary and exchange rate policies, with possible inflationary consequences. Having already been forced to abandon monetary aggregates as a policy tool because of the effects of financial innovation and the operation of Goodhart's law, and to forsake the exchange rate anchor because of the general move to floating exchange rates, central banks may find themselves further deprived of reliable indicators if long-term interest rates cease to reflect deep-seated market expectations about future inflation, but rather are determined by the technical analysis of a few like-minded institutional investors with the power to initiate a "one-way market" on the basis of whatever news item appears on the Reuter screen.[12]

---

10. Rough calculations using data from table 3 show that if the ratio of foreign assets to total assets recorded by leading fund managers in Britain were applied by the same category of intermediaries of the other European countries and the United States, total cross-border flows resulting from portfolio diversification would be on the order of $2 trillion.

11. Between the EMS crisis of September 1992 and the bond market turbulence of February 1994 the number of hedge funds increased sharply, reaching a total of about 800.

12. Interestingly, the dominance of institutional investors in market opinion making seems to take to the extreme Keynes's idea that the rationality of the market resolves itself more in the recourse to conventions than in the adoption of behaviors consistent with "true" models. In fact, the stronger the market position of the institutional investors (leaders) and their price-making power, the more would rational small agents (followers) turn their expectations into

Table 4   Distribution of assets managed by leading fund managers in Europe and the United States, 31 December 1991

Country	Total assets (billions of US dollars)	Equity plus fixed-income assets			
		Domestic		Foreign	
		Billions of US dollars	As a percentage of total assets	Billions of US dollars	As a percentage of total assets
Europe	3,701.50	1,633.40	44.10	706.00	19.10
United Kingdom	1,191.20	603.10	50.60	408.00	34.20
Switzerland	844.80	141.80	16.80	58.40	6.90
Germany	408.40	168.70	41.30	111.10	27.20
France	632.80	360.40	56.90	23.20	3.70
Netherlands	329.50	167.30	50.80	48.20	14.60
Denmark	30.80	27.40	89.00	1.60	5.20
Sweden	160.40	124.10	77.40	16.00	10.00
Belgium	23.40	14.80	63.20	5.00	21.40
Italy	55.20	22.80	41.30	24.90	45.10
Liechtenstein	25.00	2.90	11.60	9.50	38.00
United States	4,486.60	3,084.70	68.70	224.30	5.00
Total	8,188.10	4,718.10	57.60	930.30	11.40

Source: Goldstein et al. (1993).

Policy Response

The response of the international community to the monetary implications of the M-IMS has been developed in the context of multilateral institutions' surveillance of macroeconomic policies. However, the institutional pillar of monetary cooperation in the system, the IMF, has gradually lost its grip on the policymaking processes of the major industrial countries, as these no longer need its financial assistance, thanks to floating exchange rates and their high creditworthiness in financial markets. The OECD, for its part, was never endowed with financial "teeth" and has continued to rely on peer pressure as an instrument for achieving policy consistency. Although IMF consultation procedures have involved the full membership in a fruitful exchange of views, the IMF is increasingly focusing its attention on the policies of those countries that it can influence

---

guesses as to where the former want prices to move. To put it another way, it would be irrational for followers to adhere to their "true" model in lieu of trying to guess what prices the leaders will make. Thus, if followers behave rationally, institutional investors' price-making decisions are eventually confirmed by the market, even if the resulting (conventional equilibrium) prices differ from their competitive equilibrium level.

through its conditional lending. Thus the only systemic role played by the IMF in recent times has been related to issues such as Latin American debt and the transition of the former centrally planned economies to a market system.[13]

International monetary cooperation among industrial countries since the mid-1980s, conducted with a view to reducing payments imbalances among the three leading poles of the industrial world without jeopardizing noninflationary growth or rekindling protectionism, has thus taken place in smaller forums such as meetings of the finance ministers and central bank governors of the Group of Seven countries (G-7) and has assumed a noninstitutional character. Such cooperation nevertheless acquired an operational quality in September 1985 in the context of coordinated monetary and exchange rate policy action to correct the overvaluation of the dollar (the Plaza Agreement). The experience was repeated two years later, in February 1987 (the Louvre Accord), with the aim of averting a hard landing of the dollar. The coordination honeymoon lasted until 1990 when, after a failed attempt to turn the intervention strategy into a quasi-formal system of target zones for exchange rates and other indicators, it became clear that major countries were not prepared to back exchange market intervention with consistent monetary policies (Gomel et al. 1990). Since then, the G-7 has occasionally promoted coordinated intervention of limited scope in foreign-exchange markets but has mostly concentrated on multilateral consultations, refraining even from issuing formal press communiqués.

Monetary cooperation since Bretton Woods has thus traveled the full distance from an approach based on an institution empowered to establish and implement rules to one consisting in informal exchanges of views. Monetary issues of systemic relevance are only occasionally studied by the IMF staff (see, e.g., IMF 1991, Goldstein et al. 1992, and Fieleke 1993) or in forums such as the Group of 10 (G-10) deputies (see, e.g., Group of 10 1985, 1993), the G-10 governors, and the Bank for International Settlements (BIS).[14]

Two features of monetary cooperation in this new context may be noted: on the rare occasions when monetary initiatives have been taken, they have been part of crisis management exercises and, moreover, have affected the sphere of central banking rather than that of intergovernmental

---

13. The World Bank has also been active in this field. An assessment of the roles of the IMF and World Bank was conducted by the Group of Ten (1989), and guidelines were approved to avoid overlapping of responsibilities and inconsistencies of action. A more radical opinion, calling for the merger of the two institutions, was presented in *The Economist* ("Sisters in the Wood: A Survey of the IMF and the World Bank," 12 October 1991).

14. One valuable example of such activity is the periodic surveys of the turnover in foreign-exchange markets conducted by central banks in the major industrial countries under the aegis of the BIS.

affairs. In fact, governments of the G-7 or G-10 countries have stopped short of entering into binding international agreements of a permanent nature, but have asked their central banks to "intervene" in the context of ad hoc informal arrangements. This was equally the case with the coordinated strategy to stabilize foreign-exchange markets and with the efforts to contain the debt crisis, when central banks were asked to help by extending bridge loans to certain developing countries through the BIS, prefinancing drawings from IMF or World Bank facilities.

In contrast with this overall trend, monetary cooperation was actively pursued at a regional level in Europe immediately following the collapse of the Bretton Woods fixed exchange rate regime, first with the currency "snake" in 1973 and subsequently with the EMS in 1979. Significantly, the members of the EMS came to recognize that the inherent fragility of their exchange rate arrangement could be remedied only with transition to a full monetary union, with a European central bank responsible for the conduct of a single monetary policy and a single currency.[15] At the European level as well, therefore, monetary cooperation on a regional scale has emphasized the performance of central banking functions (see Padoa-Schioppa and Saccomanni 1992).

Payment Services

Market Developments

During the 1980s and especially in the last few years, the internationalization of trade and finance has boosted the volume of payments.[16] Payments related to financial transactions, in particular, have increased exponentially in recent years[17] as the M-IMS came into being, owing to the globalization of markets with round-the-clock trading, the growth in the use of derivatives, and the development of technology that allows payments to be made in real time, at negligible transaction cost, irrespective of the amount involved, the unit of account used, and the locations of buyer and seller. The annual flow of interbank payments is several times GDP in the

---

15. For an overview of the process of European monetary cooperation and integration see Padoa-Schioppa (1994c) and Papadia and Saccomanni (1994), as well as the other contributions in Steinherr (1994).

16. International payments instructions through an international network, the Society for Worldwide Interbank Financial Telecommunications (SWIFT), have increased by more than 60 percent over the last five years.

17. By the beginning of the 1990s the value of transactions in the foreign-exchange markets was more than 30 times greater than that of world imports and exports. Transactions through Cedel and Euroclear—the international settlement systems for securities transactions—have more than tripled in the last five years.

main industrial countries (Padoa-Schioppa 1994a),[18] with the growth rate of the former largely outpacing that of the latter.

The market has organized itself so as to be able to effect cross-border payments as efficiently as possible. Across frontiers, payment obligations are discharged by transferring deposits held with banks chartered in the issuing country. As it would be neither practical nor feasible for every institution to hold accounts with all the others, major international banks (money center banks) act as clearing and settlement agents for smaller or regional correspondent banks and nonbanks. Money center banks have access to national settlement procedures and to the accounts of their home central banks and thus supply liquidity to correspondents through collateralized or uncollateralized credit lines, through repurchase agreements, or through revolving lines of credit to issuers of securitized debt instruments[19] (Folkerts-Landau 1990, 1991). Moreover, for all practical purposes, money center banks provide the connecting link between national systems, as they "transform" cross-border payments into domestic payments.

In a line of evolution similar to that of domestic payment systems, the dramatic increase in the volume and size of international transactions to be handled daily has led money center banks to opt for so-called netting schemes that shorten the correspondent chain and permit them to economize on liquidity and operational costs. In such schemes each participant has only one balance to settle for each value date, instead of having to settle as many balances as there are counterparties. In this context, money center banks have de facto become multilateral clearinghouses that, at the moment of settlement, transfer to creditor banks funds deposited with them by correspondents with net debtor positions.[20]

---

18. According to estimates of the Committee of Governors of the EC central banks, intra-EC payments increased by 63 percent between 1988 and 1991, rising from ECU133 trillion (or about 33 times Community GDP) to ECU200 trillion (about 40 times GDP). Also, with the complete liberalization of capital movements in many EC countries, the growth of cross-border deposits in foreign currencies has accelerated considerably: their share of the money aggregates in France, Italy, and Germany increased from 9.4 percent in 1984 to 14.7 percent in 1990. At the G-10 level, international payments increased from 43 percent of GDP in 1988 to around 53 percent in 1992 (BIS estimates).

19. These lines of credit ensure the holder that the security will be redeemed even in the event of market disturbances.

20. The largest domestic net settlement system is CHIPS (the Clearing House Interbank Payments System), handling international dollar payments. Its operational features are described in Folkerts-Landau (1991). In Europe, in addition to domestic multilateral netting systems, more structured arrangements for international payments are in operation: Europe offers the only example of a multilateral clearing system involving an international currency, the ECU, supported by SWIFT and settled through an international institution (BIS). The ECU Banking Association and the BIS set the criteria that must be met to acquire ECU clearing bank status. Also, in the Eurobond market, Euroclear and Cedel provide competing but mutually compatible services for international transfers, and the Eurocheque system has standardized rules and guarantees for cheque payments.

The international payment system has thus developed in a much less structured fashion than national systems have established, where legal rules and operational procedures for clearing and settlement are under the supervision of the local central bank. At the international level, payment transactions are mainly based on practices and on bilateral or multilateral agreements whose enforceability is uncertain in different jurisdictions. Settlements reflect the heterogeneity of domestic payment systems in terms of regulation, payment techniques, working hours, and finality. Information on counterparties' credit standing is much harder to obtain than domestically; there is no lender of last resort, nor is there a supervisory authority; currencies are traded largely outside of their country of issue, and multiple clearing and settlement arrangements coexist.

Unlike in national payment systems, where the central bank plays a key role, at the international level central banks' involvement is still limited, with the result that, under the large and increasing weight of international payments, even national systems have increased their risks. Disturbances in one payment system reverberate to others, and disruptions in offshore markets may affect domestic clearing procedures and monetary policy. If a financial institution is unable to settle its obligations in one of the major national payment systems, the consequent loss of confidence could spill over into other national systems.[21]

Furthermore, the development of private netting arrangements outside of home central banks' jurisdiction has made national payment systems more vulnerable to failures of participating institutions. The operation of such arrangements has also raised fears of a worsening trade-off between the monetary policy function of the central bank whose currency is being netted and the stability of its "home" payment system, as the demand for central bank money from an offshore clearinghouse in a situation of stress may confront the central bank with the dilemma of either forgoing money supply control or precipitating a systemic liquidity crisis.

Finally, multilateral netting schemes in which participants retain responsibility for gross transactions are exposed to systemic risk, or a domino effect, when a participant fails to settle its obligation at the end of the netting process. The repetition of the netting procedure with the exclusion of the defaulting participant (so-called unwinding) has turned out not to be a remedy. Systemic risk in fact is bound to grow to the extent that the total amount of gross transactions to be settled increases in relation not only to central bank money balances but also to the net capital of the participants (Padoa-Schioppa 1994b). As systemic risk has outgrown individual risk, netting systems have gradually moved to a situation where participants reap most of the benefits while central banks bear the costs.

---

21. Quoting Alan Greenspan, Folkerts-Landau (1991, 49) recalls that "the greatest threat to the stability of the financial system . . . during the [1987] October stock market crash was the danger of a major default in one of the clearing and settlement systems."

Policy Response

Historical experience has shown in the case of domestic economies that, to be safe and efficient, payment systems require a "public" institution, the central bank, playing the dual role of overseer and provider of settlement services in "final" money. Payment systems generate externalities that cannot be internalized by market mechanisms and that therefore require the intervention of a public agent. A market-alone payment system where a few large players are both competing among themselves and attempting to provide market stability is intrinsically flawed by an internal inconsistency.

First, a few large private banks acting as suppliers of clearing and settlement services, and thus performing key central banking functions, may find themselves confronting the hard dilemma recalled above: either to accommodate the demand for central bank money with their own resources whenever they are required to close the settlement procedure, or to deny accommodation and let a crisis start.[22] It is not appropriate for private, profit-seeking agents to be burdened with public policy decisions of this sort, or with the task of extending credit for public purposes in times of stress.[23] Second, while they compete with other banks in the market for financial services, banks operating as clearinghouses have to decide on their rivals' access to settlement and hence on their ability to stay in the market—hardly a desirable situation. Moreover, they need to collect information about their competitors that the latter may understandably be reluctant to provide; or they might seek to adopt regulations and access limits with which other participants might refuse to comply. The institutional configuration of a stable payment system poses a problem of leadership (Goodhart 1985), to which the interagent conflict of interest involved does not admit a solution with a private, profit-making quasi-central bank.

Other reasons suggest that market forces alone may not marshal enough resources for an efficient international payment system. First, payment infrastructures entail externalities that may reduce the incentives for individual intermediaries to invest in their improvement. Second, market concentration and economies of scale, which have always been inherent in payment systems, have so far not reduced the pressure on individual

---

22. In principle, the dilemma could be solved if there were a rule establishing that no agent may go bankrupt and by extending the deadline for payers in difficulty. Of course, while stability would be preserved, the overall efficiency of the system would suffer.

23. See Padoa-Schioppa (1989). One should also consider the arguments put forward by Goodhart (1985) for domestic systems: lender-of-last-resort functions at critical times might be operationally difficult if they are provided by a consortium of clearing banks with conflicting market interests and with different views on how to share the cost of intervention. Similarly, the control of money aggregates might be complicated by clearing banks having diverging market strategies.

agents to improve the quality of payment infrastructures, thanks to the rapid expansion of the market for payment services and competition to maintain a leading market position. In the future, however, with shrinking profit margins and sizable investment required to upgrade networks, the market could fail to generate sufficient incentive for further improvements.

Central banks have increasingly perceived the systemic implications of a rapidly growing network of international payments operating in a vacuum of public monitoring and control. They have responded to the new challenges through international cooperation and coordination. Cooperation has stepped up from low-profile exercises, involving the mere exchange of general information, to a joint effort aimed at policy decisions. It started in 1980 with the constitution of the Group of Experts on Payment Systems of the central banks of the G-10 countries. The group was formed by computer experts who were asked to study the problems related to physical circulation of different payment instruments and systems for electronic fund transfer. Only in 1989, following the release of the Report on Netting Schemes (also known as the Angell Report), did the G-10 central banks' involvement in this area take on the policy issues relating to international clearance and settlement systems.

In 1990, a report on interbank netting schemes (the Lamfalussy Report) was agreed upon that recommended the adoption of a set of minimum standards for international clearing systems and of principles for cooperative international oversight. As a consequence of the minimum standards, some of the initiatives envisaged in the main financial centers were shelved, and the measures that now seem imminent appear to have embodied most of the recommendations. Two systems are now at an advanced stage of preparation: ECHO in the United Kingdom and Multinet in the United States. Both are private multilateral netting schemes for spot and forward foreign-exchange transactions and involve banks in a number of countries.

In 1992 the Group of Experts on Payment Systems was transformed into the Committee on Payment and Settlement Services and given a broader mandate. Its Delivery versus Payment Report studied ways to ensure the simultaneous exchange of securities for money. In 1993 a report on central bank payment and settlement services with respect to cross-border and multicurrency transactions (known as the Noel Report) provided a detailed account of options in this field. The report considered a wide spectrum of alternatives, which escalated in terms of the degree of central bank engagement and coordination, ranging from the simple provision of settlement accounts in domestic currency to the establishment of a central bank "common agent" offering simultaneous settlement to multilateral foreign exchange clearinghouses.

In Europe, international cooperation over payments began late, but has since progressed rapidly. In 1992 the EC central bank governors established principles for cooperative oversight of cross-border participation in domestic payment systems and defined rules for overseeing the ECU Clearing and Settlement System under central banks' joint responsibility; indeed, the ECU clearing system was the first in operation to be assessed against the minimum standards of the Lamfalussy Report. More recently, EC central banks agreed on a set of principles for the harmonization of their domestic systems in the sphere of access, risk, legal, technical, and operational features. The report setting such principles calls for the establishment of real-time gross settlement systems in all member countries and recommends that access to systems be restricted to credit institutions subject to supervision. Meanwhile work is under way to prepare the payment systems that the European Union will need when it moves to a single currency and a single central bank—in other words, for the time when what is now "cross-border" will become "domestic." It should be noted that the Maastricht Treaty confers on the European Central Bank the power to make "regulations to ensure efficient and sound clearing and payments systems within the Community and with other countries." In the transition to the final stage of monetary union, the European Monetary Institute has the task of promoting the efficiency of cross-border payments and of overseeing the smooth functioning of the ECU clearing system.

In the field of international payment systems, a most interesting development is the heightened attention of the central banks of the Eastern European countries who are members of the BIS. Important initiatives in regional cooperation on payment systems are under consideration, such as the creation of a "Central and Eastern Europe ECU-Linked Clearing System" linking the Czech and Slovak Republics, Hungary, Poland, and Russia. The system would operate via SWIFT, settlements would occur through ECU clearing banks, and a central entity would be set up to take common action, negotiate with SWIFT, and conduct relations with EU institutions.

Notwithstanding the considerable progress so far achieved, the road ahead is still a long one. Although full recognition of the systemic implications of international payment failures is now widespread, current G-10 positions taken in the field of payment systems are no more than recommendations for non-G-10 countries, and a considerable portion of international payments takes place outside safety nets. The resulting institutional configuration is, we believe, still largely suboptimal and thus unable to guarantee adequate efficiency and stability in the system.

Banking and Finance
Market Developments

International banking is as old as international trade: when Italian merchants first set foot in the major markets in Europe in the 13th century, the Lombard bankers soon followed. Problems of bad loans are equally old.

The loan granted by Peruzzi & Bardi, a banking firm of Florence, to King Edward III of England to finance his share of the Hundred Years' War was not repaid, as in 1348 the borrower defaulted, leading to the bankruptcy of the lender (Kindleberger 1984). Only in the first decades of the 20th century was the need for a banking supervisory function fully recognized and its assignment to central banks or to other agencies decided. However, supervision was deemed a strictly national affair, in spite of considerable evidence that lending to international customers could be as risky as lending to national borrowers and could have far-reaching repercussions. Although in the interwar period banking crises and financial crashes played a major role in precipitating the worldwide recession, the issue of multilateral prudential supervision of international banking was not addressed in the Bretton Woods negotiations.

International cooperation in the field of banking supervision started only in the 1970s, largely as a consequence of the rise of the M-IMS. The growth of the Eurocurrency and Eurobond markets in the 1960s had already shown the importance of the desire by both borrowers and lenders to circumvent national regulation in the exchange, monetary, or prudential field as a driving force for international banking and financial activity. The uneven pace of deregulation among countries and among segments of the market created additional impulses in the 1970s and the 1980s for banks to carry out "regulatory arbitrage" (see Folkerts-Landau 1990). Although financial liberalization and internationalization have been largely imposed upon governments by market forces and technological developments, they have received support over the last fifteen years from the market-friendly policy stance that has spread to much of the industrial and the developing world.[24] Financial innovation has resulted in strong growth in banks' off-balance-sheet operations and, more specifically, in the market for derivative products such as swaps, options, and futures. At the same time, banks and financial intermediaries have produced a globalization of markets, by opening more branches and affiliates in foreign countries and in offshore centers, and managing customers' affairs on a round-the-clock basis, moving from market to market with the sun.

Policy Response

The rapid expansion of international banking has exacted a toll in the form of a variety of crises or near crises. Just as they were for domestic banking systems, events have been a driving force behind the establishment of

---

24. At the European level, a decisive step toward the integration of financial markets was the 1988 EC directive on the freedom of capital movements. The liberal approach of the Community toward financial relations with non-European countries and the various EC directives that paved the way for the single market have stimulated the process of financial integration not only within the Community but worldwide.

prudential supervision at the international level. It was in effect the foreign-exchange-related collapse of Bankhaus Herstatt in 1974 that led the G-10 central banks to establish a Committee of Banking Supervisors in Basel under the aegis of the BIS to examine the international implications of the crisis.[25] This led to the Basel concordat in 1975, which established that the responsibility for supervision over the activities of banks' foreign establishments and their solvency and liquidity requirements should be shared between national authorities on the basis of mutually agreed principles.

Another banking crisis, the Banco Ambrosiano case, led in 1983 to a revision of the Basel concordat, setting out the two fundamental principles that no banking establishment should escape supervision and that supervision should be adequate. The implementation of these principles requires effective division of responsibilities among host and parent authorities, the former being responsible for foreign bank branches and the latter for the larger banking groups to which such branches belong. More recently, in 1992 in the wake of the Bank for Credit and Commerce International (BCCI) case, the Basel Committee has approved so-called minimum standards intended to ensure effective supervision on a consolidated basis and reciprocal satisfaction with the efficacy of other authorities' supervision. Supervisors have agreed to enforce minimum standards, and the committee will monitor their implementation in its constant review of international bank supervision.

The committee has also endeavored to establish a level playing field for banks operating internationally. The Capital Accord of 1988, possibly the most impressive achievement of the Basel Committee, sets out the details of a framework for measuring capital adequacy and the minimum standards that international banks should achieve; more recent steps aim at introducing capital requirements to cover market risks in order to reduce distortions in competition between banks and other financial intermediaries. Whereas the 1988 accord is aimed at assessing capital in relation to credit risk (i.e., the risk of counterparty failure), the new proposed measures cover other risks, notably interest rate risk and investment risk on securities, which have to be considered by supervisors when assessing the overall capital adequacy of banks.[26]

---

25. Alongside their concerns in the field of prudential supervision, the G-10 central banks have also devoted close attention to developments in international banking practices and instruments liable to have systemic implications. Among the more recent contributions are the reports on "Recent Innovations in International Banking" of April 1986 (the Cross Report) and on "Recent Developments in International Interbank Relations" of October 1992 (the Promisel Report). The macroeconomic implications of the working of derivatives' markets are among issues currently occupying the G-10.

26. This form of international coordination of supervisory policies had the effect of limiting the negative externalities deriving from regulatory arbitrage. Financial internationalization,

The action of the Basel Committee has been paralleled by developments in the European Community. Until the mid-1980s the Basel Committee led the way and the Community followed suit—witness the principle of consolidated supervision and the accord on capital, both of which anticipated the relevant European directives. Near the end of the 1980s, however, as a result of the leap to European integration brought about by the Single European Act, steps toward the integration of supervisory patterns accelerated in Europe. With the approval of the Capital Adequacy Directive, agreement has been reached with securities supervisors, while in Basel no accord has yet been found. On the whole, the interaction between the two forums can be judged positively in the light of progress toward greater cooperation.

Some aspects of the method of international cooperation in banking supervision are worth mentioning. The Basel Committee has maintained an informal character, in line with its original task of providing a forum for supervisory authorities to exchange views and become personally acquainted. Its institutional arrangements have also remained much less structured than those of other international forums for cooperation: there are no by-laws or formal criteria concerning, for example, the calling of meetings or procedures for voting. Only central banks and banking supervisory authorities are represented on the committee—no government officials participate. The authority of the committee is not a formal one: its official documents are not legally binding. Rather than issue detailed and rigid regulations, the committee established general supervisory standards, or "best practices," or guidelines and recommendations for the supervisory authorities, thus promoting convergence toward high standards of prudential control in a pragmatic and evolutionary way. This flexibility and informality, which might have been a weakness, turned out to be an element of strength: the recommendations of the Committee have been widely implemented in the G-10 countries, often through legislative changes. They have also spread all over the world: Basel Committee rules have been adopted by a vast number of non-G-10 countries; regional groups of supervisors of non-G-10 countries have multiplied and have regular contacts with the committee.

To explain the role of the Basel Committee, two main aspects have to be highlighted. First, the committee is basically oriented to respond to a

---

in fact, had induced governments to liberalize regulatory constraints in the more strictly regulated activities and jurisdictions, in an attempt to protect the market share of domestic financial institutions: often, market share considerations have taken the place of stability objectives. Although this process has, on the one hand, contributed to enhancing the efficiency of domestic financial systems, it has, on the other, increased the risk that the regulatory competition arising from a noncooperative approach might lead to a suboptimal level of overall regulation, thus implying a less-than-desirable level playing field for systemic stability.

demand for rules in international banking, not to carry out any discretionary action to forestall or manage banking crises. Secondly, unlike the equivalent bodies in the European Community, it is not the task of the committee to open national markets for banking and financial services. The basis for international action in opening markets rests more with the OECD through its code of conduct for capital movements, although in the future an expanded role will have to be played by the World Trade Organization (WTO).

Despite the institutional limitations, the Basel Committee has undergone a profound transformation in the twenty years of its existence, moving from its initial role of forum for exchanges of views to increasing involvement in rule making. In the future, the process of convergence of prudential rules should continue as banking becomes a more global and homogeneous business; even if its customary practices of voluntary cooperation remain, the effectiveness of the committee in shaping a regulatory environment for safe, sound, and competitive international banking should be preserved and enhanced. The road ahead is very long, and the primary objective is to ensure that no banking establishment escapes the supervisory net; non-G-10 countries and offshore centers must adhere to the commitment to satisfy minimum standards.

A major task ahead is the setting of uniform prudential rules for banks and nonbanks (covering securities houses in the first instance but eventually other players such as insurance companies as well) when the same type of risk is incurred by both. This is the case for market, or price, risk in foreign-exchange, securities, and commodity trading in spot and derivatives markets. A dialogue between the Basel Committee and the equivalent committee of securities regulators under the International Organization of Securities Commissions (IOSCO) started some years ago, but it has not yet produced the results required by a financial world in which the barriers of specialization are rapidly eroding.

The Institutional Dimension

The consolidation of the M-IMS will increasingly expose the inadequacy of the institutional setup conceived in the 1940s to manage relations among nation-states operating in an environment of fragmented markets and restricted capital mobility. This inadequacy certainly does not imply that the institutional framework of the M-IMS would or should be dismantled. Far from it. In any country that, almost by definition, has a single internal market, there exists a unitary institutional framework concerning all aspects of economic, monetary, and financial relations: a unified commercial law, governing the basic rights to engage in economic activity, to own and dispose of real and financial goods; a single currency, managed by a central bank, with responsibility for the proper functioning of the payment and banking systems; and rules governing access to and the working of markets, to ensure fair competition, avoid improper practices, protect savers, investors, and consumers, and promote transparency.

In a world economy that is still fragmented in political and institutional terms, the common framework could conceivably be minimal, basically one in which intergovernmental relations could be handled within a restricted set of rules and informal codes of conduct. As markets become the unifying factor of the world economy, despite the permanence of sovereign nations, the institutional requirements of the M-IMS will tend to resemble more the framework applying *within* a single nation-state than the loose arrangements applying today *among* nation-states. These requirements will not be recognized and fulfilled immediately, however. Initially, the expansion of multinational enterprises and intermediaries has led to a growing tendency for business to become stateless, conducted outside national institutional or regulatory frameworks. This has generated a proliferation of duty-free zones, tax and regulatory havens, and offshore markets competing to attract a growing share of international trade in goods, capital, and services. Subsequently, with the intensification of international integration, the perception of a need for firmer rules and institutions has become more acute. We have summarized in this paper numerous examples of ways in which this need has been met, some taken from past experience, others from current developments. It is sufficient to recall a few main points.

In the field of banking and finance, the need for common, international, and prudential regulation led to the rule-making activity of the Basel Committee described in the preceding section. A similar need has begun to be felt in the field of international payment and settlement systems, as described in the section on that topic above, prompting market participants to create spontaneous forms of cooperation and, more recently, central banks to move from merely exchanging information to designing common rules and strategies. As a result, the production of important public goods such as systemic stability and the internalization of payments externalities, as well as more advanced institutional arrangements, are now being actively considered at the official level.

Paradoxically, it is in the area of international monetary relations, where rules and institutions were assigned a fundamental role in the Bretton Woods system, that the process was first halted and then reversed, as described above. And it is in this area that dissatisfaction with the working of the current set of arrangements is becoming increasingly widespread (see Kenen et al. 1994). Even central bank cooperation in exchange rate policies, which under certain circumstances appears to be more effective than previously assumed (Dominguez and Frankel 1993, Catte et al. 1994), has been undermined by ad hockery and failures of coordination.

The future evolution of the institutional arrangements of the M-IMS is likely to extrapolate trends that have been visible since the end of the

1980s. The driving factor in shaping future arrangements is likely to be the further expansion and increased globalization of financial markets. This process will gradually involve more and more countries as they "graduate" into the global market economy; at the same time, major banks and financial intermediaries will be able to compete successfully only to the extent that they become global players, operating worldwide across the full spectrum of currencies and financial instruments.

The M-IMS, however, will not operate in a riskless environment. The main sources of concern are the disturbances that may have an impact on the stability of the financial system or lead to a revival of inflation. The management of these risks lies within the sphere of competence of central banks (Sanford 1993), while the risks themselves concern the average layperson, who wonders whether a global market system operating solely on the basis of profit motivations is adequately responding to his or her interests (Kennedy 1993).

Yet the preceding sections have shown that the M-IMS has eroded the power of national central banks and the effectiveness of their instruments, thus opening an institutional gap with potentially destabilizing implications. The question is, therefore, how to fill that gap.

Our analysis provides some clues as to how an "institution," or, more loosely, a set of institutional arrangements, for managing the M-IMS should look. The "institution" should, in our view, possess the following fundamental characteristics:

- It should be able to perform the policy functions discussed earlier in the three areas of monetary management, payment systems, and banking supervision.

- It should have jurisdiction on a global scale.

- It should belong to the category of central banks rather than governments.

- It thus should have rule-making authority.

- It therefore should be a bank and thus be able to "stay in the market" and operate flexibly with major intermediaries.

The IMF could have taken this direction. On some occasions it has come close to doing so. But in reality it did not, and it seems unlikely to become the institution where the key monetary and financial policy functions of the M-IMS are carried out.

Today, the institution that comes closest to the ideal one just described is the BIS, where some key central banking functions are performed on an international scale. The BIS is in fact the institution where regular meetings of the G-10 central bank governors are held to review developments in foreign-exchange and financial markets and in the international banking and payment systems. It serves as the permanent secretariat for the Gold and Foreign Exchange Committee, the Euro-Currency Standing Committee, the Committee on Banking Supervision, and the Committee on Payment and Settlement Services. In these bodies national central banks are represented by the relevant experts, and reports are regularly prepared and submitted to the governors for their consideration. Finally, although the central banks of the G-10 countries (among which are the founders of the BIS) play the major role in its management, the BIS has established close relations with central banks of other important regions (Eastern Europe, Saudi Arabia, the Far East). At the time of the Latin American debt crisis the BIS played a crucial role in linking the provision of liquidity support to wider actions in the fields of private and official financing and macroeconomic policies. The BIS is also active in foreign-exchange and financial markets as an agent of the central banks.

What the BIS lacks, measured against the ideal sketched above, is the special strength possessed only by institutions born of intergovernmental treaties, such as the IMF and the World Bank. In principle, it is hard to deny the superiority of a written contract over informal understandings as the backbone of an institution. However, when looking at a possible agenda for the foreseeable future, especially in such a delicate area as central banking, one must be cautious not to run too far ahead of the times and make hasty proposals that would risk undoing the good that has already been done. It should not be forgotten that new institutions do not necessarily emerge from formal agreements or international treaties: they often develop from cumulative minor adjustments to existing arrangements as a result of the restless, everyday problem-solving activities of policymakers.

Summary and Conclusions

The Bretton Woods system was established to restore order in international economic and financial relations following the trade anarchy and competitive currency devaluations of the interwar period. Its founders sought a combination of free trade, fixed exchange rates, official liquidity and financial support, and restrictions on private capital movements. The outcome was a G-IMS with a built-in asymmetry between an integrating world market for goods and commodities and domestically insulated, government-regulated financial markets.

The success of the Bretton Woods G-IMS in achieving most of its goals until the 1960s set the stage for the reawakening of financial markets, and the inability to adapt the management of its rules led to the eventual collapse of the fixed exchange rate regime. Floating exchange rates and the recycling of large imbalances after the oil shocks contributed to the further expansion of international financial relations. So did the process of exchange liberalization and market deregulation. A truly global financial market emerged. And like Aladdin's genie, once out of the bottle it will not go back to rest.

Thus, the G-IMS bred its converse, the M-IMS. This system, too, suffers from a structural weakness arising from the asymmetry between the globality of the financial market and the fragmentation of policy institutions, which are based on nation-states—an asymmetry that generates an institutional gap.

We have analyzed the M-IMS by looking at each of the three policy areas that characterize modern domestic financial systems: monetary management, payment services, and banking supervision. The analysis shows that the M-IMS raises significant public interest issues in each of these areas. Indeed, in each of them there has been some response from monetary authorities or market participants at the international level. This response has been weak in the field of monetary and exchange rate policies, and surprisingly strong and innovative in the fields of international payments and banking supervision.

We have refrained from inventing detailed institutional arrangements that could cope with the M-IMS. As we stated at the outset, a return to the old Bretton Woods system is neither possible nor desirable. What is necessary is to pursue the public interests and policy functions required by the M-IMS that has replaced the G-IMS.

Although we suggest no precise blueprint, it is possible to read in the recent evolution and present practices of international cooperation the direction of the arrangements that will prevail in the coming decades. In the background there will be a further evolution of the institutional arrangements—global and regional—created in the heyday of institution building of the 1940s and 1950s. At the global level, the successful conclusion of the Uruguay Round, the decision to create the WTO, and the signing of the General Agreement on Trade in Services (GATS) are important steps forward. The activity of the international financial institutions (the IMF, the World Bank, the European Bank for Reconstruction and Development, and others), as their money-lending functions are gradually taken over by the market, will focus increasingly on their policy advisory and surveillance functions, in a world with a growing number of important players. At the regional level, country groupings (ranging from the European Union to the North American Free Trade Agreement), where the demand for international policy dialogue and cooperation is bound to grow, will have to strengthen their bonds, and new ones may be created. The global and the regional level of multilateral cooperation will have to be linked in a consistent overall framework.

Turning to money and finance, it may be expected that the world economy will move further toward an institutional setting capable of covering the three policy areas for which central banks have responsibility. The G-10 central bank committees operating within the BIS should exploit to the fullest extent possible the available room for maneuver to make further improvements in the coordination of the various policy functions, taking increasingly into account their interactions and overall implications for the stance of monetary policy. The objectives could be, first, to strengthen and expand rule making, linking with other regional monetary institutions (such as the European Monetary Institute and later the European Central Bank) and central bank groupings in the common policy area; and second, to establish appropriate operational procedures for the provision of liquidity to banks and clearinghouses (and through them to the entire financial system) and for the conduct of coordinated interventions in exchange and bond markets designed to contain volatility and movements unrelated to fundamentals.

We are convinced that the institutional arrangements envisaged here for the performance of central banking functions would be more effective than the traditional forums of intergovernmental monetary cooperation in coping with systemic instability in the M-IMS and in controlling inflation. In this new arrangement, the shared commitment of its participants to monetary stability and their independence from national governments would ensure the time consistency that is key to credible and effective policy performance.

Much can be done in a pragmatic way to set up such an institutional framework without requiring the negotiation of an international treaty, using the powers already vested in the BIS and its member central banks. The timing and the form of the actual steps taken can only be determined as the situation evolves and experience is gained. Great caution should be exercised in any attempt to reach more formal arrangements. A scene from one of Federico Fellini's movies comes to mind, in which construction workers excavating a tunnel for the Rome subway discover a beautiful 2,000-year-old fresco, only to see it dissolve into dust as soon as strong electric lights are brought in to illuminate it better. The elaborate but still fragile framework for central banking policy that is gradually taking shape under the friendly roof of the BIS could be jeopardized by too hasty, albeit well-meaning, initiatives.

References

Catte, P., G. Galli, and S. Rebecchini. 1994. "Concerted Interventions and the Dollar: An Analysis of Daily Data." In P. B. Kenen, F. Papadia, and F. Saccomanni, eds., *The International Monetary System*. Cambridge, England: Cambridge University Press (forthcoming).

Corrigan, E. G. 1982. "Are Banks Special? A Summary." In *Annual Report*. Minneapolis: Federal Reserve Bank of Minneapolis.

De Cecco, M. 1979a. "Origins of the Post-War Payments System." *Journal of Economics* 3: 49–61.

De Cecco, M. 1979b. *Moneta e impero. Il sistema finanziario internazionale dal 1890 al 1914*. Torino: Einaudi.

De Cecco, M. 1985. "Relazioni finanziarie tra internazionalismo e transazionalismo." In Cassa di Risparmio di Torino, *Moneta ed economia internazionale*. Torino: Piemonte Vivo Ricerche.

Dominguez, K. M., and J. A. Frankel. 1993. *Does Foreign Exchange Intervention Work?* Washington: Institute for International Economics.

Eichengreen, B. 1993. "Epilogue: Three Perspectives on the Bretton Woods System." In B. Eichengreen and M. D. Bordo, eds., *A Retrospective on the Bretton Woods System: Lessons for International Monetary Reform*. Chicago: University of Chicago Press.

Emminger, O. 1977. "The D-Mark in the Conflict between Internal and External Equilibrium, 1948–75." Princeton Essays in International Finance 122. Princeton, NJ: Princeton University.

European Economic Community Commission. 1966. *The Development of a European Capital Market* (the Segré Report). Brussels: European Economic Community.

Federal Reserve Bank of San Francisco. 1985. *The Search for Financial Stability: The Past Fifty Years*. Proceedings of a conference sponsored by the Federal Reserve Bank of San Francisco, Asilomar, CA (23–25 June).

Fieleke, N. S. 1993. *International Capital Transactions: Should They Be Restricted?* IMF Papers on Policy Analysis and Assessment. Washington: IMF (December).

Folkerts-Landau, D. 1990. "The Case for International Coordination of Financial Policy." In W. H. Branson, J. A. Frenkel, and M. Goldstein, eds., *International Policy Coordination and Exchange Rate Fluctuations*. Chicago: University of Chicago Press.

Folkerts-Landau, D. 1991. "Systemic Financial Risk in Payment Systems." In International Monetary Fund, *Determinants and Systemic Consequences of International Capital Flows*. Occasional Paper 77. Washington: IMF Research Department (March).

Goldstein, M., D. Folkerts-Landau, P. Garber, L. Rojas-Suárez, and M. Spencer. 1993. "International Capital Markets." Washington: IMF (April).

Goldstein, M., P. Isard, P. R. Masson, and M. Taylor. 1992. *Policy Issues in the Evolving International Monetary System*. Washington: IMF (June).

Goldstein, M., and M. Mussa. 1993. *The Integration of World Capital Markets*. WP/93/95. Washington: IMF (December).

Golembe, H. G., and J. J. Mingo. 1985. "Can Supervision and Regulation Ensure Stability?" In Federal Reserve Bank of San Francisco, *The Search for Financial Stability: The Past Fifty Years*. Proceedings of a conference sponsored by the Federal Reserve Bank of San Francisco, Asilomar, CA (23–25 June).

Gomel, G., F. Saccomanni, and S. Vona. 1990. "The Experience with Economic Policy Coordination: The Tripolar and the European Dimensions." In *Temi di Discussione* 140. Rome: Banca d'Italia (July).

Goodhart, C. A. E. 1985. *The Evolution of Central Banks*. STICERD Occasional Papers. London: London School of Economics and Political Science.

Goodhart, C. A. E. 1987. *Why Do Banks Need a Central Bank?* Oxford Economic Papers 39 (March).

Group of 10. 1985. "The Functioning of the International Monetary System." Report to the Ministers and Governors (June).

Group of 10. 1989. "The Role of the IMF and the World Bank in the Context of the Debt Strategy." Report to the Ministers and Governors (June).

Group of 10. 1993. "International Capital Movements and Foreign Exchange Markets." Report to the Ministers and Governors (April).

Hicks, J. 1967. *Critical Essays in Monetary Theory*. London: Oxford University Press.

International Monetary Fund. 1991. *Determinants and Systemic Consequences of International Capital Flows*. Occasional Paper 77. Washington: IMF Research Department (March).

Kenen, P. B., F. Papadia, and F. Saccomanni, eds. 1994. *The International Monetary System*. Cambridge, England: Cambridge University Press (forthcoming).

Kennedy, P. 1993. *Preparing for the Twenty-First Century*. New York: Random House.

Kindleberger, C. P. 1984. *A Financial History of Western Europe*. London: Allen and Unwin.

Organization for Economic Cooperation and Development. 1967. *Capital Markets Study: General Report*. Paris: OECD.

Nurkse, R. 1944. *International Currency Experience: Lessons of the Inter-War Period*. Geneva: League of Nations.

Padoa-Schioppa, T. 1988. "Towards a New Adjustable Peg?" Paper presented at the Symposium to Commemorate Twenty-Five Years of Per Jacobsson Lectures on the International Monetary System: The Next Twenty-Five Years, Basel (12 June).

Padoa-Schioppa, T. 1989. "International Payments Systems: The Function Begets the Organ." Paper presented at the 75th Anniversary of the Federal Reserve System, International Symposium on Banking and Payment Services, Board of Governors of the Federal Reserve System, Washington (9 June).

Padoa-Schioppa, T. 1994a. "Adapting Central Banking to a Changing Environment." Paper prepared for the Central Banking Seminar on Frameworks for Monetary Stability, sponsored by the International Monetary Fund, Washington (1–10 March).

Padoa-Schioppa, T. 1994b. "Central Banking and Payments Systems in the European Community." Paper presented at the International Symposium on Banking and Payment Services, Board of Governors of the Federal Reserve System, Washington (10 March).

Padoa-Schioppa, T. 1994c. *The Road to Monetary Union in Europe*. Oxford, England: Oxford University Press (forthcoming).

Padoa-Schioppa, T., and F. Saccomanni. 1992. *Agenda for Stage Two: Preparing the Monetary Platform*. CEPR Occasional Paper 7. London: Centre for Economic Policy Research.

Papadia, F., and F. Saccomanni. 1994. "From the Werner Plan to the Maastricht Treaty: Europe's Stubborn Quest for Monetary Union." In A. Steinherr, ed., *30 Years of European Monetary Integration: From the Werner Plan to EMU*. London: Longman.

Panizza, R. 1985. "Alle radici dell'instabilità monetaria internazionale: gli accordi di Bretton Woods." In Cassa di Risparmio di Torino, *Moneta ed economia internazionale*. Torino: Piemonte Vivo Ricerche.

Sanford, C. S., Jr. 1993. "Financial Markets in 2020." Paper presented at the Economic Symposium of the Federal Reserve Bank of Kansas City, sponsored by the Bankers Trust Company, New York (20 August).

Steinherr, A., ed. 1994. *30 Years of European Monetary Integration: From the Werner Plan to EMU*. London: Longman.

Triffin, R. 1991. "Lo SMI (Sistema Internazionale. . .o Scandalo?) e lo SME (Sistema Monetario Europeo. . .o Successo?)" *Moneta e Credito* 176.

US Congress. Joint Economic Committee. 1964. *A Description and Analysis of Certain European Capital Markets, Economic Practices, and Policies*. No. 3. Washington: Government Printing Office.

Yeager, L. B. 1976. *International Monetary Relations: Theory, History, and Policy*. 2d ed. New York: Harper and Row.

6

International Direct Investment: Strengthening the Policy Regime

DeANNE JULIUS

Today multinational companies and private banks—not governments and international institutions—are the major weavers of the world economy. Its fabric is an intricate pattern of goods and services that reach consumers after crossing borders or through local production by companies whose ownership and financing originates elsewhere. By 1990 such international production totaled $5.5 trillion while world exports of goods and nonfactor services were $4 trillion.[1] Some parts of the fabric are denser and stronger than others. The continent of Europe, the North Atlantic, and the trans-Pacific region are heavily embroidered, while Africa and the broad mass of the former Soviet Union are nearly threadbare.

Things looked very different in 1944 when the Bretton Woods institutions were set up. The fabric of the world economy was in tatters. The disruption of two world wars, separated by a period of global depression and collapsing international trade and investment, left most European and Asian countries destitute and economically isolated. A revival of trade and capital flows was urgently needed. But a key lesson of the interwar period was that governments, acting independently of one another, could not be

---

DeAnne Julius is chief economist at British Airways. The author is grateful for comments on an earlier draft from Richard Brown, Kwang Jun, Peter Kenen, John Merrett, Peter Muchlinski, and Stephen Thomsen, as well as the IIE conference participants. The author retains sole responsibility for the opinions expressed.

1. UNCTAD (1993). These figures compare with a gross world product of $22.6 trillion.

relied upon to eschew such collectively disastrous policies as protection-ism and competitive devaluation. Even without the theoretical tools of game theory, the Bretton Woods participants recognized that a new re-gime to foster cooperation and commitment was needed. The Interna-tional Monetary Fund (IMF) and what eventually became the General Agreement on Tariffs and Trade (GATT) had this as their essential ratio-nale.

A second need in 1944 was to prime the investment pump that had run dry when private businesses and banks withdrew from international mar-kets. This was the basic justification for the International Bank for Recon-struction and Development (IBRD). It was to be a risk-pooling and publicly guaranteed mechanism to restart lending to otherwise non-creditworthy governments. Initially this applied mostly to Europe, but the focus soon shifted to the developing countries.

To what extent do these two justifications for international public institutions still apply? Today huge and integrated global financial markets exert a discipline on governments' fiscal, monetary, and ex-change rate policies that is both greater and more immediate than that achieved by the IMF even in its pre-1971 heyday. Indeed, since the breakdown of fixed exchange rates and the aftermath of the debt cri-sis—as Eichengreen and Kenen show elsewhere in this volume—the role of the IMF has converged on that of the World Bank as a provider of medium-term loans to governments of poor countries. Meanwhile, private risk-pooling mechanisms such as emerging market funds and the trading of sovereign debt have overtaken the volume of financing available from the Bank and the Fund. The number of noncreditworthy countries (from the viewpoint of the private market) represents only a fraction of Bank/Fund borrowers. It must be time to consider merging, downsizing, and refocusing the IMF and World Bank on the current areas of capital market failure. This is a subject addressed by other papers in this volume.

The same argument cannot be made for the GATT. There is no private equivalent of the international financial market to discipline governments' policies on trade and investment. Such governments are inevitably hos-tage to domestic politics where a few local but vocal potential losers can prevail over the many but mostly silent—and sometimes unknowing—winners. To facilitate wealth creation through trade and investment, inter-national agreements, peer pressures on ministers, independent proce-dures for dispute settlement, and the ultimate discipline of sanctions are still needed—perhaps more than ever as these flows increasingly shape, as well as respond to, comparative advantage.

The purpose of this paper is to examine and propose changes in the policy framework for international direct investment (IDI). It takes as a premise that in the vast majority of circumstances, IDI is a positive-sum game at the country level of aggregation.[2] Thus the primary concern of governments should be IDI's promotion, not its restriction or control. This accords with the political reality of the 1990s, but not with that of many countries in earlier decades. Indeed, the current convergence of international opinion on the desirability of IDI may have created a window of opportunity for a change in regime in order to encourage investment.

The next section of this paper summarizes the cyclical phases of IDI pre– and post–Bretton Woods. It identifies the new features of the 1980s/1990s and draws the implications for regime design from this historical review. A subsequent section sets out policy objectives for IDI and other international business transactions. These are then developed into a proposal for granting multinational companies access directly—not through governments—to dispute settlement panels in the new World Trade Organization (WTO).

The paper does not cover the future role of the IMF or the World Bank except as they relate to IDI, and it sees only a small pump-priming role for them there. Although the paper does not develop the author's view that there should be a refocused and reduced IMF/Bank role, its proposal for an enlarged mandate for the WTO should be placed in that context. The combination would represent a radical departure from the current distribution of international public resources and authority among the IMF, World Bank, and GATT. The currently preeminent institutions, the IMF and the World Bank, played a vital post-1944 role in rebuilding an integrated world economy after the devastation of war. But their very success has undermined much of their original rationale. We now have a tightly woven world economy, built largely and increasingly on private-sector agents: banks, businesses, and investors. The greatest scope for wealth creation post-1994 lies in expanding international trade and investment, not in exchange rate reform or public-sector lending. This implies a redistribution of scarce international public resources towards the WTO.

120 Years of IDI

Although the purview of this volume is 50 years, in the case of direct investment it is instructive to look back a bit further. The heyday of foreign investment was the pre–World War I period of rapid economic growth

---

2. Recent support for this premise can be found in Graham and Krugman (1991), Julius (1993), and Thomsen and Woolcock (1993). However, the popular literature contains many contrary views; see, for example, Franz and Collins (1989) or Glickman and Woodward (1989). There are also conflicting trends at present. Nigeria has reintroduced exchange controls, and India has outlawed sales of shares in subsidiaries of multinationals at "undervalue."

and even more rapid international economic integration. The limited data available for that period do not clearly differentiate between direct and portfolio investment. However, according to Dunning (1983), both types of flows increased dramatically. Before World War I—and not again until the 1980s—private capital flows were the main driver of growth in the world economy. Lessons from that era have relevance for regime design today.

With hindsight it is possible to distinguish five historical periods in the development of IDI. The first runs from approximately 1870 (recovery from the Civil War in the United States) until the outbreak of World War I. During this period both trade and IDI expanded rapidly, feeding on and stimulating each other. The second period encompasses the two world wars (1915–45) and was one of shrinking trade and weak IDI.[3] During the third period (1945–73), trade grew very rapidly and IDI began to recover. However, it was very much a one-way flow from the United States to Europe, stimulated originally by the Marshall Plan and the IBRD funding of infrastructure. The fourth period (1973–83) is defined by the two oil-price shocks and their recessionary aftermaths. IDI flows during that era were dominated by oil company investments and, during the 1970s, nationalizations. Finally, the decade since 1983 has seen an explosion of IDI along with its maturing into a multicountry, multisector pattern. For the purposes of this paper, the instructive periods to examine are the first and the last.

IDI Pre–World War I

In the late 19th century the industrial revolution was in full swing in the world's major economy, Great Britain. British companies were active overseas investors. They regularly exported capital amounting to 5 to 10 percent of the country's GDP.[4] France and Germany also became significant capital exporters. This outward investment from Europe was widely spread over North and South America, Australia, and parts of Africa and Southeast Asia. It was not unusual for Europe's wealthier Victorian house-

---

3. There are conflicting views about this period as well. Dunning (1983) suggests that by 1938 the overall stock of IDI had risen by at least 50 percent over 1914 levels. However, in 1937 a Chatham House Study Group, chaired by H. D. Henderson and including J. M. Keynes, published *The Problem of International Investment*. The problem to which their book referred was the failure of investment flows to revive sufficiently after World War I to effect the rebuilding of Europe, in the same way that prewar investment from Europe had accelerated the development of the Americas. Without flows from abroad to relieve capital and foreign exchange constraints, they warned, protectionism would grow, trade would shrink, and more countries would face depression.

4. The growth of domestic production during this period in Britain averaged less than 2 percent; Britain was already a *rentier* economy.

holds to have part of their savings in Argentine railroad bonds and Asian trading companies. The capital-importing countries serviced their debt by exporting agricultural commodities and raw materials back to Europe. During the 1870s, 1880s, and early 1890s, the expansion in world output of all kinds of commodities far outran that of any previous period of history.[5] All this was accomplished by private households, banks, and businesses, without government guarantees or international institutions.

In two important respects, however, there was official regime support for international investment. First, there was a near universal system of currency convertibility via the gold standard and its stepchild, the sterling area. Not only could dividends be easily remitted, but exchange rate risk was probably lower for a longer period than it has been before or since. The second factor was low (perceived) political risk. Many of the European investments were in colonial territories, which operated under home-country rules. Disputes would be settled under the laws of the home government, and if property damage or other losses were incurred illegally, then avenues for cross-retaliation were plentiful. In those countries, such a regime drew strength from the close alignment of interests between the private investor and the home government, which could generally overwhelm any objections from the host country. In independent host countries, such as Argentina and the United States, legal systems were relatively well developed and based on European models.

At first glance there may seem to be few lessons from such an unreplicable, if highly successful, regime. No one today would seriously suggest a return to the gold standard or to the tyranny of colonial relationships. However, it is worth examining the *ends* that these served, even while rejecting the means.

The gold standard aimed to provide broad country coverage and predictability of exchange rates. These are two of the key objectives of any fixed rate system. Modern versions, such as the European Monetary System (EMS), also aim to provide an inflation anchor and a symmetric method of adjusting to disequilibria, both of which were perceived weaknesses of the gold standard (Williamson 1983). These aims address different constituencies. The first two aims—coverage and predictability— are important to international investors—while the other two—inflation and symmetry—are important to governments. We therefore concentrate on the first two aims.

The question is how to achieve them in the absence of a widespread system of managed exchange rates. The answer lies in actions by both governments and companies. Governments that wish to attract IDI and to expand their tradeable sectors must give priority to stabilizing their currency and removing restrictions on capital account transactions. Stabiliza-

---

5. Sir Walter Layton, *The Study of Prices* (1912), as quoted in Hale (1993).

tion may be pursued vis-à-vis a single major currency (e.g., Hong Kong and Argentina with the US dollar, Austria with the German mark) or a basket of the currencies of major trading partners (e.g., the European Currency Unit for EMS members). Freeing capital account transactions is necessary to reassure investors that they will be as free of government interference in investment/divestment decisions in the host country as they are at home or in other countries with free convertibility. Without that assurance, they are less likely to invest. A country that chooses the discipline of a currency stability target without the shelter of foreign exchange control has accepted an obligation to place international considerations on at least a par with domestic ones, and this is ultimately what reassures the foreign investor.

In such a decentralized system, predictability ultimately rests on government commitment. However, this is also true in managed exchange systems (Kenen 1988). For companies today, predictability can be enhanced by foreign exchange hedging to deal with financial risks and investment diversification to deal with risks arising from production and marketing decisions. The growth of hedging instruments during the last decade to cover more currencies, especially of Asian countries, is testimony to the growing ability of private financial markets to meet the former demand. The major expansion of IDI flows over this period may have been driven partly for the latter reason (Ohmae 1985). I have argued elsewhere that IDI-related trade is less sensitive to exchange rate movements than is autonomous trade (Julius 1990). For the United States and Japan, more than half of trade is now IDI-related in the sense that it involves either foreign (US or Japanese) subsidiaries in other countries trading with the home country or foreign-owned firms importing or exporting from the United States or Japan. Direct investment provides a natural insulation against exchange rate losses by a closer matching of costs and revenues in the same host country currency.

As to coverage, the necessarily voluntary nature of any regime that is compatible with national sovereignty means that universality can only be approached incrementally. Coverage will expand only as countries perceive the net benefits of participation. Once the benefits are perceived, however, countries' ability to "join" is entirely self-determined and can therefore be rapidly implemented. The widespread shift in developing countries that is taking place now toward more open and market-friendly policies suggests that the coverage of this sort of decentralized and market-enforced regime may encompass 80 percent of the world's economic activity by the end of this decade.

The second important aspect of the pre–World War I regime was low political risk. This was derived from the close link between home- and host-country governments and the direct access by companies to a mechanism for dispute settlement. Often that mechanism was simply the home-country legal or political system (e.g., for French investors in West Africa,

Spanish in Latin America, and British in India). Where the host country was not a colony, it sometimes had a legal system that was closely modeled on that of the home country (e.g., for British investors in the United States and Australia). The relative importance of these legal factors in facilitating IDI, compared with the economic or even linguistic links that bound imperial systems together, is probably impossible to determine. Certainly the preeminence of imperial over colonial law was one of the distinguishing features of the political regime of the period (Lipson 1985).

Again, although the means of this mechanism are not replicable, its ends are worth examining. Those ends include a set of accepted laws or principles against which the perceived wrong can be judged, a clear process for raising a complaint, and confidence that the judgment reached will be enforced. In a world of sovereign states, the first end is clearly best approached by governments multilaterally. No one country's laws will be accepted by another, and bilateral agreements tend to proliferate into a cobweb of partially incompatible arrangements that complicate and limit multinational companies in their pursuit of global strategies.[6]

Multilateral agreements, however, cause problems with the next two ends. The process for raising a complaint when the agreement is violated is then naturally a government-to-government one. Many companies today have shareholders in several major countries and commercial interests that may not always coincide with the political interest of their "home" government. Even where that is not a problem, the home government may be reluctant to press a complaint if it feels that its broader relationship with the other country might suffer. Furthermore, there are so many other claims on politicians' and officials' time that they are unlikely to give the matter the priority that the company itself does. The public-choice literature suggests that a government official has far fewer incentives to undertake a speedy and effective pursuit of a complaint affecting only one company and few domestic voters than does a company management that sees shareholders' funds at risk or draining rapidly away. This makes representation by government an unsatisfactory solution to IDI dispute settlement. It is also unsatisfactory on the grounds of enforcement. The concept of international law has always been plagued by the fundamental sovereignty of individual states. Only very recently, through the North American Free Trade Agreement (NAFTA) and Uruguay Round agreements, has progress been made at raising the cost of noncompliance. In NAFTA, but not the new WTO, companies are allowed direct access to dispute settlement. These developments are discussed later in this chapter.

---

6. An example of this is the 1944 Chicago Convention on air transport, which set up a system of bilateral agreements on international flights that still operates today.

IDI since 1983

The decade since the recession of the early 1980s has seen a remarkable surge in cross-border investment. From 1983 until its peak in 1990, IDI grew at an average annual rate of 26 percent (18 percent in real terms), reaching $234 billion. With the onset of recession in the major investing countries, it has since fallen back to an estimated $140 billion in 1993.[7] The (cumulative) stock of IDI has thus multiplied over this period and now exceeds $2 trillion.

The characteristics of this growth have been documented elsewhere.[8] For the purposes of this paper, there are three salient features to note. First, the bulk of the investment growth during this period involved new home and host countries. Thus the cross-country distribution of IDI changed significantly. Between 1960 and 1975 the United States was the only significant net exporter of IDI. European countries were the main recipients. By the late 1980s, Japan had become the largest net exporter and the United States had become a net recipient. Particularly after the strong rise in the yen in 1985–86, Japanese companies became major overseas investors and the United States was their favorite destination. A further broadening of flows took place towards the end of this period. Flows into the United States slowed (along with the economy) while those to developing countries accelerated dramatically. The share of IDI captured by the developing world rose from 17 percent in 1987 to 33 percent in 1992.

The second striking feature of the 1983–93 period was the rise of new and smaller firms undertaking international investment. While only limited sample data are available, it appears that the number of firms investing internationally grew even faster than total IDI flows. In the 14 major home countries, the number of multinational enterprises more than tripled during the last two decades: from around 7,000 in 1969 to nearly 24,000 in 1990. A more general estimate puts the number of parent MNEs worldwide at 37,000 in 1990, with interest in some 170,000 foreign affiliates. Extrapolating from data on US and Japanese MNEs, nearly 60 percent of these parent firms are in manufacturing, 37 percent are in services, and 3 percent are in primary production. However, the sectoral breakdown of foreign affiliates is strikingly different: 60 percent of them are in services with just 36 percent in manufacturing.[9]

---

7. The recession is probably not the only factor in the reversal of the IDI growth trend, but it is likely to be the most significant. A regression relating IDI growth and GDP growth of the major countries for the period 1963–88 yielded a statistically significant income elasticity of 3.44 and an R^2 of 0.53 (Julius 1990).

8. See 1991, 1992, and 1993 editions of the *World Investment Report* (UNCTAD), Julius (1990), and Levy and Dunning (1993).

9. All data in this paragraph are from UNCTAD (1993).

The third salient characteristic of IDI flows during the past decade is this shift toward services. Deregulation of the financial and telecommunications sectors in the United States, UK, and Japan stimulated a major increase in outward investment flows. Between 1980 and 1988, for example, the share of services in Japan's outward investment stock rose from 25 to 58 percent. For the G-5 countries as a whole, it grew from 34 to 42 percent (Julius 1991). This was a reversal from the focus on manufacturing in the 1960s and early 1970s, and oil in the mid- to late 1970s. A second wave of service-sector IDI began in the late 1980s with the privatization drive in developing countries. Between 1988 and 1992, IDI from privatizations amounted to $14.5 billion or 10 percent of all IDI into developing countries. The largest privatization sectors were telecommunications, energy, and transport (IBRD 1993).

It should not be surprising that IDI grew so rapidly when deregulation or privatization of domestic service companies took place. In many service industries, proximity to the customer is necessary for the producer-consumer transaction. Conventional cross-border trade without prior investment is impossible. Yet IDI in services—and thus trade—has been severely limited until recently by the domestic regulatory structures that govern sectors such as telephones, natural gas, electricity, airlines, banking, and insurance. As a result, international competition is far less advanced in services than in manufacturing. While services account for 60 percent of world consumption, they make up only 20 percent of world trade. In manufactures, about half of world production is traded. Even if one assumed that services were only half as tradeable as manufactures, that would still imply scope for more than a doubling of service trade at today's output levels.

In summary, the past decade has seen IDI spread to and from more countries, involve more firms both large and small, and cover services as well as manufacturing and commodities. Like trade, it has become a multicountry, multifirm, multisector flow, but it is still far from maturity, particularly in the service sectors. Opening those sectors for further growth of IDI and trade is of critical importance to the Organization for Economic Cooperation and Development (OECD) countries as comparative advantage in manufacturing increasingly shifts from those countries to the developing world. The resulting job loss in manufacturing is likely to accelerate in Europe, Japan, and North America (Brown and Julius 1993). Enlarging the scope for trade in services—which often requires IDI—presents the best counterargument to the protectionist pressures that will come from manufacturing interest in the OECD.

Policy Objectives for IDI

For nearly 20 years, the main international initiative on IDI was the UN-led effort to negotiate a Code of Conduct for Transnational Corporations.

Its intent was to restrict corporate behavior and impose universal conditions that would sometimes go beyond those applying to domestic firms competing in the same industry. For these reasons the code was opposed by MNEs. Finally, in 1992, the negotiations were abandoned. By then, so many developing countries were trying to attract IDI that support for a restrictive code had evaporated. This change in attitude has cleared the way for a new examination of the policy objectives of IDI. It is no longer appropriate to assume that government and corporate objectives conflict and that therefore a balance of rights and responsibilities for each must be sought.[10] Today the situation is similar to trade policy objectives. Although mercantilist sentiments lurk in both political and corporate camps, their leaders share a broad belief in the mutual benefits of freer trade. This provides a common expectation that trade barriers will be lowered through negotiation, and it creates a shared acceptance of the basic trade principles (e.g., national treatment, most-favored nation) against which complaints can be brought.

If we are at a point in economic history, 50 years after the Bretton Woods Conference, when a large number of governments agree that IDI should be promoted because of its wealth-creating attributes, what policy objectives should they pursue to accomplish this? There are three broad principles that derive from the efficiency-seeking benefits of cross-border investment:[11]

- **Market access.** Foreign firms should be allowed to establish themselves in the host country in order to undertake any activity that is legally permissible for domestic firms. Strictly applied, this would permit 100 percent foreign ownership in any sector where there were private domestic firms.

- **National treatment.** Once established, foreign firms must obey the same laws as domestic firms and they should be accorded the same rights. This principle would be violated by local content restrictions and reporting requirements that apply only to foreign firms.

- **Free choice of means.** Government policies should be neutral among trade, direct investment, cross-border licensing, and other forms of joint ventures or strategic alliances as alternative means of access to a market. Company decisions about the access route should be as free as possible from government incentives or restrictions that favor one route over another. Voluntary export restraints are an example of a policy that

---

10. This is the structure proposed in Bergsten and Graham (1992) although their proposal is not as restrictive towards MNEs as the proposed UN Code.

11. These are outlined in Julius (1991) except that the third has been made more general to cover additional market access modes beyond trade and investment.

violates this principle by skewing business decisions towards investment rather than trade. Ideally, all means of access should be fully open (e.g., free trade, full foreign ownership allowed), but this principle could also be applied where one access route is more closed than others, due perhaps to the regulatory regime of a particular industry.

All three principles are ideals to be approached rather than strict codes that countries can be expected to meet. Derogations would be common as a starting point for negotiations. For example, the OECD Code on the Liberalization of Capital Movements enshrines the principle of the progressive introduction of the right of establishment (market access), but also contains within it rights of derogation and deferral. National treatment is probably the closest to being recognized and met at present because it has long been a basic principle of GATT negotiations.

Free choice of means, a phrase borrowed from the legal profession,[12] is an attempt to grapple with the multitude of forms that the globalization of industry is taking. Trade and direct investment are the two most prevalent, but there is actually a wide range of market entry strategies in many industries. The policy objective should be to allow the firm to choose the profit-maximizing one, subject, of course, to competition policy constraints. From the corporate viewpoint, the strategic problem is how best to integrate a geographically dispersed value chain (Levy and Dunning 1993). Too often today, it is divergent government policies—not industry economics—that result in the choice of a wholly owned subsidiary in one country, a joint venture with a local firm in a second, a technology licensing arrangement in a third, and a nonequity marketing alliance in a fourth. It is possible that the combination of the market access and national treatment principles could avoid this situation as long as the institution through which they were enforced covered all forms of market entry. Even then, however, separate negotiations on trade, investment, and intellectual property, for example, could inadvertently result in divergent treatment.

The current reality is a long way short of these three principles in most countries. Any country could adopt them unilaterally, but progress is more likely through a multilateral bargaining process. The regional groups of countries in western Europe and North America have made considerable progress in liberalizing investment flows over the past five years. On a broader front, lists of acceptable exceptions could be negotiated, as suggested by Bergsten and Graham (1992). Julius (1991) has proposed a type of sectoral reciprocity in the initial bargaining phase to shift the negotiating incentives from long to short exception lists. However, all these suggestions concern the process rather than the principles of a new

12. The author is grateful to P. T. Muchlinski, barrister and lecturer in law at the London School of Economics, for suggesting this phrase.

IDI regime. With the signing of the Uruguay Round accord in Marrakesh in April 1994, we also have a new beginning on that issues. I would therefore like to put on the table the following.

A Modest Proposal

In 1970 Goldberg and Kindleberger proposed a "GATT for Investment: A Proposal for Supervision of the International Corporation." Since then, many scholars have put forward their ideas for a new or extended international organization to cover IDI.[13] Most of the early proposals focused on constraining the activities of MNEs or defining their rights and obligations. These are of little relevance today when the objective is to facilitate IDI by inducing governments to remove discriminatory treatment of foreign-owned firms. The focus of any new institutional arrangement clearly has to be on government action, not corporate behavior.

Yet corporations must be involved, as they are the ultimate decision makers on private direct investment. The institution must have credibility with its ultimate corporate customer in order for any new rules that it negotiates to have the desired effect on IDI.

An informal survey of 12 such customers (MNEs in Europe, Japan, and the United States with a government affairs director or chief economist known by the author) revealed a unanimous distaste for any new international institution to deal with IDI. They felt that start-up costs (including costs for their own time) would be high, benefits would be slow in coming if they came at all, agreements reached would have little chance of enforcement, and there was a real risk that any new institution would be twisted in a negative direction (or tied up in fruitless internal debates) as happened with the UN Center for Transnational Corporations. There was a further risk that a new international institution would merely duplicate work already being done at the OECD on the wider investment instrument and that, unless closely coordinated with the GATT, it could create jurisdictional confusion over disputes involving both trade and investment.

Among this group there was considerable support for the GATT as a small and "ideologically sound" organization, and most (eight) were neutral (three) to positive (five) about the idea of expanding the remit of the GATT to cover investment issues. The other four felt that the current patchwork of bilateral investment treaties, while not ideal, was at least more enforceable than anything multilateral that they had yet seen. Those who favored a GATT expansion also said their greatest concern was the

---

13. These include, among others, Bergsten (1974), Vernon (1978–79), Camps (1980), Julius (1991), and Bergsten and Graham (1992). For a review of the dispute settlement aspects of these, see Brewer (1994).

complexity and uncertain enforceability of the dispute settlement mechanism.

Our earlier reviews of the IDI boom before World War I also highlighted the importance of effective dispute resolution. The new Uruguay Round agreements represent an important breakthrough in this area. The WTO Agreement establishes the umbrella framework for all other agreements and administers the Dispute Settlement Understanding (DSU). The DSU considerably strengthens the enforceability of judgments by reversing the requirement for a unanimous vote of GATT members to approve a dispute panel report. In the past the guilty party was able to veto the report and avoid whatever penalties had been recommended. In the future, a unanimous vote of WTO members will be needed to *reject* a dispute panel report. In addition, investment disputes can be linked to trade disputes through the cross-retaliation provided for in DSU Article 22.3(c). This expands the range of remedies available on investment matters and recognizes the close commercial relationship between trade and investment.

In addition to the DSU, the Uruguay Round agreements extend substantial coverage to direct investment. The most important are the Agreement on Trade Related Investment Measures (TRIMs), the General Agreement on Trade in Services (GATS), and the Agreement on Trade Related Aspects of Intellectual Property Rights (TRIPs). The TRIMs agreement applies national treatment principles to foreign-owned firms, although it does not cover IDI in services. The GATS agreement explicitly includes IDI by defining trade in services to include, inter alia, "the supply of a service . . . by a service supplier of one Member, through commercial presence in the territory of any other Member."[14] It provides a list of policies that are inconsistent with national treatment and market access principles, among others, and like TRIMs, it specifies that a future review and round of negotiations will be held within five years to achieve a progressively higher level of liberalization. Such provisions are a natural opening for broadening the WTO's coverage of investment issues.

Finally, the TRIPs agreement is important to IDI because intellectual property is often a core "ownership advantage" (Dunning 1988) that enables firms to expand successfully in foreign markets. Technology licensing agreements are increasingly used both between parent and offshore affiliate and as an alternative to IDI through an arm's-length arrangement with a local firm in the host country. Intellectual property is broadly defined in the TRIPs agreement, which could provide the base for future integration with TRIMs in pursuit of the modal neutrality principle described above. Already the cross-retaliation provision in the DSU and the fact that TRIPs, TRIMs, and GATS are all linked to the same dispute

---

14. Article I, 2(c) as quoted in Brewer (forthcoming 1994).

settlement mechanism under the WTO represent a huge advance towards comprehensive coverage of international commercial transactions.

Is anything more needed? Of course, the first requirement is to have the Uruguay Round package passed by governments over the course of this year. It would be a political failure of the highest order if this torturously negotiated package were to be rejected by the US Congress or the parliament of some other major country.

The second requirement is for governments to give high priority to the sectoral negotiations in GATS. As it stands now, GATS is a very weak instrument. It contains only the framework of principles governing trade in services, with a reference to separate sectoral negotiations to follow. These sectoral agreements will be critical to liberalizing IDI and trade in services. Competitive barriers in services are often unique to a particular sector because they derive from domestic regulations rather than trade restrictions per se.

International companies from that sector could play a direct, advisory role to the GATS Secretariat staff in these negotiations. Companies operating internationally are often better able than governments to compare different regulatory systems and to understand the true nature of investment impediments. It should not be assumed that companies always prefer the regulatory framework of their home market (as government negotiators tend to). By directly seeking out the views of companies in a sector that they know well, GATS may be able to steer governments more rapidly towards global best practice.

However, domestic regulations are so complicated and differentiated that liberalization will often require an approach based on mutual recognition rather than harmonization of regulation.[15] Mutual recognition may involve departures from national treatment, often in ways that benefit the foreign firm. In order to agree on mutual recognition of regulatory regimes in a sector, countries must have a high degree of trust in each others' legal and political institutions. This, in turn, can only be achieved among a set of like-minded and equally committed countries. Sectoral agreements have the flexibility of plurilateral membership, without which very little multilateral liberalization in services is likely to take place.

Beyond these essential tasks of "completing" the Uruguay Round agreements, there is one further institutional innovation needed at this point. Firms should be given direct access to the dispute settlement procedure in the WTO. When they have a complaint against a host government, they should be able to raise it directly and to plead their case without the filter of their home government's views and broader priorities. The WTO should be as accessible to international private corporations as the domes-

---

15. This was an important lesson of the 1992 process in Europe. Progress in liberalizing services began only after the attempt at harmonization was put aside (except for minimum standards) and mutual recognition was adopted as the way forward (Bressand 1990).

tic court system is to national private citizens.[16] Thus, if a company felt that a host government was applying its law in a way that violated its own WTO commitments in that sector, it could apply for a hearing by a WTO dispute settlement panel as an alternative to the host-country courts.[17]

While this may seem a striking departure from the postwar diplomatic tradition of government-to-government relations, there is a precedent in the recent NAFTA. It extends the dispute resolution procedures in the US-Canada FTA to provide for disputes between firms and governments as well as between governments. Chapter 11(B) provides that an investor's complaint against a government can be submitted to a three-member tribunal with the authority both to take a final decision and to award damages. Each side selects one member of the tribunal with the remaining member agreed to by both parties. A similar arrangement could be instituted at the WTO, perhaps with a prepanel hearing on the technical merits of the case in order to screen out insignificant or frivolous suits.

This proposal is not intended to replace or supersede the network of private conciliation and arbitration arrangements such as the International Court of Arbitration of the International Chamber of Commerce or the international arbitration centers in London, Stockholm, or Hong Kong. These private centers arbitrate disputes based on investment contracts between firms and host governments (common only for large resource-based investments) and also those covered under bilateral investment treaties (BITs) that have been signed between home and host governments. There are over 400 such bilateral treaties and the vast majority provide for both government-to-government and investor-government disputes. Many BITs mention the International Center for the Settlement of Investment Disputes (ICSID) as a possible venue, but it has rarely been used. ICSID was created in 1965 as part of the World Bank group specifically as a dispute resolution forum between investors and governments. It has been an important reference point, but only very large cases tend to go to it because of its lengthy and complex processes. At last count, it had dealt with 23 claims since it was established nearly 30 years ago.

Would companies be more likely to use the WTO? The advantages of the WTO over ICSID include the former's status with developed as well as

---

16. It has been suggested that if the WTO dispute settlement mechanism were to be extended to corporations there would be pressure to extend it also to nongovernment organizations (NGOs) such as unions and consumer groups. This would be a misinterpretation of the proposal since such NGOs are not directly involved in trade or investment and thus have no commercial interest at risk from government decisions in those areas. NGOs could be allowed to attend hearings as observers, but they would not have the grounds to bring complaints.

17. In sectors such as natural resources where foreign investment often takes place under specific agreements between the foreign firm and the host government, this remedy would not generally be sought since arbitration forums are specified in the agreement. However, most IDI is not covered by specific firm-government agreements.

developing countries, its authority on trade and investment matters, and the potential for cross-retaliation. In the service sectors especially, much remains to be done in liberalizing IDI in Europe, North America, and Japan. As global competition in those large markets intensifies, disputes relating to differences in regulatory systems are likely to multiply (Ostry 1990). Discussions on this subject take place at the OECD, but that organization is poorly equipped to enforce agreements reached, and of course, any such agreements would not include developing countries. It is likely, in any case, that the focus of action on IDI will shift to the sectoral negotiations in the WTO. Linking those explicitly with a dispute settlement procedure open to investors would greatly strengthen the role and credibility of that organization.

Conclusions

There is little disagreement today over the importance of international direct investment as a wealth-creating and welfare-enhancing flow. It is central to the process of technology transfer and to the growth of international competition in the service industries. Those industries make up 60 percent of world production and provide more jobs than manufacturing or agriculture in most countries of the world.

By themselves, however, these positive attributes do not imply that action is required of the international community to facilitate IDI. A clear lesson of the 1980s is that private companies are more likely to invest and expand into new markets when the number of regulations and institutions governing them is reduced, not increased. Institutional interventions, especially at the international level, should be limited to areas of clear market failure and should not duplicate existing structures.

The areas of market failure for IDI have been greatly reduced over the half century since the Bretton Woods Conference. Private financial markets have developed hedging instruments and diversification techniques that allow investors to manage exchange rate risks. Beginning in the late 1970s, many OECD countries deregulated or privatized many of their service industries, creating market-led multinationals out of moribund state monopolies. More recently this trend has spread to developing countries, providing access for IDI into many new sectors and industries. With the possible exception of parts of Africa and the former Soviet Union, it is hard to identify countries today that would meet a strict definition of market failure.

Yet there are clearly many industries, especially in the service sectors, whose international markets are far from integrated. The failure is that of governments to fully liberalize access to their markets and to apply national treatment to those in them. Even when there are international commitments, the process for settling disputes is a complex and indirect one for a company with a complaint.

Further efforts both to negotiate more liberal rules—sector by sector—and to improve the enforcement of those rules are clearly needed. However, it is not necessary to devise a new institution for this. The Uruguay Round agreements of the GATT, signed this year, represent a major breakthrough in the coverage of investment issues. The WTO that will encompass the GATT as well as the new agreements provides a strong skeleton on which to build sectoral codes that expand from and integrate the new areas of intellectual property, trade-related investment, and services.

The next step is to recognize the important contribution that MNEs can make to those negotiations through their knowledge of the effects of the different regulatory environments in which they operate. Often both their detailed understanding and their own interest will be broader than those of any particular home or host government. The WTO would benefit from involving them directly in defining and prioritizing the negotiating agenda for governments.

In addition, the time has come to grant MNEs direct access to the dispute settlement process in the WTO. As international corporate citizens, they require an impartial judicial forum where disputes with governments that relate to international commercial transactions can be heard and where a case law of such judgments can be built to guide future action. Their shareholders' funds are at stake when they make an investment, and they have a greater interest than does a government representative in ensuring that agreements are kept or redress is provided.

The benefit to the international community of this change would be twofold. First, the increased assurance and clarity provided by direct access to WTO dispute settlement would add to investors' confidence in committing money to countries without a long record of liberal policies towards IDI. And second, if WTO dispute settlement proved to be an effective means to open markets, then direct access would enlist the multinationals on the side of liberalizing (host) government policies. At present they can act only through their home governments, with whom they may be more ambivalent about liberalization. This reversal in their litigation relationships could make the dispute settlement procedures of the WTO as effective a crowbar for international market opening as the European Court of Justice has been in Europe.

References

Bergsten, C. Fred. 1974. "Coming Investment Wars?" *Foreign Affairs* 53 (October): 135–52.
Bergsten, C. Fred, and Edward M. Graham. 1992. "Needed: New International Rules for Foreign Direct Investment." *The International Trade Journal* 7, no. 1: 15–44.
Bressand, Albert. 1990. "Beyond Interdependence: 1992 as a Global Challenge." *International Affairs* 66, no. 1: 47–65.

Brewer, Thomas L. 1994. "International Investment Dispute Settlement Procedures: The Evolving Regime for Foreign Direct Investment." Forthcoming. Georgetown University Business School, Washington, DC.

Brown, Richard, and DeAnne Julius. 1993. "Is Manufacturing Still Special in the New World Order?" In R. O'Brien, *Finance and the International Economy: 7*. Oxford: Oxford University Press.

Camps, M. 1980. "The Case for a New Global Trade Organisation." In M. Camps and C. Gwin, *Collective Management: The Reform of Global Economic Organizations*.

Dunning, John. 1983. "Changes in the Level and Structure of International Production: The Last One Hundred Years." In Mark Casson, *The Growth in International Business*. London: George Allen & Unwin.

Dunning, John. 1988. *Explaining International Production*. London: Unwin Hyman.

Franz, Douglas, and Catherine Collins. 1989. *Selling Out: How We Are Letting Japan Buy Our Land, Our Industries, Our Financial Institutions, and Our Future*. Chicago: Contemporary Books.

Glickman, Norman, and Douglas Woodward. 1989. *The New Competitors: How Foreign Investors Are Changing the U.S. Economy*. New York: Basic Books.

Graham, Edward M., and Paul Krugman. 1991. *Foreign Direct Investment in the United States*, 2d ed. Washington: Institute for International Economics.

Hale, David. 1993. The World Economy after the Cold War. Unpublished paper. (October).

IBRD. 1993. *World Debt Tables*. Washington: IBRD.

Julius, DeAnne. 1990. *Global Companies and Public Policy: The Growing Challenge of Foreign Direct Investment*. London: Pinter Publishers for the Royal Institute of International Affairs.

Julius, DeAnne. 1991. *Foreign Direct Investment: The Neglected Twin of Trade*. Occasional Papers 33. Washington: Group of Thirty.

Julius, DeAnne. 1993. *Liberalisation, Foreign Investment, and Economic Growth*. London: Shell Selected Paper.

Kenen, Peter B. 1988. *Managing Exchange Rates*. London: Routledge for the Royal Institute of International Affairs.

Levy, David, and John H. Dunning. 1993. "International Production and Sourcing: Trends and Issues." In *STI Review*, No. 13 (December): 13–59. Paris: OECD.

Lipson, C. 1985. *Standing Guard: Protecting Foreign Capital in the Nineteenth and Twentieth Centuries*. Los Angeles: University of California Press.

Ohmae, Kenichi, 1985. *Triad Power: The Coming Shape of Global Competition*. New York: Macmillan, Inc.

Ostry, Sylvia. 1990. *Governments and Corporations in a Shrinking World*. New York: Council on Foreign Relations Press.

Thomsen, Stephen, and Stephen Woolcock. 1993. *Direct Investment and European Integration: Competition among Firms and Governments*. London: Pinter Publishers for the Royal Institute of International Affairs.

UNCTAD. 1991. *World Investment Report 1991: Triad in Foreign Direct Investment*. New York: United Nations.

UNCTAD. 1992. *World Investment Report 1992: Transnational Corporations as Engines of Growth*. New York: United Nations.

Vernon, R. 1978–79. "The Multinationals: No Strings Attached." *Foreign Policy* 33 (Winter): 121–34.

Williamson, John. 1983. *The Open Economy and the World Economy*, chapter 1. New York: Basic Books.

7

The Case for a Global Environmental Organization

DANIEL C. ESTY

The creators of the Bretton Woods international order showed extraordinary vision in confronting the crises of their day and in establishing institutional structures to address them. A number of new international issues have, however, surfaced in the half century since the post–World War II order took shape. Looming large among these new issues is concern for the environment, particularly in response to the emergence of global environmental problems. In this chapter I examine the environmental challenge, review the currently existing international environmental management system, and find it wanting. I then make the case for augmenting the international management structure established at Bretton Woods with a new international body—a Global Environmental Organization (GEO)—to respond to the "collective action" problem that arises when pollution spills across boundaries and to promote optimal national environmental policies centered on the "polluter pays" principle.

The Environmental Challenge

Fifty years ago, environmental issues, to the extent they were recognized, consisted largely of local public health matters (controls on garbage dumping) and modest conservation efforts (the establishment of parks).

Daniel C. Esty was Senior Fellow at the Institute for International Economics in 1994 and is director of the Center for Environmental Law and Policy and associate professor in the Schools of Law and Forestry at Yale University.

Few national programs of environmental protection existed; international efforts were even more rare. Thus, the General Agreement on Tariffs and Trade (GATT), the World Bank, and the International Monetary Fund (IMF) were set up without any explicit reference to the "environment" and with few provisions aimed at what we would now consider environmental problems.

Over the past 25 years in particular, the public's focus on environmental issues has grown dramatically and our understanding of the public health and ecological effects of pollution has evolved considerably. Air and water pollution and the handling of waste and hazardous substances are all now major policy issues. Eight out of ten Americans today consider themselves environmentalists.[1] Similar levels of interest in environmental concerns can be found throughout the world.[2] As national politicians fall over themselves to show how "green" they are, the environmental agenda has begun to compete on the international stage with other more traditional issues of foreign affairs. One measure of this interest was the attendance of more than 120 presidents and prime ministers at the 1992 Earth Summit in Rio de Janeiro, making that the largest gathering of world leaders ever.

The emergence of the environment as a policy priority has developed not only as our understanding of the potential harm of pollution has progressed (e. g., Carson 1963), but also because policymakers have come to realize that environmental degradation need not be the inevitable price for economic progress. "Sustainable development"—the belief that economic growth can occur without the sacrifice of environmental quality—has become the environmental watchword (World Commission on Environment and Development 1987).

Ironically, as our scientific knowledge about what actions and conditions harm the environment and the desire to avoid them has grown, so has the recognition of how relatively little we know about the human relationship with nature. In fact, uncertainties about the size, scope, speed, origins, effects, interactions, and optimal policy responses to pollution problems are a dominant feature of environmental policymaking.

The need to share data in order to better understand ecological and public health risks has resulted in significantly expanded international environmental policy activities. The recognition that some environmental problems such as depletion of the ozone layer and climate change are inherently global in scope—with emissions and resulting damage spilling across political boundaries without regard to the pollutants' origin—has highlighted the ecological interdependence of the planet and further internationalized environmental policymaking.

---

1. Wall Street Journal/NBC News Poll, *Wall Street Journal*, 2 August 1991, A1.

2. George Gallup International Institute, The Health of the Planet Survey, May 1992.

Expanding international trade and economic interdependence have also contributed to the internationalization process. In particular, as more and more companies compete in the global marketplace, differences among countries in how local pollution problems are handled have become significant as a competitiveness issue.[3] Indeed, the focus on the environment as a point of attack on the North American Free Trade Agreement (NAFTA)—especially fears that Mexico would become a "pollution haven" sucking away American production facilities and jobs and putting downward pressure on high US environmental standards—shows the salience of these competitiveness concerns (Esty 1994a).

Reasons for Establishing a Global Environmental Organization

The internationalization of the environmental challenge can be separated into three separate strands, each of which provides a fundamental reason to consider establishing a GEO: (1) to address global environmental issues (i.e., inherently worldwide pollution spillovers), (2) to promote shared learning in addressing common (but localized) environmental problems, and (3) to reduce competitiveness tensions and the resulting "political drag" on national environmental policy decisions.

Global Issues

The need for government intervention to address market failures in the environmental realm is well-established. The ease with which emissions (to the air, water, or land) can be pushed into the physical space of others (i.e., "externalized") has been understood for a long time. Moreover, environmental amenities such as clean water or clear air are classic public goods. Such goods are inevitably underproduced or misused, due to the gap between private marginal costs and benefits and public or social marginal costs and benefits, unless collective action to regulate market forces is generated.[4] To make the market work on behalf of the environment, there must be a recognized authority to enforce property rights and to regulate behavior.

All this is not new. In fact, the Organization for Economic Cooperation and Development (OECD 1972) endorsed the "polluter pays principle"— the notion that environmental harm should be internalized in the prices producers and consumers pay—more than two decades ago. And envi-

---

3. Local problems refer to pollution that does not spill across political jurisdictions.

4. The collective action can take any number of forms—taxes (Pigou 1918), establishment of property rights (Coase 1960), or emissions controls.

ronmental policymakers have developed an abundance of environmental regulatory tools—tradeable emissions permits, effluent fees, subsidies, etc.—designed to internalize costs and thus to overcome environmental market failures and to align the incentives private actors face with a socially optimal allocation of resources. What is new is the scale at which collective action and market intervention to address environmental issues are required (Hahn and Richards 1989). While mechanisms aimed at correcting environmental market failures are well established at the national level, the international institutional structure for collective action is much more limited.

This is significant because over the last decade, we have identified a number of important transboundary and, particularly, global environmental issues such as ozone layer depletion and climate change.[5] To be effective, policy responses to such issues must also be international in scope. Indeed, the defining characteristic of global problems is that nations cannot protect themselves from harm without cooperation from and parallel action by other nations. For example, early US efforts to protect the ozone layer (e.g., the 1978 ban on chlorofluorocarbons [CFCs]—the primary ozone-layer-destroying chemicals—in aerosols) were doomed to failure without a corresponding phaseout on the use of CFCs by other countries.[6]

The emergence of such global issues has given us a new appreciation for the ecological interdependence of the planet. More importantly, the inherently worldwide nature of these problems has raised serious doubts about the sufficiency of existing of international environmental policy coordination mechanisms.

Deficiencies in the Existing International Environmental Structure

The management of international environmental affairs has little structure and is marked by policy gaps, confusion, duplication, and incoherence (Wirth 1992). A dozen UN agencies, the secretariats to a number of environmental treaties and conventions, the multilateral development banks, regional political groups, and the world's 190 countries acting individually try to cope with the planet's environmental problems. For example, at least five separate organizations are developing methodologies for green-

---

5. Other global or potentially global problems include ocean pollution, the spread of radiation, the need for Antarctic protection, and pollution of outer space. Scientific advances are constantly identifying new elements of the "connectedness" of ecosystems (National Commission on the Environment 1993). For example, DDT recently found in the Great Lakes is believed to have been transported by high-level winds from Mexico (Rapaport et al. 1985).

6. In fact, the ozone layer over the United States continued to thin throughout the 1980s, threatening more cases of skin cancer and cataracts, among other harm.

house gas emissions inventories to follow up on the 1992 Climate Change Convention signed in Rio de Janeiro: the UN Environment Programme, the Global Environment Facility, the Organization for Economic Cooperation and Development, the Intergovernmental Panel on Climate Change, and the International Negotiating Committee that put together the Climate Change Convention. Any collaboration that occurs is on an ad hoc basis.

The difficulty is that the international institutions that address environmental issues, such as the UN Environment Programme and the recently created UN Commission on Sustainable Development, have narrow mandates, small budgets, and limited support. No one organization has the authority or political strength to serve as the central clearinghouse or coordinator for all international environmental efforts. Nor does any organization have the mission or resources to respond to global environmental externalities and to establish norms for behavior in international environmental relations.[7]

In addition, the management of international environmental problems suffers from what Edith Brown Weiss (1993, 697) calls "treaty congestion." With more than 900 legal instruments addressing international environmental issues now in place (Brown Weiss, Magraw, and Szasz 1992), it cannot be surprising that disconnects arise in the handling of environmental matters. Moreover, this multiplicity of institutions makes systematic analysis of risks across problems, budget priority setting, and other aspects of coordination nearly impossible (Hajost 1990; Wirth 1989).

The UN Environment Programme (UNEP), in particular, has far too narrow a mandate to coordinate effectively across the spectrum of global issues that require unified management. Its budget is small (about 1/100th of the US Environmental Protection Agency's funding level), and its staffing is inadequate for the many tasks that need to be undertaken. Moreover, despite the valuable political signal sent by having the organization in a developing country, there is growing sentiment that UNEP's ability to succeed is compromised by its location in Nairobi, where communications too often break down, political instability disrupts work, and crime and other quality-of-life issues make it hard to attract and retain a first-rate staff.

The institutional legacy of the Earth Summit—the UN Commission on Sustainable Development (CSD)—has an attractive dual mandate to promote both environmental protection and economic growth. But the CSD has even more limited authority than UNEP, suffers from a lack of political and financial support, and is further hobbled by its unwieldy charge of following up on Agenda 21, the sweeping Earth Summit compendium of

---

7. There nevertheless have been some successes in achieving agreements in specific international environmental niches such as ozone layer protection (Haas, Keohane, and Levy 1993).

environmental concerns and needs. Since Agenda 21 covers every imaginable environmental issue without differentiating priorities and often reflects contrary points of view, this mission is a bit like being told to follow up on the Bible. In addition to weak political support and lack of focus, the CSD suffers from the belief in many developed countries that it has been "captured" by developing countries and as a result will not act with the economic and analytic seriousness requisite for a major role on the world scene.

Despite the manifest inadequacy of the existing decentralized institutional structure, some international observers still argue for issue-by-issue management of global environmental problems, with individual international agreements and separate secretariats for each. Since this model mirrors the local decision-making tradition embedded in the philosophy of America's grassroots environmentalism, it attracts many "old school" environmentalists as well. But decentralized issue-by-issue decision making is not always the right answer. As Carol Browner, administrator of the US Environmental Protection Agency, recently told a business audience (speech to the US Chamber of Commerce, Washington, 19 November 1993): "The old piecemeal approach . . . doesn't work for me as a regulator, and it doesn't work for you." And long-time environmental policy observer Terry Davies (1994) notes: "As the deficiencies of the current environmental laws become ever more obvious, the chances for a new integrated approach steadily improve. Such an approach is urgently needed."

There are a number of reasons to avoid reliance on ad hoc environmental policymaking in the international realm. Notably, a central aspect of today's understanding of environmental issues is the connectedness of problems. Deforestation is of concern not only because of the loss of trees as a "sink" for carbon dioxide but also because forests are essential for species preservation and biodiversity. CFCs are a problem not only because they deplete the ozone layer but also because they are a greenhouse gas and cause global warming. Without a comprehensive approach to solving environmental problems, opportunities for efficiency and synergies across issues will be lost.

Efforts to protect the environment are always plagued, moreover, by competing issues and limited resources. The result is often haphazard decision making without any clear sense of priorities or understanding of which issues pose the greatest risks and deserve attention first. International environmental policies that promote separate conventions for every issue exacerbate this policy confusion. With a single, coordinated international environmental regime, risks across problems could be compared, budgets rationalized, and priorities intelligently set.

There is, in addition, growing evidence that the patchwork of US national environmental laws is a source of many shortcomings of US environmental protection:[8] overlapping issue coverage, regulatory gaps, limited ability to set priorities, inconsistent treatment of risks, reliance on conflicting and noncomparable data bases, a failure to comprehensively update policies as scientific knowledge advances, redundant activities, and inefficient spending of scarce environmental resources.

Replicating internationally the US issue-by-issue approach to environmental regulation is thus an invitation to long-term policy failure. To quote the report of the Train Commission (National Commission on the Environment 1993, xxvi), a blue-ribbon panel set up to reexamine America's environmental agenda: "Efforts to halt pollution should become more integrated and holistic." The commission goes on to suggest (65): "the proliferation of complex international agreements on the environment and resources will lead to a crazy-quilt of laws and policies." The overlaps and disconnects evident in the international efforts on the related topics of climate change, ozone layer depletion, deforestation, and funding through the Global Environment Facility make clear that this problem already exists.

This difficulty in coordinating international environmental activities may not have been a serious problem in the past because the threatened environmental harm was not perceived as major. Today, however, when we recognize the potentially significant scale and seriousness of the issues, the lack of structure to support collective action on the international scene in response to environmental market failures is an important problem indeed.

Common Problems

There is no inherent need to address *local* environmental problems internationally. Each individual country could do its own scientific work and policy analysis of the ecological and public health problems it encounters. But failure to cooperate on common issues is inefficient.[9] Research is needlessly and expensively replicated. Breakthroughs in environmental science come more slowly, and policy advances are not shared systematically. Moreover, environmental assistance to developing countries is allocated haphazardly. Given the limited budgets for environmental protec-

8. One of the earliest articulations of the problems with decentralized, ad hoc environmental policymaking is Davies (1970). For more recent developments of this theme, see Irwin (1992) and Haigh and Irwin (1990). The United Kingdom has recently moved to an integrated approach to environmental regulation, with some early signs of success.

9. "Common" problems, as used here, are those that are generally local in scope and that do not spill across borders (except for countries in close proximity) but that are found in many countries and are thus of interest to environmental policymakers the world over.

tion in all countries and the rising public aspirations for better environmental quality that exist in all countries, broader international environmental policy collaboration makes a great deal of sense.

The existing structure of international organizations fails to meet the world's need for coordination. The spread of responsibility for data exchange and information sharing across a wide range of institutions—OECD, UNEP, CSD, UN Conference on Trade and Development (UNCTAD), UN Development Programme (UNDP), and others—hampers policy collaboration and administrative efficiency. Serious and wasteful overlaps in efforts exist. There are, moreover, troubling gaps where no international organization is providing adequate attention and international information sharing is thereby limited. Thus national governments are duplicating each others' work and squandering precious environmental resources. For example, hundreds of millions of dollars are spent in dozens of countries to separately test and to regulate pesticides. The relatively small amount of collaborative work being done on lead provides another example of underattention to a critical issue.

The lack of an overarching international environmental management structure to address common environmental problems is also a problem when environmental issues compete with other policy goals on the international scene. When trade and environmental goals clash, for instance, the resulting disputes are settled in the GATT—on terms established by the international trade regime—because there is no established or recognized forum for environmental dispute settlement.

A GEO would help to ensure that environmental values are not overwhelmed by more established interests such as trade liberalization. In doing so, a GEO would provide a counterweight to the GATT and address the fear of many environmentalists that when trade and environmental principles clash, trade goals trump. If the environment had its own effective international body, the GATT's narrow focus on trade principles (or the World Bank's focus on development issues) would not seem so oppressive to environmentalists. A GEO with an appropriate mandate would provide a counterbalance to the GATT's international stature and influence. It would be able to work with the GATT and the World Bank to establish a functional division of responsibilities where trade, development, and environmental policies intersect and to set up procedures for weighing and balancing trade, development, and environmental goals and programs when they conflict.

Opportunities to link the work of a GEO to the existing international economic structure abound. For example, the GATT already has provisions that require it to incorporate into its legal framework decisions made by other international organizations. Specifically, Article XXI requires the GATT to take cognizance of certain actions required by the UN; Article XV mandates that the GATT accept findings of the IMF, and Articles XII–XIV provide for GATT acceptance of balance of payments safeguards undertaken by countries in coordination with the IMF. It would not be difficult to add a provision requiring the GATT to incorporate into its decision processes judgments concerning environmental policies advanced by a GEO.

Such provisions are of considerable value to the GATT, relieving the trade regime from responsibility for assessing the legitimacy, for example, of a nation's claim of a balance of payments crisis as justification for trade-restrictive actions. Similarly, the presence of a GEO with authority to adjudicate the validity of environmental claims that result in trade-restrictive policies would be of great benefit to the GATT. In particular, a shared "trade and environment" decision-making structure would relieve the GATT of the burden of trying to make environmental policy judgments, which are demonstrably outside its established realm of expertise and recognized legitimacy.

Competitiveness and Political Drag

A third reason to consider establishing a GEO is to confront competitiveness concerns arising out of divergent environmental policy choices and to mitigate the political backlash against freer trade and environmental policies that internalize pollution harms. Many businesses view differences in environmental standards (and therefore compliance costs) as a significant issue, particularly in the context of trade liberalization efforts. Traditional economic analysis suggests that variations in the rigor of air, water, or waste controls will not have much effect on national competitiveness or trade balances because spending on pollution control is too small a percentage of value added to matter much and because currency fluctuations will adjust for any broad-based difference in production costs. Nonetheless, worries about environmental policy impacts on competitiveness remain a major issue.

The political attention stems from the fact that even if, on a macroeconomic basis, variations in environmental standards do not affect the siting of facilities or trade flows, wide disparities in environmental standards can have significant sectoral effects. When policy variables beyond the narrow category of spending on pollution control, such as energy prices, are factored in, competitiveness impacts may become more pronounced.

From an environmental perspective, more importantly, the economic exposure of trade-sensitive industries is not the issue. What matters is how this affects the political process of determining the appropriate level of environmental standards. Competitiveness concerns tend to deflect the political debate from identifying the optimal level of emissions control (i.e., fully internalizing pollution costs) by interposing the constraint that environmental policies not be made so stringent that the nation's industries are at a competitive disadvantage in the global marketplace.

It cannot come as a surprise that this competitiveness dynamic and worries about the pressure on high environmental standards created by competition with low-standard jurisdictions have become an issue. The same fears of lost jobs and of a "race to the bottom" in environmental standards among states led the United States in the late 1960s and early 1970s to create a federal environmental authority (the Environmental Protection Agency) and to adopt minimum federal environmental standards. Although some commentators (Revesz 1992) have dismissed the seriousness of the threat of a "race to the bottom," the political pressure on states with high standards was undoubtedly real.[10]

This prisoners' dilemma dynamic, driving countries away from optimal cost-internalizing environmental policies, bears considerable similarities to the competitiveness-driven, beggar-thy-neighbor threat to collective action in the international realm in support of freer trade. In fact, sound environmental policies are hard to advance politically for the same reason free trade is—an asymmetry in political activity and influence between those who benefit (everyone a little bit) and those who perceive themselves as losers (certain special interests). Specifically, the benefits of both environmental protection and trade liberalization are diffused so widely across society that individuals do not see their value, and relatively few groups are organized or motivated to systematically defend environmental protection or freer trade.[11] In contrast, the short-term costs of trade liberalization (e.g., dislocation of uncompetitive producers and their workers) or environmental protection (e.g., the expense of meeting pollution control requirements) are often concentrated on well-organized groups (e.g., companies or unions) with political power.[12] This makes the policy process vulnerable to special interest interventions and "political

---

10. See, for example, the statements of Senator Edmund Muskie, worried about the competitiveness of Maine's paper mills in the face of higher state environmental standards, defending the 1970 Clean Water Act (cited in Esty 1994b, 22 n. 10). This same dynamic of "political drag" is now at work internationally. Witness the inability of President Clinton to get his 1993 energy tax adopted in the face of competitiveness concerns raised by many industries or the European Union's failure to advance its proposed new energy taxes for the same reason.

11. There is a long political science and economics literature addressing the important role of interest groups (e.g., Downs 1957; Olson 1965; Buchanan and Tullock 1971; Lowi 1969). Ackerman and Hassler (1981) demonstrate the risk of special interest manipulation of environmental policymaking. Destler's study (1992) of trade politics in America offers an insightful and provocative view of Congress's vulnerability to protectionist pressures. The explosion of environmental legislation in the United States over the past 25 years might seem to belie the suggestion that environmentalists are disorganized and thus politically weak. But as Elliott, Ackerman, and Millian (1985) explain, these developments may actually be attributable to other factors.

12. The passage of the NAFTA and the success of the United States in eliminating import barriers (Hufbauer and Elliott 1994) might also seem to belie the suggestion that pro–free trade interests will inevitably be weak. But the level of opposition to the NAFTA, despite the demonstrable benefits to the country, make clear the difficulty of organizing the "dispossessed."

failures" in which policy choices are made to the benefit of narrow groups rather than the broad public.

Even when environmental groups are politically effective, their successes may be narrowly focused and may not translate into implementation of the polluter pays principle through a comprehensive program of cost internalization. In the United States in particular, Congress often reacts strongly to media-inflamed environmental scandals (e.g., toxic chemicals seeping into homes along Love Canal, residue of the pesticide Alar on apples), skewing priorities to the hot issue of the moment and rendering long-term, risk-based priority setting and coordinated policy responses difficult.

The architects of the Bretton Woods economic order saw that the international noncooperation on trade and the economic failure it produced were really a function of domestic political pressures. "No policy is as domestic as international trade policy," notes Sylvia Ostry (1990). In response, these leaders set up the GATT as a government-to-government contract centered on principles of mutual forbearance in support of freer trade, eventually encompassing an international system to reinforce the agreed-upon rules promoting trade liberalization.

By enshrining the principles of liberal trade in an international regime, the creators of the GATT not only built a mechanism for reducing friction among nations; they also elevated the commitment to "nondiscrimination" and therefore to freer trade to a nearly "constitutional" level (Petersmann 1992). In moving principles that support freer trade—most notably the "nondiscrimination" obligations—to a higher plane of authority and providing a buffer against protectionist pressures, the GATT limits the power of governments around the world (and legislatures in particular) to give in to the pleadings of rent-seeking domestic interests desiring shelter from the rigors of global competition. It thereby provides a mechanism for addressing the collective-action problem that plagues domestic trade policymaking. By "tying their own hands" and joining an international regime based on mutual commitments to cooperative behavior, governments enhance the overall economic well-being of their people, promote international stability, and serve the long-term public interest.

No comparable system exists to advance optimal environmental policies. Notably, governments tend not to require polluters to compensate society fully for the environmental damage they cause because these interests can effectively lobby the government for relief, particularly in the context of international competitive pressures. As with the losses from protectionism, the costs of environmental degradation are spread widely across society, making it difficult to systematically organize those affected in response. In contrast, the price of pollution controls in the form of higher costs or taxes is often easily calculated and visible to the affected interests, making it relatively easy to mobilize opposition.

The existence of threshold effects and sometimes substantial time lags between emissions and the detection of environmental problems further reduces the apparent urgency of limiting environmental harms or of charging polluters for their actions. Environmental issues are often marked, moreover, by substantial scientific uncertainties, which make the damage from environmental degradation and the benefits of pollution control easy to dismiss as too distant or speculative—and the price to be paid under the polluter pays principle hard to assess.

Governments also recognize that burdening their own domestic industry with cleanup costs, which would largely benefit others around the world, fails on the relevant political calculus (i.e., domestic costs compared with domestic benefits) and might disadvantage their own producers competing in the global marketplace against companies whose governments do not require similar spending on pollution abatement. Thus, governments choose not to adopt stringent environmental standards.

The difficulty of getting the US Congress to adopt real cost internalization in the 1990 Clean Air Act and the special treatment given numerous industries (e.g., coal mines, steel producers) in the legislation offer one example of this phenomenon, but there are many others. This distribution of political costs and benefits leaves governments with a nearly irresistible temptation to push pollution burdens onto the ultimate inactive and unorganized interest group—generations yet unborn.

When all nations make the same calculation and engage in "free riding," the cumulative results can be disastrous for the environment. This collective-action problem and its parallel to the beggar-thy-neighbor threat to freer trade makes the GATT an important case study for efforts to advance international environmental protection.

What Sort of GEO?

The three separate arguments for a GEO—to address global environmental harm, to facilitate cooperative approaches to common environmental problems, and to reduce competitiveness tensions and the stresses such tensions place on efforts to achieve rigorous environmental policies on a national basis—argue for several different elements in a new international environmental regime. In particular, a strong GATT-like institution would be required to promote collective action in response to global environmental issues. Specifically, the GEO would need to have broad rule-making authority to address the market failures that arise in the context of global pollution spillovers. The primary role of such a GEO would be to facilitate negotiations on international standards to be implemented by all countries in response to global environmental problems. To prevent "free riding" and to ensure that international environmental agreements were adhered to, the GEO would need mandatory powers and an ability to penalize those who fail to live up to their obligations. To carry out this role, the body would have to be supported by a dispute settlement mechanism, again perhaps modeled on the GATT.

For one examining other possible sources of inspiration for the GEO in its role as the international mechanism for addressing problems that spill across national boundaries, the experience of the World Health Organization (WHO) might be instructive. The WHO's coordination of worldwide immunization campaigns has helped to eradicate a number of infectious diseases such as smallpox and polio. An essential element of WHO's success—and an important precedent for the GEO—is the significant financial and technical assistance that the WHO (and individual developed countries in coordination with the WHO) has provided to developing countries. In addition, the WHO plays a major role in sponsoring research and promoting collaborative programs in response to global health threats.

To the extent that the GEO would serve to integrate the existing web of international agreements and separate organizations, the World Intellectual Property Organization (WIPO) provides a further interesting parallel. Set up in 1967 to respond to the thicket of intersecting patent and trademark agreements and other bilateral and multilateral intellectual property accords and "unions" that had grown up around the world, WIPO helped to rationalize the global protection of intellectual property and to unsnarl the "treaty congestion" that plagued this realm. Unification of the intellectual property regime helped to ensure both efficiency and coherence in addressing the problems at hand—important attributes for the GEO as well.

A less coercive and more "cooperative" international regime based on voluntary participation would suffice to promote the exchange of information and data on common (as well as global) environmental problems. In this information-sharing mode, the GEO would need an organizational infrastructure like that of the OECD, the Food and Agriculture Organization of the UN (FAO), or the World Bank. In particular, it would need a staff of dedicated scientific and technical experts. The key function, in this regard, would be facilitating the flow of scientific discoveries, risk analyses, and policy evaluations among countries. A second aspect of this role would be the building of environmental management capacities in developing countries.

Coordinating technical and financial assistance from the more developed world to the less developed world would be another potentially significant role of the cooperative GEO. Better coordination among the parties (multilateral development banks, individual countries, and nongovernment organizations) providing environmental assistance would help to maximize the reach and efficacy of the limited resources available. Of course, in dealing with global harm where mandatory pollution control obligations have been established, a purely altruistic and voluntary funding mechanism may eventually prove inadequate. The existing Global Environmental Facility has, for example, only $2 billion available for the period 1994–98. The estimates of the resources needed to address worldwide environmental harm range from $10 billion to $15 billion per year (Brown 1988) or even higher (Earth Summit Secretary General Maurice Strong put the figure at $625 billion per year; Petesch 1992). Thus, to be effective and responsive to global environmental externalities, some more assured source of funding will likely be required.

In some regards, the best existing model for the cooperative GEO would be the OECD. Although its environment directorate is small, it contains a highly trained and competent core of environmental experts. This group, drawing on national officials to support its efforts, is able to advance environmental learning with conferences, meetings, and reports of various kinds through which information on the latest approaches to common problems is exchanged. As a facilitator of information exchange, the GEO would not need strong authority or power. The participation of national environmental ministries in the work of the GEO would be voluntary and would be motivated by the benefit that each country could expect to receive from participating in the international dialogue.

To carry out the third role identified above—mitigating competitiveness pressures and special interest distortions that leave national environmental policymaking short of optimal—the GEO would need to provide an ongoing forum for negotiation on environmental norms, best practices, and standards. In this role, the GATT again provides an interesting parallel for the GEO. Specifically, the GATT's evolution from being simply a framework of basic rules into a home for ongoing trade negotiations in support of cooperative international economic behavior and finally, 50 years later, into a full-fledged international organization may be a useful model. By providing a forum for cooperation, setting out overarching principles such as the cost internalization concepts embedded in the polluter pays principle, and reminding governments of the need to keep a long-term perspective, a GEO might help governments attain better national environmental policies. In particular, as the GATT has helped governments overcome their tendency to slide toward protectionism, a GEO might help countries resist special interest pleadings in the environmental realm that result in the noninternalization of pollution harm.

Governments, moreover, are often able to move together toward optimal policies in a way that no government would dare move alone. The logic for collective action is particularly strong in the context of the prisoners' dilemma dynamic in which any country that steps out in front to adopt cost internationalization strategies for environmental regulation fears competitive disadvantage to its industries competing globally. The Montreal Protocol experience—negotiations leading to a worldwide phaseout of CFCs and other ozone-layer-destroying chemicals—provides a concrete example of a cooperative process producing better results than any country could have achieved on its own.

Agreement on baseline environmental standards would not only promote optimal levels of environmental protection, but would also deprive protectionists of the potent "environmental competitiveness" anti–openmarkets argument in future debates over further trade liberalization. To achieve these benefits, efforts at environmental standard setting need to be made more unified, transparent, and scientifically rigorous. Today, a variety of bodies—e.g., the International Standards Organization (ISO), World Bank, and Codex Alimentarius—are engaged in standard-setting exercises. These efforts would benefit from being formalized, made more open, broadened, and linked. A GEO would serve to advance this process.

The International Labor Organization (ILO) provides one standard-setting model, having adopted more than 350 "conventions" and "recommendations" in its 75-year history.[13] In particular, the ILO's tripartite structure, drawing on business, labor, and government representatives, might be followed in the GEO with structured roles for business, environmental groups, and governments. Unfortunately, the ILO's notable lack of success in getting countries to adopt its standards (the United States, for example, has endorsed only six ILO conventions) provides a cautionary note as well.

In the standard-setting realm, the OECD, rather than the ILO (or the GATT), provides perhaps the most apt model. Notably, the work of the OECD chemicals group in identifying common approaches to the regulation of toxic substances has proven to be a very helpful addition to the individual environmental regulatory efforts of the nations of the OECD. The OECD's efforts, moreover, to establish broad policy "guidelines" (such as the polluter pays principle) to steer its member nations in the execution of their environmental programs has also proven to be a valuable voluntary element of cooperation.

Moving toward a GEO

From the perspective of economic theory, the case for a strong and comprehensive GEO is overwhelming in the context of transboundary pollution spillovers. Specifically, the presence of global environmental externalities, the public goods nature of worldwide environmental programs, and the intergenerational dimension (time lags before problems become visible) of many environmental problems are all classic "market failures" necessitating an overarching regulatory regime to avoid welfare losses.

---

13. Charnovitz (1993) has called for an International Environmental Organization modeled on the ILO and focused on establishing environment and trade rules.

Some kind of international environmental structure is needed to limit self-serving, irresponsible, and destructive behavior (focused on local or national burdens, not global consequences) and to ensure that all of the relevant environmental actors participate in a unified regulatory program. As discussed above, ad hoc regulatory arrangements are inevitably limited and weak. A GEO thus provides the best hope for establishing a regime of global cooperation and the most efficient way of coordinating the programs of collective action required to respond to the panoply of global environmental threats the world now faces.

Negotiations to establish a GEO might initially focus on defining a limited set of mandatory environmental obligations. Requiring adherence to the existing set of broadly supported international agreements—e.g., the Montreal Protocol on ozone layer depletion, the Law of the Sea,[14] the Basel Convention on hazardous waste exports, the Convention on International Trade in Endangered Species of Wild Fauna and Flora agreement on trade in endangered species, and the 1992 Climate Change Convention—would be a valuable starting point.

Over time, the GEO might move on to the identification of general environmental principles or norms to guide the world community. For example, universal acceptance and application of the polluter pays principle and environmental cost internalization could reinforce incentives for pollution prevention and ecological care, consistent with the long-term interest of the public in a healthy environment and ongoing economic growth. Other guiding principles that might be developed include the following:

- a commitment to good science and to life-cycle analysis of environmental issues (OECD 1993, 1994; Moss 1993) so that policies are based on a comprehensive view of environmental effects from production through consumption to disposal of a product;

- a "precautionary" approach to environmental regulation that skews policymaking errors toward protection of public health and ecology, especially in the face of potentially great environmental harms (Bodansky 1991; Cameron and Abouchar 1991);

- an emphasis on "pollution prevention" rather than end-of-pipe treatment (EPA 1993).[15]

---

14. The Clinton administration has recently announced plans to sign this treaty, long objected to by prior US administrations.

15. Feketekuty (1993) reviews several possible guiding principles. Roht-Arriaza (1992) also discusses some of the principles—e.g., precaution, participation, access—that are essential for good environmental policymaking.

As has been made clear above, a GEO need not begin life all-powerful. The new organization should have a sliding scale of authority depending on the global reach, severity, scientific certainty, and time urgency of the various environmental problems it took up. Such a structure would allow the GEO to grow into its job—with a mandate that expands (or contracts) as our understanding of environmental issues and our analytic capacity evolve.

Over time, a GEO might add to the existing body of international environmental law and develop a more cohesive set of norms, rules, methodologies, and procedures for countries to follow in carrying out a shared commitment to the protection of the planet.[16] By serving as a focal point for work to improve the scientific understanding of ecological problems, gather data on environmental trends, refine analytical tools, and develop environmental "indicators" to track the success of different policies, the GEO would be able to build a record of success in its "softer" cooperative mode.

Institution Building on the Regional Level

The importance of institution building in the environmental realm is increasingly being recognized. For example, the European Union recently established an environment agency in Copenhagen to facilitate the coordination of environmental policy and the harmonization of environmental standards among its 12 member states. The EU goal is to facilitate collaborative efforts in data gathering, testing, risk analysis, and other areas in support of the unified European market.

Similarly, Mexico, Canada, and the United States have set up a Montreal-based Commission on Environmental Cooperation under the NAFTA with many of the powers a GEO might possess (Esty 1994a). It is charged with examining cases where poor environmental performance has become a trade issue. It contributes to dispute settlement where environmental issues are at stake. And it has a mandate to try to harmonize environmental standards (upward) over time. Because the NAFTA countries are neighbors, the incentive to find cooperative solutions to environmental problems, as well as the potential for trade-related problems, is at a maximum (Johnson and Beaulieu 1994). Extending this regional model to other parts of the world, such as to the Asia-Pacific Economic Cooperation (APEC) forum would be fruitful.[17] In fact, environmental institutions

---

16. Wirth (1992) highlights the need for advancing international legal processes in support of the environment. Dunoff (1994) also analyzes the need for better international environmental legal structures and concludes that such needs argue for a new international environmental institution.

17. Since much of the progress in international relations, particularly the trade realm, is being

tied to regional trade agreements may offer the best mechanism for moving in the short run toward a new international environmental regime.

Why Create Another International Organization?

The proposal for a GEO is certain to engender stiff opposition. Why add another ineffective organization to the already troubled UN bureaucracy? What's wrong with existing international environmental organizations? Can't the UNEP or the CSD play the global coordinating role? Shouldn't environmental decisions be made at the national or even the local level? What rules could a GEO agree upon and enforce? Wouldn't UN-style, one-country, one-vote principles lead to worse rather than better environmental policies? Isn't it unrealistic to expect nations to surrender sovereignty over their natural resources and environmental policy to a GEO? Can a GEO function without leadership from a strong nation? Is the United States willing to lead? Is anyone else?

This skepticism is legitimate. Establishing another low-productivity international body of highly paid global bureaucrats makes no sense. But retaining a nonfunctioning status quo is even more illogical. Rather, Thomas Jefferson's call for revolution (institutional reform) in every generation should be heeded, and we should dismantle the organizations that are not performing or are outmoded.

To respond to the concern about the multiplicity of international organizations, it would be useful in setting up a GEO to recharter, eliminate, or consolidate three or four existing groups (National Commission on the Environment 1993, 65).[18] Many of the current world order's multilateral organizations have outlived or outgrown their mandates (Roberts and Kingsbury 1993; Williams and Petesch 1993) and should be candidates for restructuring or creative destruction. It would also be a step in the right direction if the GEO were to be set up with a "sunset" clause, putting the organization out of business in 20 years unless it were then deemed to be serving a useful purpose and the world community then affirmatively voted to extend its mandate.

Some objections to a GEO reflect general hostility to all international organizations as forerunners of a world government and as potential

made at the regional level (EU, Mercosur, NAFTA, APEC, etc.), it makes considerable sense to explore regional environmental initiatives at the same time.

18. Candidates for reinvigoration, consolidation, or creative destruction include the UN Environment Programme (UNEP), the UN Development Programme (UNDP), the UN Industrial Development Organization (UNIDO), the UN Conference on Trade and Development (UNCTAD), the World Meteorological Organization (WMO), the UN Institute for Training and Research (UNITAR), and the Commission on Sustainable Development (CSD).

threats to national sovereignty. Such calls have an attractive political ring, appealing as they do to individuals' sense of national identity. But in an ecologically interdependent world, to protect one's own environment requires global cooperation so that others do not foul shared resources. Just as absolute "sovereignty" for smokers threatens the ability of others in the same room to breathe fresh air, unbounded national sovereignty would be devastating to worldwide efforts to address global environmental problems. Such sovereignty would, for example, free countries to ignore the CFC controls of the Montreal Protocol, destroying the ozone layer for everyone. Thus, in dealing with global environmental problems, it is only by surrendering a bit of national sovereignty and by participating in an international regime that we can ensure our freedom from environmental harm and the protection of our own natural resources.

Indeed, blind calls to protect national sovereignty are a red herring. American sovereignty provides no guarantee of adequate US environmental protection. While the public often feels a strong sense of national identity, allegiance to a particular flag does not necessarily translate into an ironclad principle about the optimal governmental level at which to set environmental policy. To the contrary, one can be a loyal American (or a loyal citizen of any other nation) and still want effective environmental protection, something that may at times require decisions made by authorities at other than the national level. In fact, it is quite clear that environmental policy decisions are best made on a geographic scale commensurate with the problem to be addressed. Some issues should therefore be handled at the local level; others require broader perspectives and should be dealt with at the national or international levels. A GEO would help to ensure that, where appropriate, international decision-making mechanisms would be available and that global environmental programs would be as scientifically sound, economically efficient, and environmentally effective as possible.

Operational Issues

There is a more serious question about how democratic international institutions are and thus how decisions might be made in a new GEO. The GATT, for instance, has been severely criticized for its closed decision-making processes. More pointedly, legitimate questions are often raised about ceding political judgments to international bureaucrats, who are not readily answerable to elected officials.

There are several ways to address this issue in the context of a new GEO. First, it is important to recognize that all international organizations are run by their member governments, not by their secretariats. Given this reality, it is critical that decision making in the new body be made transparent to increase governments' confidence that the interests of the general publics they represent are being served. All reports and analyses should be public documents. Most meetings should be open to the public. Nongovernment organizations should be provided access to decision makers and should be able to submit views on any matter under discussion. Second, there should be more regular reporting on work and accountability to national elected officials, who in turn should be held responsible for seeking the removal of international officials who are not performing adequately. Finally, oversight hearings on GEO staff performance would be useful, perhaps conducted by Global Legislators for a Balanced Environment, the international environmental legislators' group.

A second important operational question relates to decision making, specifically, voting mechanisms. Many existing UN bodies suffer serious credibility problems because one-country, one-vote procedures are inefficient and do not reflect the realities of power on the international scene. In contrast, one of the strengths of the GATT is its consensus decision making. Formal votes are almost never taken and there exists an unspoken recognition that the views of the biggest trading nations will be given particular weight and that objections by small nations will not hold up work. Another alternative would be the "double majority" voting procedure of the Montreal Protocol Executive Committee by which projects do not go forward unless a majority of both developed and developing country committee members approve.

As discussed above, funding would be a critical issue for the GEO. To the extent that the organization operated in its "coercive" mode enforcing mandatory environmental controls aimed at global harm, support for developing country compliance with the standards would be required. The most economically efficient funding mechanism would be fees imposed on global pollution—internalizing global environmental harm. This concept, however, has a number of serious practical, political, and administrative problems and therefore other funding prospects must be explored (Esty 1994b).

Whether even the first steps toward a GEO can be taken without strong leadership from the United States is a serious question. The answer is probably not. The failure of the Earth Summit to address institutional issues despite the interest of many countries in updating the mechanisms of international governance relating to the environment demonstrates the difficulty of moving forward without the United States.[19] Of course, since the summit, the United States has elected an administration with a decidedly more environmental cast. Doubt nevertheless remains about the in-

---

19. Early on in the preparations for the Rio conference, White House Chief of Staff John Sununu made it clear that the United States would not accept any major institutional initiative.

terest of the United States in exercising bold international leadership on environmental matters.

Conclusion

There are forces at play internationally that may broaden the base of support for a GEO sooner rather than later. More clear evidence and scientific certainty that climate change or other global ecological threats mandate unified worldwide action could be one trigger for action.[20] The government budget pressures of this deficit-constrained era and a recognition of the efficiency gains and cost savings to be obtained by coordinating policy responses to common environmental problems offer another potential catalyst. Finally, fears of a loss of political support for further trade liberalization and a recognition of the economic, political, and administrative benefits of common environmental standards may lead to calls for more coherent and comprehensive international environmental management—and creation of a GEO. Whether there exists among today's world leaders sufficient foresight or gumption to move forward with a GEO remains in doubt. Most assuredly, if the visionaries of the Bretton Woods era were here today, they would act now.

References

Ackerman, Bruce, and William Hassler. 1981. *Clean Coal/Dirty Air*. New Haven: Yale University Press.

Barrett, Scott. 1990. "The Problem of Global Environmental Protection." *Oxford Review of Economic Policy* 6, no. 1.

Bodansky, Daniel. 1991. "Scientific Uncertainty and the Precautionary Principle." *Environment* 33 (September).

Brown, Lester R. 1988. *State of the World: 1988*. New York: W. W. Norton.

Brown Weiss, Edith. 1993. "International Environmental Law: Contemporary Issues and the Emergence of a New World Order." *Georgetown University Law Journal* 81, no. 3 (March): 675.

Brown Weiss, Edith, Daniel Barstow Magraw, and Paul C. Szasz. 1992. *International Environmental Law: Basic Instruments and References*. New York: Transnational Publishers.

Buchanan, James, and Gordon Tullock. 1971. *The Calculus of Consent*. Ann Arbor: University of Michigan Press.

Cameron, James, and Julie Abouchar. 1991. "The Precautionary Principle: A Fundamental Principle of Law and Policy for the Protection of the Global Environment." *Boston College International and Comparative Law Review* 14.

Carson, Rachel. 1963. *Silent Spring*. New York: Houghton, 1962.

20. Richard Cooper's (1985) analysis of the time (nearly 70 years) it took to mobilize an effective worldwide response to contagious diseases such as cholera and smallpox demonstrates both the difficulty of coordinating action internationally and the importance of doing so in the context of problems that are inherently global in scope.

Charnovitz, Steve. 1993. "Environmental Harmonization and Trade Policy." In Durwood Zaelke, *Trade and the Environment: Law, Policy and Economics*. Washington: Island Press.

Coase, Ronald. 1960. "The Problem of Social Cost." *Journal of Law and Economics* 3.

Cooper, Richard. 1985. "International Economic Cooperation. Is It Desirable? Is It Likely?" *American Academy of Arts and Sciences Bulletin* 39, no. 2 (November): 11–35.

Davies, J. Clarence (Terry). 1970. *The Politics of Pollution*. New York: Pegasus.

Davies, J. Clarence (Terry). 1994. "Reforming Federal Environmental Laws." In William K. Reilly, *Environment Strategy America: 1994–1995*. London: Campden Publishers Ltd.

Destler, I. M. 1992. *American Trade Politics: Systems under Stress*. 2d ed. Washington: Institute for International Economics.

Dixit, Avinash, and Barry Nalebuff. 1991. *Thinking Strategically*. New York: W. W. Norton.

Downs, Anthony. 1957. *An Economic Theory of Democracy*. New York: Harper & Row.

Dunoff, Jeffrey L. 1994. "Institutional Misfits: The GATT, the ICJ, and Trade/Environment Disputes." *Michigan Journal of International Law* 15, no. 4. Forthcoming.

El-Ashry, Mohamed. 1993. "Funding for Global Environmental Concerns." *Ecodecision* (March).

Elliott, E. Donald, Bruce A. Ackerman, and John C. Millian. 1985. "Toward a Theory of Statutory Evolution: The Federalization of Environmental Law." *Journal of Law Economics and Organization* 1, no. 2 (Fall).

Environmental Protection Agency (EPA). 1987. *Reducing Risk*. Washington: Environmental Protection Agency.

Environmental Protection Agency (EPA). 1993. *Transforming Environmental Permitting and Compliance Policies to Promote Pollution Prevention: Removing Barriers and Providing Incentives to Foster Technology Innovation, Economic Productivity, and Environmental Protection*. Report and Recommendations of the Technology Innovation and Economics Committee. Doc. no. EPA 100-R-93-004. Washington: Environmental Protection Agency.

Esty, Daniel C. 1994a. "Making Trade and Environmental Policies Work Together." *Aussenwirtschaft* [Swiss Review of International Economic Relations] (April).

Esty, Daniel C. 1994b. *Greening the GATT: Trade, Environment, and the Future*. Washington: Institute for International Economics.

Feketekuty, Geza. 1993. "The Link between Trade and Environmental Policy." *Minnesota Journal of Global Trade* no. 2 (Summer): 171–205.

Haas, Peter M., Robert O. Keohane, and Marc A. Levy, eds. 1993. *Institutions for the Earth: Sources of Effective International Environmental Protection*. Cambridge, MA: MIT Press.

Hahn, Robert W., and Kenneth R. Richards. 1989. "The Internationalization of Environmental Regulation." *Harvard International Law Journal* 30, no. 2 (Spring): 421–46.

Haigh, Nigel, and Frances Irwin. 1990. *Integrated Pollution Control in Europe and North America*. Washington: American Economic Association.

Hajost, Scott. 1990. "The Challenge to International Law and Institutions." *EPA Journal* 16, no. 4 (July/August): 23–24.

Hufbauer, Gary Clyde, and Kimberly Ann Elliott. 1994. *Measuring the Costs of Protection in the United States*. Washington: Institute for International Economics.

Irwin, Frances H. 1992. "An Integrated Framework for Preventing Pollution and Protecting the Environment." *Environmental Law* 22, no. 1.

Johnson, Pierre Marc, and Andre Beaulieu. 1994. "NAFTA's Green Opportunities." *Journal of Environmental Law and Practice* 1, no. 5 (March/April): 5–15.

Lowi, Theodore. 1969. *The End of Liberalism: Ideology, Policy and the Crisis of Public Authority*. New York: W. W. Norton.

Mayhew, David. 1974. *Congress: The Electoral Connection*. New Haven: Yale University Press.

Moss, Ambler. 1993. "Global Trade as a Way to Integrate Environmental Protection and Sustainable Development." *Environmental Law* 23, no. 2.

National Commission on the Environment. 1993. *Choosing a Sustainable Future* (The Train Commission Report). Washington: Island Press.

Olson, Mancur. 1965. *The Logic of Collective Action: Public Goods and the Theory of Groups.* Cambridge, MA: Harvard University Press.

Organization for Economic Cooperation and Development (OECD). 1972. "Guiding Principles Concerning International Economic Aspects of Environmental Policies." Paris, 26 May.

Organization for Economic Cooperation and Development (OECD). 1993. Life Cycle Management Conference Papers. Paris, July.

Organization for Economic Cooperation and Development (OECD). 1994. *Summary Report of the Workshop on Life-Cycle Management and Trade.* Paris.

Ostry, Sylvia. 1990. *Governments and Corporations in a Shrinking World.* New York: Council on Foreign Relations.

Petersmann, Ernst-Ulrich. 1992. "National Constitutions, Foreign Trade Policy, and European Community Law." *European Journal of International Law* 3, no. 1: 1–35.

Petesch, Patti L. 1992. *North-South Environmental Strategies, Costs, and Bargains.* Overseas Development Council Policy Essay no. 5. Washington: Overseas Development Council.

Pigou, Arthur Cecil. 1918. *The Economics of Welfare.* London: Macmillan.

Rapaport, R. A., N. R. Urban, P. D. Capel, J. E. Baker, B. B. Looney, S. J. Eisenreich, and E. Gorham. 1985. "'New' DDT inputs to North America—Atmospheric Deposition." *Chemosphere* 14: 1167–73.

Revesz, Richard L. 1992. "Rehabilitating Interstate Competition: Rethinking the 'Race-to-the-Bottom' Rational for Federal Environmental Regulation." *New York University Law Review* 67 (December): 1210.

Roberts, Adam, and Benedict Kingsbury. 1993. *United Nations, Divided World: The UN's Role in International Relations.* Oxford: Oxford University Press.

Roht-Arriaza, Naomi. 1992. "Precaution, Participation, and the 'Greening' of International Trade Law." *Journal of Environmental Law and Litigation* 7: 57–98.

Susskind, Larry. 1994. *Environmental Diplomacy: Negotiating More Effective Global Agreements.* New York: Oxford University Press.

Williams, Maurice J., and Patti L. Petesch. 1993. *Sustaining the Earth: Role of Multilateral Development Institutions.* Washington: Overseas Development Council.

Wirth, David. 1989. "Climate Chaos." *Foreign Policy* 74: 3.

Wirth, David. 1992. "The International Trade Regime and the Municipal Law of Federal States: How Close a Fit?" *Washington and Lee Law Review* 49, no. 4 (Fall): 1389–1401.

World Bank. 1993. *Terms of Reference: Evaluation of the Global Environment Facility Pilot Phase.* Report of the GEF Administrator. Washington: World Bank.

World Commission on Environment and Development. 1987. *Our Common Future.* Oxford: Oxford University Press.

8

Migration

GLENN WITHERS

> The scale and diversity of today's migrations are beyond any previous experience. Responses to the questions they raise will help to determine the course of the 21st century. (United Nations Population Fund 1993, 6)

Migration is a choice that has shaped the destinies of individuals, families, and nations. According to recent UN calculations (United Nations Population Fund 1993), 100 million people were living outside their countries of birth in 1993, compared with fewer than half that number only a decade earlier. This figure included some 17 million who were refugees, having fled direct persecution, and 20 million who had fled general civil violence, drought, or environmental destruction. The rest were economic migrants, having voluntarily sought work or a better life in another country.

Despite these statistics, international economic analysis and policy have largely ignored the international flow of labor. Standard international economics textbooks devote many chapters to commodity trade, finance, and foreign investment, but spare a few passing pages at best for population movements across borders. Similarly, the discussions at Bretton Woods and the processes established there gave little or no attention to migration. For most of the postwar era, policy toward international flows of people was largely unilateral or bilateral, without any substantive reference to any central need for multilateral arrangements. This was not because labor was free to move. On the contrary, substantial restrictions prevailed around the world.

Glenn Withers is director of the Economic Planning Advisory Council in Canberra.

The neglect of migration as a global economic phenomenon and as a focus for international policy concern does seem to be ending. Important academic economic analyses of migration are now emerging (e.g., Simon 1989 and 1990, Borjas 1990, Layard et al. 1992, Stark 1991), as are official reviews (e.g., Australia Bureau of Immigration and Population Research 1994, OECD SOPEMI 1993, US Department of Labor 1989, United Nations Population Fund 1993).

The magnitude of contemporary flows has obliged high-level bodies from the Group of Seven (G-7) to the Organization for Economic Cooperation and Development (OECD) Ministerial Council (in June 1991) to add the topic to their agendas. New regional economic arrangements have also had to address these issues, for example, at the EC Summit in December 1991 and in the North American Free Trade Agreement (NAFTA). At the national level, states are becoming more concerned about the movement of people across their borders. In Europe, racist attacks against migrants have focused public attention on the issue of migration. Political parties and movements have arisen whose policies and positions give prominence to immigration matters. Migration has become a source of controversy and an emotional and divisive issue, with its implications for competitiveness and economic growth as well as for social and cultural development.

Eichengreen and Kenen give attention to these concerns only once. Their recitation of the postwar history of managing the international economy does not mention migration. Goods are produced, investments are made, and finance is provided, all without people crossing borders—except to attend meetings dealing with goods, finance, and investment! Only in looking to the future do they offer some recognition of migration issues, concluding, "The early growth of international trade, the more recent growth of international capital mobility, and the prospective growth of international migration have all heightened the need to choose between adherence to international rules and independent pursuit of domestic economic and social policies."

Yet this sums up the situation well. The economic imperative is that enhanced liberalization of population movements offers the potential for great gain. Using global general-equilibrium modeling, Hamilton and Whalley (1984) estimated that removal of all barriers to migration would double world GDP. The gains claimed for continued liberalization of commodity trade (e.g., in OECD 1994) do not come anywhere near such magnitudes.

However, political considerations may dictate that labor flows continue to be treated in a very different way from those of capital and commodities. Migration challenges national sovereignty and identity much more directly than do other international movements. Its embodiment in foreigners who come to live among native citizens is its distinguishing characteristic. An increase in world output through migration can cause distinctive external social costs in both the receiving and the sending countries.

This paper seeks to develop these issues by looking at the nature of migration flows and like movements, reviewing their determinants and consequences, and by looking at international institutions relevant to managing this aspect of the international economy.

Historical Background

Migrant flows have reached global levels of 7 million to 8 million persons in recent years—equivalent to the total populations of many medium-sized countries. Shortly before this conference, upward of 250,000 people were reported to have fled to Tanzania from Rwanda in one weekend.

Of course, mass population movements have been an intermittent but enduring feature of human geography and history, and internal migrations can be as important as, or even more important than, international migrations. Industrialization and urbanization are associated with massive internal migration in some countries. The urban population of developing countries is projected to increase some 16-fold between 1950 and 2025 (United Nations Population Fund 1993).

In the 19th century, substantial free population movements occurred, including the sustained colonization from Europe of Australia, Canada, and the United States. Restrictions on Asian entry did develop in these countries (often after gold rush inflows), but Asian guestworker movements continued to many European colonies elsewhere, especially in Asia and in Africa.

Greater restriction on movement emerged in the period between the world wars. For instance, after World War I German emigration was curtailed and the Soviet Union and the Eastern European countries effectively stopped all in- and outmigration. The Great Depression increased this trend, because of widespread fears that immigrants would take scarce jobs from nationals.

The more buoyant economic conditions after World War II allowed for greater numbers of migrant movements again, but the mechanisms for national control of entry remained firmly in place. On the one hand, passports and visas became standard requirements; these were more forcefully used to keep down migration to Europe after the oil shock of the mid-1970s. On the other hand, pressure to remove racially discriminatory laws succeeded in changing many national migration policies, for example in Australia and Canada. Provisions favoring movement within regional trading arrangements such as the European Union and the Australia–New Zealand Closer Economic Relations (CER) group have emerged more recently.

Regional Dimensions of Migration

North America and Australasia

The "classic" 19th-century migrations from Europe to North America and Australasia revived after World War II. These were voluntary movements of persons intending to settle permanently in nations that welcomed them as new residents and, potentially, as citizens.

The United States has been admitting an average of half a million immigrants a year over the last two decades, thereby increasing its population by about 0.2 percent a year; currently it receives over 700,000 settlers a year. Australia and Canada have taken even larger flows relative to their base populations. For some time the Australians and Canadians distinguished themselves from the United States by an explicit policy of seeking out highly educated and highly skilled youthful settlers and successful business migrants. But beginning with the Kennedy-Simpson Act in 1990 the United States also built such criteria into a significant component of its migrant programs.

For these traditional host countries, European sources of migration came increasingly to be supplemented by flows from other sources. These included the Middle East and Asia for Australia and Canada, and Latin America for the United States.

Europe

Meanwhile Western Europe itself became a major destination for migrants after World War II, as many millions traveled northward from the Mediterranean countries and then from the Maghreb, the Levant, and now from Eastern Europe as border controls there have collapsed.

In contrast with the migrations to North America and Australasia, migration into Europe was often either a reflection of the colonial past of the host country or of a perceived need for guestworkers to supplement local labor during a period of sustained expansion. That the guestworkers often opted to stay on and become de facto permanent settlers was a source of ongoing policy difficulty to European governments, since this was not their intent in allowing the migrations and it raised issues of social integration that did not apply to temporary entrants.

Attempts to restrict permanent migration into Europe grew in the 1970s. But family reunification, liberal asylum laws, and porous borders have maintained substantial inflows. In recent years western Germany has received the biggest migrant inflows in Europe, most notably of course from the former East Germany. Layard et al. (1992) predict that the changes in Eastern and Central Europe will ensure that 1 million migrants a year or more will flow into Western Europe for the next 15 years, representing an average annual population increase of 0.3 percent for

Western Europe, exceeding the ratio for the United States in previous decades.

The Middle East

The European practice of allowing guestworker immigration was also adopted by some of the oil-rich countries of the Middle East during the 1970s. Significant labor shortages in the region attracted large numbers of migrants, and while initially there was some inter-Arab permanent migration, for example from Jordan, by 1985 the Gulf Cooperation Council states together hosted approximately 5.1 million migrant workers (and 7.2 million foreign residents), with East and South Asian guestworkers accounting for 63 percent of these. Migrants comprised 70 percent of the Gulf work force at this time. The Asian guestworkers were often younger and better educated than the host country population and came on fixed contracts, without their families, from Pakistan, Sri Lanka, India, China, Korea, and the Philippines.

East and South Asia

Asian migratory movement is not just a phenomenon of the 1970s. The large-scale migration of Asian peoples goes back many centuries. The colonial experience of the late 19th and 20th centuries, mentioned above, saw several associated large waves of Chinese and Indian migration in particular. But the Gulf experience represented the postwar reentry of Asia into the world migration arena, a reentry that has been strongly sustained into the 1980s and 1990s but with a focus on intraregional flows.

Pang Eng Fong (1993) distinguishes three major flow concentrations in Asia: within the Northeast Asian economies, within the Southeast Asian region, and between the developing South and Southeast and the industrialized Northeast. The flows are complex, involving both documented and undocumented workers and often proceeding in both directions. Two-way flows usually reflect professional and skilled workers going in one direction and unskilled in the other, which suggests that older concepts of "immigration-receiving" and "immigrant-sending" countries should perhaps be discarded.

These flows are typically seen as temporary. Most Asian countries do not see a need for active immigration programs offering foreign workers permanent residence or citizenship, although Singapore in recent years has begun to seek permanent settlers, at least from Hong Kong.

Other Regions

There have been major pan-African migrations to South Africa, Zimbabwe, Nigeria, Côte d'Ivoire, and Gabon; there have also been substantial migrations within South America as well as north to the United

States. Mexico, Colombia, and El Salvador provided the largest totals of emigrants in the later 1980s.

Overview

Overall, international migration flows can be characterized as large and growing. Whether these flows will continue to expand rapidly is unknown. The trend is encouraged by the ease of communication and travel in the contemporary world, the opening of previously closed borders, humanitarian disasters, and economic pressures, as well as rising individual aspirations. Yet easing of restrictions does not make migration inevitable—populations can remain stable even where restrictions on movement are removed. For example, not all Scots went to London when the English and Scottish kingdoms were united, nor did all Victorians move to Queensland following Australian federation in 1901. Just as most economies produce the bulk of their goods and services for domestic consumption, so most populations are not internationally mobile, actually or potentially. The questions are instead, how large is the responsive margin of migrants—that is, how many people are likely to respond to lowered restrictions and increased pressures to migrate—and is that margin growing?

Whether the responsive margin will be large enough to represent a "third wave" in the evolution of the international economy remains an open issue. But the significance of these flows seems evident, and the need for greater attention than has been given in the past seems clear. Also evident is the fact that intraregional movements are at least as important a focus for international migration policy today as interregional flows.

Types of Migration

Economic Migration

As was noted at the outset, the dominant migratory flows are those of individuals voluntarily seeking jobs or a better life in another country. These migrations can be temporary or permanent. Such migration best matches economists' conventional choice-theoretic analysis of migration. One compares the streams of pecuniary net returns for alternative locations, suitably discounted for time and risk, and maximizes accordingly, perhaps with a monetary allowance for nonpecuniary preferences added in (Sjaastad 1962). This approach is helpful in understanding why continuing disparities in world wealth and income distribution will sustain an ongoing demand for movement. Overlaying these basic disparities will be divergent rates of growth of output and employment opportunities, which will influence many migrant job seekers both in motivation and in timing.

Globally, the contrasts are strong between countries with high living standards but aging and declining populations, rapidly growing and industrializing countries undergoing economic and population transitions, and poorer countries with large rapidly growing populations. There is pressure for migrants to seek to move either to those richer countries that may be wishing to offset the aging of their populations, or to those countries needing to meet short- or medium-term labor supply constraints while also promising longer-term sustained real income growth prospects.

The nature of these pressures can be conveniently illustrated for the Asia-Pacific region using the annual labor supply and demand projections for selected Pacific Rim countries prepared for the Pacific Economic Cooperation Council (PECC), as outlined in table 1. These leave out South Asia, but even so the disparate patterns of labor structure show the potential for economically based intraregional labor movement. Disaggregation into specific skills and sectoral needs would show even greater disparities and hence pressure for movement.

Within the category of economic movements, migration connected directly with foreign investment is of note. Freer global movement of skilled personnel is clearly associated with trade and investment flows. Table 2 shows the direct correlation between size of foreign investment and numbers of associated guestworkers, using the example of Japanese investment in Asia. There are over 85,000 Japanese living outside Japan in the Asian region, of which 34,000 work for Japanese-owned companies. Although these workers may not constitute a large share of total migration movements, their high-level skills and their link with the investment process raise a range of important policy issues such as whether this "crowds out" training of higher level domestic workers by multinational companies.

Family and Refugee Movements

Two additional types of migrants can be distinguished: families seeking reunification, and refugees. Family reunion can be seen as derivative of economic or other migration, where dependents and other relatives seek to follow earlier migrants. The link leads to the phenomenon of chain migration, and there is some interesting demographic and socioeconomic analysis of the factors determining the "multipliers" for such chain effects (Goering 1989).

In contrast with economic and family migration, refugee movements can be characterized as involuntary. The term "refugee" here covers both persons defined as such by the United Nations—that is, individuals suffering a well-founded fear of persecution—and other persons such as those fleeing civil disorder, group persecution, and environmental disasters. The growth in ecological consciousness in the Western industrialized countries and renewed predictions of dramatic global environmental deg-

Table 1 Projected growth in labor demand and supply in 18 Pacific Rim economies, 1994 and 1995

Country	Labor force (millions) 1993	Labor demand growth (percentages) 1994	Labor demand growth (percentages) 1995	Annual labor supply growth	Excess supply growth (percentages) 1994	Excess supply growth (percentages) 1995
Australia	8.6	1.1	1.0	1.2	0.1	0.2
Canada	14.0	1.1	0.6	0.7	−0.4	0.1
China	695.9	1.1	1.3	1.8	0.7	0.5
Taiwan	8.9	2.7	2.8	2.3	−0.4	−0.5
Hong Kong	2.9	1.5	1.6	1.3	−0.2	−0.3
Indonesia	78.1	2.1	2.4	3.0	0.9	0.6
Japan	66.0	0.1	0.2	0.3	0.2	0.1
Korea, Rep. of	30.2	0.3	0.4	1.8	1.5	1.4
Malaysia	7.6	3.1	3.3	2.8	−0.3	−0.5
New Zealand	1.6	0.8	0.6	0.6	−0.2	0.0
Philippines	24.8	2.2	2.3	2.4	0.2	0.1
Singapore	1.6	2.7	2.8	1.6	−1.1	−1.2
Thailand	33.0	3.8	4.0	1.8	−2.0	−2.2
United States	128.5	0.8	1.0	1.1	0.3	0.1

Source: PECC (1994).

radation have given particular salience to the prospects for an upsurge in so-called environmental refugees. The potential consequences of global warming for countries such as Bangladesh, Egypt, or the Pacific island states have been used to illustrate these concerns.

In the meantime, humanitarian flows caused by civil disruption continue to emerge. According to the United Nations High Commissioner for Refugees (UNHCR), since the start of hostilities in 1991 a total of 690,000 people have fled from the former Yugoslavia to other European countries. In the broader Eastern European context, some nations, such as Hungary, Poland, Slovakia, and the Czech Republic, have themselves become receiving countries for migrants and asylum seekers both from within the region and from the developing world. Table 3 provides a global snapshot of refugee numbers, and table 4 shows their growth since 1983 for those formally applying for asylum.

Illegal Migration

Unlike economic settler and guestworker movements, movements of refugees are not readily amenable to planning and orderly processing. Similarly the growing phenomenon of illegal migration defeats the endeavors of countries to maintain the orderly entry of migrants.

Table 2   Japan: foreign direct investment and Japanese nationals working for Japanese-owned companies in Asia

Country	Foreign direct investment, 1951–91 (billions of US dollars)	Number of workers, 1992 (thousands)
East Asia	19.4	12.0
Korea, Rep. of	4.1	1.6
Taiwan	2.7	1.7
Hong Kong	9.8	6.3
China	2.8	2.4
Southeast Asia	27.1	19.9
Indonesia	11.5	3.7
Malaysia	3.2	2.7
Philippines	1.5	1.2
Singapore	6.5	5.5
Thailand	4.4	6.8
Rest of Asia	0.6	1.3
Total	47.1	33.2

Source: Pang Eng Fong (1993).

Illegal migration is undoubtedly a major political issue in many countries. The scale of this migration is by its nature hard to pin down, but even in countries without land borders and with tight visa systems, it is significant. It has been estimated that there are from 80,000 to 150,000 illegal residents in Australia, and from 150,000 to 300,000 in Japan. Taiwan may have over 200,000 illegal residents, and estimates run as high as 700,000 for undocumented migrants in peninsular Malaysia (Hugo 1991). The recent Malaysian offer to "regularize" the status of illegal residents on a fixed-term guestworker basis allows an opportunity to test these estimates.

Trade in Services

A broader conception of migration can embrace other international movements of peoples. In fact, the numbers of permanent settlers and guestworkers are dwarfed by movements across borders of people involved in trade in services. Even for older notions of migration, these service-related flows are important, because students, tourists, and other visitors can often change their category and become settlers or guestworkers or seek asylum or family reunification. More important for understanding the evolution of international economic and other integration, the magnitude and growth of these flows must be understood and their place in the management of the international system better addressed.

Table 3 World flows of refugees and other displaced persons, 1986 and 1992 (thousands)

1986		1992	
Refugees and asylum seekers (host regions)			
Africa	3,112	Africa	5,698
Europe	70	Europe and North America	3,423
Latin America and the Caribbean	323	Latin America and the Caribbean	107
East Asia and the Pacific	573	East Asia and the Pacific	398
Middle East and South Asia	7,617	Middle East	5,586
		South and Central Asia	2,341
Total	11,698	Total	17,556
Refugee-like situations (selected host countries)			
United States	750	Jordan (Palestinians)[a]	750
Turkey	400	Iran (Iraqis)	500
Kuwait	300	Mexico (Central Americans)	350
Other Arab peninsula states	300	Pakistan (Afghanistanis)	300
Internally displaced persons (selected countries)			
Mozambique	900–1,800	Sudan	5,000
Ethiopia	700–1,500	South Africa	4,100
South Africa	3,500	Mozambique	3,500
Sudan	1,300	Somalia	2,000
Afghanistan	1,000	Philippines	1,000

a. Nationalities of the migrants are given in parentheses.

Source: World Refugee Survey (1986 and 1993).

There is a wide range of services, from medical services to engineering consultancies, whose trade might involve human movement across borders, but the most important single category is undoubtedly travel and tourism. According to the World Tourism Organization (1993), the world recorded 455 million international arrivals in 1991, up from 288 million arrivals in 1980 and representing an average annual increase of 4.25 percent for 1980–91. Table 5 provides further data on international tourism and travel. Although growth was significant in all regions up to 1990, a slowdown accompanying the recession in many countries in 1991 is evident, as is the higher overall rate of growth in East Asia than in Europe.

Not as large, but also growing rapidly and of interest, is the international movement of persons for purposes of training and education. Many of these movements are short-term, but particular interest lies in movements of people engaged in longer, tertiary-level studies, which are also better monitored and recorded in international data. Figures from the UN Educational, Scientific, and Cultural Organization (UNESCO) for 1985 and

Table 4 Estimates of asylum applications in Europe, North America, and Australia, 1983–91 (thousands)

	1983	1984	1985	1986	1987	1988	1989	1990	1991	Total 1983–91
Europe	75	110	178	214	203	243	321	461	599	2,407
Western	65	98	164	194	172	220	306	426	544	2,192
Central, Eastern, and Southern	9	11	14	20	30	23	15	35	55	215
North America	25	31	28	41	61	102	122	109	100	621
Canada	5	7	8	23	35	45	22	36	30	212
United States	20	24	20	18	26	57	100	73	70	409
Australia	negl.	negl.	negl.	negl.	negl.	negl.	negl.	3	16	20
Total[a]	100	141	206	256	264	345	444	574	715	3,049

negl. = negligible
a. Totals may not add precisely due to rounding.

Source: United Nations Population Fund (1993).

Table 5 International tourist arrivals, by regions (thousands except where noted otherwise)

Region	Arrivals					Average annual rate of increase 1980–91	Share of world total (percentages)	
	1980	1988	1989	1990	1991		1980	1991
World	287,771	393,865	427,884	455,584	455,100	4.3	100.0	100.0
Africa	7,337	12,463	13,751	14,973	15,845	7.3	2.6	3.5
Americas	61,387	83,463	87,462	93,532	97,503	4.3	21.3	21.4
East Asia and Pacific	20,945	45,077	45,549	52,253	53,892	9.0	7.3	11.8
Europe	189,830	243,020	270,548	284,178	277,904	3.5	66.0	61.1
Middle East	5,992	6,961	7,519	7,479	6,712	1.0	2.1	1.5
South Asia	2,280	2,881	3,055	3,179	3,244	3.3	0.8	0.7

Source: World Tourism Organization (1993).

1993 are given in table 6 and show an increase in "third level" (i.e., post–high school) student numbers from 892,000 in 1985 to 1,217,000 in 1993. The major host countries include the United States, France, Germany, Canada, and Australia, and the largest sources have been Asia and Europe.

The Uruguay Round of the General Agreement on Tariffs and Trade (GATT) saw the signing of a new General Agreement on Trade in Services (GATS). This agreement brings the fastest growing area of world trade under GATT-style rules for the first time. One ministerial decision in the GATS related to "movement of natural persons" where, for the purposes of further liberalizing movement of people to enhance services trade, negotiations aiming at securing "appropriate commitments" would be entered into for conclusion by the end of 1995.

Impacts of Migration

Economic Issues

Migration expands the overall scale of an economy. The interesting question is what it does in the shorter run to macroeconomic variables such as inflation and unemployment, and in the longer run to per capita incomes and their distribution.

Much of the evidence on these questions comes from the United States, Canada, and Australia. And for these countries a certain uniformity of results is observed (see, e.g., Australia Bureau of Immigration and Population Research 1994, US Department of Labor 1989, Employment and Immigration Canada 1989):

- Migrants create as many jobs as they take.

- Migrants do not generate substantial inflation or upward nominal wage pressure.

- Migrants pay their way for government services received.

- Migrants contribute to short-term and long-term balance of payments improvements but medium-term deteriorations.

In the longer term:

- Migrants may enhance per capita income in the presence of a strong skill focus in migration and/or the presence of economies of scale.

- Migrants will benefit themselves, local property owners, and complementary workers most.

Table 6 Post–high school students studying abroad, by country of origin and host country, 1985 and 1993 (thousands)

Country of origin	Host country	1985[a]	1993[b]
Africa	Total	176	201
	France	73	74
	United States	33	21
North America	Total	66	87
	United States	33	43
	United Kingdom	4	7
South America	Total	46	44
	United States	23	19
Asia	Total	360	573
	United States	144	277
	Germany	29	46
	United Kingdom	22	33
	Australia	8	23
Europe	Total	148	271
	United States	22	51
	Germany	28	43
	France	22	29
Oceania	Total	6	10
	United States	3	3
	Australia	1	2
Former Soviet Union	Total	1	5
	United States	negl.	2
Total		892	1,217

negl. = negligible
a. 45 host countries.
b. 50 host countries.

Source: UNESCO (1985 and 1993).

These results are subject to numerous qualifications, but I believe they nevertheless add up to a conclusion that the economic effects of migration are benign. Whether such results would carry over to other receiving countries and to different magnitudes and speeds of migration, and how they apply to source countries as well as receiving countries, are more open questions. The research also primarily relates to settler and guestworker migration; other temporary movements have received comparatively little scrutiny. There remains much scope for research on these matters.

A study by the OECD SOPEMI (1993) tried to cast the net a little wider than the "New World" countries (the United States, Canada, New Zealand, and Australia), and Layard et al. (1992) have provided an overview of East-West migration impacts. The OECD study concluded:

> Economists have never reached a real consensus on how to assess the economic impact of immigration on host countries. However, amongst the majority of those who have attempted to identify and measure every possible effect, there is little doubt that immigration has made a significant and positive contribution to growth. (OECD 1993, 157)

Layard et al. express a somewhat more qualified view, which seeks to make allowance for their focus on fairly dramatic inflows from the East to Germany. But their qualifications are largely a priori or cautionary. It is therefore of interest that subsequent detailed empirical analysis of European migration coordinated by the Centre for Economic Policy Research (CEPR) found at its November 1993 meeting:

- "Immigration's adverse effects on unemployment and per capita income will be minor, even with no growth in the EC capital stock. Capital growth and wage flexibility will alleviate its effects on labour markets." (16)

- "Foreigners concentrate in areas that do well in terms of employment but the foreign share had no impact on native unemployment." (17)

- "The contribution of the average foreign household to net public revenue exceeded that of the native household. . . . Immigrants benefit the native population through their impact on the public transfer system." (19)

There were no findings presented to the contrary (CEPR 1994).

Another large and highly reputable research team that looked at these issues was a group organized by the National Bureau of Economic Research under Richard Freeman (Abowd and Freeman 1991). They extended their ambit to comparing migration effects with those of foreign investment and imports, and they concluded for the US labor market:

- "Immigrants were absorbed with little adverse net wage or employment effect on native residents.

- Foreign firms paid wages higher than or equal to those paid by domestic firms.

- In contrast, the impact of import increases on US wages and employment was severe, both in the aggregate and in specific sectors and regions.

It would seem that international integration through migration and investment may be preferable to that through trade. That poses a worthy challenge for international economic management.

Social Issues

A reason offered above for the continued restriction of international movements of people was that the real issues are the social, not economic, consequences of migration. Correspondingly, there is a growing literature on the social consequences of migration.

To attempt a global characterization of the findings of such studies would be too ambitious here. But it may be helpful to illustrate their value by reference to the Australian case. A recent survey of the Australian sociological literature on immigration (Holton 1990) reports the following findings, many of which challenge some cherished beliefs of those who oppose immigration:

■ Migrants are no more closely linked with crime than other residents.

■ Migrants are no more prone to welfare dependence than other residents.

■ Migrants are no more prone to back injuries and accident compensation than other residents.

■ Migrant families are not more prone to intergenerational conflicts of values.

■ Marriages between Australian men and Filipino women are not less successful than most Australian marriages.

■ There is no evidence that migrants from more patriarchal cultures favor sons over daughters in education.

■ Migrants of non-English-speaking background actually have higher take-up rates for citizenship.

To be fair, many of those who favor liberal migration programs probably also indulge in myths, and these too need to be countered with facts. Among the findings reported in the same survey are the following:

■ Migrants may not significantly slow the aging of the population.

■ The population would not shrink for a considerable period if migration were stopped.

■ Labor market discrimination against migrants is small and mostly concentrated within the more skilled groups.

■ The voting patterns of ethnic minorities do not differ significantly from those of native-born groups with otherwise similar characteristics.

■ Migration for the purpose of family reunification is no more closely linked with settlement success than are other forms of migration.

In the Australian case, I take these findings as constructive. Dislike or fear of those who are different is often nurtured by ignorance or myth, to which effective research is an important antidote. When the resultant outcomes are less benign, the research can as much be a stimulus to improvement in migration and settlement policies as to restriction and exclusion. Here, too, further pursuit of knowledge is needed, although its power to change deeply entrenched attitudes quickly must not be exaggerated. Its effect is much more gradual, and the underlying problem of fear of foreigners will remain a basic issue for a very long time and be a source of major perceived negative social consequences of migration.

Environmental Issues

Expanded knowledge could also be of benefit to a final burgeoning area of concern beyond the economic and social spheres, namely, the environmental consequences of migration. Population growth in individual nations can bring with it serious deterioration of the natural environment and complex problems in the human-made environment. Some elements of national environmental movements (e.g., in Canada, Australia, the United States, and Germany) hold that population increase, to which immigration is an important contributor (see figure 1), is a major source of continuing damage to the environment. Since immigration is also very much more tractable by policy decision than are other dimensions of population change, there is a corresponding view that immigration should be drastically reduced.

Much of this argument is too simplistic. Much of the inappropriate land use, degradation, and pollution decried by environmentalists was already in train when Australia's population was much smaller. And there is no clear evidence that Canada, with a similar geography and institutions but twice Australia's population, has suffered greater environmental damage. Clearly, then, environmental problems are caused by much more than population pressure. At the same time, there are also benefits from immigration, such as expansion of the tax base, that can assist in both finding and funding solutions for environmental difficulties.

My point is not to assert the certainty of net environmental benefits from immigration, but only to point out the complexity and our present ignorance—of the process by which human behavior is linked to our environment. Understanding of the two is at present far too segmented. We should proceed cautiously on policy in these areas, but not so cautiously as to permit migrants to become scapegoats in a search for simple solutions to real problems. Vague appeals to environmental concern, like appeals to asserted but not thoroughly quantified economic costs, can too easily provide cover for those wishing to pander to less worthy motives.

This must certainly be so at the global level. It should be evident that the global impact of national population increase caused by people moving

Figure 1   Population growth by natural increase and net immigration in 19 selected OECD countries, 1980–91

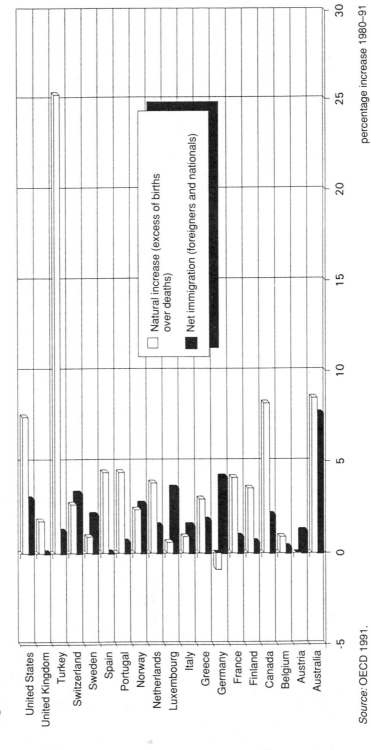

Source: OECD 1991.

from one country to another is quite different from that of an equal increase through natural causes. In the first case, but not the second, global population is not increased, just relocated.

It is sometimes said that liberalizing migration is inimical to global environmental responsibilities because use of energy and other resources in receiving countries is many times that of the less developed countries that are the sources of migration. Table 7 indeed indicates that per capita emissions of carbon dioxide from fossil fuel combustion are many times higher in developed countries such as Australia or Canada than in developing countries such as India or Indonesia.

Further research is needed on this issue, since migrants come from many countries, not all of them less developed, and many of those who do come from less developed countries tend to be highly skilled, hence relatively affluent, and hence likely to use resources relatively intensively wherever they locate. Also, there are other environmental impacts of consumption in source countries that may be less well managed than in most countries—for example, deforestation, water pollution, and poor solid waste disposal—so that despite their smaller per capita consumption, they might be imposing greater environmental costs. There is also some potential for reduced family size from population relocation to richer countries. These considerations would all counterbalance the suggestion that global emissions will increase through population relocation. But the exact extent of any such offset is unknown.

A related view is that acceptance of migration should be sensitive to the loss of skilled human resources that less developed source countries suffer when their residents move to richer countries. But whether source countries are necessarily losers from emigration is unclear. Some developing countries actively seek to place skilled labor overseas, seeing it as a valued source of foreign remittances, while others have substantial surpluses of some types of highly trained workers, despite their other economic difficulties. Such matters are ultimately the concern of national policy in the source countries, which would benefit from first-best policies that seek to tackle environmental and skill issues at the source for all of the population, rather than rely on a blunt and indirect instrument like migration control. But responsible international involvement does suggest that the issues could well be beneficially discussed in international forums concerned to enhance cooperation on international population movements.

Policy Responses

Conditioning Factors

Several fundamental principles govern an appropriate policy response to migration issues. The first is the recognition that no country is isolated

Table 7   Carbon dioxide emissions from fossil fuel combustion, selected countries, 1987[a] (tons of carbon per capita)

Country	Oil	Gas	Coal	Total
Developed countries				
United States	2.6	1.0	2.1	5.7
Canada	2.4	1.1	1.3	4.8
Japan	1.4	0.2	0.6	2.1
Germany	1.5	0.4	1.3	3.2
United Kingdom	1.1	0.5	1.2	2.8
Australia	1.5	0.5	2.3	4.3
Total OECD	1.6	0.5	1.0	3.1
Developing countries				
India	<0.1	<0.1	0.1	0.2
Indonesia	0.1	<0.1	<0.1	0.2
Brazil	0.4	<0.1	0.1	0.4
Mexico	0.8	0.2	0.1	1.1
Korea, Rep. of	0.6	<0.1	0.6	1.2
Rest of world	0.2	0.1	0.2	0.5
Total world	0.5	0.2	0.6	1.2

a. Does not include carbon dioxide emitted by other human activities such as deforestation.

Source: New South Wales Government (1990).

from migration. Movement is increasingly easy and migration can affect all. Even Myanmar has refugee and guestworker problems. There are underlying pressures that can affect all countries, albeit in different forms and with different intensities at different times.

Australia, for instance, has no land borders with other countries. It operates an orderly permanent migration program. Yet it is estimated that up to 150,000 illegals may be resident in the country. Almost all of these are persons who entered as visitors or students and chose not to leave after their visas expired.

Besides the permeability of borders, "category jumping" by entrants makes these problems inevitable. Students will seek to become settlers, as will tourists. Guestworkers will seek to stay and be joined by their families. Persons granted asylum will similarly want family reunification in the host country.

A second principle is that there is a convergence in migration experience. The blurred distinctions between types of migrants indicate that there is not only a common set of pressures and problems, but that much can also be learned from the experience of others. For instance, Germany for a long period felt that it had little to learn from "New World" migration: it received temporary guest workers, not settlers. Yet of the 30 million guestworkers who came to Europe, 13 million stayed permanently. Asian countries such as Japan and Malaysia are grappling with these same phenomena today. This is not to say that divergences are not important, but only that there are some instructive commonalties and, equally important, that migration in any one country can change its character very rapidly.

A third principle is that migration should be viewed as a broad concept. The phenomenon of "category hopping" has been mentioned. But aside from this, even groups of migrants who stay within their different categories can have like effects. In the refugee context, the distinctions made by the UNHCR between "Convention" refugees, other asylum seekers, refugee-like persons, displaced persons, and so on are confusing even to initiates. And where the focus is on national environmental protection and population movement, it is just as relevant to focus on tourist entry as on the country's permanent migrant population.

Equally, if there is a desire to restrict international population flows, understanding the links between population, trade, and investment may be essential. For example, aid may facilitate emigration by providing the wherewithal to move and creating networks that give people the opportunity to move. So in the long haul, addressing the root causes of migration in situations where a culture of emigration has not yet emerged is essential. In this sense migration is seen as related to the objectives of cooperative economic development.

What will be the objectives of policy in response to international migration? It will not be completely open borders in any foreseeable global future, however clearly researchers might establish the neutrality of the shorter-run economic effects and the significant gains in world per capita income from migration in the longer run.

It is true that substantial liberalization has occurred, for example in the European Union. But other barriers remain and are unlikely to be dismantled quickly. Their form could change—for example, we may someday see auctioning of immigration permits. But even this is unclear. The reason is that migration is more of a social process than is either trade or investment. It is embodied in human beings. In many cases the social elements are seen as enriching—a meeting of ideas and development of cultural synergies. But in other cases there is a fear of loss of social cohesion and the production of social disharmony. Large-scale migration may also be seen in political terms, threatening a loss of national identity and sovereignty. Countries such as the United States, Australia, Canada, and Israel define themselves at least in part through their immigration experience. But even in those countries, and more so elsewhere, there are those who are less certain of these benefits.

To return to the question posed by Eichengreen and Kenen: How then can national concerns be best integrated with global realities? To ask the question implies the answer: through a new and cooperative regime of international migration management.

International Institutions

How can such a regime proceed? The major international agencies presently operating in this field are the UN High Commission for Refugees and the International Organization for Migration (IOM). Both of these have been primarily refugee-oriented.

The Office of the UN High Commissioner for Refugees was established by the UN General Assembly in 1950 in order to provide for the protection of refugees. The IOM was established in 1951 in Brussels as the Intergovernmental Committee for European Migration (ICEM); it changed its name in 1989. It was established to assist in the orderly movement of persons in need of international migration services.

Like many UN agencies, UNHCR has had a checkered history, but so has IOM. There also remains a problem of adequately differentiating the roles of the two agencies. The UN Bureau of Humanitarian Affairs also has some activities in this same area.

It seems clear that a single overall international agency dealing with refugee matters would be a step forward; the UNHCR could be that agency. At the same time, if the IOM could move from a traditional European and refugee focus to embrace broader international migration issues, it could take on a new function and role presently unoccupied but much needed. However, not all the donor countries to IOM support such a broadened role at present.

A broader embrace would require some delicate negotiation with other agencies and groups such as:

- the Informal Consultations, a group of 16 migrant-receiving countries that meet to discuss common migration concerns;

- the International Labor Organization, which has been looking at the position of migrant workers and their rights and working conditions— an issue not unrelated to worker rights and trade issues now emerging on the trade agenda—and which has established a Migrant Workers Convention;

- the UN Center on Human Rights, which administers the UN Covenant on Civil and Political Rights;

- the OECD, which provides some analysis of migration and basic detailed international statistics in its so-called SOPEMI reports;

- the UN Population Fund, whose annual *Population Review* documents the scale and form of world migration;

- the soon-to-be-established World Trade Organization (WTO), which must oversee implementation of the General Agreement on Trade in Services (GATS), which includes horizontal schedules of commitments relating to temporary movement of personnel and sector-specific schedules in areas such as professional services, education, and tourism;

- UNESCO, which deals with information on international student movements;

- the UN World Tourism Organization, which deals with information on international tourist movements.

The best overall outcome might be for UNHCR to encompass refugee movements broadly defined; for the IOM to dominate international coordination on guestworkers, illegals, family reunion, and economic settler migration matters; and for the World Tourism Office to take responsibility for tourist, student, and related services trade movements.

However desirable and perhaps even necessary for enhanced management of global migration matters, an effective multilateral initiative will not be easy. Nor will it be sufficient. Much of the observed trend in international migration reflects strong growth in intraregional migration. Given the greater manageability that comes from smaller numbers and greater homogeneity among participants, regional groupings may be better able to initiate progress in these matters. The success of the European Union in incorporating internal freedom of movement in its provisions, despite historical enmities and other concerns, gives cause for optimism on this front. But it must go further. There is clearly a pressing need for regional discussion of the desirability of a common European migration policy. National immigration laws in Europe can only have limited effect with increased integration of EC labor markets, because if one country in the European Union allows substantial immigration, these new residents can soon migrate to other member countries.

Of course, existing global agencies such as the IOM or the UN Economic and Social Commissions could themselves develop a regional structure, perhaps even along federalist lines. Alternatively, separate instruments could be developed, for example under the auspices of PECC or the Asia Pacific Economic Cooperation (APEC) in that region, or by the development of a new Asia-Pacific Migration Council or Committee.

The Asian example is particularly pertinent because the countries of that region have been among the most restrictive in regulating foreign residence. When I delivered a paper on this topic a year ago and suggested that migration should be on the APEC agenda, it was suggested to me that this was premature and that the region was not ready for significant steps on migration.

I am pleased to be able to report that on 11 April 1994 the first Regional Consultations on Illegal Migration were held in Canberra. Seventeen countries from the Asia-Pacific region plus UNHCR and the IOM were represented at the meetings, hosted by the Australian government. The aim was to exchange information and increase the level of knowledge among participants of the ways in which illegal migration operates. Agreement was reached among participants to continue these consultations on a regular basis and to extend their agenda to other migration issues. If similar regional initiatives could proceed for other areas, preferably under a broad IOM umbrella, this would be a major advance.

The key to success, as evidenced here, is to begin with discrete topics within the broader domain of migration (and preferably topics where win-win solutions are possible), such as illegal migration and visa documentation. Once trust and constructive engagement have been built up, more problematic topics can be approached. Table 8 lists the sort of topics that could constitute the terms of reference for such meetings. The table provides an illustrative list of actions of various kinds, beginning with attempts to understand problems, moving through loose forms of cooperation such as exchanges of information, and ending with others that involve formal commitments.

It is notable that Japan has also sponsored regular technical meetings on migration among countries in its region to deal with specific microissues such as visa processing and document forgery detection. The most difficult step will be moving from entry-exit migration policies to settlement (postarrival) policies. Yet the most enduring lesson is the need for fair and just settlement policies if migration is to enrich the host country and minimize the social costs. Such policies need not preclude suitable user-pay policies (e.g., language training) to reduce costs to residents. A current symptom that these issues are being addressed is the establishment of reviews of laws governing citizenship in many countries including Australia, Canada, the United States, Germany, and France.

If these issues are resolved constructively, international economic integration will have a good chance of moving beyond trade and investment toward the integration of peoples. In this sense the management of migration may actually be the key to a sustainable international economic order.

Conclusions

International migration may or may not be the "third wave" of international integration. But it is of substantial and growing significance, and therefore worthy of much more analysis and policy attention than it has received in the past. Migration between regions has been very important, but intraregional migration is becoming even more so and is likely to be an important focus for the future.

Although a distinct range of primary motives for migration can be identified (e.g., economic, family reunification, humanitarian), these distinctions become increasingly blurred in practice. A broad view of population movements is therefore helpful. In fact, as we have seen, the biggest growth in population movements between countries is not in traditional

Table 8 Illustrative terms of reference for regional migration discussions

To better understand how migration relates to trade, aid, and investment policies in terms of both causes and effects (e.g., aid to education unintentionally facilitating skilled emigration).

To minimize economic and social shocks to other countries (including third parties) by means of prior discussion of policy changes, their intentions, and likely consequences.

To minimize foreign policy conflict resulting from misunderstanding of migration policies, including criteria for entry and treatment of migrant residents (e.g., outdated perceptions of racial criteria in entry regulation).

To better track, detect, and repatriate clandestine and fraudulent movements of persons through information exchange and other forms of cooperation.

To exchange information on administrative devices and arrangements in immigration such as point systems, grievance procedures, automation, and postarrival services.

To negotiate better-informed policies regarding recognition of education, trade, and professional qualifications.

To discuss and understand the cultural basis for family reunion policies (family definition, de facto status, adoptions policies, etc.) and to coordinate policy with respect to reunification of family members in multiple locations.

To protect national sovereignty in matters of administration of migrant residents, citizenship, emigré return issues, change of migrant status, bonding policies, and others.

To improve mutually beneficial international skill transfers, mitigating concerns about brain drain and lack of local training offsets.

To review tax and related rights and obligations for migrants engaged in business and others residing in multiple locations.

To protect all human beings, and especially low-skilled migrant laborers, crossing international borders from exploitation and abuse in work conditions and rights, remittance policy, and administration.

To reach agreement on mechanisms for repatriation of asylum seekers who may face persecution in their home country merely for having sought asylum.

permanent or guestworker migration or refugee movements, but in newer, often short-term movements linked to investment and to trade in services such as tourism and education.

The economic effects of these movements have generally been found by researchers to be benign. But the social and political consequences may be more problematic, and environmental consequences open up new issues so far little touched by research. The Bretton Woods conference and the subsequent 50 years of formal international economic arrangements neglected international migration. But modern transport and communications make porous borders inevitable. International arrangements for the 21st century must come to terms with the rapidly growing mobility of the world's peoples.

These characteristics determine the desirable policy responses. The blurred nature of migration categories, their increasing intraregional focus, and the crucial social dimension of their impacts make the development of an international regime for migration more problematic than for trade, investment, and even the environment. Full international rule making and global regulation will be difficult. A more authoritative effort to aid and protect refugees broadly defined is the essential starting point for international organizations. This should be supplemented by better integration of the functions of the array of international agencies dealing with different aspects of migration, and by strong complementary regional structures.

The keys to these institutions' success in addressing migration issues as a basis for sustainable international integration will be early and successful issue-by-issue negotiation and effective development of fair and efficient settlement policies. Joint efforts on the more positive-sum issues, such as documentation coordination, dealing with illegals, training offsets, student exchange conditions, child adoption arrangements, and child custody and support issues, could provide the basis for developing early trust and cooperation. Then increasingly tougher issues could be embraced. In the process, nations would need to examine closely their postarrival settlement policies to ensure that appropriate "social compacts" are in place to reassure both the existing resident population and the new migrants that their arrival will be to their overall mutual benefit. If this fails, the vacuum may well be filled by populist, protectionist parties inimical to liberalization on many fronts. In this sense, a more effective international regulatory regime for migration may well be an important component of sustaining a broader liberal economic order.

Increasingly porous borders mean that unilateral national regulation of migration is increasingly ineffective and that migration issues will not go away. On the other hand, the social consequences of migration mean that full liberalization of the movement of people is unlikely as a politically viable global goal for some time. The obvious conclusion is that more international cooperation is needed to bring about open and informed recognition of this problem, and thereby to better regulate the flows and deal with their consequences.

References

Abella, M., and L. L. Lim. 1993. "Internal, Intra-regional and International Migration." Paper presented at the Conference on Asia-Pacific Migration Affecting Australia: Temporary, Long-Term, and Permanent Movements of People, Darwin (14–17 September).

Abowd, J., and R. Freeman, eds. 1991. *Immigration, Trade and the Labor Market*. Chicago: University of Chicago Press.

Athukorala, P. 1993. "Literature Survey: International Labour Migration." *Asian-Pacific Economic Literature* 7, no. 2 (November): 54–57.

Australia Bureau of Immigration and Population Research. 1994. *Australian Immigration: A Survey of the Issues*. Canberra: Australian Government Publishing Service.

Borjas, G. 1990. *Friends or Strangers: The Impact of Immigrants on the US Economy*. New York: Basic Books.

Centre for Economic Policy Research. 1994. "European Integration: Economics of Migration." *Bulletin* No. 59 (Winter): 16–19.

Employment and Immigration Canada. 1989. *Immigration to Canada: Economic Impacts.* Ottawa: Official Print.

Goering, J. 1989. "The 'Explosiveness' of Chain Migration: Research and Policy Issues." *International Migration Review* 23, no. 4: 809–12.

Pang Eng Fong. 1993. *Regionalisation and Labour Flows in Pacific Asia.* Paris: OECD.

Hamilton, B., and J. Whalley. 1984. "Efficiency and Distributional Implications of Global Restrictions on Labour Mobility." *Journal of Development Economics* 14: 61–75.

Holton, R. 1990. "Social Aspects of Immigration," in M. Wooden et al., *Australian Immigration: A Survey of Issues.* Canberra: Australian Government Publishing Service.

Hugo, G. 1991. "Recent International Trends in Asia: Some Implications for Australia." In J. W. Smith, *Immigration, Population and Sustainable Environments: The Limits to Australia's Growth.* Adelaide: Flinders University Press.

Jupp, J. 1991. "From Free Entry to Tight Control: The Entry of Immigrants to Australia since 1788." In G. Withers, *Commonality and Difference: Australia and the United States.* Sydney: Allen and Unwin.

Layard, R., O. Blanchard, R. Dornbusch, and P. Krugman. 1992. *East-West Migration, The Alternatives.* Cambridge, MA: MIT Press.

New South Wales Government. 1990. *A Greenhouse Strategy for New South Wales.* Sydney.

OECD. 1991. Labour Force Statistics, 1980–91. Paris: OECD.

OECD. SOPEMI. 1993. *Annual Report: Trends in International Migration.* Paris: OECD.

OECD. 1994. *Trade Liberalisation: Global Economic Implications.* Paris: OECD.

Pacific Economic Cooperation Council. 1993. *Human Resource Development Outlook 1993–94: Migration and Labour Flows in Selected Pacific Economies, 1993–94.* Singapore: Times Academic Press.

Pacific Economic Cooperation Council. 1994. *Human Resource Development Outlook 1994–95: Investment and Labour Flows in Selected Pacific Economies, 1994–95.* Singapore: Times Academic Press.

Simon, J. 1989. *The Economic Consequences of Immigration.* Oxford: Basil Blackwell.

Simon, J. 1990. *The Economics of Immigration.* New York: The Free Press.

Sjaastad, L. 1962. "The Cost and Returns of Human Migration." *Journal of Political Economy* 70 (October): 80–93.

Stark, O. 1991. *The Migration of Labour.* Oxford: Basil Blackwell.

UNESCO. 1985. *Statistical Yearbook.* Paris.

UNESCO. 1993. *Statistical Yearbook.* Paris.

United Nations Population Fund. 1993. *The State of World Population 1993.* New York.

US Department of Labor. 1989. *The Effect of Immigration on the US Economy and Labor Market.* Washington: Government Printing Office.

World Travel and Tourism Council. 1993. *Travel and Tourism: A New Economic Perspective.* New York.

World Tourism Organization. 1993. *Yearbook of Tourism Statistics.* Madrid.

IV

THE FUTURE

9

Managing the World Economy of the Future

C. FRED BERGSTEN

The Case for Reform

A comprehensive review of the institutional framework for international economic cooperation has become essential. The 50th anniversary of the Bretton Woods system provides a convenient point of departure for conducting that review. So does the imminence of a new century. The Group of Seven (G-7) leading industrial democracies called for such a review at their annual summit in Naples in July 1994 and have inscribed the issue on the agenda for their next meeting at Halifax in mid-1995.[1]

The case for assessing the adequacy of the present regime rests on three substantive historical transformations, however, rather than on chronological coincidences. First, the end of the Cold War has totally altered the security foundations of the existing international economic order, including the global institutions devised at the end of the Second World War—the International Monetary Fund (IMF), the International Bank for Reconstruction and Development, and the General Agreement on Tariffs and

---

C. Fred Bergsten is director of the Institute for International Economics.

1. In its summit communiqué of 9 July, the heads of state and government of seven major industrial nations and the president of the European Community declared,

> As we approach the threshold of the 21st century, we are conscious of our responsibility to renew and revitalize these [Bretton Woods] institutions. . . . To carry out this responsibility, we have agreed that, in Halifax next year, we will focus on. . . . What framework of institutions will be required to meet these challenges in the 21st century? How can we adapt existing institutions and build new institutions to ensure the future prosperity and security of our people?

Trade (GATT)—and the main regional bodies (centered on the European Union, as it has now become). The demise of the Soviet Union has eliminated much of the security "glue" that compelled the major industrial democracies, across both the Atlantic and the Pacific, to maintain their strong institutional ties and, partly through those institutions, to resolve their economic disputes cooperatively to preserve alliance solidarity against the communist threat.

Second, the economic foundations of the global order have changed at least as dramatically. American economic dominance has given way to a world of three relatively equal economic superpowers, with the European Union and Japan joining the erstwhile hegemon. In addition, a rapidly growing number of countries have become important players on one or more global economic issues—for example, Saudi Arabia and some other OPEC members on energy and finance and Korea and other newly industrialized economies (NIEs) on trade. China, Russia, and India could join the ranks of the economic superpowers within the next few decades. In short, pluralism has replaced hegemony in undergirding the international economic order.

Third, global commerce and finance have changed beyond recognition from that of half a century ago. Financial flows have been liberalized throughout the world, and their magnitude swamps that of trade transactions. Market forces now largely determine economic outcomes almost everywhere, even in the former command economies of the communist world and in previously closed economies elsewhere (such as India and Mexico). International economic negotiations now routinely address, and even sometimes alter, policies traditionally viewed as "purely domestic." The share of trade in the world's largest national economy, the United States, has doubled in the past quarter century and now equals that of the European Union (as a group, excluding trade among its members) and Japan.

All these changes suggest a compelling need to reassess the adequacy of the international economic order. At the same time, however, the end of the Cold War tempts countries to shift their focus from international and security problems to domestic and economic problems. The economic slowdown and growing social problems of the past two decades, which have been pronounced in Europe and North America, add to the case for domestic orientation. The growing reliance on market forces, both domestically and internationally, leads to doubts in some quarters about the need for extensive institutionalization of (or even explicit cooperation on) international economic issues.

The answer to this debate is surely that, in a world of increasing economic interdependence, each individual country will be more prosperous and more stable if the international economic order can more effectively promote trade and financial flows that support world and national welfare. Desired domestic progress will be facilitated by global economic success and may even require it. The issue for this paper is whether reforms of the international economic institutions can contribute to such an outcome.

The sweeping global transformations described above have already prompted extensive change in the world's economic arrangements. Most of those changes have been incremental. But some have been systemic: the shift from pegged to flexible exchange rates in the early 1970s, the adoption of a comprehensive global response to the debt crisis in the 1980s, the inclusion of services trade under the GATT in the 1990s. A central issue is whether these adaptations have provided an effective international economic regime for the period ahead.

I conclude that "the Bretton Woods system"[2] of the past half century has worked quite well. No systemic crises have been permitted to devastate the world economy, as in the 1930s. Unprecedented prosperity and stability have been achieved and maintained in most countries. The system has adapted with impressive flexibility to many of the new issues it has been forced to face. Countries have learned to use the international regime constructively in promoting sensible national policies, notably liberalization of trade and capital movements.

The Bretton Woods system embodied widespread international commitment to central economic goals, including freer trade and currency convertibility, and a framework for the coordination needed to achieve those goals. Hence it produced crucial support for world peace, both directly through its impact on relationships among the key countries and indirectly by promoting economic progress throughout most of the world.

On the other hand, the system worked better in its first quarter century than it has more recently. Some of its earlier achievements, including monetary stability and steady progress toward freer trade, have eroded over the last decade or two. The effectiveness of the international monetary regime declined substantially after the demise of the adjustable peg system at the global level and the associated decline in the role of the IMF. Trade protectionism, often taking new forms, made a comeback in some of the larger countries, and pressures for new governmental intervention remain intense in many of them. World growth has been much slower since the end of the "golden period" of the postwar era in the early 1970s; the slower growth has undoubtedly made it harder to sustain the system, but the causality may run at least partly in the opposite direction as well.

Some new issues, such as the oil shocks of the 1970s, have not been handled very effectively. Newly rising economic powers, notably Japan

---

2. I define the "Bretton Woods system" as the entire institutional framework created to guide the world economy at the end of the Second World War. This definition is considerably broader, and I think more useful, than the alternative favored by some analysts that emphasizes the specific regime of pegged exchange rates, which was the main monetary variant of that system during its first quarter century.

and now China, have yet to be integrated into the system. Interrelationships between issues often have not been handled well. Some of the institutions have undergone sweeping changes in their functions and geographical locus of operation, raising doubts about the continued effectiveness of their original design.

But the system may be making a comeback. The Uruguay Round was concluded successfully: new issues were brought under the trade regime, the core trade institution should be more effective in the future, and developing countries played a far greater role in the process than in any previous GATT negotiation. Unilateral trade and investment liberalization has become widespread, including in some of the previously most protectionist countries. Most of the former communist countries, including the largest, are groping toward market reform. Protection in the United States, the largest market of all, has fallen dramatically over the past decade with the abolition of all import quotas (auto, steel, machine tools, and prospectively textiles and apparel and several agricultural products via the Uruguay Round).

Beyond trade policy, the G-7 has evolved a de facto system of target zones (as described below) that has maintained a fair degree of currency stability. The IMF and IBRD have helped many countries adjust to the debt crisis of the 1980s and to the transformation from command to market economies in the early 1990s. The debt crisis was resolved without systemic damage. The Montreal Protocol on CFCs, the Basel Convention on hazardous wastes, and, with respect to broad goals, the Earth Summit in Rio de Janeiro in 1992 represent initial steps toward a global consensus on environmental problems. The Basel Accord has begun a process of international cooperation in the prudential supervision of global capital markets. The trend line is unclear, but some of the recent news is encouraging.

Moreover, some of the earlier problems of the system are understandable and are in fact inevitable results of its own initial successes. As private financial flows increased with the liberalization of capital markets, the role of institutions whose clout derived largely from their ability to provide official financing—including the Fund and the Bank—was bound to decline. As the agenda of "international economic" issues spread to include topics previously regarded as "purely domestic," due to the continued expansion of interdependence and the system's success in liberalizing traditional border barriers, it would inherently take time for the institutions (and the countries and people who run them) to catch up. As world growth slowed, partly due to the end of the period of postwar reconstruction and easy "catch-up" by poorer countries, both of which were supported importantly by the Bretton Woods system, cooperation became more difficult to sustain.

I thus conclude that the international economic order does not require sweeping overhaul. But it requires more than fine tuning. I will call for a series of modest evolutionary reforms of four types: further adaptation to new circumstances by some of the existing institutions,[3] creation of a few new institutions to deal with issues that are not now handled effectively, abolition of several institutions that have outlived their usefulness, and new management techniques for using the organizations better.

The paper will proceed in turn to each of these four sets of recommendations after initially suggesting a set of general lessons drawn from our half century of experience with "the Bretton Woods system." All of my institutional conclusions and proposals will of course derive from judgments concerning the substantive requirements of each issue area (or the interactions among them) as well as the effectiveness of the current institutional framework in meeting those requirements. My time frame is essentially the next decade or two, though a few of the proposals may take longer to evolve, and I would hope that the reformed framework could provide the foundation for another half century of international economic progress.

General Lessons from the Past

Institutions can only work when they are based on an agreed conceptual framework. The widespread global consensus on the costs of protectionism, in both economic and political terms, underpinned the success of the GATT. The burden of proof was placed squarely on the opponents of liberalization. Both politicians and bureaucrats had a guiding principle to rely upon (or hide behind). Virtually all countries, including former command economies and former bastions of protectionism, have largely embraced the global consensus.

The absence of similar consensus on the impact of multinational enterprises has limited progress in setting agreed rules on international direct investment. The failure to achieve intellectual accord on a central principle, such as the internalization of pollution costs, has impeded international advance in dealing with global and transborder environmental questions. The advent of substantial intellectual support for floating exchange rates in the 1960s, and growing doubts about the viability of systemic reliance on the dollar, contributed importantly to the rejection of pegged currencies and the original postwar monetary regime in the early 1970s. One cannot overemphasize the importance of intellectual consensus in inspiring effective political action.

The system has functioned largely through its impact on national economic policies. The chief purpose of any international regime is to tilt national policies in an internationally consistent, and thus sustainable,

---

3. I define "institutions" as encompassing both agreed international rules, such as those embodied in the Articles of Agreement of the IMF and the General Agreement on Tariffs and Trade, and the organizations that were created to help implement those rules.

direction. The GATT, for all its imperfections, has played an important role in tilting the balance of domestic debate against protectionism in most countries. So have regional arrangements, notably the European Community (most explicitly when France in 1982–83 rejected a protectionist strategy that would have sought to preserve the new Socialist government's "dash for growth"). At the margin, this impact was probably more important for larger and more closed economies (such as the United States and the European Community), which were not as predisposed to liberal trade policies by their economic openness.

The monetary regime has been less successful in this regard. Even here, however, there is substantial evidence of systemic impact on domestic policies. This was especially true under the adjustable peg rules of the original IMF and the European Monetary System (EMS).

Some skeptics argue that the existence of international institutions deserves little, if any, credit for the sensible economic policies undertaken by individual countries in the postwar period. After all, unilateral trade liberalization and monetary stability are good for a country, so such actions must be motivated primarily by domestic calculations.

This view ignores the domestic political problems of implementing "sensible policies" and the role of the institutions in helping accomplish them, as just noted. Domestic groups that used the international regimes to promote their own objectives in turn became supporters of the international regimes. Cases in point include exporters, importers, financial institutions, and other beneficiaries of free international trade and capital movements. The international-domestic interaction has thus become a self-supporting, if not always self-sustaining, process.

Moreover, the appeal of qualifying for participation in desirable international regimes had an important impact on some of the more important liberalizations in recent history. Mexico was motivated partly by the lure of NAFTA. Other Latin American countries were enticed by the prospect of President Bush's Enterprise for the Americas Initiative, which envisaged an ultimate Western Hemisphere Free Trade Area. The ex-communist countries in Eastern Europe liberalized partly to qualify for participation in the European Union. China has been driven partly by its desire to become a charter member of the new World Trade Organization.

Though Eichengreen and Kenen note the absence of any comprehensive "development regime," the moral pressure of the postwar system (along with the security objectives of the Cold War era) also helped produce unprecedented transfers of real resources from richer to poorer countries. Global aid targets and the like have attracted much skepticism, but constant systemic pressure, including via the key international institutions, contributed substantially to these transfers. Trade concessions to the poorer countries, through the Generalized System of Preferences and Part IV of the GATT, were widespread as well. Results can again be seen both globally (e.g., through the IBRD, GATT, and the Organization for Economic Cooperation and Development's Development Assistance Committee) and regionally (especially the EC transfer mechanisms but also the regional development banks).

Functionally specific international economic institutions work best. The IMF has been most effective when managing the international monetary system. Its effectiveness has declined and its image has suffered as it has become viewed as "an aid institution"—an erroneous view, as the Fund continues to finance balance of payments problems rather than long-term development and extends very little of its credit on concessional terms. The view, nevertheless, is widespread and understandable, in light of the very modest IMF involvement in international monetary affairs and the total absence of IMF programs in high-income countries for almost two decades.

The lesson of functional specificity derives from the evolution of other international economic institutions as well. The World Bank has been more effective at promoting economic growth than at social engineering. The GATT has faltered when attempting to move from trade into related areas, such as investment or the environment. The International Energy Agency (IEA) represents the successful creation of a new institution to deal with a sharply focused problem. By contrast, the world wound up substantively altering the IMF to deal with the debt crisis instead of creating a new institution (as some proposed at the time).

The success of functional specificity at the international level reflects the organization of most national governments. As demonstrated by the literature of the 1970s on "transnational coalitions," cooperation is often more successful among functional counterparts in *different* countries (e.g., central bankers) than among those responsible for different functions within the *same* country. Cooperation (and even coordination) within a specific issue area is the most likely route to successful international regimes.

I therefore reject proposals to merge the IMF and the GATT, or other efforts to achieve better coordination across issue areas at the cost of forgoing the benefits of functional specificity. But I would also note that functional specificity is not a sufficient condition for institutional effectiveness: Emile van Lennep pointed out in his comment on this paper that many of the economic organs of the United Nations are organized functionally but that they have nevertheless been largely ineffectual.

Linkage across issue areas has been generally ineffective. The flip side of the success of functional specificity is the disappointing record of integration across issue areas. The international problem again reflects the domestic situation in most countries: few governments integrate well across different substantive topics.

One acute example is the relationship between monetary and trade policies. The IMF and GATT are supposed to work together but do so sporadically at best. The tension between these issue areas has long been evident: the greatest protectionist threats in the postwar period have resulted from large currency disequilibria, notably the huge dollar overvaluations of the late 1960s and middle 1980s (which triggered, respectively, the American import surcharge and Burke-Hartke pressures in the early 1970s and the Super 301 initiative in the Trade Act of 1988). Dramatic last-minute monetary initiatives, the Nixon abandonment of gold convertibility for the dollar in 1971 and the Plaza Agreement of 1985, were required to save the trading system but generated crises of their own.

Eichengreen and Kenen raise another example by noting that there has been a failure to integrate elements within the development issue area, such as its trade and commodity-price dimensions. "Development" (like "world growth") is such a pervasive and important consideration that it must be injected frontally into decisions in each individual issue area, whether it be the pursuit of global trade liberalization or international monetary stability. This has clearly not been done in practice. The overall management of the system (addressed below) must always take developmental concerns into account, even though the implementation of its individual institutional components follows a functionally specific course.

The Group of Five (and subsequently G-7) was created in part to deal with these problems of linkage. At its two main levels, the annual summits and the more frequent meetings of finance ministers, this steering committee has recorded some notable successes, such as the Bonn summit agreement of 1978 and the Plaza Agreement. But the G-5 has failed to achieve continuing cooperation (let alone coordination) across the key issue areas, its finance ministers have been much better at managing crises than preventing problems or improving the architecture, and its record has deteriorated over the past decade or so. Nor do the international economic institutions themselves cooperate directly in any systematic manner.

One promising technique for achieving linkage has been to deal with new issues by creating separate "windows" within existing institutions. The World Bank, for example, responded to the need for concessional capital flows to the poorest countries by creating the International Development Association (IDA), to the interest in promoting the private sector via the International Finance Corporation (IFC), and to new environmental concerns by creating a Global Environmental Facility. The GATT added a General Agreement on Trade in Services (GATS) in the Uruguay Round.

In some instances, such intra-institutional innovations may be the best way to combine the benefits of functional specificity with the need for better linkage across issue areas. Such innovations could help avoid excessive institutional proliferation: more timely expansion of the World Bank's role in Eastern Europe and the former Soviet Union, for example, would have obviated the need for the latest international economic institution, the European Bank for Reconstruction and Development (EBRD).

Leadership is essential. A key reason for both the pervasive systemic problems in the more recent period, and the failure of cross-issue linkage in particular, has been the difficulty of replacing the American leadership of the earlier postwar period. Effective collective leadership is clearly required by the pluralization of economic power and the diminished salience of security issues, which helped provide the United States with both the capability and will to guide the economic order throughout the Cold War era. But the other major industrial actors, the European Union and Japan, have been slow to accept systemic responsibility (even when grudgingly paying the bills), and their internal situations suggest it may be some time before they can do so. Hence the United States has, in fits and starts and with tactics that are frequently inconsistent with stable systemic leadership, attempted to maintain its previous role and the world may have no good alternative for a while.

There is a second, extremely important, relationship between systemic leadership and international institutions. As noted by Joseph Nye in his comments on this paper, the United States might well have exercised much of its postwar leadership in the absence of the Bretton Woods system; hence the question of how much success is attributable to the system itself can never be definitively resolved. But the existence of that system enabled the United States to exert at least part of its leadership through an institutional framework that was far more legitimate politically than its unilateral action alone would have been. In addition, the existence of the system frequently tilted internal policy outcomes within the United States in directions that supported its systemic role and thereby reinforced its capacity to provide the needed leadership. Hence there again appears a self-supporting cycle between modalities through which the international rules are implemented and the strength of the institutions themselves.

Filling the present leadership vacuum is one of the most crucial challenges facing the system as it enters the 21st century. In such an environment, the institutions themselves will need to play a much more important role. I will suggest below that institutional management is extremely important and can generate results that are internationally greater than the sum of their national parts. But the institutions are largely a reflection of their members, primarily those with the greatest economic power. Much of the "leadership lesson" is that the key countries must be willing to use the international institutions constructively if they are to exercise their systemic responsibilities effectively.

Rising powers have not generally been integrated in an effective manner. The history of both the late 19th century and the interwar period suggests that a failure to integrate legitimate new powers into the international management structure is a recipe for disaster. But the Bretton Woods regime was created by a small number of relatively homogenous countries. Hence it is not surprising that its record to date in assimilating "competing models of capitalism," as in Japan and the NIEs—let alone economies that are in transition from a totally nonmarket orientation, such as China and Russia—is checkered. In this context, the relative success of the postwar system cuts in both directions: it promotes a degree of convergence between the "competing models" and now the former command economies, but its success in reducing border barriers also exposes (and highlights the effects of) key differences in national economic systems, such as those of the United States and Japan.

The Bretton Woods regime has attempted to respond to this issue through a combination of cooptation and confrontation, with limited success. Japan was the first major new actor. It was readily accepted into all the institutions, becoming the first non-European member of the OECD in 1962. But it was only grudgingly and belatedly accorded its rightful (second) place in the hierarchy at the IMF and World Bank (and, along with Germany, is not yet a permanent member of the UN Security Council). Europe and the United States have repeatedly taken unilateral actions against Japan that they would not think of taking against each other. The GATT, after three rounds of far-reaching multilateral trade negotiations, still does not address some of the main access problems in Japan.

Nor has the system done much better in assimilating other new powers. Saudi Arabia and the other oil producers were essentially confronted, via the IEA and referral to the private markets to invest their surpluses, rather than incorporated (though Saudi Arabia was proffered a de facto permanent seat on the IMF's Executive Board). The NIEs may repeat some of the Japanese experience. The general North-South problem, emphasized by Eichengreen and Kenen, is less important in this systemic sense, but there, too, the newcomers—despite the aid programs, trade concessions, and increased participation of less developed countries in the GATT—have been largely invited to accept the trickling down of growth and trade liberalization from the industrial world.

China is a partial exception. It was accepted into the IMF and World Bank soon after it turned toward market economics in the late 1970s, and the Bank in fact played a major (if largely unsung) role in the development and implementation of China's reforms. But China has not yet been permitted to rejoin the GATT, and its resentment toward the established order will fester if entry is postponed long beyond the startup of the new World Trade Organization.

This is another of the central challenges for the period ahead. Japan is still to be assimilated, and several NIEs are en route. China may represent one of the cardinal systemic problems of the 21st century (with important security as well as economic implications). So could Russia, and its partial participation in recent G-7 summits represents a halting first step toward its systemic engagement. The European Union will require a different type of international restructuring if it achieves effective monetary and macroeconomic union, permitting it to be represented by a single spokesperson rather than a number of member states as in most of the institutions to date.

Systemic stability cannot be taken for granted. As noted above, systemic collapse like that of the 1930s has been avoided. But there have been numerous close calls: the outbreak of strong protectionist pressures, notably in the United States in the early 1970s and middle 1980s; the breakdown of the monetary order in the early 1970s; the oil shocks of the 1970s; and the related debt crisis of the 1980s. The system must be nurtured and constantly renewed.

This is particularly true in periods like the present that confront historic transformations in both the economic and security underpinnings of the global edifice. It is particularly true when leadership is missing, and when new actors and new issues are forcing their way onto the agenda. We next turn to an appraisal of what should be done to strengthen the system, applying these general lessons from the past to the prospective new conditions of the years and decades ahead.

Proposals for the Future: Reforming Existing Regimes

The International Monetary System

The international monetary system lies at the heart of the world economy just as national monetary policies lie at the heart of individual economies. The international system clearly needs reform. Substantial misalignments occur with distressing frequency and persist for prolonged periods, often with severe costs for national economies and open trade. Short-term volatility is less important but can disrupt other financial markets that in turn affect real economic activity. The G-7's management is episodic, and the IMF's is virtually nonexistent. The decline in effectiveness of the international monetary regime correlates with the sharp slowdown in world growth and increased inflation over the past two decades and, as noted above, has contributed directly to major outbreaks of protectionism.

The two extremes—exchange rates that are "fixed" (mainly via adjustable pegs) and "freely flexible" (truly free only under Beryl Sprinkel in the first Reagan administration)—have been tried and found wanting. Governments perennially seek halfway houses that will work: "dirty floats," wider bands, crawling pegs, and innumerable other variants. The major industrial countries have operated a more-or-less de facto target zone/reference range system for the major currencies since early 1987, and the G-5 "formally" adopted such a regime at the Louvre in February of that year (though some participants deny even that limited degree of coherence). Almost simultaneously, the EMS abandoned its previous resort to frequent realignments and sought to achieve truly fixed parities. The key global and regional groups were thus seeking, at about the same time, to sharply reduce the extent of currency variability and to establish a system more effective than the status quo.

The "formal" G-5/G-7 effort lasted less than a year, and the narrow EMS bands became untenable in 1992–93. However, both were replaced by de facto target zones rather than abandoned. The trade-weighted dollar has been quite stable, remaining within 10 percent on either side of its trade-weighted average since the end of 1987. The dollar and mark have fluctuated between about 1.40 and 1.80 marks to the dollar since 1989—with joint intervention at both extremes to preserve the range. The dollar and yen fluctuated between 120 and 160 yen to the dollar until being "rebased" to about 100–115 in 1993–94. At the regional level, the EMS responded to its crises in 1992–93 by widening its margins—thereby adopting target zones de jure—rather than by eliminating its parities. All these ranges (except the most recent dollar-yen zone, which was narrower) were centered on notional midpoints with bands of ±10 to 15 percent. The increased effectiveness of intervention (except, of course, when trying to defend patently unsustainable parities, as with the EMS in 1992–93) has permitted maintenance of these ranges without significant deflection of monetary policy from its pursuit of domestic goals.

One option for the future is simply to maintain the present de facto regime. This would avoid committing governments to explicit targets that speculators, with far larger resources, might attack. It would enable officials to maintain a maximum element of surprise in the intervention efforts that they do decide to launch.

But the de facto regime has key defects. First, some of the ranges have been so wide that they could permit substantial misalignments to occur and persist. Second, the markets cannot be fully confident that the ranges will be maintained and hence are tempted to bet against them; by contrast, credible announced margins would induce private capital to help defend the ranges and reduce the need for official action. Third, there is no orderly mechanism for altering nominal or (more importantly) real rates as underlying economic circumstances change. Fourth, implementation of the de facto regime depends almost totally on the individuals who are in office at particular points in time and cannot be counted on for the long haul. The present regime should thus be viewed as a way station en route to lasting reform rather than a satisfactory terminus.

The best step would be to convert the present de facto regime into a de jure system of target zones among the major currencies. Such a system would synthesize the virtues of the extreme systems and avoid the shortcomings of both. It would be defended primarily through agreed intervention strategies but supported as needed by domestic monetary and fiscal policies. During the present period, when governments seem to be searching for new regimes to discipline their own fiscal policies—such as the Maastricht Treaty in Europe and balanced budget amendments or Gramm-Rudman-Hollings and subsequent procedures in the United States—agreement on global rules that promoted such results might become feasible or even viewed as desirable.[4]

Now is clearly not the time to adopt the full blueprint for policy coordination described in the Williamson-Henning paper in this volume. However, history suggests that such extensive cooperation is most likely to be achieved by first agreeing on a monetary regime, as proposed here and by Williamson-Henning as well, and letting the implications for macroeconomic policy emerge in the course of its implementation. The initial decade of both the Bretton Woods and EMS adjustable peg systems demonstrates the potential payoff of such a strategy.

Over time, successful implementation of the proposed system could permit a progressive narrowing of the margins (which should commence at about ±10 percent). Over a *very* long time, such a system could lead to a return to fixed exchange rates and consideration of a global currency and central bank. The European Union could continue to provide the lead to this global process—an example of the positive regional-global interaction described below with respect to trade policy—by pushing forward with its convergence plans *a la* Maastricht and perhaps eventually achieving its objective of a common currency.

Such a reformed system would need more structured management than could be offered by current G-7 practices. But conversion of the G-7 into a formal independent institution would be a huge mistake, both because of the political illegitimacy of any such group in a pluralizing world and because the G-7 itself is the wrong steering committee. Systemic responsibility should be returned to the IMF, with new mechanisms devised *within* the institution to permit effective implementation of the new task. The primary requirement, as described in detail in the Williamson-Henning paper, is to create an informal steering committee within the Executive Board, comprising representatives of the G-7 (or preferably the G-3, as soon as Europe can speak on these issues with a single voice) with full

---

4. In his address to this conference, Treasury Under Secretary Lawrence Summers argues that "the consensus in favor [of such schemes] tends to collapse when substance is brought in" by citing differences between Paul Volcker and myself on intervention efforts by the Treasury in the spring of 1994. Those differences were very minor and wholly tactical. There is in fact a growing consensus in support of fundamental monetary reform as proposed here, as evidenced *inter alia* by the Report of the Bretton Woods Commission—convened by Mr. Volcker and including a large number of former high officials and private sector leaders from Germany, Japan, the United States and other key countries—in July 1994.

participation by the managing director, to implement the international monetary component of the group's systemic leadership.

On the substance, the IMF should calculate (and monitor implementation of) the "fundamental equilibrium exchange rates" that would form the core of the system. These would in turn be based on judgments concerning sustainable internal and external equilibria in the participating countries, which the countries themselves would, of course, have to accept. With such agreement on goals among the participants, the IMF could conduct meaningful surveillance of national policies and effectively promote systemic stability.

In the absence of such substantive reform of the international monetary system and restoration of the original function of the IMF, there will continue to be calls for merger of the Fund with the World Bank. Some observers believe that the IMF has lost its monetary role over the past 20 years. As noted above, some even characterize it as an "aid institution." Pressures for merger under current circumstances are understandable and will continue.

I believe that proposals for Fund-Bank merger are misplaced. The IMF's activities in developing and transition economies remain primarily monetary, addressing these countries' balance of payments and other stabilization problems. Its enormous expertise on these issues is a huge asset for the international community.

But it is essential to clarify the relationship between Fund and Bank and to coordinate their activities much better. In particular, all long-term and structural functions should be assigned to the Bank. All IMF offices and personnel that have become engaged in such activities should be shifted to the Bank. The most important change, however, is for the IMF to resume managing the international monetary system, which would clearly preserve the functionally specific role of that institution while achieving the needed substantive improvements.

The Trading System

Three additional lessons from the past half century should undergird future reforms of the trading system. First, the bicycle theory works. Continuing liberalization is necessary to avoid backsliding into protection. The GATT went into prolonged periods of inaction after the conclusion of the first large postwar negotiations—the Kennedy Round and the Tokyo Round—and protectionist pressures escalated everywhere.

Second, the theory of "rounds" has also worked. Despite the complexities involved, deliberate broadening of the agenda has promoted inter-issue trade-offs that have produced much greater liberalization than issue-specific negotiations could ever have delivered. The Uruguay Round was so comprehensive that it came perilously close to overloading the circuits, but its ultimately successful conclusion provides fresh validation of the concept.[5]

Third, globalism and regionalism have been mutually reinforcing—despite widespread fears that regional entities would undercut the global system and promote "attention diversion" (which is almost surely more important than actual trade diversion). The creation and subsequent expansion of the European Community were key factors in prompting the world to launch the Kennedy and Tokyo Rounds, respectively, and the Community's single voice in those negotiations undoubtedly contributed to their impressive results. The creation of the North American Free Trade Agreement (NAFTA), and especially the Asia Pacific Economic Cooperation (APEC) forum, in the late 1980s were catalysts to a successful Uruguay Round in the early 1990s because they demonstrated to the European Community, the main holdout on that occasion, that the United States and other major countries could and would pursue alternative trading arrangements if the GATT effort were to fail. The continued strengthening of the global system has in turn made the world much safer for regionalism, although further strengthening of global surveillance of regional accords is needed to ensure continued positive interaction between the two.

The World Trade Organization (WTO) created by the Uruguay Round is by no means a substantive replication of the International Trade Organization (ITO) developed in the Havana Charter of 1947 (and subsequently rejected by the United States), but the new institution in a sense completes the original triumvirate of functionally specific international economic organizations envisaged at Bretton Woods. The Uruguay Round enables the trade regime to address the new issues of the late 20th century: intellectual property (quite well), services (with excellent principles but little application thereof as of yet) and the trade aspects of international investment (only a start, albeit a useful one). The WTO's new dispute settlement procedures and Trade Policy Review Mechanism should greatly improve the effectiveness of the global trade system.

But it is now necessary to "make the WTO work," and substantial further institutional reform is needed in this arena as well. One key priority is the integration of additional major countries, notably China and Russia. Another is the further evolution of arrangements to deal effectively and comprehensively with the issues initially incorporated via the Uruguay Round, although new institutions to cover nontrade aspects of some of these issues, such as international investment, may be needed as well.

In addition, the WTO will have to address the new issues of the early 21st century. One set includes competition policy, technology policy, and other microeconomic issues, where the interactions of national policies

---

5. Trade-offs among issues *within* a functionally specific regime, such as the GATT for trade, are quite different from trade-offs *across* issue areas, such as monetary and trade policy, which we saw above have not generally been handled well during the postwar period.

increasingly lead to international problems. Another set encompasses the linkages between trade and broader social concerns including the environment, labor conditions, and human rights. The WTO will need to cooperate with other functionally specific institutions in these efforts, such as the International Labor Organization (ILO) on labor issues and existing (or perhaps new) institutions on environmental issues. Such collaboration can emulate (and even improve upon) the GATT's historical arrangements with the IMF, to deal with the interactions between trade and monetary issues, but those arrangements, too, need substantial elaboration to improve the system's response to cross-issue linkages.

The key operational need on trade is continued forward momentum of the bicycle toward liberalization. In addition to the usual systemic considerations, new global negotiations are required to redirect the United States away from its contentious "aggressive unilateralism" of early 1994 (vis-à-vis Japan, China, and a number of other countries) back to its "aggressive multilateralism" of 1993 (embracing NAFTA and APEC as well as the Uruguay Round).

The primary choice for restoring the momentum is between continued reliance on all-encompassing negotiating rounds, as in the previous half century, and an emphasis on continuing negotiation on discrete topics. A set of the latter has already been launched through agreed follow-ups to the Uruguay Round. This is highly desirable in order to avoid the long periods of negotiating hiatus that spawned widespread protectionism after the Kennedy and Tokyo Rounds.

However, the same logic that produced the decisions to launch the three major postwar rounds—despite widespread declarations of "never again" at the end of each preceding round—should prevail once more: that is, the inescapable value of broadening the agenda sufficiently to permit trade-offs across enough issues to maximize the systemic benefits of the total package. The optimum combination would be a periodic series of rounds, perhaps one per decade as has occurred since the 1960s, connected by ongoing negotiations to both "fill in the details" from the predecessor and "prepare the ground" for the successor. Such a combination offers the best prospect for keeping the bicycle moving and the system both open and globally oriented.

The other key substantive issue is whether future progress would be enhanced by adoption of a "big picture" goal—perhaps free trade in industrial goods and some services either among industrial countries alone or including the NIEs by a specific deadline, say 2000 or 2010. Such a goal would in essence seek to completely eliminate border barriers. It could provide the cornerstone of the next major round, which could be deferred for a few years if the continuing negotiations from the Uruguay Round (and the regional initiatives described below) prove to be adequate to keep the bicycle moving until that time. Such goals can seize the imagination of political leaders and galvanize the entire process, paradoxically making it easier to pursue large-scale initiatives (as the three major rounds were) than to take incremental steps.

As with the monetary system, a key question is: who will take the lead? This question of overall systemic leadership will be discussed below.

The trade system can also benefit, however, from continued exploitation of the constructive interplay between regional and global liberalization. The enormous expansion of GATT/WTO membership makes it far easier to proceed at the regional level. In addition, "neighborhood effects" have become more important in economic terms (and easier politically, in some cases, with the end of the Cold War). Hence, "GATT-plus" initiatives, which can push the frontier of trade liberalization beyond what can be negotiated at the global level at a given time, may best be pursued via regional groupings rather than—as has often been proposed—via groups that mainly reflect similar levels of development (notably the OECD).

The European Union has been the front-runner in this sense, as its deep regional integration has carried it far beyond the level of global accord that could be agreed in the GATT or elsewhere. Its continued strides in this direction may provide further models that can usefully be emulated on a number of topics, such as competition policy and industrial standards. Other regional initiatives, such as the Canada–United States Free Trade Agreement and now NAFTA, may provide more relevant precedents on such issues as dispute settlement, however, because their agendas are less ambitious and hence more consonant with feasible global efforts.

A primary candidate to assume this leadership role is APEC, both because it is the newest regional organization (and thus has the farthest to go) and because its membership accounts for virtually half the world economy and trade. APEC decided, at its Seattle summit in late 1993, to consider the vision of free trade in the region and is developing detailed means to that end. It is also contemplating "GATT-plus" items such as a regional investment code.

APEC is committed to open regionalism—that is, it would almost certainly be willing to generalize its regional liberalization to the world as a whole. Some APEC members might even extend their commitments to outsiders on an unconditional most-favored nation (MFN) basis, but at a minimum the group would presumably open its agreements to participation from nonmembers on a reciprocal basis in an explicit effort to ratchet up the process of liberalization from the regional to the global levels. Such offers could apply to the entire WTO and hence provide a de facto foundation for the next global negotiation.

Other regional initiatives could also contribute to this process. The European Union will of course be expanding further, clearly into Eastern Europe and probably into the former Soviet Union as well. The NAFTA may be extended into other parts of the Western Hemisphere and could link with APEC through their three (and possibly more) common members.

This regional proliferation, while potentially quite constructive, requires parallel progress at the global level to avoid undercutting the broader regime. A central and fairly urgent element of future global trade negotiations should thus be a substantial strengthening of GATT Article XXIV, which governs the conformity of regional agreements to the GATT/WTO regime. That article should henceforth require regional entities to reduce their barriers to outsiders as well as insiders rather than simply refraining from raising them to outsiders, as is called for at present. It should authorize the WTO to exercise firm and active surveillance, through the new Trade Policy Review Mechanism, of all regional entities. The regional entities should cooperate in making sure that their own subregional entities, such as the NAFTA and the ASEAN Free Trade Area (AFTA) within APEC, conform to the global requirements as well. Oversight of this process should be one of the chief tasks of the informal global steering committee, discussed below.

Like the IMF, the WTO may need changes in its decision-making procedures to permit effective pursuit of this agenda. It would run better with an Executive Board, like those at the IMF and World Bank, and with weighted voting as in those institutions (though based on substantially different criteria). But the WTO already encompasses a new dispute settlement mechanism, as agreed in the Uruguay Round, that should be given a chance before any additional procedural changes are considered. Moreover, any effort to install such sweeping reforms in GATT/WTO decision making could take a long time and could totally absorb the energies of the organization—thus derailing rather than propelling substantive trade liberalization. If the new procedures do not fulfill expectations, the entire decision-making structure of the institution should be reviewed as part of the next major set of substantive trade negotiations.

Proposals for the Future: Creating New Institutions and Abolishing Old Ones

A key lesson of the past half century is that increased interdependence propels new issues onto the international economic agenda. The original postwar regime primarily addressed traditional border barriers: tariffs, quotas, and exchange controls. As the system succeeded in removing or at least reducing those barriers, it was increasingly recognized that many "purely domestic" issues had significant international effects. Hence there commenced a second wave of systemic focus, beginning in the 1970s and accelerating since, on nonborder economic measures that have transborder effects such as subsidies, government procurement, and more recently competition policy and financial regulation. As interdependence continues its inexorable expansion, especially in the United States, a third wave of nonborder, noneconomic (even "social" or "cultural") measures now seems poised to join the agenda (or even dominate it, as in the final stages of the NAFTA debate): the environment, labor conditions, and human rights.

This "agenda shift" has raised major problems for the international economic order. It requires the involvement of new players: different government agencies, different private-sector constituencies, different researchers in the intellectual community. Its rapid onset over the past two decades helps explain why the original Bretton Woods system faltered for a while. The world's growing ability to cope with the new agenda, to at least a degree, helps explain the recent systemic comeback, cited above. But many new issues have not yet been effectively addressed, and others will find their way onto the agenda over the years ahead.

The international economic order can integrate new issues into its institutional arrangements in two ways. It can graft them onto the existing structures. Or it can create new institutional arrangements to handle newly important functions and—particularly where entire new regions become prominent—to cover additional geographical areas. This section will address both approaches.

Some of the expanded agenda of international economic issues has been embraced by existing international institutions: the IMF took on developing-country debt, and the GATT has incorporated trade-related intellectual property and trade-related investment issues (TRIPs and TRIMs). Some "new issues" have spawned new institutions: for example, the first energy crisis led to the creation of the International Energy Agency and environmental concerns to the United Nations Environment Programme. Some have been handled by setting up "windows" within existing institutions, as with the World Bank on a number of functions, as described above. Proposals for other new institutions were rejected either because the topic was not deemed important enough to justify any new architecture (e.g., a World Resources Bank in the middle 1970s) or because it was thought better to annex it to an existing body (e.g., the debt crisis into the IMF).

It is always difficult to decide whether a new issue should be added to the responsibilities of an existing organization or addressed by a new one. There is understandable distaste for "creating yet another international bureaucracy" (though this concern might be at least partially assuaged by simultaneous termination of some existing bureaucracies). Moreover, adding to the roster of independent institutions can increase the problem of coordination across issue areas. On the other hand, as noted above, the principle of functional specificity has been demonstrably successful—and rests on a strong foundation in terms of the makeup of most of the constituent national governments.

Our first general lesson from the past suggested that an agreed conceptual framework was needed to provide a firm foundation for any successful international economic institution. At the same time, the existence of such an institution can be extremely helpful in widening support for the "agreed concept" and implementing it around the world. One guidepost to whether a new issue should beget a wholly new institution is thus whether there is widespread support for the principles underlying an international response to it. If the consensus is less sweeping, the issue might be handled better within an existing institution—perhaps with linkages to "old issues" that are widely understood—at least for an initial or interim period.

There are two major gaps in the current network of international economic institutions. Several functional issue areas that have become quite important remain uncovered, with a consequent risk of economic costs and policy conflict. In addition, some geographical areas have failed to create the kind of institutional ties that have enhanced both welfare and security in other parts of the world.

There are four functional issue areas that should now be serious candidates for the creation of new international institutions (and are addressed in issue-specific chapters in this volume): supervision and regulation of international financial markets, international investment and multinational enterprises, the environment, and migration. Parts of each are now addressed by existing organizations, and it is possible that additional parts could be handled in a similar manner. But none of these new issues fits wholly or comfortably into any of those entities. Hence the existing institutions could be substantially distorted, and risk losing their present focus and resultant effectiveness, if they were asked to take on the additional tasks. Creating institutions to address these problems should thus be seriously considered, based on an assessment of whether there is sufficient conceptual consensus in each case to support a wholly new organization as well as the trade-off between the merits of functional specificity and the costs of institutional startup and proliferation.

International Portfolio Capital

The issue area that most urgently requires new institutional innovation is supervision and regulation of capital markets. Flows of international portfolio capital have reached massive dimensions. The markets are virtually global, and future financial crises could be widespread. Nonbanks have come to rival, or even exceed, banks in their impact on international financial markets; they generate systemic risk but are subject to virtually no internationally coordinated supervision. The interactions between banks and nonbanks are equally devoid of prudential international action. There have been promising beginning steps toward cooperative international responses but most regulation—especially outside banking—remains national and uncoordinated.

Three options could be considered. The first approach would be simply to make changes at the margins of the existing supervisory framework.

This could include extending the 1988 Basel Capital Accord to include market risk; improving accounting and disclosure standards for derivatives; strengthening payments and settlement systems; and encouraging financial firms to upgrade their own risk-management systems. Much of this is already in progress.

A second approach would be to address potential systemic risk in the nonbanking sector more aggressively. The activities of banks and nonbanks have become much more similar over the past decade. The influence of institutional investors—mutual funds, hedge funds, life insurance companies, pension funds—and securities houses has increased markedly relative to banks. The activities of all these major players have now become much more international. The next systemic problem is as likely to arise in capital markets as in the banking sector.

Yet the existing supervision of nonbanks deals almost exclusively with investor protection. It does not address the safety and soundness of individual institutions and associated systemic risk. Nor has international coordination among nonbank supervisors developed very much. At a minimum, nonbank supervisors need to meet regularly and frequently—as bank supervisors do monthly at Basel—to discuss potential problems and emerging risks. Some nonbank entities that are not now regulated, such as off-shore subsidiaries of US securities houses, should be subjected to greater supervision.

A third and more fundamental approach would be to shift the regulatory system away from distinctions between the providers of financial services (banks, nonbanks, etc.) to functional regulation. All providers of a given service (insurance, depository services, risk management, etc.) would become subject to the same codes of conduct and regulatory oversight. Users of each service would then know that all aspects of the service were being regulated in a consistent manner.

Who should implement the selected approach? One possibility is simply to graft new rules onto existing institutions. Expanded banking agreements, for example, could naturally be added to the current Basel Accord and housed at the Bank for International Settlements (BIS). But the "central bank for central banks" would be an unnatural home for cooperation on other components of the capital markets, such as securities and insurance, or any integrated approach as just outlined. The International Monetary Fund could play a new role in this area.

But interrelationships among the different markets have an important impact on the world economy, one that must be considered in developing international regulation and supervision. Indeed, the interrelationships themselves would be a focal point of the more ambitious reform approach just described. Hence there is a strong case for creating a new International Capital Markets Supervisory Authority. Such an institution could build on the pioneering efforts of the European Union in this area and thus represent another instance of constructive regional-global interaction.

International Direct Investment and Multinational Enterprises

Offshore production by multinational enterprises exceeds $5 trillion annually, more than the annual level of world trade. The foreign assets of such companies are valued conservatively (i.e., at book value) at about $6 trillion. The Havana Charter included international direct investment (IDI) in the original plan for the ITO, yet IDI enjoys no comprehensive institutional support.

To be sure, aspects of IDI are addressed in a variety of quarters. The new TRIMs in the GATT cover some performance requirements levied on companies by host countries. The Multilateral Investment Guarantee Agency (MIGA) and International Center for the Settlement of Investment Disputes (ICSID) in the World Bank provide mechanisms for settling disputes in specific IDI cases. There are extensive provisions on IDI in some regional arrangements, such as the far-reaching chapter 11 of the NAFTA and the potential APEC Investment Code. The OECD's Code of Liberalization of Capital Movements and its Committee on International Investment and Multilateral Enterprise provide a framework for partial liberalization of IDI for a very important group of countries. There have also been efforts to develop global arrangements on IDI, primarily during the 1970s negotiations in the United Nations on a Code of Conduct for Transnational Enterprises.

Two sets of issues arise in this context. One is conflict between firms and governments, a problem of inherently increasing scope as business globalizes while governments necessarily retain their focus on national boundaries. Host countries—mainly but not solely in the developing world—often fear that multinationals will use their global networks to exploit local workers and consumers. Home countries fear that the firms will use these same networks to transfer jobs to low-wage areas and potential revenues to tax havens.

The second problem is conflict among governments over the activities of firms. Governments will sometimes clash over the types of corporate activities just cited, such as the international allocation of tax revenues and corporate pricing practices. In addition, host countries traditionally fear that powerful home countries (notably the United States) will use "their multinationals" as instruments of foreign policy. Home countries increasingly worry about export of jobs because of host-country actions to suppress wages and permit pollution. The widespread competition among host countries to attract footloose international investment through various incentives, and to maximize the contribution of such investment to national goals through explicit performance requirements, raises the specter of "investment wars"—both among host countries and between home and host countries—akin to the traditional trade wars that the GATT was designed to avoid.

New international institutional arrangements are thus needed to avoid both the potential economic costs of excessive governmental interference in the investment process and the intergovernmental conflicts that can arise from competition via and for multinational firms. Such rules would need to establish several key principles: transparency of the rules that govern IDI, right of establishment for foreign firms, national treatment of those firms once they have entered, and avoidance of incentives and performance requirements—both of which distort the international location of production and hence transfer economic benefits across political jurisdictions. Rights and obligations of both home and host countries, in such areas as tax policy (including transfer pricing) and competition policy (antitrust), should be spelled out. Obligations of the firms, particularly with respect to restrictive business practices, could be included as well. A dispute settlement mechanism would be needed to implement the rules.

Julius, who shares most of my substantive views, makes a strong case in her chapter in this volume that the new WTO could handle IDI effectively. But this listing of the relevant international investment issues suggests that many of them fall far outside the scope of the WTO and that no existing institution could easily absorb them. Nor would it makes sense to distribute the different issues among current organizations that might conceivably be able to handle some of them, because no cohesive approach to the overall phenomenon of IDI would then be possible. The world should create a new World Investment Organization (WIO).

The widespread receptivity to international direct investment that now exists throughout the world, including in most developing countries, suggests that the needed conceptual consensus may be emerging for the creation of a functional organization in this issue area. The continuing globalization of business, especially the proliferation of firms now "going international," suggests substantial demand for such an effort in the private sector. The structural shift of the United States toward becoming the world's largest host (as well as home) country for IDI provides a political opening to move in this direction that can and should be seized.

A Global Environmental Organization

A third issue area in need of a more effective institutional regime is international environmental management. Here there has been widespread attention to the problems, but the institutional evolution to date has been both inadequate and excessive: inadequate in that there are no universal, established principles to undergird a successful regime for responding to global and transborder environmental issues, and excessive in that a welter of overlapping responsibilities belong to myriad organizations that do not have the human or financial resources to accomplish their assignments.

The genius of the GATT and the IMF—the most successful international economic institutions of the era—is that each rested on a simple but widely agreed principle: the merits of avoiding, respectively, protectionism and monetary instability. Each then provided an international standard that could be used within each country to push national debates toward outcomes that would comply with, and in turn reinforce, the international regime itself. A self-sustaining process, despite the frequent lapses and setbacks along the way, was created and nurtured over decades.

Clearly, concerted international effort is needed to mount effective responses to several environmental problems. To date, that effort has resulted in an ad hoc process to deal with specific problems (e.g., the Montreal Protocol on CFCs). Such a process bears all the costs of any ad hoc approach, however. Moreover, it misses the opportunities both to build a network of cooperation over time and to exploit mutually reinforcing linkages among the different environmental topics (e.g., addressing global warming and preserving the ozone layer both require cutbacks in the emission of CFCs).

In his chapter in this volume, Esty proposes a Global Environmental Organization (GEO) based on internalizing the costs of pollution through such devices as the "polluter pays principle," which could function as the organizing idea for fostering environmental protection just as the GATT's antiprotectionism principle fostered trade liberalization. A GEO would permit consolidation of the panoply of existing environmental institutions and provide a focal point for effective action to replace the present diffused structure. It should be considered as part of the international economic architecture of the future.

Migration

A fourth issue area for possible new institutional treatment is migration. People flows have become huge: more than 100 million are now living outside their countries of citizenship. All continents are now substantially affected: previously nonimmigrant Asia, reluctantly immigrant Europe, and relatively immigrant America. Interactions with trade and financial flows are extensive and increasingly apparent, as with the West German decision to provide enormous subsidies to quell East German emigration and the US decision to negotiate NAFTA, partly in the hopes of slowing immigration from Mexico. Most national policies are extremely restrictive. Migration may be the most important—and potentially most explosive—North-South economic issue.

Perhaps most persuasively from a systemic standpoint, migration is the least institutionalized of all international economic flows. Despite the shortcomings in the regimes that address the other key factor of production, as noted above, capital has been a centerpiece of international discussion throughout the Bretton Woods era. By contrast, migration has seldom been placed on the agenda—let alone seriously addressed. As populations continue to grow rapidly in the poorer countries and age rapidly in the industrial countries, the economic pressures for migration are likely to increase further. The social consequences, absent a determined effort to come to grips with the issue at the international level, will become even more explosive than they are today.

The world thus needs to seriously consider creating an international migration regime. As noted in Withers's chapter in this volume, the agenda of such a regime would be far-reaching even if its goal were only to bring order and equity to the international flow of people rather than seeking (at least at the outset) to liberalize the very restrictive immigration laws most countries maintain: joint measures vis-à-vis illegal immigration, minimum rights for guest workers to prevent exploitation, migrant selection systems, return of overseas students, and many others. Linkages with trade, investment, and development policies—and hence other international institutions—would be essential because of the trade-offs among these issues in both sending and receiving countries.

But there is no consensus on an underlying theory in this issue area, let alone a set of operational principles ready to be implemented. Even though the current institutions are extremely weak, it will be particularly difficult to develop new arrangements, and a longer time may be needed to do so. But the broader issues inevitably relate to immediate questions of labor standards, discussed above in the trade policy context, and should be ignored no longer.

New Regional Arrangements

Regional and subregional economic arrangements have proliferated over the past decade. As noted above, they have generally represented positive forces for liberalization and cooperation. They have provided new sources of external pressure to help push domestic decision making in constructive directions in member countries. They have provided innovative answers to a number of trade questions that were later emulated in other regional groupings and generalized to the multilateral arena. Competition among them, and between them and the global system, has galvanized multilateral liberalization. Thus they have been instrumental in keeping the bicycle moving forward.

The most advanced and most effective regional organizations remain those created early in the Bretton Woods era and centered on Europe and the Atlantic (even where, as in the case of the OECD, they have added a few members from other parts of the world). The roster includes NATO and more recently the CSCE on the security side, the OEEC/OECD (and the associated Marshall Plan), and the European Union in all its incarnations and with all its associated entities.

The most striking regional gap is the absence of similar institutional architecture in Asia and the Pacific Rim. Regional trade dependence is as high among the APEC members (including both East Asia and North America) as it is in the European Union. The risk of economic conflict within the region, as indicated by the recent bilateral squabbles between the United States and Japan (and the United States and China), calls for major reconciliation efforts. The largest and fastest-growing national economies now border on the Pacific rather than on the Atlantic. Security concerns are at least as great in the Pacific region, where the United States fought three wars in the last half century, as they are in Europe. The need to solidify the links across the ocean, for both economic and security reasons, is as great in the Pacific as in the Atlantic.

From a global systemic standpoint, the creation of a second major "pole" in the Pacific would be a healthy development. Indeed, a major systemic risk is that the world could devolve into three competing blocs—centered on each of the three economic superpowers with a separate grouping in Asia coalescing around Japan and/or China—because we know from both game theory and history that three-player games are extremely unstable. By contrast, a bipolar economic system could replicate the stability of the bipolar security structure of the Cold War/Bretton Woods era without any of the associated risks of nuclear annihilation. An effective APEC could also play an important role in integrating China into the international economic order, and might assist as well in completing the integration of Japan.

Hence the rapid escalation of APEC into a meaningful community of Asia Pacific economies that liberalizes trade and investment among its members, and generalizes its benefits to nonmembers that are willing to reciprocate, could fill a major gap in the current institutional framework. It would provide a stronger foundation for continued progress in the region itself, a potential catalyst for global trade and investment liberalization, and a new source of systemic stability and leadership. Key European officials viewed the APEC summit in Seattle in late 1993 as a decisive element in bringing the Uruguay Round to a successful conclusion; this demonstrates that APEC already possesses the capacity for systemic leadership—a trait that is sorely needed, as emphasized throughout this analysis.

A Big Bang or Incrementalism?

There are two broad strategies for launching and pursuing the new international institutional arrangements recommended here. One is the "big bang" approach *a la* Bretton Woods itself: hold a "constitutional convention" to review the entirety of the international economic order and launch negotiations on each component thereof. This was the implicit goal of the advocates, mainly from the developing countries, of a New International Economic Order in the 1970s and perhaps of some who envisaged a "new international order" after the end of the Cold War. But such an approach would probably overload both the negotiating capabilities of governments and their strained budgets. Even more importantly, it might conjure up images of a "dash to world government" that would derail the entire process.

The alternative, which is much more feasible in the happy absence of cataclysmic events like those that triggered Bretton Woods, is an evolutionary process where new regimes are created *seriatim* as the perceived need for each passes a critical threshold. Keeping in mind that the first priority over the next few years is to reform the existing monetary regime and develop the new WTO in the trade field, a realistic target might be the creation of one new major international economic institution per decade during the first half of the next century. The cumulative outcome would then be about the same as for the Bretton Woods era, which wound up with five: the IMF, IBRD, GATT/WTO, OECD/IEA, and EC/EU. The five new entities of the early 21st century would be the International Capital Markets Supervisory Authority (ICMSA), the World Investment Organization (WIO), the Global Environmental Organization (GEO), a World Migration Organization (WMO), and APEC.

Some will object that such a pace would be far too leisurely. To be sure, a global financial crisis resulting from inadequate supervision and regulation could greatly accelerate the pace in that area (as earlier crises, such as the failure of Herstatt in 1974 and of Banco Ambrosiano and BCCI more recently, have triggered the international cooperation that does exist in this issue area). An acceleration of scientific evidence in support of global warming (or even three or four consecutive hot summers) could galvanize action on the environmental front. The projected timetable assumes a relatively calm world scenario within which national authorities nevertheless recognize the merits of expanding the international economic regime to additional issue areas. In practice, a more sporadic and thus uneven progression may be more likely.

Creative Destruction

Our review of the Bretton Woods era concluded that most of the existing major institutions have achieved substantial success, for part if not all of their lives to date. Even if some are in need of modification, they deserve to be preserved and improved. But several of the prior creations have failed to fulfill their functions effectively and should be abolished.

International institutions do occasionally die. A few have concluded their functions, some more successfully than others, and promptly disappeared: the European Payments Union of the 1950s and the "gold pool" of the 1960s are examples. Some have admitted failure and closed their doors, such as the East Africa Economic Community. Others have been subsumed into broader entities: the European Coal and Steel Community blended into the European Community and the Canada–United States Free Trade Agreement into NAFTA (which may itself, over time, expand into a Western Hemisphere Free Trade Area and/or Asia Pacific Economic Community).

There are a number of candidates for "creative destruction." As described above, the Bretton Woods institutions themselves need a new governing structure. A corollary of that reform is to abolish the Interim Committee and Development Committee, which have never fulfilled any substantive purpose and thus waste considerable time of busy ministers and officials.

The several international environmental organizations that have been created to date have proved largely ineffective. They should be merged into a single new Global Environmental Organization, as recommended above.

Another ineffective and costly international economic organization is the United Nations Conference on Trade and Development (UNCTAD). Its main justification is as a caucus for the developing nations on international trade and other economic issues, but it was ineffective even in that effort after the 1960s (when it played a role in achieving the Generalized System of Preferences). Moreover, differences *within* the erstwhile "Third World" are now at least as great as differences *between* "developing" and "industrial" countries—so the countries that UNCTAD sought to coalesce no longer constitute a recognizable bloc. UNCTAD should be absorbed into the WTO.

A number of other UN agencies, such as its regional economic commissions, are also candidates for termination. So are some of the other regional entities, whose functions could be rolled into the similar global institutions. The EBRD, for example, could easily be subsumed in the World Bank. My support for regionalism does not extend to regional institutions that duplicate the work of effective global institutions.

Whatever the logic, it will of course be difficult to close down institutions. Nor should termination be undertaken without an extensive analysis of the costs and benefits of doing so in each case, including an assessment of whether the functions assigned to each candidate for closure are being handled adequately elsewhere. A similar problem has existed within the United States with respect to closing military bases, even when their utility has clearly ended. The political solution in that case was to create an independent Defense Base Closure Commission, which looks carefully and objectively at each situation and whose recommendations for closure become effective unless explicitly overturned in their entirety by the president and Congress. There is no similar decision-making process at the international level, but the G-7, as part of its review of the international institutional structure launched at Naples in July 1994, could create an International Institutions Termination Commission—including members from outside as well as inside the G-7—to propose organizational closures with a presumption that its recommendations will be accepted unless a compelling case can be made to the contrary.

Systemic Management
Toward Collective Leadership

The overarching issue for systemic management over the years and decades ahead is how to replace the American leadership of the earlier Bretton Woods era. No other hegemon is available, nor is one desired. What is needed is collective leadership.

The operational question is the makeup of this leadership. At present, no such group exists. The G-7 is the closest approximation and has been a useful crisis manager. However, it has become increasingly ineffective and has paid little attention to systemic architecture (or even maintenance). Moreover, its main operational body, the finance ministers, has jurisdiction only over a limited subset of issues—excluding even monetary policy in countries with independent central banks, notably the United States and Germany, and excluding fiscal policy in the major case of the United States, with its crucial role for an independent Congress. The annual summits of the heads of government can address the entire range of topics and their interactions, and have done so on occasion, but they are not structured to provide the leadership that is needed.

A less well-known, but probably more effective, leadership committee exists in the trade area: the "Quad," comprising the United States, European Union, Japan, and Canada. It has steered the major multilateral negotiations, most recently in the Uruguay Round, and other central issues facing the global trading system. With a political push from the G-7 summits at critical junctures, as at Bonn in 1978 (for the Tokyo Round) and Tokyo in 1993 (for the Uruguay Round), it has done its job reasonably well.

There is no need to create a formal leadership structure for global economic management, nor could any such group acquire political legitimacy. What is required instead is an informal steering committee of the major economic powers, with concentric circles of decision making that radiate out from the steering committee, culminating in the formal (mainly global) institutions that this set of proposals seeks to strengthen and extend. The chief goal is to make the formal institutions work more effectively and coordinate better across their functional responsibilities through a process whereby the countries with the ability to steer the system accept and exercise responsibility for doing so. One key requirement, of course, will be for those key countries to work out formulas for burden sharing among themselves in the exercise of such systemic leadership.

The obvious candidates for initial membership in the informal steering committee are the three current economic superpowers: the European

Union, Japan, and the United States. To facilitate the process, "Europe" should have a single representative (as do Japan and the United States). In that sense, the present G-7 would be collapsed into a G-3.

High-level representatives of the G-3 should be in virtually constant contact to fulfill this role, as occurs among the member countries of the European Union today. They could build on the experience of the summit "sherpas" and that of the European Union. Issue-specific summits could be held when an issue required the leaders themselves to meet, in addition to the regular annual meetings. The group's decisions would be carried forward by corresponding groups at each of the functional institutions— for example, within the Executive Boards of the IMF and IBRD and within the new WTO.

The informal steering committee would have to operate with great flexibility in two senses. It would have to be alert to the need to broaden its standing membership as new countries, perhaps China in a decade or Russia in two, become sufficiently important to the world economy. And it would have to periodically add countries on specific issues (such as Mexico and Brazil on developing-country debt) or for temporary periods (e.g., Saudi Arabia during the energy crisis) to enable it to respond effectively to a changing agenda.

The system of concentric circles would work roughly as follows. The informal steering committee would be at the center of the process. It would attempt to guide the key functional issues, the interaction among them, and the interplay between them at regional and global levels. Each member would be responsible for close and continuing two-way consultations with the next ring, the next most important countries and those with which they had the closest relationships: the EU representative with all members of that group and its associates; the United States with NAFTA members and others in the Western Hemisphere (and some in the Middle East); and the United States and Japan together (or via an agreed division of labor) with Asia. The third ring would be the formal institutions at the regional and especially global levels, in which the final decisions would be made and implemented.

The European experience again points the way. Despite the effort to maintain appearances of equality among all members of the European Union, a three-tiered operation is clearly emerging—and may well become formalized over the next few years in the monetary area. The core group of half a dozen or so centers on Germany and France (and constitutes the likely membership of any initial move to Economic and Monetary Union). The second tier is the rest of the full members. The third tier is the growing number of associated states, possibly to include Eastern Europe and perhaps some parts of the former Soviet Union. They coordinate roughly in the manner proposed here for the global system.

Such an operation would of course generate charges of political illegitimacy and undemocratic foundation. This is a central reason for keeping the steering committee wholly informal. But the world has grudgingly gotten used to the G-7 and the management of most GATT issues by the Quad. Most countries recognize the need for effective leadership, whether by the United States in the earlier postwar period or by Germany (and especially the Bundesbank) in a uniting Europe. Moreover, a basic goal of the entire exercise is to force the G-3 countries to focus on their global responsibilities: to divert the United States from its periodic tendencies toward aggressive unilateralism, to pull Europe away from excessively regional preoccupation, and to overcome Japanese insularity by offering it a global role commensurate with its demonstrated economic capabilities.

The expansion of the role of the formal international institutions, which is a basic purpose of the entire exercise, is of course of major benefit to the smaller countries. It would be highly desirable for the informal steering committee to include a developing country or two that could represent the interests of that huge majority of the world's population. No single less developed country or even small group of LDCs, however, could purport to do so (or be accepted by the others). Perhaps the most practical possibility is to seek such representation through a respected individual, such as a national of such a country who might become head of one of the international economic institutions or otherwise possess the requisite stature. The proposed system of concentric circles seeks to most effectively mesh the central considerations of efficiency and legitimacy but should always be alert to possibilities to improve its performance on both counts.

Finally, a transitional problem of uncertain duration must be noted. It will take some time for the European Union to complete its economic integration and thus be able to participate in the proposed steering committee through a truly unified voice (and institutional locus). Likewise, Japan did not appear ready to assume a major international leadership role even before entering its present period of intense political instability. The United States has historically vacillated between dominance and withdrawal and has yet to demonstrate a capacity to participate effectively in a shared leadership consortium. Hence it may be impossible to create a fully functioning G-3 steering committee at this time.

Nevertheless, each component of the G-3 should resolve to move in this direction. A decision to do so could help speed the internal process in each (as the series of global trade rounds helped the EC Commission consolidate authority for trade policy in Brussels). The group may be able to operate effectively on some issues, such as trade, sooner than on others. As there is no effective alternative to collective leadership, every effort should be made to move toward that ultimate goal as rapidly as possible.

Meanwhile, the United States must shoulder its lingering systemic leadership responsibilities. Much as it may wish to throw off that legacy of the Cold War and its hegemonic history, and become "like any other country" in pursuing its narrower national objectives, it will remain the closest approximation to a systemic custodian until at least the European Union and Japan can begin to share such leadership to a significant extent. There are signs that the United States has in fact retained some systemic consciousness: its efforts were central in bringing the Uruguay Round to a successful conclusion (including those via the G-7 and APEC), it has sought to keep the bicycle of trade liberalization moving ahead with regional initiatives in both the Western Hemisphere and the Asia Pacific, and it has sought, at least episodically, to revitalize G-7 cooperation on macroeconomic and monetary issues. As suggested by our final lesson from the past, systemic stability cannot be taken for granted, and a modicum of American leadership will be essential until a stable collective management evolves.

Management of the Institutions

International economic institutions are created by national governments and must respond primarily to the desires of those governments. However, history has demonstrated that independent and effective leaders of international secretariats can play major roles in prodding governments to take more active and constructive positions. Eric Wyndham White and Peter Sutherland are early and recent cases in point at the GATT, as are Robert McNamara at the IBRD and Emile van Lennep at the OECD.

It is therefore time to start soliciting the best available people for the top management positions of these institutions rather than allocating them on the basis of archaic notions of geographical horse trading. Paul Volcker would be an ideal managing director of the IMF. Carlos Salinas de Gortari would be a superb director general of the new WTO. Toyoo Gyohten could effectively run the World Bank. The enhanced and expanded role for international economic institutions called for in these proposals deserves—indeed requires—tapping the widest possible pool of individual leaders to run them.

The staffs of most of the organizations, notably the international financial institutions and the GATT, are a major international asset. They provide critically useful advice to the poorer countries in Africa but also to such larger nations as China (as they did at the outset of its market reforms in the late 1970s) and some of the other transition economies. In addition to providing this international public good, the institutions represent an important training ground for future officials of numerous countries. Their staffs are drawn from all parts of the world, and similar objective considerations, rather than historical inertia or crude politics, should determine the composition of the institutions' top leadership as well.

The institutions also need to cooperate more systematically with each other. The heads of the three central organizations—the IMF, World Bank, and WTO—should meet quarterly to coordinate their programs. Their staffs should intersect much more effectively (including across 19th Street in Washington). The new institutions proposed here would need to collaborate closely with their more experienced precursors: the World Investment Organization and Global Environmental Organization would need to work closely with the World Trade Organization, for example, and the International Capital Markets Supervisory Authority with the International Monetary Fund and Bank for International Settlements. Such interorganizational coordination could complement and help with the work of the proposed informal steering committee of the major countries.

Mobilizing Public Support

Finally, both the international economic institutions themselves and the member countries need to become much more active—and much more effective—in explaining the roles and functions of the institutions to the publics of the member countries. The "democratic deficit" often cited with respect to the European Union is a far greater problem at the Bretton Woods institutions, with their traditions of closed proceedings and lack of transparency. Much of the attack on the institutions, such as the widespread characterization of the IMF as "an aid agency," is rooted in ignorance—but an ignorance that is partly due to the posture of the institutions themselves.

Some of the needed changes are substantive: the GATT should open its dispute settlement panels to testimony from nongovernmental experts, and private parties should be able to bring cases directly to it. The IMF and IBRD should release documents on their country programs and specific loans, or the member countries should do so on activities of the institutions that affect them directly—as new member Switzerland has become the first to do. But the institutions will also have to spend a good deal more time communicating their messages to the world if they are to build a solid base of support for their current operations, let alone the ambitious reforms proposed here.

Conclusion

This paper deliberately takes a long-term view of the international economic order. It seeks to identify the lessons of the last half century and apply them to the international economic scene, as the author foresees it, over the decades ahead.

The proposed program is essentially an effort to get the initially successful Bretton Woods system back on track and to extend it into new issue areas and modalities of operation that are called for by changes in circumstances. I conclude that, even in the face of sweeping changes in the economic and political underpinnings of the system, a great deal of continuity is both desirable and feasible. Moreover, most of the needed emendations can occur in an evolutionary manner within the intellectual and policy framework of the recent past. There is no need for a Bretton Woods II.

The proposed program rests on the prospect of an inexorable and highly desirable continued expansion of international economic interdependence. The chief implication for this paper is that governments will need to search continuously for new and better ways to manage that interdependence—to simultaneously maximize its benefits and limit its costs. The underlying philosophy is that economic globalization is clearly positive on balance, but that it brings attendant adjustment difficulties that must be accommodated both because of the human problems that result and, not unrelated, the political imperative of doing so if the advantages are to be retained. Modest evolutionary reforms of the institutional framework are thus essential.

Some will object that the proposed further expansion of international regimes and institutions would represent an unacceptable intrusion on national sovereignty. In truth, interdependence has already eroded *real* sovereignty to a considerable extent in virtually every country in the world—including the largest, the United States. Politicians nevertheless seek to retain a significant measure of *nominal* sovereignty, and the design of any new regimes must take that consideration fully into account. Wise policy, however, will recognize the merits of responding to the international realities through increasingly cooperative arrangements rather than confrontation (or efforts to reject the tide of interdependence itself).

Most fundamentally, leaders in the early part of the 21st century are likely to confront a deep tension between economic realities and political yearnings. Economic pressures will push both private firms and governments to operate on larger and larger scales, continuing and even accelerating globalization trends.

But political pressures will simultaneously be seeking to decentralize decision making in order to maximize responsibility at the local level. The European Union, here as elsewhere, is at the forefront of the debate and is attempting to resolve the dilemma through development of the principle of subsidiarity. As the world economy broadens and deepens the institutional framework through which it addresses the issues covered by this paper, its managers must fully recognize this political reality and the need to accommodate it through the decision-making structures they create and implement.

Comment

JOSEPH NYE

I am of two minds regarding this paper. I like Fred Bergsten's conclusions because my preferences, like his, are those of the liberal internationalist. By that, I mean someone who believes in markets, with institutions and rules to help coordinate them. But as an analyst, I am unconvinced. In earlier correspondence to me, Bergsten noted that his paper would be long on conclusions and short on analysis, and in the paper he says he is borrowing a good deal of the analysis from Kenen and Eichengreen. Consequently, he ends up borrowing their problems.

Bergsten aims to identify the lessons of the past and apply them toward creating an era as successful as he believes the Bretton Woods era to have been. But we have to look a bit more carefully at the past. I will not address all of the lessons laid out in the paper: for instance, I don't wish to get into arguments about the degree of fixity or fluctuation of exchange rates or how utopian that is. I will leave that to those who are wiser or braver than I am. But I will focus on the first two: one, that the Bretton Woods system worked, and two, that it worked through its impact on national economic policies. I have problems with both propositions.

It is true that the Bretton Woods system worked, but clearly not as designed. In fact, as designed, the Bretton Woods system worked for a brief, 12-year period—from 1958–70. Essentially, this system ended around 1970. Or in other words, the system after 1970 was very different from the original blueprint. Certainly, the architects' plans at the outset

Joseph Nye is assistant secretary of defense for international security affairs. He was formerly chairman of the National Intelligence Council.

were not fulfilled. From 1945 to 1958, when there was discrimination against the dollar, it was a good thing the system didn't work. Otherwise, domestic politics in the participating countries would have ruptured the system of liberal internationalism, as we saw when the British tried convertibility. After the United States shut the gold window, it may also have been a good thing that the system didn't work. Otherwise, shocks such as the 1973 oil crisis might have broken the system, again through domestic political responses.

Regardless of whether the Bretton Woods system was good or bad, the point is, it didn't work for long. One could take issue with this interpretation as being too narrow and say that its success lay precisely in the fact that it worked in spite of itself—because it was flexible and not bound to its initial definition, which wasn't taken all that seriously. Further, its chief success was that it let markets work and allowed for coordination at the margins in cases where the markets weren't functioning as well as they should.

Another argument, however, is that the whole idea of Bretton Woods' success is spurious. The fact that the world enjoyed a relatively stable 50 years of reasonable growth is correlation but not causation. There are several alternate explanations for this period of prosperity. As Max Corden said, the 1930s produced lessons and ideas that nations would have learned whether there were or were not Bretton Woods institutions. Second, the US side payments during the Cold War enhanced security by keeping countries that were central to the balance of power—Japan and those in Europe—from taking the wrong direction. A third alternative is technology. Given the technology of the information revolution, openness was inevitable—the forces of closedness couldn't compete.

None of these alternative explanations are really captured or encompassed in the Eichengreen-Kenen paper on which Fred rests his analysis. Therefore, we are left with a correlation rather than a clear causal statement of what it was that made the system work in the past, whatever the characteristics of that system.

The second proposition—that the system worked through its impact on national economic policies—is probably true, but it is both a truism and underdeveloped as a proposition. It is a truism in the sense that there were no supranational institutions and there was no external direction forcing governments to do certain things, and therefore the system had to work through national economic policies. But how did it work? How did these institutions make a difference? That is what is underdeveloped.

Earlier in the conference, I suggested that the institutions may have made a difference by imbedding certain ideas that then caused people to shift or reorient their expectations. It may also be that the institutions worked because they established effective rules, bureaucrats are rule-abiding creatures, and thus the burden of proof fell on those that didn't want to follow the rules. The institutions may also have been important as a focal point for aligning interest groups. Or, their major impact may have been the creation of transnational coalitions: perhaps little else happened at meetings of the OECD or IMF except that coalitions were forming of people with similar interests who then could return to their domestic political battles with allies from abroad.

I don't know which of these explanations, if any, is most valid. But the question needs more work. It cannot be completely addressed in this one paper, but I hope it will be part of the Institute's research agenda. There are several fine cases where one would have expected the system to break down; the researcher can then examine whether it in fact did break down and then ask whether institutions played any role. Bergsten does in fact raise some plausible cases on which the proposition can be tested. For instance, he suggests that if one looks at the rise in protectionism and whether the GATT made a difference, there is evidence that it did affect internal policymaking.

Similarly, he cites the European Community and the role of France in 1982–83. French Socialists, who sought a more closed system, were essentially constrained from achieving that closure, and EC rules and institutions probably played significant roles. The European Community, however, was not a Bretton Woods institution. In any case, more careful examination is needed before the first two propositions of the paper can be accepted.

Some might question my nitpicking about causation and say that I ought to turn directly to Bergsten's conclusions. My answer is that governments can spend considerable energy on prescriptions, such as those found here, only to discover later that they don't really matter. You may create the array of proposed organizations (WIO, GEO, and so on) scattered throughout the paper and still not have much effect on the future.

What about the future? I will limit myself to only 25 years out rather than 50 and ask, what are some of the ways in which we might view the future of the international economy? I have listed six, but as we should know and as I continually preach to those who prepare intelligence estimates, there is no one future. The future is indeterminate, and there are many different futures. What we try to do is understand the forces that will give us higher probabilities for one than another.

Let me name six alternative futures. One is the future that Henry S. Rowen paints: a world of enormous and spreading prosperity by 2020 driven by both technology and economic growth. It is a pretty picture of the future. Toward the other end of the spectrum, there is the prospect of ecocide. In this view, the externalities that accompany Rowen's rosy growth picture may overwhelm the earth's capacity to accommodate them and may eventually choke that growth.

A third future, described by Robert Kaplan in a recent issue of *The Atlantic Monthly*, is a bifurcation between a small, beleaguered core of rich states and a sea of failed states that surrounds and isolates the economy of the wealthy. Kaplan points to the experience of Africa, but this disintegration may be broader than one continent. We are living in an era that has seen the end of empires, which is often accompanied by disintegration. In examining 20 or 30 recent wars, it is apparent that they tend to flare up in the vacuums left by the end of the British and French empires or, most recently, the Russian or Soviet empire. This upheaval may continue for quite some time. This is a substantially different future from the others envisioned here, one in which international economic institutions such as the World Bank would have to rethink their role. How would the Bank relate to a world where a large proportion of the members are failed states?

The fourth type of future is a world of dysfunctional regionalism, which stands in contrast with Fred's functional regionalism. For Lester Thurow, it is a three-bloc world; for Jacques Attali, it is a two-bloc world—Atlantic versus Pacific. This is an implausible case, but not totally implausible.

Yet another vision could be a new cold war. A former colleague recently said he thought there was a 50 percent chance that Ukraine would collapse into internal civil war within three years because the economy is in such bad shape now. The Russians would almost certainly be drawn into it. And if they were, the West would certainly react strongly, perhaps by extending NATO to include Poland and others. The Russians, in turn, would react very badly. It would be the end of START I and START II, and it would probably propel more extremist groups to the fore of Russian politics—a situation similar in effect to that created by the fall of Czechoslovakia in 1948. Such a scenario would not be like the recent Cold War because Russia is not as strong as the Soviet Union was. But it could certainly be quite unpleasant, and it would reverberate through defense arrangements and economies throughout the world.

The sixth vision of the future is the one that Bergsten has portrayed for us: liberal international institutionalism that relies on markets and devices for coordination.

How do we judge among these futures? It seems to me that there are three major determinants. One is ideas, the second is technology, and the third is security. On technology, I think you could make a case that the information revolution in computers and telecommunications is what really broke the Soviet system. Central planning couldn't keep up with it—it was all thumbs and no fingers. One of my favorite statistics on this is that in 1985, when Mikhail Gorbachev came to power, the Soviet Union had 50,000 personal computers, and the United States had 30 million. After four years of Gorbachev, the Soviet Union had 200,000, and the Americans had 40 million.

Globalization also works to overcome barriers. But notice that the reduction of barriers has two effects: it opens up economies, but it can have a tremendous parochializing effect on society and in politics. When Marshall McLuhan discussed his concept of the global village, he should have said "global villages"—that is, in the plural—because when people feel threatened by the erosion of the barriers, they may become more parochial, not more cosmopolitan. Indeed, I would submit that the evidence in terms of ethnic conflicts in the world today is much more supportive of that hypothesis than the former. And that would coincide more closely with Kaplan's view of the future. Thus, technology's effect will differ by area and depend on how it is interpreted and used.

As for ideas, ideas and learning are tremendously important. But there can be good and bad ideas. On the good side, for example, consider the GEO or some other means of global environmental cooperation, which Daniel Esty talked about. One should look at Richard Cooper's work on the health questions in the 19th century and realize that all efforts to establish effective rules and institutions to deal with diseases on an international basis failed until there was an understanding of the underlying science—the causal agents behind those diseases. I submit the same thing is likely to happen in the environmental area. Until everybody believes what William Cline writes about global warming, for instance, I don't think there will be a GEO. Perhaps not even then. There is too much scientific uncertainty. Once the science is clearer, there may be a basis for creating the institution.

As for bad ideas, if you get a rise in neomercantilism and the forces of neomercantilism become strong enough, you could wind up with the type of world Attali envisions, in which separation is considered a good thing.

Let me turn finally to the question of security. It is probably the most important determinant and one that has not been handled sufficiently in this conference or in this paper. Security is a lot like oxygen. No one pays attention to it until it is taken away. Most people spend more time thinking about lunch or dinner. But when you are not breathing, you forget about lunch or dinner. Likewise, we have been living in a security-rich environment for quite some time that we have taken for granted, and Americans have been a major provider of that global security.

It is a commonplace view that the security system undergirds the world economy. The 19th-century liberal world economy relied heavily on the British position in the world in security terms. In that sense, we ought to be very careful about the relationship of security to our diagnoses of the international economy. The conventional wisdom, which has been put about by political scientists, picked up uncritically by economists, and repeated in the Eichengreen-Kenen paper, was that the world was hegemonic after World War II. The United States ruled the world; therefore it set up the global economy. But think carefully. The world was not hegemonic; it was bipolar. There was a thing called the Soviet Union, with enormous military force that balanced that of the United States. The United States was not a hegemon that could impose its will upon others. Witness the "loss" of China, Cuba, and many other things.

In my book, *Bound to Lead*, I argue that the world was not hegemonic and that this is a distinction of tremendous importance. The conventional wisdom has it that the United States created the world economy for basic economic reasons. I would argue that US side payments, which allowed discrimination against the dollar and opened US markets to Japanese goods, were made primarily for security reasons related to the Cold War. If there hadn't been a Soviet Union, America would likely have been much less "generous."

Now that there is no more Cold War, where does that leave us? I would argue that it leaves us with a world that is clearly no longer bipolar. Nor is it unipolar because the world doesn't revolve entirely around the United States. The post–Cold War structure of power is really like a three-dimensional chess game: There is a unipolar structure of power on the top board—the military board. The middle board, which is the economic board, is tripolar, with the United States, Japan, and Europe making up two-thirds of the world economy but rapidly becoming quadripolar if China becomes the world's second largest economy by the end of the century or shortly thereafter. In the bottom board—the board of transnational relations— there is no polarity at all. On these boards, one must play games of power that are not only horizontal across any given board but at the same time vertical.

For instance, when Japan considers the economy in East Asia and specifically whether it should support Malaysian Prime Minister Mahathir bin Mohamad's plan for an East Asian Economic Caucus, it must ask not only whether such a step is good for the Japanese economy but how the economic exclusion of Americans from Asia will affect America's security guarantee in the region. I would submit that one of the reasons Mahathir's proposals have not gone further is this relationship between the top board and the second board. The Japanese are thinking vertically as well as horizontally.

Further, I maintain that security is the key determinant shaping the future. Essentially, the United States plays the lead role in the security domain. But if the United States, bowing to public pressure or for some other reason, decided to withdraw from its position in maintaining the balance of power in East Asia between China and Japan, and if it withdrew from its role in maintaining the balance of power in Europe—that is, giving the French and Germans the reassurance that they can continue their integration without new threats from the East—you would have a very different world economy. Thus, one of the things we have talked least about may be the most important single variable determining the future of the world economy.

Comment

PAUL VOLCKER

I usually find Fred Bergsten's work provocative, direct, all-encompassing—and often wrong! This time, however, I fully agree with his conclusions about the need for "modest, evolutionary" reform of the system.

Like Joseph Nye, I was somewhat confused by the paper's reference to the Bretton Woods regime, which I tend to think of as having ended in 1971. But I gather that Bergsten is using the term more broadly to apply to international cooperation in economic management.

This raises an interesting question about the nature and implications of the break that occurred between 1971 and 1973. A break is certainly evident in terms of changes in world growth rates and other measures of economic performance. Before 1971, when the Bretton Woods system appeared to be in its heyday, we saw an increase in trade liberalization and freer movement of capital. Afterward, of course, the framework of negotiated fixed exchange rates within which the system had worked came to an end. But in terms of the extent of international cooperation or the impact of the system on domestic policy, I don't see much evidence of a decline since the early 1970s. Certainly, the United States sometimes modified its policies in accordance with international imperatives before 1971, but it has also done so since. I believe this would have happened under any system: domestic policymakers perceive threats to the international community that also undermine domestic objectives, and then they react. Thus, I question how much the Bretton Woods arrangements really achieved in terms of inducing change in domestic policies that would not have otherwise occurred, even though that was ostensibly one of the system's goals.

Paul Volcker is chairman of James D. Wolfensohn, Inc.

I would like to comment on the IMF and on the structure of the monetary system more broadly. I believe that the IMF has been effective in areas closely related to but outside what we think of as the monetary system proper. For instance, the IMF played a central role in the debt crisis of the 1980s, an issue outside its initial mandate. It is interesting to note that the IMF's Executive Board did not make an explicit decision to take on this role, nor was it the result of a debate by the total membership. Instead, individual leaders within the IMF, with the support of a few key countries, operated in a rather ad hoc way within formal IMF mechanisms to start adjustment programs on a country-by-country basis.

What should we learn from this experience? It may provide clues about how to structure a system for better management of exchange rates. I have a certain sympathy for the halfway house between fixity and floating that is represented in John Williamson and C. Randall Henning's paper on instituting target zones. There does seem to be some limited movement toward de facto target zones reflecting governments' desire to deal with excessive exchange rate volatility, which in turn feeds volatility in domestic financial markets and may relate to trends we have seen in economic activity generally. The authors craft an intelligent structure for management of this system, while attempting to answer every possible objection to its implementation. Nonetheless, I must conclude that the institutional devices they present are unworkable in practice in their full form. Perhaps 50 years from now, this will not be the case. But right now, their conception of a monetary system is too elaborate, too complicated, and depends too much on getting disparate countries to decide jointly on operational matters on which they are never likely to agree.

For making decisions on operational details, there must be smaller groups within the larger institutions that have the power to act. One case in point is the Organization for Economic Cooperation and Development, which was a source of frustration for me in the early 1970s. Despite intelligent staff and the availability of good analysis, the OECD could not arrive at operational decisions, partly because it could only act by the unanimous consent of the full membership. That suggested to me the need for the OECD to delegate some authority to an executive committee—in other words, a smaller, more cohesive group. But efforts to achieve that failed when one or more countries that would be excluded refused to agree to the procedure.

This speaks more broadly to the problems of operating any sizable international institution and to the IMF specifically. In this regard, I disagree with some specific suggestions in the Bergsten paper on the need for "creative destruction" of existing institutions. He suggests elimination of the Interim Committee and the Development Committee, which he says "have never fulfilled any substantive purpose and thus waste considerable time of busy ministers and officials." I take exception to that: I often think that the only lasting residue of my labors on the Committee of

Twenty is those two committees. They may not be perfect: they are too large and became too bureaucratic. But in concept there is a definite need for such smaller, more informal groups.

Bergsten suggests that "conversion of the G-7 into a formal independent institution would be a huge mistake." I think building on the G-7 itself is the mistake. It is the better candidate for creative destruction. The G-7 is not the institution on which to build a system that operates more effectively and has maximum influence on domestic policy. There is the question of its legitimacy; at this point, the G-7 seems to be mainly a cover for a G-3, with a couple of observers to keep it honest.

These suggestions do not get at the problem of how you structure a monetary system in which international management involves all interested parties and achieves results. You can't really have both, but, as I noted before, you can construct smaller, less formal groups in existing institutions that are fairly representative, comprise people with major responsibility for policy in their own governments, and thus can maximize the chances of affecting domestic policies. Therefore, I think no one should too casually suggest doing away with the Interim Committee or the Development Committee.

Another major theme of this paper is trade policy and regionalism. I see a limitation to the bicycle theory. Those who ride bicycles search out the smoothest roads because the pumping is easier there. Likewise, trade negotiations have put tremendous emphasis on reducing tariffs because this is the easiest course. However, we have reached a stage in which little more mileage can be achieved in tariff reduction. We may even have gone too far in reducing tariffs: it seems ridiculous that passage of the Uruguay Round legislation could be held up because Congress can't find a way to replace $3 billion in lost revenue from tariffs that weren't doing any real harm anyway—especially when compared with the effects of other threats to the international order.

Clearly, the new challenges are in the area of nontariff barriers. Bergsten has correctly identified some of these more pressing threats: subsidies, investment, the environment, and labor standards. Such issues put the bicycle on very rough terrain. Nevertheless, they deserve much higher priority than another round of cutting already-low tariffs.

I also very much agree with the general thrust of Bergsten's view of regionalism: it is possible to make more progress in some of these new areas by addressing them regionally first and then trying to expand to an international consensus. I say this despite my long-standing concerns over the dangers of the discriminatory aspects of regional agreements—something the US Treasury has worried about since the early days of the European Common Market.

Nor was I initially a great enthusiast for NAFTA, which I did not see as the highest US priority. Certainly, I am glad it was negotiated and put in place, but I feared at the outset that encouraging regionalism also risked encouraging the United States to turn inward. So far, it appears that I may have overestimated that threat. Rather than turning the United States inward, NAFTA has been a device for reduced barriers. Now, I strongly believe it is desirable to have a more multilateral arena—but something short of a global forum—to deal with the intense bilateral disagreements the United States has with Japan and China.

Nevertheless, I also believe that the danger of excessive emphasis on regional initiatives remains. So while I support the idea of a Pacific community generally and the APEC in particular as an exemplar for how to proceed into the new issue areas, I also believe that defending against inward-looking regionalism ought to remain high on the world's agenda. I don't think it is very probable that APEC will achieve the goal of free trade with China and Japan in the near term, and, in any case, this is the wrong emphasis. Such an approach risks fostering suspicions, unjustified though they may be, of an inward orientation.

I also want to comment on financial regulation, an area where globalism is most pronounced, as is evident in the recent activities of the financial markets, and where the shortcomings of purely national approaches have become very pronounced. The United States, and other countries as well, have implicitly premised their regulation of the financial system on the notion that it was sufficient to provide a safety net for banks, and in protecting the stability of the banking system, provide protection for the overall stability of the financial system. Failures of securities houses and insurance companies were not seen as potentially destabilizing to the economic system as a whole—at least not nearly to the same extent as banks. Therefore, the Securities and Exchange Commission was given responsibility for protecting consumers and policing securities fraud, and no other federal agency saw the need to be involved in regulating these industries from a safety and soundness standpoint.

This assumption is being challenged, particularly in the United States. Regulating banks alone is no longer enough; in no place is this more apparent than the derivatives market.

So what do we do about it? The situation is inherently an international one that goes beyond the traditional bounds of financial regulation. I suspect that we must address this issue on an international scale. Yet no single institution has a mandate to take it on. Do we create one? Or do we work through existing institutions?

My judgment is that it would be most practical to work with what is already there: cooperative arrangements among national systems for regulating banks, which are fairly well-developed, and systems for regulating securities firms, which are embryonic. You begin by bringing together the groups responsible for dealing with these areas nationally, so they can discuss how the problems might be addressed internationally. You build intellectual approaches to the design of an appropriate system, and this takes time. Nothing dramatic is likely to be accomplished in this area in the next few years.

Should there be one regulator for banks and other financial institutions in the United States, or a single coordination body internationally? We undoubtedly will arrive at something not quite so tidy. In any case, the potential is very real for one all-encompassing regulator to become too intrusive, too bureaucratic, and too suffocating for market development. In fact, a system with multiple regulators, and therefore a little competition among them, is probably a good idea.

Finally, I agree that leadership is a core issue for the international system. It is true, as Bergsten concludes, that the United States is for now the only viable candidate, even though it is not as powerful as it was during the early Bretton Woods period. Yet it is still in a position to take the initiative, and if doesn't do so, it is unlikely any of the difficult issues will be adequately addressed.

The world should move gradually toward a more shared basis for leadership. If we put in place a more effective system of executive committees for the international institutions, this can happen and, I believe, has begun to happen. In the meantime, the United States, even if it cannot make all the decisions, still has the initiative.

Comment

HORST SCHULMANN

A recent review of Hamish MacRae's *The World in 2020* concludes that history is full of unexpected events and that forecasts remain vulnerable to the unpredictable. There is little to add to this. Even the need for the Marshall Plan was not anticipated at Bretton Woods, let alone the problems created by the explosion of the world population in the 50 years that followed and by the specter of ecological disaster.

Fred Bergsten's paper, of course, is not so much about prediction as it is a prescription (with a dose of proscription). But prescription, too, needs a framework; it requires some assumptions about what the world is going to look like—a scenario, in short.

Henry Kissinger's new book *Diplomacy* may provide such a scenario. Its first and last chapters deal with the new world order, and they raise some awkward questions for the future of international economic relations. Number one is the contention that never before have we tried to develop an international system with so many powerful players. Kissinger's list starts with the usual three suspects—America, Europe, and Japan—and adds China and Russia as sort of a minimum. Next, the author points out that these players do not share many values. In turn, this means that it may take quite some time for the new international system to develop.

Kissinger also points out that this will be the first time in history that the international system will operate under conditions of instantaneous communications. Those of us on the financial side know all too well what that implies. I do not venture to predict what a world will look like where a

---

Horst Schulmann is president of the Landeszentral Bank in Hesse.

diplomatist will have to react to the unexpected outcome of a national election in a major country with the speed by which a foreign exchange dealer has to react to news of an unexpected change in the unemployment rate in a key-currency country. With instantaneous communications, policymaking is becoming more and more precarious with no limits in sight.

This future world that Henry Kissinger depicts is a far cry from the postwar scenario. There were two superpowers, there was a Western alliance that shared important values, and there were three "worlds." The Third World had, of course, already lost much of its homogeneity before the collapse of the Second World, but now, with only one world left, strife seems to have become the order of the day.

Maybe it was particularly easy for us Germans. The Berlin Wall made life simple: capitalists here communists there. But it of course implied much more: the threat of nuclear annihilation. Whatever differences the West had in the economic and financial sphere were subordinated to its single most important common objective: the containment of Soviet imperialism and the deterrence of nuclear war. And while there was no guarantee that subordinating policy differences in economics and finance would be mutually beneficial, the outcome has been extremely positive. It has certainly proved that it is possible to play plus-sum games over an extended period.

The 19th century nation-state still is the basic organizing principle of our international order. But as more and more problems extend beyond national borders and require common solutions, the nation-state has tended to become too small and is no longer an optimal political decision unit. Nonetheless, the nation-state will still be with us 50 years from now. It is wishful thinking that it will disappear more or less automatically as a result of economic or technological imperatives. Politics is much less logical than economists are inclined to assume. The existence of financial institutions that operate worldwide around the clock—that is, the emergence of a truly global financial market—certainly poses a challenge to the traditional nation-state but does not render it obsolete. It would make forecasting much easier if in the final analysis people's economic interest counted most. After all, that is not what people in Bosnia or Rwanda are dying for.

The real question is how much progress we will make in moving the nation-state toward transnationalism. Let me explain what I have in mind. In Europe, we have started to realize that many of our problems can only be solved at the next higher political level: the supranational level. More often than not, that means the European level. This raises the question of whether the appropriate political forum is a federation or a confederation—that is, whether we are seeking the American solution or something less binding. That has been the core of a good deal of the post-Maastricht discussion.

At any rate, we are approaching the limits of what can be accomplished through intergovernmentalism—by national governments sitting down together to resolve cross-border problems in a multilateral or supranational context. The principal reason for this is that the more complex the problems, the more questionable becomes the governments' extraterritorial legitimacy. But while all economics may become more and more international, all politics is likely to remain local.

My plan is as follows. Since the purpose of this conference is to commemorate the Washington-based Bretton Woods institutions, I will focus on their problems and neglect trade questions and all those new areas of international cooperation for which Fred Bergsten wants to create new institutions. I will conclude with a few remarks on macroeconomic policy cooperation in general.

Conservatives like to point out that Washington is full of institutions that have outlived their usefulness. Of course, that could be said of most other capitals as well. As the world changes, so does the rationale for a specific institution. Thus, if the institution is to survive, it must continually find a new purpose. To start with a general proposition: as private-sector investment and finance become the rule in middle-income countries, the need for lending by international financial institutions such as the IMF and the World Bank becomes more limited.

The need for adaptation has probably been more pronounced for the IMF than for the World Bank. That is partly a function of the breakdown of the Bretton Woods exchange rate system, which moved the world from asset settlement to liability management. The IMF's search for a new mission, some would claim, has been less than a success story. Indeed, it has become more difficult to argue that the IMF is still a monetary institution. For starters, the IMF should therefore change its policy on arrears to other lenders, official and private, and make their clearance again a condition of the IMF's own support. It would also help if the IMF were to relinquish its historical focus on current account convertibility and make capital account convertibility the centerpiece of its analyses and policies. As a practical matter, the bias in favor of capital controls needs to be removed from the IMF Articles of Agreement, which permit member states to exercise such controls.

It has become more difficult to argue that we need the IMF. Twenty years ago, everybody would have agreed that we should keep the IMF in place for the day when we would return to Bretton Woods. But since then, support for a worldwide fixed exchange rate system has shrunk, and the benefits of—and indeed the need for—a safety valve in the form of flexible exchange rates among the main trading blocs are now widely recognized. Consequently, I have little use for either formal or informal target zones. Or as Karl Otto Pöhl has put it recently: "Floating rates anchor an alliance."

In theory, an institution such as the IMF might have just as important a role to play in a flexible exchange rate system, but in practice much of the magic disappeared after 1973. This could change if several currency blocs were to develop in addition to the EMS. Conceivably, the IMF could be charged with overseeing the relations between the regional currency blocs, a role similar to the WTO's with regard to regional trading blocs. A set of common, universal rules certainly would help to keep regionalism in check.

But how do we measure the present importance of an institution such as the IMF? Is it the number of member countries, or at least the number of member countries in which it is active? On both scores, the IMF has done very well indeed in the past 50 years. It is now almost a universal institution, and according to a recent tally, about 70 (out of 178) member countries either have a program with the IMF or are negotiating one. It is debatable whether this represents progress. The fact that the institution is active in so many countries is indicative of the bad economic policies pursued in these countries. Accordingly, the 70/178 ratio would represent an international misery index and definitely not a welfare index.

The argument that the IMF has lost its monetary character and become a development agency certainly seems less far-fetched than it would have 10 or 20 years ago. This is evident in the plethora of facilities that have been created over the years: the Enhanced Structural Adjustment Facility (ESAF), Extended Fund Facility (EFF), Systemic Transformation Facility (STF), and Compensatory and Contingency Financing Facility (CCFF), to name but a few. Today, both the IMF and the World Bank group offer balance of payments support, both grant concessional assistance through ESAF and IDA, and both deal with macroeconomic policies as well as with sectoral policies. Is the IMF exempt from the principle of comparative advantage?

At any rate, the institution of 1994 is very different from the blueprint of 1944. When countries have IMF programs for 10 or 20 years in a row, little is left of the revolving nature of the IMF, and sooner or later this is bound to have an impact on the quality of the assets of those central banks on whose currencies the IMF has drawn. These concerns are reinforced by the emphasis the institution appears to be giving to a fresh allocation of Special Drawing Rights (SDRs) on the grounds of distributional equity, thereby contributing inadvertently to the impression that it may be less interested in strong multilateral surveillance.

I, for one, would be content to maintain the IMF as a fleet in drydock— perhaps to serve eventually as the nucleus of a future world central bank. Foreign exchange dealers need not worry about their livelihood. A world central bank is, at best, a project for the second half of the 21st century. But in the meantime the IMF should shed all functions that are not pertinent to its future mission. In the first instance, this means that the IMF should stop competing with the World Bank in general and IDA in particular. The longer the current situation lasts, the stronger the case becomes for a merger of the two institutions. I first made that case around 1980. Needless to say, I received a lot of flak at that time; these days, I encounter much less opposition.

If a committee were set up to propose a new mission for the IMF, it might suggest a role in maintaining the safety and soundness of the international financial system. But there is no straightforward measure of "safety and soundness." While some would argue that the system has become less vulnerable as a result of better international coordination and cooperation, others wonder whether it has not become more accident-prone as a result of the accelerating global integration of national financial markets and the advent of new financial products such as the second generation of derivatives.

Again, the prescriptive answer is simpler than the predictive answer. On the prescriptive side, it seems clear that we need better regulation—certainly more internationally oriented regulation. One practical way to proceed is to extend the idea of a level playing field that now determines the minimum capital requirements of commercial banks to other aspects of, and players in, the international financial system. Investment banks, insurance companies, and financial conglomerates are clearly candidates in this respect.

A case is sometimes made for regulatory competition—so-called regulatory arbitrage—as an alternative to international standardization. This reflects a serious misunderstanding of the role of financial institutions. Banks in particular are too central to the functioning of the economy to be treated like other businesses. Regulatory loopholes, wherever they exist, will be exploited, and the result is likely to be greater financial instability. Therefore, regulatory laxity is definitely not the way forward.

A related area is taxation. Here, too, a certain degree of uniformity is desirable. The taxation of capital income is a particularly urgent case for action. Since the national control of international capital movements has become virtually impossible, differences in national taxation of financial capital lead to systematic tax avoidance. This is not only a matter of concern for the tax collector. If one factor of production is not taxed while labor income is, this raises questions of equity—questions that are at the heart of a democratic society. Therefore, convergence of taxation across borders is a matter that goes well beyond international finance.

In both cases—the avoidance of regulation and the avoidance of taxation—governments should address collectively the standards and tax rates around which harmonization should take place. In the past, these matters have been dealt with predominantly in the BIS, the European Union, and the OECD. Taking a longer-term view, these problems are unlikely to remain confined to today's high-income countries. Whether this implies that the IMF would be a good place to deal with them is a different matter. It would certainly lead the IMF further away from its original mandate as a monetary institution.

The other day, Jacques de Larosière said that the EBRD last year faced three urgent problems: a problem of image and credibility, a lack of organization and efficiency, and insufficient clarity in the definition of its objectives and missions. Reading this, one wonders what he would have to say about the IBRD.

The various parts of the World Bank group are faced with different problems. Given its private-sector focus, the IFC is in pretty good shape; indeed, it would be in an even stronger position if its shareholders had provided it with more capital.

The IBRD and IDA have a common problem as development institutions, a problem that goes beyond the shortcomings outlined in the famous Wapenhans report (1993): that of expectations raised too high. The problem is most obvious in sub-Saharan Africa, as was revealed in the World Bank's policy research report, *Adjustment in Africa*. The upshot of that report, as I read it, is that it will take 40 years for the region to regain the level of per capita income of the mid-1970s. It seems to me that in this field, too, we need to become more modest and downsize our expectations about the quick returns that can be gained from an injection of Western know-how and capital. Incidentally, several of the so-called countries in transition (e.g., in the southern belt of the former Soviet Union) and Arab countries such as Algeria that have yet to move from statism to capitalism may share many of the problems of sub-Saharan Africa.

IDA's other problem is the chronic shortage of funds, but that is unlikely to change in a world where domestic priorities dominate the political agenda and where IDA has to compete with ESAF and other soft loan windows. IBRD's problem as a financial institution is quite different: it is running out of creditworthy borrowers. With private capital again flowing to Latin America, fewer middle-income countries than ever are dependent on official money. IBRD, we should remember, was set up as an intermediary in case of market failure. Thus, the rationale for IBRD lending becomes weaker when the market is doing the job it is supposed to do and vice versa. But when we had the biggest market failure in the postwar period—the 1980s debt problem of the middle-income countries—the IBRD was not allowed to play a decisive role by making use, for example, of its cofinancing potential.

The question today is whether the IBRD should compete with the private sector and the regional development banks for investment opportunities, say in Latin America and Southeast Asia, and whether it should lend to countries in transition whose creditworthiness is limited. There is no straightforward answer, but as more and more of world investment takes place in the private sector, the scope for an institution with a mandate to support public-sector investment is bound to shrink *pari passu*—unless the mandate changes.

For the time being, IBRD lending to potential "tigers," such as Vietnam, that have not yet gained market access makes sense. The international financial community also has to face the fact that somebody will have to look after the countries in transition, whether or not they are creditworthy. The systemic question is whether special cases are better dealt with in a universal institution such as the IMF or the IBRD or in a regional agency such as the EBRD. My impression is that the latter type of institution may be better placed to deal with special cases. There is less risk of setting an unwarranted precedent, and a universal institution may have greater difficulty in obtaining finance from public sources if it is perceived to favor certain clients. Since altruism will continue to be in short supply, regionalism may be a better way to raise funds for special as well as not-so-special cases.

I do not have much to say about the traditional areas of international policy coordination—the stuff that used to make headlines in the 1970s, when the first economic summits took place. At that time, the objective was clear: prevent a repetition of the competitive devaluations and trade wars of the 1930s. We were also much more confident about our ability to make things happen than we are today. Finally, we had at least one and at times two common enemies throughout most of the 1970s and early 1980s: the communists and the OPEC cartel.

The special factors that were the basis of international economic policy coordination in the 1970s cannot be reproduced at will. For one, it now may take more than seven to tango. But more important, the history of the past 20 years is that there are many more pitfalls than we ever envisaged. As economists, we certainly have reason to be more modest regarding our ability to manage our own economies, to say nothing of the world economy. In a technical sense, our modeling capacity is not keeping up with the growing complexity of the real world. Whenever a crisis occurs, a surprising array of factors have had a bearing on its origin.

The biggest obstacle to international macroeconomic policy coordination remains fiscal policy, partly because we are dealing with democracies and their internal inconsistencies. Most governments that promised they would do away with their deficits have yet to deliver. Nor is it likely they ever will as long as they do not face a hard budget constraint.

A related word of warning has to do with financial markets. Only when the weather gets stormy do economic policymakers appear willing, albeit reluctantly, to accept that the markets have something to tell them. By that time, it is usually too late to bring about the kind of gradualist policy changes that economists prefer. The corollary is that the scope for international economic and financial cooperation is circumscribed if policymakers are only willing to lock the barn door after the horse has been stolen.

What is the way forward? The expanded number of nation-states has also hampered traditional international economic and financial cooperation. Forty-four nations were represented at the Bretton Woods conference. Today, IMF membership totals 178. Since 9 November 1989, over two dozen states have been created, mostly as a result of the breakup of the Soviet Union. Political geographers predict that in Africa alone there will be 180 states some time during the 21st century. I think it unlikely that the world will be more peaceful for having more states and more people. I also do not believe that atomization of the world economy will make it more manageable. Small is not always beautiful.

Internationalism does not blossom without altruism, and as economic reality has finally caught up with the free-spending governments and parliaments of the high-income countries, altruism tends to be in short supply. A good example is the recent devaluation of the CFA franc, which a recent issue of *Frankfurter Allgemeine* described under the headline: "Africa becomes too expensive for France." And because Russia became too expensive for just about everybody, the IMF was pressured to provide funds without a reasonable basis. But since the supply of "other people's money" is limited, this is not a viable solution. What we need in the world economy is a group of countries that are willing to lead and to offer side payments (as Eichengreen and Kenen refer to them) that are conducive to international cooperation. As things stand, there are no volunteers. This does not bode well for internationalism.

We may also have to rethink our basic approach to international economic and financial cooperation. The European example may be instructive in this respect. The Europe of 12 may well become a Europe of 16 as early as 1 January 1995, but enlargement of the Union will continue to be on the agenda beyond the turn of the century. Enlargement will increase the need for differentiation among member states. In the monetary field, for example, we are discussing the concept of concentric circles, with the degree of integration diminishing as we move from the core to the periphery of the Union. In other words, we are discussing multiple tiers of sovereignty. That may also be the model for global economic and financial management: a world economy at variable speed and in different tracks— a sort of à la carte approach to international cooperation.

I conclude that this is not a good time for developing a new, grand strategy for international economic and financial cooperation. The vast common denominator that emerged after 1945 no longer exists. This may be a good time, however, to focus on other areas: on the deficiencies in our own societies, on how to create a level playing field in those areas where doing so has a positive impact on the international welfare function, and on putting in place safety valves for those situations that are unpredictable but are certain to arise. While this may be less optimistic than what Bergsten proposes and may appear to be a minimalist proposal for managing the world economy in the next half century, it may be the only realistic one.

References

Wapenhans, Willi. 1993. *Efficiency and Effectiveness: Is the World Bank Group Prepared for the Task Ahead?* Internal Working Paper. Washington: World Bank.

10

Summing Up and Looking Ahead

PETER B. KENEN

Themes and Highlights

In the paper with which this book begins, Barry Eichengreen and I draw a sharp distinction between the roles of the organizations established at the end of the Second World War—the International Monetary Fund, the World Bank, and the General Agreement on Tariffs and Trade—and the roles of the rules and principles imbedded in their constitutions. When we try to appraise economic performance during the postwar period and to assess the contribution of international cooperation, we attach greater importance to those principles than to the activities of the organizations themselves. Some of the main achievements, we argue, reflected ad hoc efforts to apply and extend those principles, often initiated by the United States, rather than the efforts of the organizations. John Jackson expressed the same thought with great felicity when he presented his paper to the conference from which this book derives. International economic relations, he said, "have been guided but not governed" by the basic principles imbedded in the constitutions of the Bretton Woods organizations.

Eichengreen and I suggest, however, that the vitality of those principles must be ascribed in part to very special circumstances. The advent of the Cold War paralyzed the United Nations but not the Bretton Woods organizations. It sustained and gave new purpose to the Western democracies that had fought the Second World War together and led them to bring Germany and Japan into economic partnership with them. After the First World War, the victors sought revenge. After the Second World War, they offered rehabilitation. They were motivated partly by their belief that the attempt to punish Germany after the First World War had been a major cause of the Second World War. But it was the Cold War, above all, and the belief that free markets protect free people that caused the United States to promote and abide by the principles of the Bretton Woods organizations.

The tragic history of the interwar period made another contribution to the vitality of those principles. Those who had fought in the Second World War were promised by their governments that they would not have to fight for jobs after the war was over. Convinced that Keynesian policies would work, although they had not yet been tested widely, governments undertook to foster full employment and replace class conflict with social cohesion. Furthermore, the legacy of the war itself and of the interwar period helped them to honor that pledge. Trade and capital flows were relatively small and heavily restricted, and the rules adopted at Bretton Woods, although they attached much importance to exchange rate stability and preventing predatory devaluations, did not preclude exchange rate changes if the need to maintain "external" balance threatened to interfere with the pursuit of "internal" balance.

But Eichengreen and I go on to make a familiar point: the success of the postwar system began to threaten its survival. Economic recovery in Europe and Japan diminished the will and ability of the United States to make "side payments" of the sort it had made in the early postwar years to purchase support for its initiatives and its vision of the system. By exposing key sectors and regions to import competition, the liberalization of international trade strengthened the hand of its domestic opponents. The revival of capital movements ossified the exchange rate regime by forcing governments to defend existing exchange rates tenaciously, and the exchange rate regime broke completely down halfway through the postwar period. Tensions arising from competition among the developed countries, as they became more alike in structure and influence, were compounded by tensions arising from conflict between developed and developing countries. Movements of goods, capital, and enterprise unified the international economy, but movements of ideas, images, and people divided the international community by raising aspirations and dramatizing differences. Finally, the end of the Cold War deprived the countries at the center of the system of the common purpose under which they had cooperated for so many years while posing political and economic problems that made new claims on their resources.

The papers in this book call attention to the many incongruities arising from the history of the last half century. The principles adopted at Bretton Woods continue to guide—if not govern—trade and financial policies, and they are endorsed by almost every government. Yet their scope and the organizations designed to conserve and promote them appear increasingly inadequate. Consider four such incongruities:

- The International Monetary Fund was established to regulate the exchange-rate and financial policies of the key-currency countries. Yet it has no influence over them today.

- The rules of the trading system, long housed in makeshift quarters, have been given a permanent home in the World Trade Organization, with better ways to settle trade policy disputes, and the rules are being applied to agriculture and services. Yet trade itself has been transformed during the last 50 years, with much of it conducted today within multinational firms, and disputes about familiar trade policy issues are being overshadowed by disputes about the impact of domestic policies and private-sector practices on international trade and investment.

- The World Bank was established to intermediate between private lenders in developed countries and public borrowers in developing countries. Yet the privatization of the development process has challenged the rationale for that sort of intermediation.

- With the collapse of the centrally planned economies and remarkable changes in the doctrines and policies of developing countries, the principles adopted at Bretton Woods apply to almost every country, so that we can speak today about a single world economy. On every continent, however, governments are building regional arrangements. The United States was the advocate of multilateralism for most of the postwar period, but it may cease to play that role.

Where then do we go from here?

The Case for Conserving Institutions

Robert Keohane gives us part of the answer in his thoughtful comment on the Eichengreen-Kenen paper: rely where we can on the organizations built up in the postwar period, because it would be costly to change them dramatically and very expensive to replace them entirely. He writes, "The institutions' rules shape expectations, exemplify commitments that are costly to break, reduce transactions costs of making further agreements, and help governments monitor their partners' actions." But Keohane goes on to warn that the future effectiveness of those institutions will depend on their members' ability to sustain domestic political support for the principles they represent and therefore the ability of governments to cope with the social ramifications of internationalization. "Not only does effective management of the world economy depend on domestic politics; domestic politics is deeply affected by changes in international markets," he concludes.

This book does not deal extensively with the domestic challenges posed by internationalization, but many of the papers do respond to Keohane's call for conserving and improving the Bretton Woods organizations rather than replacing or changing them drastically. A good case can be made for establishing a Global Environmental Organization, as Daniel C. Esty argues, but the case is nearly unique. John Williamson and C. Randall Henning would use the IMF to house new rules and arrangements aimed at achieving exchange rate stability; Tommaso Padoa-Schioppa and Fabrizio Saccomanni would use the Bank for International Settlements to pursue similar objectives informally. Nicolás Ardito-Barletta concludes that the traditions and methodologies of the World Bank and of the regional development banks have "much value, resilience, and flexibility" and that those organizations "should continue evolving as development requirements evolve and need not be subjected to major surgery." De-Anne Julius urges the articulation of new rules to promote direct investment, but she would use the WTO, not a new organization, to resolve disputes arising from those rules.

C. Fred Bergsten, by contrast, believes that we should expect the birth of three new organizations during the next half century, in addition to the GEO proposed by Esty: one to supervise international capital markets, a task that Padoa-Schioppa and Saccomanni would lodge with the BIS; one to deal with issues arising from international investment, a task that Julius would assign to the WTO; and one to deal with migration, a task that Glenn Withers would divide among several existing agencies, including the UN High Commissioner for Refugees and regional bodies such as Asia Pacific Economic Cooperation (APEC) forum. Bergsten believes that the new rules and principles required to address new issues will need new organizations to maintain and apply them. He also forecasts a growing role for APEC, even though he also reminds us that functionally specific organizations appear to have been more effective than those that have tried to deal with a multiplicity of issues.

Although the papers in this book do not call for a drastic revamping of the existing organizations, one paper calls for a major change in the priorities of the international community. Mahbub ul Haq is gravely concerned about the small flow of financial resources to the developing countries. In recent years, he notes, interest and amortization payments to the World Bank and its affiliates have exceeded the flow of new loans to the developing countries. Large amounts of private capital have been invested in developing countries, but most of it has flowed to a small number of relatively prosperous countries in Latin America and East Asia. He also charges that the IMF and World Bank have been too tolerant of policies that squeeze the poorer and weaker segments of society. The Fund and Bank should insist on the slashing of subsidies to the rich before subsidies to the poor are touched, and they should deal as frankly with land reform and other sensitive issues as they do with distorted prices. The two institutions, he says, are often criticized for interfering excessively in the affairs of developing countries. In fact, "they interfere too little or certainly not enough in the key areas of policy."

This brief concluding essay cannot summarize or comment on each paper in the book, nor would that be appropriate. Each paper deserves to be read very carefully. So do the discussants' comments. But I will say something about the four incongruities listed earlier and the papers that address them.

The IMF and the Monetary System

Reviewing recent monetary history, Fred Bergsten detects what he calls a "revealed preference" for a more orderly exchange rate regime. We already have de facto target zones for the Group of Seven (G-7) currencies, he says, and the European Monetary System came to resemble a target zone regime with the widening of the EMS margins in 1993. Together with Williamson and Henning, however, Bergsten believes that the present arrangements are unsatisfactory: some of the zones are too wide to preclude the emergence of harmful misalignments, the boundaries of the zones are not sufficiently credible, there are no reliable rules for shifting the zones, and the governments' responsibilities are not defined clearly enough. Hence, they recommend more formal arrangements.

Bergsten would convert the existing de facto target zone regime into a de jure system for the major industrial countries. More comprehensive forms of policy coordination are likely to develop naturally, he argues, as governments start to understand the implications of the target zone regime for their monetary and fiscal policies. For Williamson and Henning, by contrast, a move to a formal target zone regime would be the prelude to adopting a comprehensive "blueprint" for exchange rate management and policy coordination. A target zone regime by itself can deal with the damage done when markets make mistakes; the full-fledged blueprint is required to deal with the damage done when governments make mistakes.

Other contributors to this book raise important questions about these proposals, especially about the comprehensive blueprint. Richard Cooper, for example, doubts that the governments involved would be willing or able to agree on the compatible current account targets required for them to reach agreement on the "fundamental equilibrium exchange rates" (FEERs) that are vital for the blueprint. Padoa-Schioppa and Saccomanni emphasize the operational problems that will bedevil any effort to stabilize exchange rates under conditions of very high capital mobility.

There are, in addition, differences concerning the transition to the new regime and about organizational matters. Bergsten would lodge an operating arm of the G-7 within the IMF as an informal steering committee of the Executive Board, with the full participation of the managing director, and would have the IMF calculate and monitor the FEERs on which the target zone regime would be based. Williamson and Henning would embody their blueprint in a formal treaty and give the IMF a larger role in choosing and changing the FEERs. They would replace the Interim Committee with a council, which would meet at the ministerial level to make key decisions about the functioning of the new regime, and they would upgrade the Executive Board by appointing ministerial deputies as executive directors. There would still be important work for the G-7, to which the IMF would "delegate" the organization and management of the new regime. But the managing director of the Fund would attend G-7 meetings, and the staff of the Fund would prepare the documentation for them.

In brief, Williamson and Henning would give the IMF duties and powers akin to those it had before the move to floating exchange rates and the Second Amendment to its Articles of Agreement. But Padoa-Schioppa and Saccomanni believe that the conduct of exchange rate policy should be transferred gradually from governments to central banks, and they therefore propose that exchange rate policy be made and implemented under the aegis of the Bank for International Settlements (BIS). If this were done, of course, there would be no way back for the IMF. It could continue to provide the balance of payments financing required by developing countries and might do other useful work. But it would have no role whatsoever in the affairs of the major industrial countries.

It has never been easy to define the appropriate division of responsibility for exchange rate policy because it impinges importantly on monetary policy. But the Williamson-Henning blueprint reminds us clearly that exchange rate policy is also linked tightly to fiscal policy. Governments cannot hope to manage exchange rates over the long term unless they engage in comprehensive policy coordination. That is the main message of the blueprint itself. It is also my chief reason for doubting that governments will agree to Padoa-Schioppa and Saccomanni's proposal. (Under the Maastricht Treaty, the EC governments left the responsibility for exchange rate policy divided between the Council of Ministers and the future European Central Bank.)

It should be emphasized, however, that none of the contributors to this book dissented from the basic premise underlying the proposals summarized above: freely floating exchange rates do not work well enough, and there is a compelling case for exchange rate management.

Trade, Investment, and the WTO

The aims of the Uruguay Round were far more ambitious than those of earlier GATT rounds, and the achievements were impressive, although they fell short of the goals. When implemented fully, the tariff cuts themselves will be larger than those of the Kennedy or Tokyo Rounds. Furthermore, the Uruguay Round was much more comprehensive, not only because it covered services, intellectual property, and agriculture, but also because it covered many more countries. John Jackson's paper, however, is focused on the two achievements that are likely to be most important in the long run: the decision to establish the WTO and thus codify the rules and practices that have governed trade relations and the resolution of trade policy disputes, and the decision to abandon the approach, introduced during the Tokyo Round, of offering "GATT à la carte" and thus to insist instead that every participating country accept almost all of the outcomes of the Uruguay Round.

Many issues remain unresolved, and Jackson suggests that 50 more years may be needed to liberalize trade in services completely. But a larger, more difficult task lies ahead, and we have barely begun to define it. There would be no basis for international trade if countries were identical in every respect. Yet many cross-country differences in laws, institutions, and private-sector practices are often regarded as "unfair" trade barriers. In Jackson's own words, countries with different domestic arrangements may require an "interface mechanism" to trade together harmoniously. The problem, moreover, is two-sided. On the one side, a country's domestic arrangements may be seen by foreigners as barring access to its markets, whether through trade or investment measures. On the other side, a country's domestic arrangements may be seen by foreigners as conferring an unfair advantage on its own producers when they compete abroad. Environmental standards loom large on the list, and labor standards are attracting a great deal of attention. (See Martin's Wolf's politically incorrect but sensible comments on dolphins, cows, greenhouse gases, and child labor.)

Another aspect of the "interface problem" is raised by Julius, who calls for a new international regime to promote direct investment. That regime, she argues, should be based on three basic principles: A foreign firm should be free to engage in any activity that domestic firms may undertake. A foreign firm should obey the same laws as domestic firms but must be accorded the same rights. A foreign firm should have "free choice of means," meaning that a country's policy regime should not distort the firm's choice among trade, direct investment, cross-border licensing, and other means of access to the country's markets—a principle which, carried to its limit, requires the elimination of all trade barriers. These are not operational rules, but they are the standards by which such rules should be judged. Julius goes on to suggest that the newly revised dispute settlement procedures of the WTO should be used to handle complaints arising from those rules and that individual firms should be allowed to bring complaints directly to the WTO.

One complicated question is missing from these papers, however, and it is rarely mentioned elsewhere in this book. How should multinational firms be taxed? The internalization of trade within the multinational firm and the globalization of production make it hard to defend the existing tax regime, and it is becoming increasingly hard to administer. Yet there have been few attempts to reconsider the regime. Mahbub ul Haq urges the World Bank to explore new ways of funding the International Development Association (IDA), including perhaps a global tax on foreign exchange trading, on the use of nonrenewable energy, or on trade in armaments. Why not take a bigger step by turning the taxation of corporate income over to an international institution—Bergsten's World Investment Organization, for example—and using the revenues for international purposes, including peacekeeping, development, and environmental protection?

Development and the World Bank

Two themes run through much of the criticism recently leveled at the World Bank and the regional development banks. First, critics say that the privatization of the development process has rendered these banks obsolete—not merely the privatization of publicly owned firms but the new emphasis on private investment, including foreign investment, guided primarily by market forces. Second, critics charge that the Bank and the regional development banks have not been attentive enough to the actual implementation of the projects they have supported or to the impact of those projects on the environment—using that term broadly to include economic and social dimensions as well as strictly ecological dimensions. Both objections convey the same message: the Bank and the level of its lending should shrink. At times, indeed, the shrinking of the Bank seems to be the main aim of its critics, rather than the consequence of carefully reassessing the Bank's basic mandate and strategy. I am no less troubled by this view than by the very different view implicit in ul Haq's suggestion that the Bank should always lend enough to rule out "negative transfers" from the developing countries.

I am more sympathetic to the position taken by Ardito-Barletta in his paper and by Lawrence Summers in his address to the conference. The privatization of development necessarily involves a narrower role for governments in the developing countries, but it also affords them an opportunity to focus more intensively on those tasks that the private sector does not normally perform. The point is made broadly by Ardito-Barletta, when he says that "development should empower both peoples and nations" and is concerned with "building the capacity, structures, institutions, and sense of purpose to widen horizons." The lessons for the multilateral banks are drawn clearly by Summers when he says that they must "help people endure the difficult macroeconomic and structural policy necessary to promote long-term growth," that they must allow for the human consequences of development projects, and that they must promote development "from the bottom up" by working to involve local communities in project development and implementation and by undertaking many more small-scale programs—"from local environmental and poverty reduction initiatives to financial support for microenterprises." This is not a call for shrinkage but rather for renewal and reorientation.

Horst Schulmann may be right. The Bank may face a shortage of creditworthy borrowers. But this may merely mean that the Bank will have to reconsider the way in which it raises and uses its money. Instead of soliciting subscriptions for IDA, it should perhaps solicit subscriptions to subsidize the Bank's own lending, so that it may borrow at market-determined interest rates but step up its lending at less than market rates.

Schulmann may also be right to say that "internationalism does not blossom without altruism, and as economic reality has finally caught up with the free-spending governments and parliaments of the high-income countries, altruism tends to be in short supply." Refugees, however, are not in short supply—not from Bosnia, Haiti, or Rwanda—and there will be many more if the developed countries cannot supply the resources required to sustain democratic development in the developing countries and the countries in transition. Of the latter, Marek Dąbrowski notes that we can observe a very close relationship between the progress of individual countries in making a market-oriented transition and their progress in building democratic institutions. Countries such as Ukraine, by contrast, that have not undertaken comprehensive economic reforms have very uncertain political futures, and are potential sources of regional and global instability.

There is no certainty of success in every country. Stephan Haggard warns that the task will be daunting indeed in Africa and much of South Asia, where the central institutions of government themselves are crumbling in a number of the poorest, war-torn countries. "It is still unclear," he says, "how the Bretton Woods and UN institutions will manage these failed states." It is quite clear, however, "that the IMF and the World Bank will not be able to operate solely on the near-commercial criteria that govern the bulk of their operations, nor with the resources presently available to them. The successes of the last two decades in East Asia and the sweeping reforms in Eastern Europe and Latin America should not obscure the profound environmental, social, and economic deterioration that has taken place in other parts of the developing world."

The Rise of Regionalism

The papers in this book deal mainly with the worldwide organizations, and some of them devote a good deal of attention to the problems and opportunities arising from the fact that those organizations have finally become—or are now becoming—worldwide in membership. Yet a number of papers also deal with the problems and opportunities posed by the proliferation of regional arrangements and by proposals for new ones.

Bergsten is greatly impressed by the achievements of the Uruguay Round. Although the agenda was so long that "it came perilously close to overloading the circuits," the round showed that more can be achieved by cross-issue bargaining at the global level than by issue-specific negotiations. He also believes that global and regional bargaining can be mutually reinforcing. He argues, indeed, that the creation of NAFTA and APEC were crucial for the success of the Uruguay Round, just as the creation and expansion of the European Community were important for the launching and success of the Kennedy and Tokyo Rounds.

In Bergsten's view, moreover, "GATT-plus" initiatives, which can carry liberalization beyond what can be achieved at the global level, may be pursued more effectively by regional groups than by other groups of seemingly like-minded countries. He is, of course, sensitive to the risk that regional arrangements can be attention-diverting as well as trade-diverting, but he has high hopes for the "open regionalism" to which APEC is committed, believing that some APEC members might even extend their commitments to outsiders on an unconditional MFN basis and that APEC as a whole will presumably open its agreements to nonmembers on a reciprocal basis in order to "ratchet up" the liberalization process from the regional to the global level.

Other contributors to this book are less optimistic about the outlook for regionalism and less sanguine about its possible effects. Eichengreen and I note that the European Community was an outgrowth of the need to tie Germany closely to its Western neighbors, especially to France, before the regeneration of German industry and that it was part of the broader Atlantic partnership based on NATO. Joseph Nye asks whether we can realistically expect that a Pacific partnership will be equally cohesive in the long run if its members do not have similar security concerns. And Paul Volcker finds it rather hard to believe that we will have free trade with China and Japan in the near term. I have the impression, moreover, that Washington has not even decided how NAFTA should be opened up to other countries in the Western Hemisphere—whether those countries should be invited to subscribe to it *in toto* or should instead be linked to it by less comprehensive free trade agreements.

Martin Wolf and Emile van Lennep are even more skeptical. Wolf notes that the rapid growth of intraregional trade in Asia has occurred without the benefit of regional arrangements. In his view, moreover, "a deliberate focusing of trade on neighbors is not self-evidently sensible," as trade between neighbors is likely to flourish anyway, whereas interregional trade may have to be nurtured. "An alternative to regional discrimination," he suggests, "is an open arrangement, available to any country, wherever located, that is willing to make the necessary commitments." (But Wolf also notes that free trade arrangements require rules of origin, which are not easy to negotiate and tend now to involve investment-related issues. Hence, the very notion of an "open arrangement" may prove less simple that it sounds.)

When we turn from trade to some of the new issues, moreover, the case for cooperation among like-minded countries, rather than regional groups, takes on more strength. No regional group could have negotiated the Basel Accord on bank capital. The process had to be initiated by the rather small group of large countries that have the biggest banks. Furthermore, the solution to many aspects of the "interface problem" may call for the use of new bargaining techniques. Julius suggests, for example, that "mutual recognition" may be more effective than an attempt to agree on common rules or standards when dealing with many differences in national laws and practices. But that approach may not work well when the differences themselves are very large, and geographic proximity does not always imply institutional similarity.

A Concluding Note

Looking back over the papers and comments in this book, I have one concern. It might have been better to start the book differently—not by assessing the past but by forecasting the future. All of the papers acknowledge that the end of the Cold War has altered the international system fundamentally. Most of them, however, are chiefly concerned with ways to consolidate and supplement the system as we know it now, as though it were in some sort of sustainable equilibrium. That may not be true.

The Bretton Woods Conference took place a full year before the bombing of Hiroshima and four years before the Berlin blockade. Fewer than 50 countries were represented at the first annual meeting of the IMF, which had 178 members at last count. And the world is bound to be different 25 years from now. Joe Nye lists six very different futures, ranging from one with enormous and spreading prosperity to one choked by ecocide. It may be divided between wealthy, stable states and a sea of failed states. There could be another Cold War. Even in the absence of cataclysmic change, moreover, there will be unpleasant shocks. Prosperity may not promote democracy. Russia and China may reject the market.

No one can plan confidently for these possibilities. Nevertheless, we can be sure that the modest reforms proposed in this book, even if fully adopted, will be considered insufficient when the Bretton Woods institutions or their successors are reexamined once again. We may have to replace them or reform them drastically far sooner than this book would lead us to expect.

V

ANNEX

The Bretton Woods Institutions and Global Governance

MAHBUB UL HAQ

As we celebrate the 50th anniversary of the Bretton Woods institutions, I wonder whether John Maynard Keynes and Harry White, were they to rise from their graves, would recognize their own creations. Probably there would be neither instant recognition nor immediate affection, for the Bretton Woods institutions have drifted too far from their original vision. Before I offer a few concrete proposals for the future functioning of these institutions, let me briefly review the gap between the original vision and the current reality. And I will focus only on the International Monetary Fund and the World Bank, leaving the General Agreement on Tariffs and Trade out of my analysis.

The IMF in its present form is merely a pale shadow of Keynes's original vision:

- Keynes proposed a Fund equal to one-half of world imports so it could exercise a major influence on the global monetary system. Even White's more conservative proposal suggested IMF reserves equaling one-sixth of world imports. In actual practice, IMF today controls liquidity equal to only 2 percent of world imports.

- Keynes envisioned IMF as a world central bank, issuing its own reserve currency (the "bancors") and creating sufficient international reserves whenever and wherever needed. The IMF was authorized in the 1970s

The writer is a former finance minister of Pakistan, as well as a former senior official of the World Bank, and is currently serving as special adviser to the United Nations Development Programme administrator and as the chief architect of UNDP's annual Human Development Reports. This is the text of a speech given at the conference.

to create Special Drawing Rights (SDRs), but the experiment was still-born because of persistent US trade deficits and because the United States chose to finance its deficits by creating more dollars rather than accepting the more painful path of real adjustment. When their interest rates were raised nearer to the market rate during the 1970s, SDRs became somewhat unattractive holdings. Now SDRs constitute only 3 percent of global liquidity. The world economy is dollar-dominated. The United States continues to be the informal central banker of the world. Not surprisingly, the global financial markets hold their collective breath for the words of Federal Reserve Chairman Alan Greenspan, not those of IMF Managing Director Michel Camdessus.

■ Keynes regarded the balance of payments surpluses as a vice and deficits as a virtue since deficits sustained global effective demand and generated more employment. This led him to advocate a penal interest rate of 1 percent a month on outstanding trade surpluses. The situation today is exactly the reverse: deficit nations, particularly those in the developing world without a reserve currency of their own, come under tremendous pressure for real adjustment. There is no similar adjustment pressure on the surplus nations.

■ The heart of the IMF-led global monetary system was fixed exchange rates. That system died in the early 1970s with the delinking of the dollar from gold and with the introduction of floating exchange rates. All attempts to introduce a modicum of stability in the volatility of exchange rates have since proved largely futile.

Has the World Bank stuck closer to its original vision than the IMF? Let me take up its role only vis-à-vis the developing nations. The World Bank was supposed to stand in between the global capital markets and the developing countries and to recycle market funds to the countries by using its own creditworthiness, as well as by gradually building up the creditworthiness of these nations over time so they could have direct access to the private markets. Again, the reality is a long way off from the original vision:

■ In some respects, the World Bank has done better than originally expected. It helped raise market funds at lower cost, for longer maturity periods, and for some social sectors (such as education, health, population, and nutrition) that private markets would not have touched. It introduced the International Development Association (IDA) in 1960 to subsidize its lending for poorer nations. It kept graduating from a bank into a development agency.

■ Where the World Bank is beginning to fail is in the transfer of resources to developing nations. Recently, its net resource transfers, including

IDA, have been a negative $1 billion to $2 billion a year. The role of the World Bank in recycling market funds is by now a marginal one. Private lending to developing countries has increased rapidly—that is certainly a good development. But three-fourths of this private market lending still goes to about 10 relatively better-off economies in Latin America and Southeast Asia. What about the other 117 developing countries? The Bank's role has been a modest one in these countries, and negative net resource transfers by the Bank in some poor nations have raised real questions about its developmental mandate.

■ The original Keynesian vision for the World Bank would have envisaged the Bank as an institution for expansion of global growth and employment levels, rather than as an instrument for deflationary policies. One of the most scathing criticisms of the Bank in the developing countries these days is that the Bank gets greatly browbeaten by the IMF in prescribing demand management and deflationary policies, particularly as conditionality for its structural adjustment loans. Instead of offering healthy competition to the IMF, it has chosen a path of intellectual subservience.

We may well ask what is so wrong about the offspring departing from the hopes and aspirations of their parents. After all, it is an all-too-familiar experience in our own personal lives. The real question is, was the original vision flawed in itself? Or has the international community opted for some inferior options?

I believe that there are two aspects of this 50-year evolution that should particularly concern us.

First, the IMF and the World Bank are no longer institutions of global management; they are now primarily institutions to police the developing world. The industrial world is largely independent of their policy prescriptions or management control. The Group of Seven (G-7) and private capital markets have taken over the job of global economic management. No real institutions of global economic governance exist today. The proposed World Trade Organization (WTO) may be an exception. We shall see. But as far as the IMF is concerned, isn't it somewhat charitable to call a money manager with influence on the monetary policy of developing countries responsible for only about 10 percent of global liquidity an *international* monetary fund? And isn't it somewhat optimistic to describe an institution that recycles almost negligible net financial resources as a "World Bank"? The plain truth is that both these institutions have been totally marginalized in global economic governance.

Many conference participants discussed the remarkable global prosperity of the postwar period. But how much did the Bretton Woods institutions have to do with industrial-country policies after 1970? Do they have much of a role now in what the Federal Reserve Board or Bundesbank does, or in private capital markets, or in the $1 trillion that travels the globe every 24 hours, or in global monetary expansion and in global interest rates, or in setting an expansionary or deflationary tone in global policies? Most industrial countries largely ignore these institutions, except when it comes to regulating the developing world or recently in relation to the transition economies of former communist countries. In fact, multilateral institutions have weakened just when global interdependence has increased.

That is not what was envisaged at Bretton Woods. With memories of the Great Depression of the 1930s still fresh, the battle cry in the Bretton Woods Conference was "never again." Unemployment had been heavy, so the new objective was full employment. Trade and investment rules had broken down, so the new objective was to prevent beggar-thy-neighbor policies. The international monetary system had collapsed, so the new objective was to have stable currencies with agreed procedures for adjustment. Unilateral national policies had created a world chaos, so the basic idea was to fashion new institutions of global monetary and economic governance, with clear objectives and with changes in global policies engineered through broad international consensus.

We have strayed many miles from that original vision. A basic question today is whether we need Bretton Woods institutions only to influence the policies of the developing countries—which account for one-fifth of global output and one-tenth of global liquidity—or whether we need them as genuine institutions of global governance. Should we leave the fate of the global economic system to the ad hoc improvisations of the G-7 or to the free workings of the international markets? Or do we need a minimum of global economic management, conducted through professional analysis and consultative processes within international financial institutions? Incidentally, some of the criticisms of these institutions in the enlightened lobbies of the developing world arise from a perception that the industrial countries are largely independent of the discipline of the Bretton Woods institutions. Further, many believe that the industrial countries not only set their own rules, they also set the framework within which Bretton Woods institutions and developing countries can operate.

A second concern is that industrial nations' macroeconomic problems drive the institutions' policy agenda. The founders of the Bretton Woods institutions were searching for expansionary economic policies after a prolonged global deflation. Full employment was on top of the international agenda in the 1940s. But in recent decades, it appears that the world leaders, particularly in the industrial nations, have been far more preoccupied with inflation than with jobs. The pendulum is beginning to swing once again, and jobs are now moving to the top of the policy agenda.

The developing countries, unfortunately, have to live with the consequences of the changing policy agendas in the industrial world. The Bretton Woods institutions have subjected most of the developing countries to deflationary-policy conditionality when their real need was expansion of jobs and output. The demand management school often won out over the supply expansion school, partly because adjustment through supply expansion often takes longer and requires greater resources than the Bretton Woods institutions could afford.

I do not suggest that demand management is unnecessary. It may sometimes be even a precondition for sound supply expansion policies. After all, budgets must be balanced, and borrowing must be curtailed. But the Bretton Woods institutions compounded their error of overemphasizing demand management by accepting wrong policy choices for slashing budgetary expenditures. It does not take a genius to figure out how to balance budgets without unbalancing the lives of the people: there are many low-priority budget items. Military expenditures exceed expenditures on education and health in many developing countries. Budgetary subsidies to the rich often far exceed such subsidies to the poor. Yet education and health expenditures have often been cut ahead of military expenditures during periods of adjustment, and food subsidies to the poor have been slashed in preference to cutting the tax and interest rate subsidies to powerful landlords and industrialists. The social and human costs of the adjustment programs have been unnecessarily high, and the Bretton Woods institutions have been blamed for the consequences.

I personally believe that this image of political insensitivity has been rather unfair to both the IMF and the World Bank. I do not seriously accept the notion that staff members in the Bretton Woods institutions chuckle over the harsh human conditionality of their loans. I have watched this game of mirrors from both sides—as a staff member of the World Bank for 12 years and as the finance and planning minister of Pakistan for 8 years. What really happens is that the developing-country governments find it politically convenient to squeeze their poorer and weaker sections of society while pretending that such policies are a part of external conditionality.

But the Bretton Woods institutions must accept some responsibility. They must pressure governments to cut military spending rather than their social spending, something they have started doing only in the last few years. They must analyze subsidies to high- and low-income groups in a national budget and stand firm on slashing subsidies to rich, elitist groups in a society before subsidies to the poor are touched. They must spend as much time discussing politically sensitive issues of land reform and credit availability as they now do on price distortions.

These are not easy issues. Such a stance would require skillful engineering and political alliances for change within the system. But unless the Bretton Woods institutions are willing to take some political heat on these issues, the cause of the poor—which is always poorly defended in their own systems—may suffer by default. In any case, since the Bretton Woods institutions are already criticized for exacting human costs they do not wish to cause, they may as well become more directly involved in these politically sensitive areas. The general criticism of the policy conditionality of the Bretton Woods institutions is that they interfere too much in the economic management of the developing countries. My own perception is that they interfere too little or certainly not enough in key policy areas.

Let me turn now to the second issue I want to explore: what reforms can reposition these institutions for the challenges of the 21st century?

I will discuss the IMF first. We do need a global institution that can ensure sound macroeconomic management and global monetary stability. In fact, such an institution should perform five functions:

- help stabilize global economic activity;

- act as a lender of last resort to financial institutions;

- calm the financial markets when they become jittery or disorderly;

- regulate financial banks and institutions with an international reach;

- create and regulate new international liquidity.

These five functions, as Richard Cooper has often pointed out in his excellent analyses, are the proper roles for a world central bank. Even if we deemphasize the last function—of creating an international reserve currency—as it may be overly ambitious at this stage, the other four functions lie at the very heart of sound macroeconomic management, and the IMF must carry them out if it is to reclaim its legitimate role in the global monetary system.

Whether or not we eventually move toward a world central bank in the 21st century is an issue that is likely to excite a good deal of debate in the next decade. I am firmly on the side of those who believe that such a development is inevitable. But this is not what I wish to discuss here. Let me present to you instead four somewhat cautious steps—and I believe eminently logical ones—that can initiate a reform of the IMF in the right direction.

First, we must seriously consider a new issue of SDRs—in the range of 30 billion to 50 billion SDRs—now while global inflationary pressures are low, primary commodity prices have hit rock bottom, most industrial countries are reducing their budget deficits, and an extra dose of global liquidity can help fuel world economic recovery. There could also be some innovation in the distribution of SDRs, with some industrial countries passing on part of their allocations to developing countries through overdraft facilities.

Second, the Compensatory and Contingency Financial Facility (CCFF) of the IMF needs to be changed in several directions. There should be no quota restriction so that a country can obtain full compensation for a shortfall in its exports. The loan period needs to be extended so that countries do not have to repay before the contingency is over. Even more important, it is somewhat illogical to attach policy conditionality to borrowing. If a country is reeling from external shocks outside its control, why add the shock of IMF conditionality as well?

Third, in collaboration with the Bank for International Settlements (BIS), the IMF should acquire some regulatory control over international banking activities. I personally believe that the IMF should also be administering the proposed "Tobin tax" of 0.5 percent on international currency transactions to curb excessive speculation if this eminently sensible proposal begins to catch the imagination of the international community. This would not only give the IMF some control over international flows of capital that are sweeping global markets with hurricane force. It would also yield enormous revenue—about $1.5 trillion a year—which could help finance World Bank and UN development operations. In this way, global prosperity would be taxed in an invisible and nondiscriminatory manner to finance an attack on global poverty.

Fourth, the IMF needs to acquire a greater role in global macroeconomic management, reviewing the policies of all countries—whether or not they are active borrowers—and particularly influencing the macroeconomic policies of major industrial powers to at least some extent. One possible mechanism may be for the IMF to persuade BIS to link the level of reserves that banks are required to hold against country loans to IMF evaluations. This would affect the industrial countries' ability to raise funds from private banks and give the IMF important leverage on their policies.

These four steps represent only an initial move toward IMF reform. They are not a blueprint for converting the IMF into a world central bank. I offer these proposals in the hope that it may be possible to act on at least some of them in the current environment.

Let me turn now to the World Bank. I believe that it needs to consider several areas of reform. First, the Bank, though certainly the finest institution for advising developing countries on economic growth policies, needs to develop much greater sensitivity and expertise in linking economic growth to human lives, in analyzing the distribution and sustainability of growth, and in examining more participatory patterns of development. The issue is not growth per se. To address poverty, economic growth is not an option: it is an imperative. But what type of growth? Who participates in it? Who derives the benefits? These are the real issues. To benefit the masses, growth opportunities must be more equitably distributed, and they must be sustainable from one generation to the next. The World Bank certainly talks about these issues. But its critics allege that its embrace of the issues of sustainable, people-centered development is less than enthusiastic. It appears to regard such issues more as an irritation than as central themes. I believe that we could all gain a great deal if the Bank were to turn its professional rigor to the emerging concerns for sustainable human development.

Second, the Bank must find new ways of recycling much larger resources to the developing countries. The resource profile of the Bank and the poverty profile of the developing world are getting out of sync. According to the Bank's own estimates, the number of absolute poor has been increasing in the developing world. Yet real IDA availability per poor person has been shrinking, greatly limiting the Bank's options. This is not a fault of the Bank's management but of its donors, who have refused to see the implications of such an imbalance.

But the point I wish to make is a different one. We are reaching the end of an era where legislatures in the rich nations will keep voting larger IDA resources. In the 21st century, we will have to start looking for more innovative ways of raising global financing to address the issues of global poverty. Proposals such as the Tobin tax, an international tax on nonrenewable energy or on armaments trade, or proceeds from environmental emission permits—which are still regarded with a good deal of healthy skepticism—are the kind of proposals that may move to the center of the international debate when it is recognized that the new dimensions of global human security require some form of global financing. The Bank has been fairly conservative in its approach to new financing sources. In fact, after the launching of IDA in 1960, it has considered no significant innovation in its modalities. I would certainly like to see the Bank as a leader in exploring new avenues for raising international finances.

Third, I personally believe that the Bank must start considering prudent ways to restructure its own debts. The Bank has advised all other creditors to restructure their debts to developing countries, but it has expressed an inability to reschedule its own because of its charter limitations and concerns about its triple-A credit rating in the capital markets. The result is obvious. The Bank will end up owning more and more debt of its member countries, its net transfers will decline significantly, and after some time it will be recycling its own debts rather than transferring new resources. It has already reached that position with several developing countries. Whenever I have discussed this issue with my friends in the World Bank, I have generally received the compassionate looks normally reserved for the mentally ill. But I still believe that the Bank can persuade its contributors and the capital markets to act as a development agency, and not as a global money lender, and that prudent rescheduling of debts must be a part of its operations.

Fourth, I have been urging for some time now that the Bank take on the role of an International Investment Trust—selling bonds to nations with a surplus and lending the proceeds to developing countries. Developing countries could borrow from the trust on terms appropriate to their level of development. The newly industrializing countries could pay commercial rates, while low-income countries would pay less—a subsidy that richer members of the international community should be persuaded to cover. If some of the proposals regarding international fees or taxes prove to be acceptable to the international community, a pool of resources would become available for such a subsidized recycling of market funds.

I have been deliberately restrained in my proposals for reforms in the IMF and the World Bank over the coming decade. Somehow, we have all been chastened by the imperatives of realpolitik.

I have stayed away from the exciting discussion of what institutions can be created or which existing ones merged. C. Fred Bergsten has an extremely stimulating paper on this subject with many innovative, creative proposals. I would support many of his conclusions. But let me offer two specific comments at this stage.

First, any proposal for a merger of the IMF and the World Bank will be extremely unpopular in the developing world. Rightly or wrongly, there is much more goodwill toward the World Bank in the developing countries than toward the IMF. The IMF is seen as an institution that will insist on strict demand management and harsh policy conditionality. Moreover, it is seen as an institution driven primarily by the interests of the rich nations that would be reluctant to relinquish their control. Rather than a merger, the developing countries would like to see the World Bank emerge from under the intellectual dominance of the IMF.

Second, I firmly believe that one international mechanism we must create fairly soon is an Economic Security Council in the United Nations to manage the new imperatives of global human security. Increasingly, the conflicts are within nations rather than between nations, and their resolution requires socioeconomic development, not soldiers in UN blue berets. We also need a much broader consultative process than the G-7 for global economic decision making, as well as a forum in which policy initiatives for global development can be discussed and practical compromises made on a regular basis. Such an Economic Security Council should supervise the policy direction of all international institutions, including the Bretton Woods institutions.

Let me now conclude with one final observation. The founders of the Bretton Woods institutions and the United Nations were neither inhibited nor timid 50 years ago. While bombs were still raining on London, John Maynard Keynes was preparing the blueprint for the Bretton Woods institutions. When Europe was still at war, Jean Monnet was dreaming about a European Economic Community. The dust of war had not settled when the Marshall Plan for the reconstruction of Europe was taking its shape. The hostility of nations was still simmering as President Truman approved the hopeful design of a United Nations.

We must admire the vision and courage of those people today. We see so little of this intellectual ferment these days, even though we have seen some unprecedented changes in the global environment—from the fall of the Berlin Wall to the end of apartheid in South Africa. The unthinkable is already becoming commonplace. And yet our sources of creativity are curiously passive regarding the future shape of global economic governance. Maybe it is time to begin designing the global institutions of the 21st century.

Shared Prosperity and the New International Economic Order

LAWRENCE H. SUMMERS

I've been asked to discuss the international economic system and how it needs to be changed now at the 50th anniversary of the Bretton Woods conference. Before we can talk about how the system should be changed, it seems to me we have to be clear about how the world has changed, and about how our objectives have changed. I will reflect on just what is new about the new international economic order, what are and what should be the goals of American international economic policy, and then offer some reflections on the missions of some crucial international economic institutions.

What Is New?

In thinking about the challenges that lie ahead, three features of the new international economic order stand out.

First, the most remarked on difference between the policy environment of today and of a few years ago is that the Cold War is over. No longer is the containment of the communist threat the preeminent challenge facing the industrial democracies. The industrial countries are reaping a peace dividend measured in the hundreds of billions of dollars.

But the end of the Cold War is not an unmixed blessing. With the passage of the communist threat, an important adhesive binding industrial democracies to each other and to their allies in the developing world

Lawrence H. Summers is under secretary of the treasury for international affairs. This is the text of a speech delivered during the conference.

has been lost. And conflicts which the superpowers could and would have prevented in an earlier era have been allowed to fester.

Second is the rise of the developing world. It is normally assumed that when the history of the last quarter of the 20th century is written a century from now, the defining story will be the victory of capitalism over communism. I would suggest that a story of equal importance will be the fact that this was the period when developing nations with a combined population of nearly 3 billion people stepped onto an economic growth escalator toward modernity—an event that may rank in economic history with the Renaissance and the Industrial Revolution.

Of course the rise of the developing world is closely related to the fall of communism, for it reflects in large part the increasing recognition that a market system supported by a strong government that performs essential public functions is the best way mankind has yet found to harness productive energy.

The rise of the developing world is an event with profound consequences for human welfare. It is a staggering commercial opportunity for businesses around the world. And it has the potential to be an enormous contributor to human freedom. But the rise of the developing world also carries with it risks. As prosperity spreads, those left behind are ever more embittered. And as the roots of the First World War in German economic expansionism, and the roots of the Second World War in the Pacific in Japanese economic expansionism, remind us, new economic powers frequently do not fit easily into the world economic system.

The third great change is that the world is getting smaller in so many ways. With current long distance phone rates, CNN, and fax machines, I think it is fair to say that a Washingtonian traveling in Tokyo today finds it easier to be in touch than a Washingtonian traveling in Denver just 25 years ago. As Alan Greenspan is fond of pointing out, the mass per unit of value added keeps falling, facilitating international trade. And with all the problems in the international trading system, trade growth continues to significantly outstrip income growth, and foreign investment growth far outstrips income growth.

Technology has enormous potential. But those enamored with globalization would do well to remember that while trade and investment rates are now far greater than they were a decade or two or three ago, they are about where they were a century ago. Much of the integration of the last 50 years represents repair of the disintegration caused by misguided policies and ideologies during the dark 1914–45 years.

What Are Our Goals?

It is natural that with these profound changes in the world, the search for new paradigms to guide international policy in general, and international economic policy in particular, is on.

Some would have the United States and other industrial democracies borrow from the defense area and pursue policies directed at containing threats posed by foreign commercial rivals in an effort to preserve something called "economic security."

In my view, this is a profoundly misguided vision. It fails to recognize the fundamental difference between prosperity and power. Power can be gained only at someone else's expense. Prosperity can be shared. We gain when other nations grow and their markets expand. We gain when other nations innovate and our firms and our consumers gain access to new technologies. We gain when foreign companies choose to invest in the United States and compete for American workers.

The United States has the most productive workers on this planet. As President Clinton has said, we must "compete not retreat." We have little to fear from foreign competitors and much to gain from an open world system.

Others would make the competitive advantage of American producers the sole goal of international economic policy. Certainly the 1992 election delivered a clear verdict that the American people's number one priority was the creation of more high-wage jobs.

Notwithstanding Paul Krugman,[1] competitiveness is important. People who talk about competitiveness want to see America produce more, better products at lower cost, and sell them into more rapidly growing and more open markets. What is wrong with that?

American policymakers have an obligation to promote US exports by reforming domestic policies, and by working to bring down foreign trade barriers. Asymmetries in the degree of protection in the United States and some of our major trading partners that may have been justifiable decades or even a decade ago are no longer appropriate today.

But competitive advantage of American producers cannot be the sole or the overarching goal of our international economic policy, for the world's only remaining superpower has a major stake in the international economic system and in the success of other nations.

Rather, the overriding goal of American international economic policy and a central goal of American economic policy has to be the creation of shared prosperity around the world.

■ Shared prosperity means prosperity at home and expanding markets for American producers and more jobs for American workers.

■ Shared prosperity means a reduction in the possibility of conflicts rooted in economic frustration. From Pretoria to Palestine, and from

---

1. See Krugman's 1994 article, "Competitiveness: A Dangerous Obsession," *Foreign Affairs* 73, no. 2 (March/April): 28–44.

Russia to Rwanda, we have a stake in creating prosperity as a route to preserving peace.

- Shared prosperity advances human freedom. Think about the differences in life choices of a child born today and one born 25 years ago in Korea or China or Chile. It cannot be an accident that most of the world's rich countries are democratic, and most of the world's poor countries are not.

- Shared prosperity preserves our planet's environment. As nations develop, population pressures are reduced. And more prosperous nations gain both the way and the will to address environmental concerns.

Achieving the Goal of Shared Prosperity

The international economic institutions are as important to the new world order as the security organizations were to the old one. Just as the security organizations were directed at the then central challenge of combating communism, the economic institutions are directed at the now central challenge of creating shared prosperity.

The merits of multilateralism in the military sphere have been much debated. But the role of multilateral institutions in the economic sphere has been much less discussed. Yet multilateral activity has enormous benefits for the United States: It leverages our limited resources. It allows us to disseminate our ideas and our values. It fosters international cooperation. It is striking to reflect on the fact it is the international financial institutions that allocate more than $60 billion a year to accomplish these goals: they have provided the lion's share of financial support for central Europe and the former Soviet Union, are coordinating the efforts to rebuild the Palestinian economy, and are the principal source of funding for efforts to preserve biodiversity.

That is why President Clinton and his administration worked so hard to complete the Uruguay Round and are absolutely determined to pass it this year. And that is why Secretary Bentsen has made seeking the full funding of American commitments to the international financial institutions, and a start on paying down arrears, a top legislative priority this year.

The topic of international economic coordination is an enormous one. So I want to concentrate in the remainder of my remarks on the three areas that are particularly important for the Department of the Treasury— macroeconomic cooperation and coordination, the role of the IMF, and the role of the World Bank and the other development banks.

Macroeconomic Coordination

Secretary Bentsen has laid out the US approach to macroeconomic coordination in the Group of Seven (G-7). It starts from the reality that it is policy fundamentals that are ultimately important for real economic performance. And it relies on informal, quiet communication and persuasion to produce results rather than seeking to pull regular rabbits out of hats at the time of meetings. I hope that our actions two weeks ago demonstrated that the G-7 lives and can when appropriate act quickly, strongly, and in concert.

I have carefully studied proposals such as the Williamson-Henning blueprint for bringing greater stability by formalizing the cooperation process. I have very little sympathy for such ideas.

- In a world of proud legislatures and independent central banks, I see little prospect for the implementation of such an arrangement.

- Such blueprints presume a degree of precision in economic forecasting that seems to me almost wholly unrealistic. And they fail to recognize just how long and variable the lags between policy actions and results can be.

- History suggests the law of unintended consequences is likely to bedevil formal cooperative schemes. And my experience is that consensus in their favor tends to collapse when substance is brought in. I note that the front page of the *Wall Street Journal* recently cited Fred Bergsten and Paul Volcker as seeing a need for more cooperation to stabilize exchange rates, even as the inner pages cited Bergsten as seeing no reason why the dollar was undervalued and Volcker as calling for more active efforts to raise its value.

I believe that widening the process of macroeconomic cooperation will ultimately be found to be more fruitful than deepening it. I mean this in two senses. First, increasingly macroeconomic outcomes are dependent on microeconomic policies in areas ranging from financial regulation to manpower training. There is much to be gained from more international cooperation in the structural area—something the Clinton administration sought to initiate with the Detroit jobs conference, and which will be carried on in Naples. Likewise, I believe concerns of the kind that have recently been raised about derivatives point up the need for greater internationalization in the area of financial regulation.

Second, widening macroeconomic cooperation means broadening the set of countries that are involved. I believe that the US action to support Mexico following the tragic Colosio assassination was very constructive, although the ultimate reason for success was Mexico's deep commitment to reform and its reinforcement through NAFTA. The North American Financial Group announced last month will be an important adjunct to NAFTA. In a similar vein, the agreement of the APEC finance ministers to hold their second annual meeting in Indonesia next year points towards the possibility of greater cooperation especially to assure that flows of capital in the region prove to be as sustainable as they have been strong.

The IMF

Historians note that democracies do not go to war with one another. Economic historians add the corollary that democracies do not survive hyperinflation. With more countries experiencing inflation rates in the hundreds and even the thousands of percent, the IMF's role is more important now than at any previous point in history.

The basic premises on which the IMF operates in support of stabilization are absolutely right. It is the fundamentals of fiscal and monetary policies and not gimmicks that determine national inflation rates. Domestic policies, not foreign assistance, ultimately determine stabilization outcomes. Financial support has to be conditional if it is to be effective.

The conspicuous improvements in Russian economic policy in recent months and the successful conclusion of the negotiations for the second tranche of the STF bear out the wisdom of a strategy of measuring the pace of support with the pace of reform while at the same time engaging as intensively and at as high a level as possible.

While the basic premises on which it operates are right, I do believe that the nature of the problems we face will over time compel some evolutionary change in the way in which the IMF operates. It is impossible to generalize intelligently about the whole world, but let me suggest some directions of change:

- Increasingly, we are coming to understand that austerity is no substitute for adjustment, that the quality as well as the quantity of fiscal deficit reduction matters for both the immediate impact and sustainability of financial programs. This means that the IMF will have little choice but to be more intensively engaged in monitoring and perhaps even supporting the structural as well as the purely financial aspects of economic reform. The development of the Systemic Transformation Facility was a visionary step in this regard.

- Increasingly, economists are coming to understand that outcomes depend on policies and on their credibility. Addressing policies is not enough if their credibility is not addressed as well. In part, credibility is enhanced when macroeconomic and structural reforms such as privatization are linked. But there is also a need for more active support of institutions such as currency boards, managed exchange rates, and independent central banks that can reinforce credibility.

- Increasingly, as fiscal problems in the major industrialized countries mount, their capacity to support reform efforts in the world's trouble spots is more limited. This means that the international financial institutions in general and the IMF in particular will have to take on more of the burden. Fortunately, the IMF's liquidity and reserve position is extraordinarily good by absolute and historical standards. As the Interim Committee communiqué recognized, it is high time to consider how the Fund's resources can be more fully and effectively mobilized in support of its crucial mission.

I have emphasized the role of the IMF in supporting stabilization in the developing world and in the economies in transition because I think that is where the IMF will make its greatest contribution in the next few years. But I do not intend to slight its role in supporting sound macroeconomic performance within and sensible dialogue among the industrial countries.

The Development Banks

The development banks face a different but no less important challenge in the new international economic order. The growing importance of the developing world makes their jobs more important to the world economy than ever before. And the increased availability of private capital changes the world in which they operate. The banks must evolve to reflect this reality, as well as the unfolding challenges facing developing countries— what some now call the second generation of reforms.

The development banks have a continuing role to play in providing support for economic reform and sound policies. They have proven themselves in this role. The World Bank, to name one example, has been the agent through its adjustment lending of more unilateral tariff reduction than the Uruguay Round—for instance in Mexico and China.

But there are also some changes to be made in the way they do business.

Just as here we are seeking to reinvent our government, the development banks—and the IMF as well—need to reinvent themselves. They need to produce the services they provide in a more efficient and cost-effective way. Considerable progress has already been made in this area with the change in travel policies, the more realistic approach to salaries, the move toward more transparency, and the effort to strengthen self-criticism. But to be effective—and to set a good example for those they are trying to help—the banks and the IMF must make reinvention a continuous process.

And just as the challenges facing the developing world and transition economies are evolving, so must the priorities and approach of the development banks adapt.

First, the banks must promote policy frameworks that put people first. People are one of the greatest resources of any country. And this is certainly true in the developing world. The banks must help people endure the difficult macroeconomic and structural policy changes necessary to promote long-term growth. They must take into account the impact on people of development projects—from large dams that may uproot people from their homes to industrial facilities that have environmental side effects to construction of health facilities that need to be accessible to those who need them most. And the banks must also concentrate on what can be done to help people be productive contributors to the quest for sustained economic growth. They must invest in people—their education, health, and broader well-being.

The recently negotiated replenishment of the Inter-American Development Bank demonstrates the direction that the banks need to take in this area. The IDB has decided to increase the share of resources dedicated to social and environmental programs. The IDB and its members have also laid out objectives on governance—in order to help governments do their jobs of collecting revenues, enforcing laws, and serving their citizens. Indeed it is in these areas that many of the challenges of second-generation reforms lie.

Second, the development banks need to refine their approach to private-sector development. It is vital that they support but not supplant a strong role for private-sector finance in infrastructure and other projects.

The IDB, as an example, will now allow 5 percent of its resources to be lent to support infrastructure projects. This can help recently privatized entities make the transition to private capital markets. The IDB is also looking for appropriate ways to increase cofinancing for its projects—to bring the private-sector into areas where it can and should be playing a profitable role.

Third, the development banks need to promote development from the bottom up. Experience demonstrates the importance of ensuring early and meaningful involvement of local communities in project development and implementation. Local participation gives affected parties a vested interest in development and increases project effectiveness. For the banks, this underscores the importance of maintaining a strong field presence and an active dialogue with local communities. It also means we need more small-scale programs—from local environmental and poverty reduction initiatives to financial support for microenterprises.

Conclusion

What are the stakes? Let me use a comparison that President Clinton has used a number of times. The Cold War is the third war that has ended in this century. Everything went wrong after the First World War. Most things went right after the Second World War. What was the difference? We worked for shared prosperity after the Second World War. We must do no less today.

Conference Participants

Authors

Nicolás Ardito-Barletta
International Center for Economic
Growth

C. Fred Bergsten
Institute for International
Economics

Barry Eichengreen
University of California, Berkeley

Daniel Esty
Institute for International
Economics

Mahbub ul Haq
United Nations

C. Randall Henning
Institute for International
Economics

John Jackson
University of Michigan

DeAnne Julius
British Airways

Peter Kenen
Princeton University

Tommaso Padoa-Schioppa
Bank of Italy

Fabrizio Saccomanni
Bank of Italy

Lawrence H. Summers
Department of the Treasury

John Williamson
Institute for International
Economics

Glenn Withers
Australian Economic Planning
Advisory Council

Panelists

William R. Cline
Institute for International
Economics

Richard N. Cooper
Harvard University

Marek Dabrowski
Center for Social and Economic
Research

Klaus Engelen
Handlesblatt

Stephan Haggard
University of California, San Diego

Robert Keohane
Harvard University

Moisés Naím
Carnegie Endowment for
International Peace

Joseph Nye
Department of Defense

Shijuro Ogata
Yamaichi Securities

Kenneth A. Oye
Massachusetts Institute of
Technology

Richard Portes
Centre for Economic Policy
Research

Horst Schulmann
Landeszentral Bank in Hessen

Niels Thygesen
University of Copenhagen

Emile van Lennep
The Netherlands

Paul Volcker
James D. Wolfensohn, Inc.

Martin Wolf
Financial Times

Alan Wm. Wolff
Dewey Ballantine

Participants

Masood Ahmed
World Bank

Michael Aho
Prudential Securities

Lazzeri Antonalla
World Bank

James Arrowsmith
Texaco

Gail Attridge
Putnam Investments

Howard Banks
Forbes

Thomas Bayard
Institute for International
Economics

Zanny Beddoes
The Economist

Peter Bekx
Commission of the European
Communities

James Boughton
International Monetary Fund

Ralph Bryant
Brookings Institution

Alan Cathcart
International Monetary Fund

Clay Chandler
Washington Post

Benjamin Cohen
University of California, Santa
Barbara

Max Corden
Johns Hopkins University

Kenneth Courtis
Deutsche Bank Capital Markets

Clive Crook
The Economist

Charles Dallara
Institute of International Finance

Richard Debs
Morgan Stanley

Susan Dentzer
US News and World Report

Gina Despres
Capital Strategy Research

I. M. Destler
Institute for International
Economics

Joly Dixon
Commission of the European
Communities

Wendy Dobson
University of Toronto

John Dorrington
International Monetary Fund

Neil Dunay
ITOCHU

Kimberly Elliott
Institute for International
Economics

Mike Elliott
Newsweek

Dean Foust
Business Week

Henry Fowler
Goldman Sachs

Jonathan Francis
Putnam Investments

Yoshihiro Fujii
Nihon Keizai Shimbun

Tommy Fukuda
Marubeni

Glen Fukushima
AT&T Japan

Michael Gadbaw
General Electric

Raymond Garcia
Rockwell

Jean-Daniel Gerber
World Bank

Robert Gilpin
Princeton University

Paul Gleason
International Monetary Fund

Jeffrey Goldstein
James D. Wolfensohn, Inc.

Morris Goldstein
International Monetary Fund

Norio Gomi
Matsushita

John Goodman
National Economic Council

Catherine Gwin
Overseas Development Council

David Hale
Kemper Financial Services

Carl Hartman
Associated Press

Edward Hoyt
J. P. Morgan

Gary Hufbauer
Institute for International
Economics

Nancy Hunt
Industrial Bank of Japan

Chang-Ik Hwang
Export-Import Bank of Korea

Hidehiko Ide
Fuji Bank

Paul Jolles
Bern, Switzerland

Miles Kahler
University of California, San Diego

Carola Kaps
Frankfurter Allgemeine Zeitung

Robert Keatley
Wall Street Journal

Edward Keene
Knight-Ridder

Tae-Han Kim
Bank of Korea

Hirotsugu Koike
Nihon Keizai Shimbun

Jae Ouk Lee
Bank of Korea

Marc Leland
Marc Leland & Associates

William Lewis
McKinsey & Company

Robert Liberatore
Chrysler

Lawrence Malkin
International Herald Tribune

Philip Martin
Migration News

Hayes McCarthy
Bretton Woods Committee

Bailey Morris
Institute for International
Economics

William Murray
Dow Jones Economic Report

Joan Nelson
Overseas Development Council

Richard Neu
National Intelligence Council

Seamus O'Cleireacain
Ford Foundation

John Odell
University of Southern California

Yasushi Onoda
Tonen

James Orr
Bretton Woods Committee

Henry Owen
Consultants International Group

Karim Pakravan
First National Bank of Chicago

Jay Patchen
Nissho Iwai

Louis Pauly
University of Toronto

Valerie Ploumpis
Nissho Iwai

Jacques Polak
International Monetary Fund

Ernest Preeg
Center for Strategic and
International Studies

Louise Price
Asahi Shimbun

Michael Prowse
Financial Times

Jean-Francois Rischard
World Bank

Howard Rosen
Competitiveness Policy Council

Tadahiro Sakai
Marubeni

Gary Sampson
General Agreement on Tariffs and
Trade

Nancy Schwartz
Office of Management and Budget

Mark Seagel
Putnam Investments

Koh Sera
Sumitomo

Hyun Kyu Shin
Hyundai

Michelle Smith
Department of the Treasury

Robert Solomon
Brookings Institution

David Stanton
International Monetary Fund

Ernest Stern
World Bank

Joseph Stiglitz
Council of Economic Advisers

Bruce Stokes
National Journal

Tsuneharu Takeda
ITOCHU

Charles Taylor
Group of Thirty

Amos Tincani
Commission of the European
Communities

Edwin Truman
Federal Reserve System

Chris Wada
Sony

John Walsh
Group of Thirty

Robert Warne
Korea Economic Institute

Sidney Weintraub
Center for Strategic and
International Studies

Paul Wonnacott
Institute for International
Economics

Other Publications from the
Institute for International Economics

POLICY ANALYSES IN INTERNATIONAL ECONOMICS Series

1 The Lending Policies of the International Monetary Fund
   John Williamson/*August 1982*
                         ISBN paper 0-88132-000-5   72 pp.

2 "Reciprocity": A New Approach to World Trade Policy?
   William R. Cline/*September 1982*
                         ISBN paper 0-88132-001-3   41 pp.

3 Trade Policy in the 1980s
   C. Fred Bergsten and William R. Cline/*November 1982*
   (out of print)   ISBN paper 0-88132-002-1   84 pp.
   Partially reproduced in the book *Trade Policy in the 1980s.*

4 International Debt and the Stability of the World Economy
   William R. Cline/*September 1983*
                         ISBN paper 0-88132-010-2   134 pp.

5 The Exchange Rate System, Second Edition
   John Williamson/*September 1983, rev. June 1985*
   (out of print)   ISBN paper 0-88132-034-X   61 pp.

6 Economic Sanctions in Support of Foreign Policy Goals
   Gary Clyde Hufbauer and Jeffrey J. Schott/*October 1983*
                         ISBN paper 0-88132-014-5   109 pp.

7 A New SDR Allocation?
   John Williamson/*March 1984*
                         ISBN paper 0-88132-028-5   61 pp.

8 An International Standard for Monetary Stabilization
   Ronald I. McKinnon/*March 1984*
                         ISBN paper 0-88132-018-8   108 pp.

9 The Yen/Dollar Agreement: Liberalizing Japanese Capital Markets
   Jeffrey A. Frankel/*December 1984*
                         ISBN paper 0-88132-035-8   86 pp.

10 Bank Lending to Developing Countries: The Policy Alternatives
   C. Fred Bergsten, William R. Cline, and John Williamson/*April 1985*
                         ISBN paper 0-88132-032-3   221 pp.

11 Trading for Growth: The Next Round of Trade Negotiations
   Gary Clyde Hufbauer and Jeffrey J. Schott/*September 1985*
                         ISBN paper 0-88132-033-1   109 pp.

12 Financial Intermediation Beyond the Debt Crisis
   Donald R. Lessard and John Williamson/*September 1985*
                         ISBN paper 0-88132-021-8   130 pp.

13 The United States-Japan Economic Problem
   C. Fred Bergsten and William R. Cline/*October 1985, 2d ed. January 1987*
   (out of print)   ISBN paper 0-88132-060-9   180 pp.

BOOKS

Economic Sanctions Reconsidered (in two volumes)
  Economic Sanctions Reconsidered: Supplemental Case Histories
  Gary Clyde Hufbauer, Jeffrey J. Schott, and Kimberly Ann Elliott/*1985, 2d ed.*
    December 1990

ISBN cloth 0-88132-115-X	928 pp.
ISBN paper 0-88132-105-2	928 pp.

  Economic Sanctions Reconsidered: History and Current Policy
  Gary Clyde Hufbauer, Jeffrey J. Schott, and Kimberly Ann Elliott/*December 1990*

ISBN cloth 0-88132-136-2	288 pp.
ISBN paper 0-88132-140-0	288 pp.

Pacific Basin Developing Countries: Prospects for the Future
Marcus Noland/*January 1991*

ISBN cloth 0-88132-141-9	250 pp.
ISBN paper 0-88132-081-1	250 pp.

Currency Convertibility in Eastern Europe
John Williamson, editor/*October 1991*

ISBN cloth 0-88132-144-3	396 pp.
ISBN paper 0-88132-128-1	396 pp.

Foreign Direct Investment in the United States
Edward M. Graham and Paul R. Krugman/*1989, 2d ed. October 1991*

ISBN paper 0-88132-139-7	200 pp.

International Adjustment and Financing: The Lessons of 1985-1991
C. Fred Bergsten, editor/*January 1992*

ISBN paper 0-88132-112-5	336 pp.

North American Free Trade: Issues and Recommendations
Gary Clyde Hufbauer and Jeffrey J. Schott/*April 1992*

ISBN cloth 0-88132-145-1	392 pp.
ISBN paper 0-88132-120-6	392 pp.

American Trade Politics
I. M. Destler/*1986, 2d ed. June 1992*

ISBN cloth 0-88132-164-8	400 pp.
ISBN paper 0-88132-188-5	400 pp.

Narrowing the U.S. Current Account Deficit
Allen J. Lenz/*June 1992*

ISBN cloth 0-88132-148-6	640 pp.
ISBN paper 0-88132-103-6	640 pp.

The Economics of Global Warming
William R. Cline/*June 1992*

ISBN cloth 0-88132-150-8	416 pp.
ISBN paper 0-88132-132-X	416 pp.

U.S. Taxation of International Income: Blueprint for Reform
Gary Clyde Hufbauer, assisted by Joanna M. van Rooij/*October 1992*

ISBN cloth 0-88132-178-8	304 pp.
ISBN paper 0-88132-134-6	304 pp.

Who's Bashing Whom? Trade Conflict in High-Technology Industries
Laura D'Andrea Tyson/*November 1992*

ISBN cloth 0-88132-151-6	352 pp.
ISBN paper 0-88132-106-0	352 pp.

Currencies and Politics in the United States, Germany, and Japan
C. Randall Henning/*September 1994*
ISBN paper 0-88132-127-3   432 pp.

Estimating Equilibrium Exchange Rates
John Williamson, editor/*September 1994*
ISBN paper 0-88132-076-5   320 pp.

Managing the World Economy: Fifty Years After Bretton Woods
Peter B. Kenen, editor/*September 1994*
ISBN paper 0-88132-212-1   448 pp.

SPECIAL REPORTS

1   Promoting World Recovery: A Statement on Global Economic Strategy
    by Twenty-six Economists from Fourteen Countries/*December 1982*
    (out of print)   ISBN paper 0-88132-013-7   45 pp.

2   Prospects for Adjustment in Argentina, Brazil, and Mexico:
    Responding to the Debt Crisis
    John Williamson, editor/*June 1983*
    (out of print)   ISBN paper 0-88132-016-1   71 pp.

3   Inflation and Indexation: Argentina, Brazil, and Israel
    John Williamson, editor/*March 1985*
    ISBN paper 0-88132-037-4   191 pp.

4   Global Economic Imbalances
    C. Fred Bergsten, editor/*March 1986*
    ISBN cloth 0-88132-038-2   126 pp.
    ISBN paper 0-88132-042-0   126 pp.

5   African Debt and Financing
    Carol Lancaster and John Williamson, editors/*May 1986*
    (out of print)   ISBN paper 0-88132-044-7   229 pp.

6   Resolving the Global Economic Crisis: After Wall Street
    Thirty-three Economists from Thirteen Countries/*December 1987*
    ISBN paper 0-88132-070-6   30 pp.

7   World Economic Problems
    Kimberly Ann Elliott and John Williamson, editors/*April 1988*
    ISBN paper 0-88132-055-2   298 pp.

    Reforming World Agricultural Trade
    Twenty-nine Professionals from Seventeen Countries/*1988*
    ISBN paper 0-88132-088-9   42 pp.

8   Economic Relations Between the United States and Korea:
    Conflict or Cooperation?
    Thomas O. Bayard and Soo-Gil Young, editors/*January 1989*
    ISBN paper 0-88132-068-4   192 pp.

FORTHCOMING

Reciprocity and Retaliation in US Trade Policy
Thomas O. Bayard and Kimberly Ann Elliott

The Globalization of Industry and National Governments
C. Fred Bergsten and Edward M. Graham

The Political Economy of Korea–United States Cooperation
C. Fred Bergsten and Il SaKong, editors

International Debt Reexamined
William R. Cline

Trade, Jobs, and Income Distribution
William R. Cline

Overseeing Global Capital Markets
Morris Goldstein and Peter Garber

Foreign Direct Investment in the United States, Third Edition
Edward M. Graham and Paul R. Krugman

Global Competition Policy
Edward M. Graham and J. David Richardson

Toward a Pacific Economic Community?
Gary Clyde Hufbauer and Jeffrey J. Schott

Measuring the Costs of Protection in Japan
Yoko Sazanami, Shujiro Urata, and Hiroki Kawai

The Uruguay Round: An Assessment
Jeffrey J. Schott

The Case for Trade: A Modern Reconsideration
J. David Richardson

The Future of the World Trading System
John Whalley, in collaboration with Colleen Hamilton

For orders outside the US and Canada please contact:

Longman Group UK Ltd.
PO Box 88
Harlow, Essex CM 19 5SR
UK

Telephone Orders: 0279 623923
Fax: 0279 414130
Telex: 81259

Canadian customers can order from the Institute or from either:

RENOUF BOOKSTORE
1294 Algoma Road
Ottawa, Ontario K1B 3W8
Telephone: (613) 741-4333
Fax: (613) 741-5439

LA LIBERTÉ
3020 chemin Sainte-Foy
Quebec G1X 3V6
Telephone: (418) 658-3763
Fax: (800) 567-5449